AMERICAN
LITERATURE
AND SCIENCE

AMERICAN LITERATURE AND SCIENCE

Robert J. Scholnick
Editor

THE UNIVERSITY PRESS OF KENTUCKY

Editorial and Sales Offices: Lexington, Kentucky 40508-4008

Library of Congress Cataloging-in-Publication Data
American literature and science / Robert J. Scholnick, editor.
    p.   cm.
   Includes bibliographical references and index.
   ISBN 0-8131-1785-2 (alk. paper)
   1. American literature—History and criticism. 2. Literature and
science—United States. 3. Science in literature. I. Scholnick,
Robert J.
PS169.S413A8 1992
810.9'356—dc20   92-373

This book is printed on recycled acid-free paper meeting
the requirements of the American National Standard
for Permanence of Paper for Printed Library Materials. ♾

Contents

Acknowledgments   vii

1   Permeable Boundaries: Literature and Science in America
ROBERT J. SCHOLNICK   1

2   "This Brazen Serpent Is a Doctors Shop": Edward Taylor's
Medical Vision   CATHERINE RAINWATER   18

3   Benjamin Franklin: The Fusion of Science and Letters
A. OWEN ALDRIDGE   39

4   Thomas Jefferson   JOSEPH W. SLADE   58

5   An Intrinsic Luminosity: Poe's Use of Platonic and
Newtonian Optics   WILLIAM J. SCHEICK   77

6   Fields of Investigation: Emerson and Natural History
DAVID M. ROBINSON   94

7   Thoreau and Science   ROBERT D. RICHARDSON, JR.   110

8   (Pseudo-) Scientific Humor   JUDITH YAROSS LEE   128

9   Traveling in Time with Mark Twain   H. BRUCE FRANKLIN   157

10   Hart Crane and John Dos Passos   JOSEPH W. SLADE   172

11   Fields of Spacetime and the "I" in Charles Olson's *The Maximus
Poems*   STEVEN CARTER   194

12   "Unfurrowing the Mind's Plowshare": Fiction in a Cybernetic
Age   DAVID PORUSH   209

13   Turbulence in Literature and Science: Questions of Influence
N. KATHERINE HAYLES   229

Bibliography: American Literature and Science through 1989
ROBERT S. SCHOLNICK   251

Contributors   273

Index   275

Acknowledgments

I am especially grateful to the contributors to this volume for their patience, support, and many valuable suggestions, from inception to completion. My William and Mary colleagues Scott Donaldson, Elsa Nettles, Christopher MacGowan, Robert Gross, Carl Dolmetsch, and Thad Tate read portions of the manuscript and offered pointed and pertinent observations. The anonymous readers of the manuscript for the University Press of Kentucky showed me how to strengthen the project in many ways. My work on this and related studies has been supported by a grant from the National Endowment for the Humanities, for which I am most grateful. I have benefited in many ways from the generous support for faculty scholarship from the College of William and Mary. Wanda Carter, who oversees the graduate studies office at William and Mary, took time to provide much-needed assistance. My son Jonathan graciously listened to my discussions of literature and science during several long automobile trips—and in more ways than one kept me awake with his comments. Joshua Scholnick, Amy Napier, and MaryKate McMaster provided crucial assistance with the bibliography. As with all my projects, my wife, Sylvia Scholnick, combined the most searching criticism of my work with the most powerful love. This book is dedicated to my parents, Ruth and Allen Scholnick, and the blessed memory of my wife's parents, Ken and Berniece Huberman, who became my parents also.

1

Permeable Boundaries:
Literature and Science in America

ROBERT J. SCHOLNICK

Reaching back to the Puritan poet Edward Taylor and forward to the contemporary novelist Thomas Pynchon, this collection of original essays explores the relationship in American culture between literature and science. These two ways of knowing are often thought to be unrelated, if not actually antagonistic. Through analyses of the ways that such writers as Franklin, Jefferson, Poe, Emerson, Thoreau, Twain, Hart Crane, Dos Passos, and Charles Olson have understood the sciences and explored them in their work as essential and powerful methods of knowing and changing the world, these essays seek to comprehend how literature and science have evolved together in American culture.

Over the more than three and a half centuries of American literature the modes of investigation that we now include under the heading "science" have changed radically, as has "literature." Up through the beginning of the nineteenth century, literature and science were understood as parts of a unitary endeavor, but by mid-century they had diverged. Science became the province of the professional, while concurrently poets, novelists, and other imaginative writers asserted the autonomy of their art. Despite moving in different directions, science and literature have continued to speak with one another in ways that have helped to shape each. Focusing on the languages that writers have used to explore the interpenetrating realms of science and literature, this collection seeks to open for wider analysis a neglected dimension of American culture.

We undertake this inquiry at a time when the familiar understanding of science as an objective, systematic, progressive, and transcultural means of investigating reality has come under increasing attack from several quarters. Historians have learned to approach science as only one among other social constructs, and so the subject has been opened to the sort of critical analysis directed at any form of cultural expression. As Clifford Geertz observes in "A Lab of One's Own," a recent essay on feminist approaches to science, "If, like everything else cultural—art, ideology, religion, common sense—science is something hammered together in some place to some purpose by partisans and devotees, it is, like everything else cultural, subject to questioning why it has been built in the way that it has. If knowledge is made, its making can be looked into."[1] In the final essay in this collection, N. Katherine Hayles looks into the making of several new sciences, including chaos theory, fractal geometry, and fluid dynamics, as a means of opening "passages between literature, science, and culture in which the influence is construed as a turbulent complexity, not a one-way street." Because American writers themselves have explored the meanings of science and its offshoot technology, literature offers us multiple new perspectives on science as a cultural expression, even as science offers new perspectives on literature.

Certain of the principles of twentieth-century physics have served to undermine from within the perception of science as an objective mode of knowing that exists apart from the human investigator. Heisenberg's famous uncertainty principle, for instance, holds that we can precisely measure the position of a subatomic particle or its motion, but not both at once. Consequently, in the words of Ilya Prigogine and Isabelle Stengers, investigators are forced "to decide which measurement we are going to perform and which question our experiments will ask the system," and so there exists "an irreducible multiplicity of representations for a system, each connected with a determined set of operators." In short, the "post-Einsteinian" physics has placed new attention on the agency of the investigator-interpreter. And since the human investigator frames his or her questions in language, the codes of science touch those of literature in unsuspected ways. Prigogine and Stengers draw the conclusion that on one level both literature and science can be understood as "fictions" or conceptualizations of reality: "One of the reasons for the opposition between the 'two cultures' [C.P. Snow's famous division between the culture of science and that of the 'humanities'] may have been the belief that literature corresponds to a conceptualization of reality, to 'fiction,' while science seems to express objective 'reality.' Quantum mechanics teaches us that the situation is not so simple. On all levels reality implies an essential element of conceptualization."[2]

Neither is literature immune to such fundamental questioning. The work of Terry Eagleton and other Marxist critics, for instance, has brought into question the very existence of the category of writing we refer to as "literature." They have argued that "literature" is a term used by dominant social groups to privilege certain kinds of writing for purposes of social hegemony.[3] Modes of investigation, conceptualization, and expression within culture, both literature and science are also instruments for the exercise of power. This is not to ignore the very real differences between literature and science as ways of knowing, but to suggest the grounds for an investigation of their interaction within a single culture.

The authors of these essays focus on the particular historical situations of the writers, asking how the writer came to understand science on its own terms and in its relationship to literature. Hence, the essays work together to define the changes in literature and science over the course of American history. Beyond a common attention to the specificity of historical circumstance, no one synthesis unites them. Given the writers' very different situations, such critical eclecticism is to be expected. However, by providing a historical grounding for discussions of literature and science as related modes of discourse within the context of a single culture, this volume seeks to establish the essential framework for that possible synthesis and to stimulate the new scholarship that will make it possible.

Given our epistemological uncertainties, however, such a critical synthesis may well be out of reach. As Josué V. Harrari and David F. Bell have written in their introduction to Michel Serres's *Hermes: Literature, Science, and Philosophy,* literary texts "are born of spaces of communication among several domains. Legend, myth, history, philosophy, and science share common boundaries. . . . The domains of myth, science, and literature oscillate frantically back and forth into one another, so that the idea of ever distinguishing between them becomes more and more chimerical."[4] While ultimate distinctions among the terms may be impossible, historical understanding of the interaction of these ways of knowing is not.

This collection identifies two closely related aspects of the interaction between literature and science over the course of American history. To use a metaphor from electricity, the first is one of resistance. Writers have opposed those destructive and controlling powers made possible by science and technology. The second is one of conduction. Writers also have drawn images and vocabularies from science and technology as powerful expressions of new ideas for their work, even as their autonomous investigations have enabled them to express ideas that have a parallel or complementary relationship to those of science.

The aspect of resistance is to be found as early as Benjamin Franklin's warning against the potential for mass destruction of bombardment from the newly invented balloon, a subject that A. Owen Aldridge treats here in "Benjamin Franklin: The Fusion of Science and Letters." And Mark Twain, in the late nineteenth century, as H. Bruce Franklin shows in "Traveling in Time with Mark Twain," symbolically "explodes" the dangers of a technological military machine, the product of industrial capitalism, by converting its powerful energies into the sort of destructive heat and electrical explosions that we witness in the apocalyptic "Sand Belt" chapter of *A Connecticut Yankee in King Arthur's Court.* Similarly, David Porush argues that what he calls "cybernetic fiction" "is an expression of literature's need to contest cybernetics' claims for an ultimate description of human communication and thought." But, as Porush demonstrates, even as cybernetics and the fiction that makes use of its methods contest the question of "who does the better job of describing how humans think and communicate?" they collaborate "in a larger postmodern mission: defining from opposite sides that gap where humanity remains inexpressible in mechanical terms."

H. Bruce Franklin argues that the American belief in an ever-improving future is closely tied to a faith in science and technology as the essential vehicles for realizing that future. However, in creating memorable images of the destruction that they have made possible, writers have exposed fundamental contradictions within the culture. For instance, Nathaniel Hawthorne's extensive gallery of mad scientists grew out of his "fascination," Taylor Stoehr has asserted, with a culture that "displayed a remarkable popular interest in science and technology, even among citizens who had little notion of the actual methods and aims of the laboratory."[5] At least from the times of Franklin and Jefferson, American writers have critically examined the complex of contradictory expectations surrounding those central terms, "science," "technology," and now "high technology," and have found languages and artistic methods to resist their potentially dangerous uses. This tradition is essential, for in the words of the historian Robert V. Bruce, "Science and technology are the prime instruments of irreversible change in the thought and life of mankind, and for much of our own century the United States had led in wielding them."[6]

Yet, as the examples in this collection illustrate, for the most part American writers have not found science and technology to be destructive per se. Their concern has been with the way human beings have used them as instruments of power and control within the industrial capitalism of the

United States. To return to the metaphor of electricity, we can say that even while resisting the destructive potential of science and technology, American writers have at the same time developed ways of conducting certain of their methods, languages, and discoveries across the shifting boundaries that now separate them.

Many of these essays focus on what precisely happens at the point of contact, when the languages or codes of the sciences touch those of art. The writer may seek a way to co-opt the scientist by demonstrating a gain when a scientific idea is amplified through an examination of its metaphorical meanings in the realm of art. Joseph W. Slade shows that John Dos Passos and Hart Crane sought both to "assimilate and reshape" the new sciences and technologies in their respective literary structures. On the other hand, little sense of rivalry between poet and scientist emerges from Steven Carter's analysis of the ways that Charles Olson used ideas from the physics of Heisenberg and Bohr to help structure *The Maximus Poems*. Carter quotes Bohr's famous assertion that "when it comes to atoms, the language that must be used is the language of poetry" to show that energy may be conducted both ways, from science to literature and from literature to science and without struggle for precedence.

Further, as autonomous investigators, writers may independently formulate in literary terms ideas that also find expression in the sciences, a point which we can approach through Bohr's principle of complementarity. An "extension of Heisenberg's uncertainty relations," Prigogine and Stengers explain, this principle is based on the recognition that "various possible languages and points of view about the system may be complementary. They all deal with the same reality, but it is impossible to reduce them to one single description. The irreducible plurality of perspectives on the same reality expresses the impossibility of a divine point of view from which the whole of reality is visible." From this perspective, we can see that multiple languages may be needed to investigate the "wealth of reality, which overflows any single language, any single logical structure."[7] Literature and science independently investigate a "reality" that exceeds any single system of explanation, any one language.

This principle is reflected in the poetry of Robert Frost. As Guy Rotella observes, Frost "was writing poems that can be described by the terms indeterminacy, correspondence, and complementarity long before he became aware of those concepts in science."[8] We may approach Frost's work and that of other writers as a place of exploration, a kind of experimental chamber, where the similarities and differences between conflicting conceptualizations of reality, between science and art, subjectivity and objectivity, and power and contemplation, are played out through the medium of language.

This collection has been organized to enable the reader to explore the interaction between literature and science over the entire course of American literary history. The essays on Taylor, Franklin, and Jefferson treat the relationship between literature and science when it was possible to pursue both as part of a unitary endeavor. The essays on three major writers from the first part of the nineteenth century, Poe, Emerson, and Thoreau, consider their responses to the growing separation between science and literature and the underlying search for new and deeper ways of relating them. The final essays, analyzing the relationship after science and literature moved apart at mid-century, treat the growing gap between popular understanding and the increasingly complex sciences. The essays also examine the attempts by writers to develop languages that are responsive to the new scientific complexities and the ever-increasing importance of science and technology as agents of change.

We begin at the outset of the Scientific Revolution with Catherine Rainwater's essay on Edward Taylor. Rainwater shows how the great Puritan poet-physician-minister was able typologically to integrate recent medical concepts with his orthodox Puritan theology. "Taylor's Paracelsian poems," she writes, "demonstrate his vision of himself as an instrument in the healing and redemptive process; his conception of himself as poet (user of words) and as reader-interpreter (of the Word) is synonymous with his sense of himself as physician, as reader-interpreter of the Book of Nature who looks for the earthly signifiers of spiritual conditions and cures." As Rainwater and other scholars have demonstrated, Taylor developed a hermeneutic system that could respond to the latest scientific intelligence from many fields, including Copernican astronomy. Her exploration of Taylor's immediate situation adds to what we know about the reception and dissemination of science at the time. But Rainwater also looks forward, identifying Taylor as the first in a tradition of physician-writers in America, which includes Oliver Wendell Homes, William Carlos Williams, Walker Percy, Oliver Sacks, and Richard Selzer. Such writers, Rainwater writes, remind us "of the sacramental dimension of healing that is also a dimension of the writer's art. Such resonance suggests that despite the persistent efforts of empirical science to abandon the metaphysical territories that science once occupied, some central mystery of speech and existence prevents any such absolute separation."

Nor did the coming of the Newtonian scientific revolution bring with it such a separation between science and the other dimensions of one's being. In his essay on Benjamin Franklin, A. Owen Aldridge explains precisely why "Newton demanded the muse." Neither in America nor England was it a mechanical universe empty of meaning and purpose that the expositors of Newton described. On the contrary, the "Enlightened theory of science," as Perry Miller has remarked, "coming to these shores with incalculable prestige, taught Americans to conceive of it as consisting in an aesthetic contemplation of a perfected universe and then to salute the comprehension of this universe (mainly through the grasp of Newton's system) as providing an entrance into the cosmopolitan culture of the West."[9] Aldridge's essay on Franklin and Joseph W. Slade's on Jefferson enable us to understand just how it was possible in the eighteenth century to integrate science and letters.

Aldridge begins by reviewing the five definitions of "science" in Johnson's dictionary. He demonstrates that only one of these definitions, "certainty grounded on demonstration," with its emphasis on method, "approaches the modern conception." The others refer to science as knowledge in a generic sense and include such definitions as "art attained by precepts" and "any art or species of knowledge." Similarly, in writing about Thomas Jefferson as both scientist and writer, Slade points out that Franklin's "1743 charter for the American Philosophical Society, which Jefferson served as president for seventeen years, gave equal weight to science and literature, as if a fluent pen were the natural extension of a curious mind. Indeed, the terms *literary* and *scientific* were virtually interchangeable as descriptions of the society's activities." The terms that were used to refer to the activities now encompassed by the sciences—"natural history" and "natural philosophy"—are themselves highly suggestive, for they specify the connection between the study of the natural world and fundamental philosophical questions.

Aldridge's analysis of Franklin's balanced approach to science gives us a new appreciation of his genius. In many ways Franklin's characteristic pragmatism, his suspicion of linking metaphysical speculation with scientific investigations, and his strong interest in experimentation helped to compensate for his limitations, particularly in mathematics. Aldridge contrasts Franklin in this regard with the theoretical Newton. At the same time, he shows that Franklin's scientific interests were remarkably similar to those of Voltaire. Perhaps the key to Franklin's achievement, Aldridge concludes, was his ability to balance his experimentalism with a wide-ranging imagination, which enabled him, for instance, to envision the possibility of space travel. He perfectly "fused" letters and science and performed experimental research that was both theoretical and applied, thereby claiming a place in international science.

By way of contrast, Slade, in reviewing the work of Thomas Jefferson as scientist, promoter of science, and writer, finds no such balance or "fusion" of writing and scientific investigation. He relates this imbalance to Jefferson's complex engagement with America. Even though Jefferson worked tirelessly to promote the development of science in America, his resistance to the growing specialization that came as a consequence limited his own achievements as scientific investigator. Convinced that there remained a need in a democracy for a common vocabulary that would enable the people at large to comprehend essential scientific intelligence, he resisted the increasingly specialized vocabularies that were another consequence of the maturation of the sciences he himself promoted. Slade, reversing Jefferson's own perception of his achievement, argues for his greatness not as a scientist but as a writer. For especially in *Notes on the State of Virginia* Jefferson registers the "crack in his Newtonian universe" represented by the presence of slavery in the American Republic: "When . . . he confronts the institution made peculiar by democratic principles that he himself had derived from a scientific reading of the cosmos, the schism shakes his world." The *Notes,* which Slade treats as "seminal for many sciences in America," responds to Count Buffon's "patronizing pronouncements" about the supposedly inferior forms of life on the American continent. In writing carefully and precisely about the natural world, Jefferson created a new literary form, the "first example of an American genre of naturalism as substratum for opinions and imagination that runs through Thoreau, Burroughs, and Muir to Annie Dillard and John McPhee in the present."

Increasingly during the eighteenth century, Newtonian science was responsible for a new attention to the natural world as a source of value. Now the "text" of the much revered American landscape was open to the same sort of reading and interpretation as were Holy Scripture and other writings. The art historian Barbara Novak has used the phrase "Trinity" to describe the way that in the first half of the nineteenth century, science, art, and religion came to be associated as parallel, mutually reinforcing modes of exploration: "Nature's truths as revealed by art, could be further validated by the disclosures of science, which revealed God's purposes and aided the reading of His natural text. At mid-century, landscape attitudes were firmly based on this unity of faith, art, and science." And she remarks that "so strong was the belief in the powers of science that there was no difficulty in aligning its aims with those of art."[10] Ironically, even as art, science, and belief seemed to find a common ground, underlying changes in all three realms would fracture this hypothetical unity by mid-century.

The essays on Poe, Emerson, and Thoreau explore how these American writers participated, if belatedly, in the quest of Romanticism to integrate science and imagination. Through developing new approaches to such sciences as biology, chemistry, and electricity, the Romantics sought to bridge the gap between the self and the external world, between the Me and the Not Me. The weight of recent scholarship on the Romantics has served to document not only the importance of the sciences for Romantic writers but also the lasting value of Romantic approaches and contributions to the sciences themselves.[11]

William J. Scheick, in "An Intrinsic Luminosity: Poe's Use of Platonic and Newtonian Optics," shows how Poe went beyond Newton's rather mechanical theory of vision to develop a theory of seeing that sought to account as well for the shaping of perception by the imagination. After analyzing Poe's wide knowledge of the sciences (and pseudo-sciences) of his time, Scheick focuses on the complex subject of Poe's ability to bring together in his work two contrasting theories of vision, the Platonic (vision results from the emanation of light from the eye outward) and the Newtonian (sight results from the reflection of light from an external source on the eye). Aware that the Platonic theory had no basis in fact, Poe still drew from it in creating characters with such active imaginations that the mind creates "images that are literally perceived by the retina. In this sense the imagination generates something like an interior luminosity behind the eyeball, and so Poe depicts the highly imaginative person as someone who evinces this interior light in large luminous eyes, eyes that therefore *seem* to emanate light from within." Such behaviors were in fact just then being described in the scientific literature, and so in drawing from the Platonic system for metaphors, Poe was able imaginatively to encompass an interior dimension of seeing absent from the Newtonian theory. Scheick's demonstration of the ways that Poe brought together these two dimensions of perception gives us a new perspective from which to understand a central point in his thinking: his "firm belief" in the essential similarities of the creative methods employed by the scientist and the artist. Poe came to realize, Scheick concludes, that "only a complete perception by means of both the light of imagination and the light of nature can bridge the gap between viewer (subject) and viewed (object), the gap otherwise manifest in the behavior of the human eye. . . . [T]his complete perception from within as well as from without, so apparent in a true scientist like Kepler or a visionary artist like Usher, suggests in microcosm something macrocosmic: Poe's belief finally in an essential Unity (an intrinsically luminous cosmic imagination, as it were) behind the phenomenological fragmentation that is the natural universe."

The central figure in exploring the complex of meanings of art, science, and religion in the nineteenth century was Emerson, who as David M. Robinson remarks, began his career when science and literature had not yet separated. However, Emerson in living until 1881 experienced their divorce in ways that Poe, who died in 1849, could not have known. At once adding to what we know about Emerson's lifelong study of the sciences and pointing to areas in need of further research, Robinson shows that Emerson's engagement with the sciences was central to his life's work. Starting from Emerson's early idealism, which in connecting nature to spirit provided a strong impetus for scientific exploration, Robinson documents the changes in Emerson's thought as he incorporated newer scientific ideas, particularly the dynamic ideas of metamorphosis, which came both from Romantic biology and from the Laplacian astronomy of John Pringle Nichol. He came to feel that "the concept of the evolutionary development of nature was itself a profound theological statement, giving powerful support to the conception of the creation as a field of dynamic energy. That energy reflected the dynamism of the soul." But the ever-increasing scientific specialization, which brought narrowly denotative languages, moved Emerson to complain that "science was false by being unpoetical." He glimpsed the alienating side of some of the newer scientific ideas as well. And so Emerson never was able to bring his speculations on science and the imagination together in a coherent formulation. But in praising "the example of his intellectual project that integrated scientific knowledge with metaphysical curiosity," Robinson concludes by emphasizing the scope of Emerson's undertaking, which required that he think beyond the sort of restrictive categories that still hamper us: "He turned to science because he needed its facts and its vision, and he was unafraid of any truth he might discover there."

Emerson's complaint about the "unpoetical" language of science reflects his distaste for the growing professionalization and specialization within the sciences during what the historian of science in America George H. Daniels calls "the emergent period, 1830-60." Daniels asserts that "by the middle of the century, the earlier pattern of gentlemanly scientific activity was rapidly becoming obsolete. The amateur was in the process of being replaced by the trained specialist—the professional who had a single-minded dedication to the interests of science. The emergence of a community of such professionals was the most significant development in nineteenth-century American science."[12] These societies explicitly excluded amateurs, who in any event found themselves being left behind by the extraordinary increases in mathematical rigor, highly technical vocabularies, and specialization now required if one were to contribute to a particular field of science. Consequently, during the 1840s both in England and America the word "scientist" came into use, Gillian Beer remarks, as a word that "begins to privilege and demarcate a particular method of coming to know and allows summary description of an enclosed professional group."[13]

At the same time, however, literature was asserting its autonomy as a way of knowing. Writers may not have been able to establish restrictive professional organizations, as did scientists, and it remained difficult at best to earn a living in the emerging literary marketplace, which gave a new status to the writer as a professional. Still, writers increasingly felt the need to assert the autonomy and power of the artistic imagination. Emerson described "The Poet," and by extension any creative artist, as "a sovereign, [who] stands on the centre. For the world is not painted, or adorned, but is from the beginning beautiful; and God has not made some beautiful things, but Beauty is the creator of the universe. Therefore the poet is not any permissive potentate, but is emperor in his own right."[14] If beauty creates the universe, who better than the imaginative writer to explore its originating power through language? The two greatest American poets of the century, Whitman and Emily Dickinson, followed Emerson in asserting the power and autonomy of the literary imagination.

Perhaps more than any other investigator, Henry David Thoreau, both as Transcendentalist writer and as practicing scientist, confronted the growing separation of the two modes of knowing. In "Thoreau and Science" Robert D. Richardson, Jr., precisely charts Thoreau's changing understandings of, and commitments to, both science and writing over the course of his career. At the outset, in the 1840s, drawing upon the heritage of such thinkers as Emerson and Goethe, Thoreau had a "bright and uncomplicated" attitude toward science, and confidently pursued "the connection between the natural and moral worlds." But increasingly during the early 1850s, as its languages became more specialized, Thoreau came to assert that science "actually gets in the way of our understanding how the world relates to us." And as science became institutionalized, he came to think that "the kind of writing he [was] interested in and the kind of work he [understood] as science [were] fundamentally opposed." Yet Thoreau could give up neither science nor writing, and there is high drama in Richardson's account of Thoreau's valiant struggle during the last decade of his life to find a way to bring these essential entities into harmony. Thoreau continued to grow as a scientist, as his "The Succession of Forest Trees" demonstrates. And so Richardson concludes by speculating that Thoreau's "late projects [tried], once again, to bridge the chasm between scientist and Transcendentalist, for Thoreau's *methods* [paid] attention to observation and detail, while his *aim* [was] nothing less than comprehensive: to describe the natural world, in a typical cross section called Concord. It is a world in which everything is interrelated, a world of change and process, a world that is above all and in all respects, alive." Thoreau was an early reader of Darwin's *Origin of Species* (1859), and Richardson offers evidence that he incorporated Darwinian ideas in his late writings. One cannot resist speculating how, if he had lived, Thoreau, as a brilliant writer who was also a brilliant naturalist, would have responded to the full implications of Darwin's thought.

We can now see that, more than anything else, the evolutionary biology of Darwin served to undermine the usefulness of science for the traditional purpose of confirming God's wise design of the universe. As Barbara Novak has written, "Pre-Darwinian science . . . accommodated discovery to design. Each new revelation was quickly enlisted as a proof of providential creation."[15] But if, as Darwin seemed to imply, humankind is a product of chance and contingency, then the enterprise of science could no longer contribute to the traditional search for underlying principles of metaphysical order and cosmic harmony. The concluding essays in this collection address from a variety of perspectives several related problems: the widening gap between the sciences and the scientific comprehension of the general public in the post-Darwinian world, the increasing power of science and technology to transform life and possibly destroy it, and the consequent challenges for the writer to find languages and structures capable of encompassing the complex new sciences.

One way to comprehend the public's attitude toward science, Judith Yaross Lee's "(Pseudo-) Scientific Humor" suggests, is to look at its comedy. Although the scope of her essay does not permit a full "scientific" sample, she does find that the dominant tradition of popular humor in America is antiscientific. Among the few exceptions to this tradition are the contemporary novelists Thomas Pynchon and Don DeLillo and the two forgotten nineteenth-century "Phunny Phellows" who are the subjects of her essay, George Horatio Derby and William Wright. Lee shows us how to "read" the language of a comedy that is both knowledgeable and appreciative of scientific understanding.

It may be that a full reading of antiscientific humor would enable us to chart a growing schism in American life betwen the complexities of the new sciences and popular understanding and reveal as well a deep unease with the destructive potential of those sciences. Henry Adams's famous warning from 1862 continues to strike a responsive chord: "Man has mounted science, and is now run away with. I firmly believe that before many centuries more, science will be the master of man. The engines he will have invented will be beyond his strength to control. Some day science may have the existence of mankind in its power, and the human race commit suicide, by blowing up the world."[16]

H. Bruce Franklin treats Mark Twain's *A Connecticut Yankee in King Arthur's Court* as projecting just such a vision of destruction as that suggested by Adams. At the novel's conclusion the "apocalyptic weapons" created by Twain's protagonist, the Yankee Hank Morgan, whose technological genius is the driving force behind the attempt to transform sixth-century Britain into nineteenth-century America, are used to destroy "everything that the nineteenth century has anachronistically introduced into the dark ages. But this resolution itself is paradoxical. The science and technology that mark progress, that distinguish forward from backward in time, become the means to annihilate all that humanity has created." Franklin argues that our basic understanding of the future in America has been made possible by the capacity of science and technology to transform life, so that history itself comes to have a "scientific design." Twain reveals the unsuspected destructive potential of a future with a "made in America" design.

Joseph W. Slade shows how Hart Crane and John Dos Passos recognized, as did Twain, that science and technology were critical elements in shaping American life and hence essential subjects for the writer. But "what made their assessments unique," Slade tells us, "was the assumption that science was not merely an essential ingredient in national life but part of what it meant to be human and American." Both understood the considerable diversity in purpose and methods among the sciences. And most importantly, each writer—Dos Passos drawing particularly from biology and Crane from physics—found in the sciences extraordinary resources for new literary languages and forms. Slade writes that "to poets like Crane, William Carlos Williams, and Wallace Stevens, the paradoxes of Werner Heisenberg and Niels Bohr restored a sense of mystery if not to the world then at least to language. Late-nineteenth-century positivists like Poincare, Mach, and Pearson had tried to purge language of metaphor; the Principles of Complementarity and Indeterminacy affirmed the indispensability of metaphor." Focusing on *The Bridge*, Slade shows how Crane "conceptualized energy as language" and created a poem in which "technology serves as a demotic plane where art and science can meet, a vernacular where spirituality can converge with everyday secular life, a non-Latinate version of the Mass." Dos Passos, starting with biology, developed the fictional techniques that make the *U.S.A.* trilogy "perhaps the first novel of the information age," a world (and here Dos Passos anticipates the novelists discussed by David Porush in "Cybernetic Fiction") where the total environment is defined by the volume of nodes of information that redefine it each moment. In complex ways, then, Crane and Dos Passos treated the new sciences and technologies both as subjects and, through metaphor, as a source for new artistic structures that could convey "the vast quantities of information that were characteristic of every sector of American endeavor."

Similarly, Steven Carter shows how in *The Maximus Poems* Charles Olson explores from the perspective of quantum mechanics some of the ways that the realms of space, time, and consciousness interact across a "quantum field" in which meaning is defined through comprehending complex, shifting relationships. In mastering the principles of the new physics and in using them to structure his poetic universe, a universe that twists like a Moebius strip around his Gloucester, Massachusetts, Olson finds new ways to bring together the realms of science and art, investigation and imagination. In its poetic reading of the universe, Olson's art, Carter suggests, is also a kind of interpretive science.

In his reading the cybernetic fiction of John Barth, Kurt Vonnegut, William Burroughs, and especially Thomas Pynchon, David Porush identifies an interpretive realm where postmodern literature and post-Einsteinian physics and other sciences come together. The cybernetic paradigm holds that "*everything in the knowable universe can be modeled in a logico-mathematical (formal) system of quantifiable information,* from the phase shifts of subatomic particles to the poet's selection of a word in a poem, to the rent in the fabric of spacetime created by a black hole, to the evanescent images flickering through the brain of a preverbal infant." In structuring their fictions around the very principles of cybernetic control that they seek to resist, the writers open closed codes to human control. And through constructing codes and deploying metaphors these authors find a common ground with certain contemporary sciences as cybernetics, quantum physics, and certain branches of mathematics. Porush refers to these sciences as "postmodern" because of their self-conscious concern with the structure of codes and their need to account for the presence of the observer. They are extremely self-conscious of their own status as models of reality, they view the reality described by their models as essentially plastic, and they must account for the role of the human observer-manipulator in their descriptions of phenomena. In short, these sciences no longer view themselves as directly involved with the stuff of nature so much as with descriptions of that stuff. We can, then, connect Porush's analysis with the comment of Prigogine and Stengers that to the extent science is a conceptualization of reality, it is a kind of fiction.

And this brings us back to the ways that literature and science interact within a common cultural field, the subject of N. Katherine Hayles's concluding essay. In challenging the usual way of understanding the question of influence in studies of literature in science—from science to literature—Hayles asserts that "influence is a construction to be explored rather than a premise to be embraced." Treating from a feminist perspective the development of such fields as fractal geometry and chaos science, she shows how underlying codes of perception and representation are transmitted through "coupling mechanisms" across the culture. These new sciences signal "a change in the ground of representation itself. The same kind of shift is apparent in many other disciplines besides physics and mathematics. It is so wide-ranging, in fact, that in my view the only adequate explanation for it is to assume that it has been authorized by reconfigurations in the cultural matrix." Hayles's essay, in challenging us to develop new and more complex ways to envision the "turbulent flow" of influence from and to literature and science, implicitly challenges us as well to envision the shape of a full history of science and literature in America, one that fully responds to the complex and multidirectional flows of meaning.

Because of lack of space, subjects have not been included here that clearly would figure prominently in that full history. More should be done with the Colonial period. From the nineteenth century, the tough-minded Hawthorne, Whitman, Dickinson, Adams, and Dreiser must be included. Marianne Moore, Robert Frost, William Carlos Williams, and Don DeLillo are some omissions that come immediately to mind from the twentieth century. Nor has the scientific essay, which in our time flourishes in the work of Lewis Thomas and Stephen Jay Gould, been adequately explored. Close analyses of the work of such women writers as Dickinson and Moore would make it possible for us to inquire into possible gender differences in the literary approaches to the scientific realm. This collection must stand, then, as both a beginning and as an invitation to others to continue the scholarly and critical investigations that will make possible a full history of science and literature in America.

We have seen how science and literature, once fused, later separated and how they continued to speak with one another across the boundaries. For the writer, language itself is the most powerful of exploratory instruments, one capable of expressing ideas and relationships that, as the essays in this book testify, come to have deep and unsuspected connections with the sciences. The writers considered here provide essential perspectives on science within the context of the larger culture of which it is an integral part. Of course, no simple account of the writer's reading or use of particular sources fully accounts for the complex interaction between literature and science within culture. Knowledge of the external world comes to the writer, as to all of us, from a variety of sources, and his or her treatment of such basic modes of perceiving as time, spatial relations, distance, and the like may be understood as expressing in literary terms concepts that may also have an expression in the language of science. The "loop" of perception is constant and moves in several directions at once; the texts that are the products of this process reflect its multi-layered complexity. However specialized, remote and removed the actual work of science may be, science is the "property" of all of us, as William Ellery Channing recognized a century and a half ago.[17] In their searching and critical explorations of science as part of culture, the writers surveyed here provide us with examples of responses to a challenge that has never been more compelling: "to live responsibly," as Helen Vendler has said about the poet A.R. Ammons, "within natural fact, scientific imagination, and ethical discovery."[18]

Notes

1. Clifford Geertz, "A Lab of One's Own," *New York Review of Books* 37 (Nov. 8, 1990): 19.

2. Ilya Prigogine and Isabelle Stengers, *Order Out of Chaos* (New York: Bantam, 1984), 225-26.

3. Terry Eagleton, *Literary Theory* (Minneapolis: Univ. of Minnesota Press, 1983), 16.

4. Josué V. Harari and David F. Bell, "Introduction," in Michel Serres, *Hermes*, ed. Harari and Bell (Baltimore: Johns Hopkins Univ. Press, 1982), xxix.

5. Taylor Stoehr, *Hawthorne's Mad Scientists* (Hamden, Conn.: Archon, 1978), 9.

6. Robert V. Bruce, *The Launching of American Science* (New York: Knopf, 1987), 3.

7. Prigogine and Stengers, 225.

8. Guy Rotella, "Comparing Conceptions: Frost and Eddington, Heisenberg and Bohr," *American Literature,* 59 (May 1987): 184-85.

9. Perry Miller, *The Life of the Mind in America* (New York: Harcourt, Brace, and World, 1965), 277.

10. Barbara Novak, *Nature and Culture* (New York: Oxford Univ. Press, 1980), 47.

11. See Andrew Cunningham and Nicholas Jardine, eds., *Romanticism and the Sciences* (Cambridge: Cambridge Univ. Press, 1990).

12. "The Process of Professionalization in American Science: The Emergent Period, 1820-1860," in Nathan Ringold, ed., *Science in America since 1820* (New York: Science History Publications, 1976), 63. The essay appeared originally in *Isis,* 58 (Summer 1967).

13. Gillian Beer, "Problems of Description in the Language of Discovery," in George Levine, ed., *One Culture* (Madison: Univ. of Wisconsin Press, 1987), 39.

14. Alfred R. Ferguson, Joseph Slater, et al., eds., *The Collected Works of Ralph Waldo Emerson,* 4 vols. to date (Cambridge: Harvard Univ. Press, 1971-   ), vol. 3, *Essays: Second Series,* ed. Slater, 5.

15. Novak, *Nature and Culture,* 54.

16. J.C. Levenson, et al., eds., *The Letters of Henry Adams,* 3 vols. (Cambridge: Harvard Univ. Press, 1982), vol. l, 290.

17. "The Present Age," in *The Works of William Ellery Channing* (1882; rpt., New York: Burt Franklin, 1970), 160.

18. Helen Vendler, "Veracity Unshaken," *New Yorker,* Feb. 15, 1988, 104.

2

"This Brazen Serpent Is a Doctors Shop": Edward Taylor's Medical Vision

CATHERINE RAINWATER

"A physitian cureth not only the body but the mind in some manner," writes Nicholas Culpeper in 1654; his statement reflects the neo-Platonic and alchemical assumptions underlying Renaissance medical theory.[1] Such holistic views of medicine prevailed in Edward Taylor's era (c. 1641-1729), despite the fact that the late seventeenth century was rapidly shifting away from an animistic cosmology, which stressed vital connections between matter and spirit, toward a Cartesian and mechanistic view, which posed few links between matter and spirit. Culpeper's and other hermetically based herbals were the primary sources of medical information during Taylor's lifetime, but the trend was increasingly to abandon the mystical underpinnings of the medical theory and to emphasize the practical, curative effects of the remedies upon the corporal "machine." Indeed, most branches of "natural philosophy" were discounting their metaphysical dimensions and becoming modern empirical sciences. The abandoned metaphysical territories eventually became the exclusive provinces of religion.

Taylor lived during an age of numerous mind-boggling challenges to the scientific status quo; the new science often generated bitter disputes, not only between science and religion, but frequently among the proponents of the new science themselves. Many of these controversies derived from arguments over factual detail, such as, in astronomy, whether the moon emitted or reflected light. But generally, controversy centered around the relative acceptance or rejection of the medieval "vitalist" cosmology. Vitalism posited an animate universe of "correspondences" between macro- and microcosm, spirit and matter, nature and humanity.

During the late seventeenth century, the Cartesian mechanical model of the universe augured eighteenth-century rationalism and began to make inroads into vitalist theories. Consequently, many scientific theories were constructed upon a shifting epistemological ground; proponents of these theories attempted to retain part of the religious and mystical foundations of knowledge, and yet to develop inductive, empirical sciences.

These and other intellectual disputes of the era received much attention at Harvard College in America, where Taylor matriculated in 1668. Indeed, Samuel Eliot Morison has shown that Harvard students, far more than their British counterparts, were encouraged to acquire the most current scientific information, which they favored over the ancient, authoritative views.[2] For example, when the tutor of Taylor's class of 1671 required his students to read *Physiologiae Peripateticae* (1610), Johannes Magirus's outdated cosmological treatise, their response was to lock him into a closet.[3] Infused by the new scientific spirit of the late Renaissance, the students complained that Magirus's work held no information "about the universe that Dante didn't know."[4] Indeed, as historian of science Herbert Butterfield has observed, the new science had challenged much more than ideas about the arrangement of the heavens; it had also "changed the character of men's habitual mental operations even in the conduct of the non-material sciences, while transforming the whole diagram of the physical universe and the very texture of life itself."[5]

Taylor later deplored his part in the little insurrection of his class, but he did so less because he accepted Magirus's views than because, as a conservative Puritan, he regretted the disrespect for authority the students had shown. Beyond this respect for authority, Taylor maintained a nostalgic fondness for the old, aesthetically appealing ideas of order that Magirus's text represented, even though the text was no longer valid. Thus, despite Taylor's up-to-date knowledge, poems in the *Preparatory Meditations* often depend for their internal structure upon medieval concepts of macro- and microcosmic design. Other poems, however, especially in the Second Series of the *Meditations*, reveal Taylor's intellectual predisposition toward the new science that was fostered in Harvard's free academic environment,[6] and that over the years he came to see as likewise aesthetically appealing. Apparently, the new scientific data posed no significant threat to Taylor, as it did to many others, for Taylor was always able, eventually, to accommodate the new information to Puritan theology. Unlike some other religious poets of his era (such as John Donne in England, who complained that the new science had "disproportion[ed]" the "pure forme" of the universe[7]), Taylor never railed against the systematic destruction of the old cosmic diagram. Instead, his works often display a spirit rallying to the new scientific challenge to the design of the universe. Though a modest colonial physician and minister spending most of his life in the remote frontier settlement of Westfield, Massachusetts, Taylor nevertheless shows a progressive attitude toward change resembling that of the great innovators of his era. Announcing the advent of the "Great Instauration," one such innovator—Sir Francis Bacon—remarked early in the seventeenth century: "I am certain of my way but not certain of my position."[8] Taylor displays Baconian confidence in the new scientific method even if, like Bacon, he is uncertain where such methodology might take him. Taylor's conservative Puritan vision repeatedly accommodates the revisions of heaven and earth that are now known collectively as the Scientific Revolution.[9]

Taylor came of age during this revolutionary time of scientific ferment and confusion. In some fields, such as astronomy, thinkers employed modern empirical methods; other fields, including medicine, remained medieval. In medicine, disputes arose between older theorists, inheritors of Galen, who believed in the humors, and the Paracelsians and post-Paracelsians, who applied new, but still not empirical, methods. These Paracelsians understood disease as the invasion of the body by foreign substances rather than as a result of humoral imbalances, and they advocated chemical cures, but they still insisted upon "spiritual" or "metaphysical" dimensions of the healing arts. This tradition proved stimulating for Edward Taylor as preacher-poet-physician, for as physician he interprets the physical signs of illness as spiritual signs. These signs are "read" by the physician just as biblical texts and poems are read. In his three-part role as poet-physician-minister, Taylor is always primarily an interpreter, who imitates the tripartite role of Christ as ultimate Physician, Embodiment of the Word, and Interpreter. Thus, language becomes one of the poet-minister-physician's essential tools. Taylor had a holistic understanding of illness and a holistic understanding of his three-in-one roles. In playing these roles, he wrote a poetry full of multiple meanings and complex puns. In fact, it is in light of the several roles that we can understand the nature of his verse forms, style, and underlying poetics, a poetics that always reveals Taylor's need to synthesize and reconcile disparate information. Perhaps ironically, it is owing to the uncertainties of Taylor's age that he was compelled so carefully to systematize and account for his own certainties.

If uncertainty characterized the age, so did philosophical and epistemological inconsistency. Butterfield remarks that "even the greatest geniuses who broke through the ancient views in some special field of study . . . would remain stranded in a species of medievalism when they went outside that chosen field."[10] Taylor's scientific understanding mirrors the inconsistencies of the day. His era was one in which more advances had been made in astronomy and mechanics than in any other field. Consequently, while Taylor sometimes reveals in his works a Copernican view of the universe, he also displays a variety of medieval views of other sciences, such as optics and chemistry, for example, which lagged behind in their development.

Another such scientific discipline late to modernize was medicine. Though some historians of science argue that, at least in the biological sciences if not in actual medical practice, a "revolution" occurred through the "chemical philosophy" of Paracelsus (Theophrastus Bombastus von Hohenheim, 1493-1541), the anatomical studies of Andreas Vesalius (1514-1564), and the physiological discoveries of William Harvey (1578-1657), Michel Foucault demonstrates in his study of the history of medical perception that modern medicine with its intense "rationality" and "empirical vigilance" has "fixed its own date of birth . . . in the last years of the eighteenth century."[11] Foucault also investigates the differences in medical discourse before and after the period of modernization and suggests some of the ways in which pre- and post-eighteenth-century medical vision derives from separate hermeneutical systems. Premodern medical vision grew out of the physician's assumption of a metaphysical relation between visible symptoms and invisible conditions (hence Culpeper's statement cited earlier: "a physitian cureth not only the body but the mind"); the modern vision, according to Foucault, stresses the accuracy of the trained physician's eye in reading the phenomenal signs—signs that are not *of* the disease, but that are themselves the disease. Although as early as the first half of the sixteenth century, Paracelsus and other physicians proposed "ontological" or nonmetaphysical theories of the sources of some diseases, Foucault reasonably concludes that only after the eighteenth century, as a general consensus, is there "no longer a pathological essence beyond the systems."[12]

For Taylor, as physician and minister, such a "pathological essence beyond the symptoms" was always an assumed part of disease, which the physician-minister treated as a phenomenon of the spirit as well as of the flesh. Taylor died in 1729, several years before the "birth" of modern medicine as Foucault identifies it. However, he certainly witnessed the numerous controversies in medical science that some historians regard as "revolutionary" moments that, according to Foucault, culminated in its modernization in the later eighteenth century. Though medical developments in general ran far behind those in astronomy and mechanics, medical science in Taylor's day was no static or complacently medieval discipline. Sanctus Sanctorius (1561-1636) had drawn insights from mechanical science and invented devices for studying temperature and respiration and for measuring pulse rate; William Harvey applied to cardiology a variety of mechanical principles; Giovanni Alfonso Borelli (1608-1679) employed mechanistic theory in his study of muscular movement; and Robert Boyle (1627-1691), whose ideas were highly regarded by the Mathers, had incorporated mechanistic concepts into his corpuscular theory of the universe. During Taylor's era, subjects of continual debate concerned the validity of Galenic and scholastic medical theories as opposed to the "new medicine" or "iatrochemical" studies of Paracelsians, as well as to the ideas of those such as Boyle, who advocated a relatively empirical study of chemistry divorced from its alchemical background.[13]

In short, medical science, like the other sciences, was struggling with the impending epistemological shift to rational empiricism. Thus, Taylor was heir to myriad and radically disjunctive influences in all areas of scientific inquiry, both between and within the disciplines. Sometimes only incipient, and sometimes overtly present in all these disputes was the tendency for what Foucault calls the invisible "essences" to disappear from the scientist's purview. Despite Taylor's scientifically progressive attitude (and perhaps encouraged by the Cambridge Platonists who probably influenced him while he studied in England[14]), he maintains a unifying vision in his works in constant resistance to the "new scientific" tendency to divorce matter and spirit. Apparently, Taylor did not accept the need for divorcing matter and spirit, for when he reconciled the new data with Puritan theology, such data only reinforced Taylor's sense of the coherence of God's design.

Such a state of affairs could reasonably have led Taylor to produce a body of literary works marred by confusion, and, indeed, some of Taylor's critics see only inconsistency and incoherence in his art. However, other scholars have discovered significant unities in Taylor's thought and artistry.[15] I intend to show how Taylor's overarching typological hermeneutic enables him to reckon with the confusion of his age; more specifically, I will demonstrate, through an analysis of Taylor's medical vision, how he developed a hermeneutic system that allowed him to employ the most recent medical concepts within the orthodox theology reflected in his poetry.

The identification of medical and ministerial roles had long antecedents, both historical and religious. Moreover, Taylor's dual role of minister and physician was by necessity a quite common one in early America. During this time, hardly anyone in the colonies had formal training in medicine, so ministers and magistrates frequently served as "physician, surgeon, and apothecary."[16] Benjamin Tompson's "A Funeral Tribute" (1676) to John Winthrop, Jr., suggests how deeply ingrained in the colonial imagination was this combined function of physician with magistrate or minister. Tompson depicts the colonies as bleeding patients aware of the loss of their Christian physician.[17]

Like his colonial contemporaries, Taylor lacked formal training in medicine, but he probably began to gather much knowledge while growing up in England on a farm in Sketchley, Leicestershire. Not much is known about Taylor's early life, but rural people of the time usually were their own physicians, and so knew quite well the medicinal properties of plants. One reason so few colonists had formal training is that in seventeenth-century England, medicine was not an established part of any university curriculum. Harvard College had no medical curriculum either, for the efforts of President Henry Dunster in 1647, and later of Jonathan Mitchell in the 1660s, to acquire medical faculty and materials for the school failed.[18] Thus we know that Taylor could not have studied medicine at Cambridge or at Harvard. Whatever he knew from common experience, however, he clearly augmented by independent study and reading throughout his life. The books in his library included a number of medical volumes: John Woodall's *The Surgeons Mate* (1617), Joseph Galeanus's *Epistola Medica* (1648), and Nicholas Culpeper's *London Dispensatory* (1649), among others. Moreover, Taylor's friendships with men such as Samuel Lee and Increase and Cotton Mather provided a channel for the exchange of current scientific information as well as opportunities to borrow books, from which Taylor often copied long passages.[19]

Taylor read widely in all the sciences and tried always to resolve intellectual conflicts between science and theology without distorting science or Puritan doctrine.[20] Taylor seemed nearly compulsive in his drive toward a unifying typological vision, unlike his contemporary and friend, Cotton Mather, for example; Mather apparently accepted a greater divergence between secular and religious life and seemed less preoccupied than Taylor with the dualisms of his era.[21] Consequently, such works as the *Magnalia Christi Americana* (1702) sometimes propose a theory of earthly experience controlled by a constantly intervening Calvinistic God, and at other times exhibit a rationalistic stance heralding an eighteenth-century mechanistic view of the universe.[22] For Taylor, however, all significant experience eventually came to fit into the Puritan typological scheme. At first it seems curious that conservative Puritan typology could accommodate new scientific information, which frequently contradicted theological paradigms. Indeed, Taylor's typological hermeneutic was drawn from the most conservative of exegetical writers, especially Samuel Mather (*The Figures or Types of the Old Testament*, 1683) and Thomas Taylor (*Christ Revealed*, 1635).[23] But the great number of typological poems in the Second Series of the *Preparatory Meditations* reveals Taylor's steady development of just such an accommodating vision; over the years, Taylor more and more confidently interprets the new and strange phenomena of a revised Book of Nature as signifiers in a system circumscribed by a constant Book of God. Taylor's medical knowledge affords him one of many opportunities to read the signs of nature, and his unified vision prevails despite the "bewildering spectrum of medical . . . views" of his era.[24]

At the center of this "bewildering spectrum" of views lies an epistemological conflict: are the body and its ailments the mere outward signs of a spiritual condition, or are diseases mere malfunctions of the corporal mechanism that houses but does not "correspond" to the soul? In the medical disputes of the seventeenth and eighteenth centuries, we see the gradual demise of notions of correspondence between spirit and matter, an epistemological shift that Marjorie Hope Nicolson calls "the breaking of the circle."[25] Proponents of the ancient views of Galen, Hippocrates, scholasticism, and medieval alchemy found themselves at odds with the new views of Paracelsians, post-Paracelsians, anatomists, and chemists, who were rapidly transforming medicine into a science based on empirical observation and analysis rather than upon scholastic paradigms that posited knowledge of matter based on metaphysical assumptions.

The new medical theories were available to Edward Taylor from a wide variety of sources. Among these were medical compendia compiled by Daniel Sennert, Charles Morton, Nicholas Culpeper, and others. Books by Jean Baptiste Van Helmont (1577-1644), Robert Boyle, and William Harvey were also generally accessible. Taylor's notebooks contain passages from other well-known sources, such as William Salmon's *Pharmacopoeia*

Londinensis (1685), Lazare Riviere's *The Practice of Physick* (1672), and Nicholas Culpeper's *Dispensatory* (1654). Taylor's "Meditation 1.4" reveals his knowledge of yet another herbal that he neither owned nor apparently copied—Gracia D'Orta's *Coloquious dos simples e drogas e sonsas medicinas da India* (1653).[26] Like Culpeper's and other pharmacopoeia, D'Orta's herbal emphasizes the practical effects of remedies. Indeed, D'Orta repudiates ancient authority in the Paracelsian manner and declares, "I am only going to say what I know to be true."[27] D'Orta's attitude follows the example set by the authors of medical compendia and by the London College of Physicians, who in 1589 had advocated compromise in the disputes between ancient and modern medical theories.[28]

Taylor likewise seems to think in a synthetic, eclectic fashion. His works are replete with Galenic terminology, and they suggest that he knew the difference between Galen's and Harvey's notions about circulation; his works especially evince Paracelsian alchemical concepts. Although this slough of nomenclature could cause confusion, careful scrutiny of Taylor's work reveals that he maintains primarily a Paracelsian vision, which harmonizes well with Puritan typology.

The foremost harmony between Paracelsian philosophy and Puritan theology lies in their mutual acceptance of the "two book" universe: rational, careful observation of the Book of Nature, subordinated to proper insights derived from the Bible, leads to truth. Paracelsus himself was driven by motives as much or more religious than scientific, though he was an early advocate of the scientific method of empirical observation. His seventeenth-century followers were even more rigorously scientific in their approaches, though they too shared significant, if diverse, religious motives. The seventeenth-century Paracelsians included Culpeper, Van Helmont, Robert Fludd, John Webster, and John Woodall, among those who directly and indirectly informed Taylor. Besides the Culpeper texts, Taylor owned Webster's *Metallographia: An History of Metals* (1641), and the 1617 edition of Woodall's *The Surgeons Mate,* a widely circulated work that was expanded and reprinted twice before Taylor's death in 1729.[29] Fortified by the many scientific developments of the late sixteenth and early seventeenth centuries, these Paracelsians surpassed Paracelsus in their knowledge of chemical properties of plants and metals, and they conjoined this knowledge with the older, Christian alchemical notions about the metaphysical "essences" of these substances.[30]

Though authorities on Paracelsian alchemy trace its origins in Platonic, Aristotelian, and Gnostic philosophy, the Christian tradition cen-

tral to Paracelsian thought seems more particularly Augustinian; this
feature of Paracelsianism largely accounts for its easy reconciliation with
Puritan theology.[31] The Augustinian notion of how God's Being pervades
nature accounts for why the Paracelsians cannot properly be termed pan-
theists, even though they sometimes appear to be so. Though seventeenth-
century Paracelsians were not a philosophically or theologically unified
group, they variously defended "natural magic," while they denied pan-
theism for reasons that Van Helmont explains throughout his works. His
argument follows Augustinian lines in proclaiming that, although there
is no gap between the corporal and the spiritual, nature is not divinely
immanent. Instead, it contains something approximating a receptivity to,
or even a yearning toward, the "Life Spirit," which comes from God.
Paracelsus himself had referred to the "archei" within the incipient forms
of nature that are responsible for transforming "prime matter" (God's force)
into "ultimate matter" (particular forms). These "archei" constitute that
part of matter that retains a divine origin. Van Helmont later revised
Paracelsus's notion of "archei" in a manner that precluded all arguments for
a pantheistic universe.[32] An Augustinian concept of divine presence that
is not immanence underlies Puritan theology as well, and Edward Taylor's
thought in particular.[33] Taylor, who is no pantheist, declares in "Meditation 2.17" that "Being Being gave to all that be." That is, deistic "Being"
permeates nature—nature partakes of the order of grace, but nature is not
divine. Moreover, when Taylor repeatedly refers in his poems to the "aqua
vitae" that flows from God throughout all nature, he likewise refers to
God's love (for St. Augustine, synonymous with Being) and recalls the
alchemical fascination with water as the element pervading all matter.[34]

Considering this common thread of Augustinian philosophy uniting
both Paracelsian and Puritan traditions, one can more clearly appreciate
Taylor's ease in assimilating Paracelsian medicine into a Puritan typological scheme; his understanding of God's grace dispensed throughout
nature comports with the Paracelsian notion of a non-pantheistic natural
magic. As Taylor explains in the seventh sermon in the *Christographia*,
"The Influences that flow from Christ are Nature's disposing influences.
He Wealds nature as he pleaseth. . . . All the influences in naturall things
come forth from him as to their flowrishing and glory. So all those Influences that actuate Nature Preternaturally, or not in a naturall way, are
from him, Whether they are Contranatural [or] Supernatural."[35]

Always maintaining this notion of the unity of matter and spirit,
Taylor in his poems depicts the source of physical illness as spiritual

malady, despite whatever immediate material causes seem apparent. Such illnesses yield to the pharmacopoeian remedies because these remedies are the vehicles of Christ's "disposing influences." That is, they are ordained channels for spiritual healing through grace.

Despite some ostensibly Galenic terminology, "Meditation 2.67B" exhibits Taylor's Paracelsian medical vision at work within this larger, encompassing theological view. As usual, illness stems from spiritual sickness: "Consumptions, Fevers, Head pains: Turns. / . . . Lythargy . . . Apoplectick Strokes: / . . . Surdity, / Ill Tongue, Mouth Ulcers, Frog, the Quinsie Throate" and a gallery of other diseases result from "Ill humors" of the spirit. The speaker in "2.67B" several times refers to "humors": "O! Sun of Righteousness Thy Beams bright, Hot / Rafter a Doctors, and a Surgeons Shop. / . . . So rout Ill Humors: And thy purges bring." Though these references to "humors" at first recall Galen's theory, one must remember that Taylor owned a copy of Woodall's *The Surgeons Mate*, in which the author paraphrases and otherwise reports on the ideas of French Paracelsian Joseph Duchesne, who revised humoral theory within a Paracelsian context.[36] Instead of an inconsistent use of Galenic and Paracelsian ideas in "2.67B," Taylor's lines demonstrate his familiarity with contemporary medical texts, some of which synthesized old and new concepts.

Thus, we see that in this poem, as in all of Taylor's poems concerning medicine, disease is a postlapsarian condition responsive to "purges," which Paracelsians, in contrast to Galenists, prescribe for ridding the body of invasive impurities and poisons. This notion of disease as the overt presence of foreign substances in the body rather than as internal humoral imbalance is the primary distinguishing feature between Galenic and Paracelsian theory. Paracelsus himself, in fact, like such Puritans as Taylor, equated the primary separation of nature and divinity—the Fall—with the "separation" of the body from health that is caused by an intrusive substance and that calls for purgation.

For Taylor, illness is spiritual in origin, and a true cure is a purging or clearing of the channels of divine grace between God and nature; grace flows through Christ (the ultimate Physician) to the human patient. In "The Reflexion," for example, the speaker requests "Med'cine" to help clear a passage for grace to his soul: "Had not my Soule's thy Conduit, Pipes stopt bin / With mud, what Ravishment woulds't thou Convay?" Likewise, in "Meditation 2.68B," the poet asks for a "heavenly Alkahest"—probably Van Helmont's coinage for the universal solvent in alchemy—to cure his

maladies by filling him with grace. In "2.149," the alchemical remedy
reconciles spirit and matter: the womb of the Bride in the song of Solomon
and the altar of the Church (type and antitype) are "basons" in which
"Spirits Chymistrie" occurs.

In Taylor's poems, healing not only cures the patient but also allows for
the glorification of God. As the speaker says in "2.67B": "When with these
Wings thou does mee medicine / I'st weare the Cure, thou th' glory of this
Shine." Christ the Healer's refining fire descends and cures, and then
reflects back to glorify its source. Once again Taylor conjoins Augustinian
and Paracelsian notions: Augustinian tradition anticipates the spiritualiza-
tion of nature and humanity when the reception of grace brings completion to all that remains incomplete (cut off from its origins) in fallen
nature; Paracelsian alchemy similarly looks forward to the gradual refining
of the universe through alchemical transformation of matter.

"Meditation 2.67B" draws together Puritan theology and Paracelsian
medicine in yet another way which demonstrates Taylor's synthesizing
vision as well as his impressive verbal dexterity:

> Doe Fables say, the Rising Sun doth Dance
>   On Easter Day for joy, thou didst ascende.
> O Sun of Righteousness; tho't be a glance
>   Of Falshoods Spectacles on Rome's nose end?
>   And shall not I, furled in thy glorious beams
>   Ev'n jump for joy, Enjoying such sweet gleams?
>
> What doth the rising Sun with its Curld Locks
>   And golden wings soon make the Chilly world
> Shook with an Ague Fit by night shade drops,
>   Revive, grow brisk, Suns Eyebright on it hurld?
>   How should my Soule then sick of th' Scurvy spring
>   When thy sweet medicating rayes come in?
>
> Alas! Sweet Sun of Righteousness, Dost shine
>   Upon such Dunghills, as I am? Methinks
> My Soule sends out such putrid sents, and rhimes
>   That with thy beams would Choke the aire with Stincks.
>   And Nasty vapors ery where, whereby
>   Thy rayes should venom'd be that from thee fly.
>
> The fiery Darts of Satan stob my heart.
>   His Punyards Thrusts are deep, and venom'd too.
> His Arrows wound my thoughts, Words, Works, each part

They all a bleeding ly by th' Stobs, and rue.
His Aire I breath in, poison doth my Lungs.
Hence come Consumptions, Fevers, Head pains: Turns.

Yea, Lythargy, the Apoplectick Stroke:
    The Catochee, Soul Blindness, Surdity,
Ill Tongue, Mouth Ulcers, Frog, the Quinsie Throate
    The Palate Fallen, Wheezings, Pleurisy.
    Heart Ach, the Syncopee, bad stomach tricks
    Gaul Tumors, Liver grown; spleen evills Cricks.

The Kidny toucht, The Iliak, Colick Griefe
    The Ricats, Dropsy, Gout, the Scurvy, Sore
The Miserere Mei. O Reliefe
    I want and would, and beg it at thy doore.
    O! Sun of Righteousness Thy Beams bright, Hot
    Rafter a Doctors, and a Surgeons Shop.

I ope my Case to thee, my Lord: mee in
    Thy glorious Bath, of Sun Shine, Bathe, and Sweate.
So rout Ill Humors: And thy purges bring.
    Administer in Sunbeame Light, and Heate.
    Pound some for Cordiall powders very small
    To Cure my Kidnies, Spleen, My Liver, Gaul.

And with the same refresh my Heart, and Lungs
    From Wasts, and Weakness. Free from Pleurisy
Bad Stomach, Iliak, Colick Fever, turns,
    From Scurvy, Dropsy, Gout, and Leprosy
    From Itch, Botch Scab. And purify my Blood
    From all Ill Humors: So make all things good.

Weave, Lord, these golden Locks into a web
    Of Spiritual Taffity; make of the same
A sweet perfumed Rheum-Cap for my head
    To free from Lythargy, the Turn, and Pain,
    From Waking-Sleep, Sin-Falling Mallady
    From Whimsy, Melancholy Frenzy-dy.

Thy Curled Rayes, Lord, make mine Eare Picker
    To Cure my Deafeness: Light, Ophthalmicks pure
To heate my Eyes and make the Sight the Quicker.
    That I may use Sins Spectacles no more.
    O still some Beams. And with the Spirits fresh
    My Palate Ulcerd Mouth, and Ill Tongue dress.

And ply my wounds with Pledgets dipt therein.
  And wash therewith my Scabs and Boils so sore,
And all my Stobs, and Arrow wounds come, bring
  And syrrindge with the Same. It will them Cure.
  With tents made of these Beams well tent them all.
  They Fistula'es and Gangrenes Conquour shall.

Lord plaster mee herewith to bring soon down
  My Swellings. Stick a Feather of thy Wing
Within my Cap to Cure my Aching Crown.
  And with these beams Heale mee of all my Sin.
  When with these Wings thou dost mee medicine
  I'st weare the Cure, thou the glory of this Shine.

The poem corroborates Thomas Taylor's notion about illness as expressed in *Christ Revealed,* and through a pun on the word "Turns," introduces Edward Taylor's unique interpretation of the Paracelsian doctrine of "signatures"—the theory that the best remedy for an illness is the one that, in essence or in literal physical form, most resembles the affected bodily part or the offending material agent of the disease. Thus, eyebright cures optical problems; orchid cures maladies of the male genitalia; liverwort cures hepatic ailments, etc.[37] (This idea about the similarity between ailment and cure, incidentally, contrasts directly with the Galenic notion that a disease demands a cure made from a substance *opposite* in character to the malady.) Thomas Taylor's theory of illness is essentially a "like-cures-like" proposition: physical illness adumbrates spiritual affliction and offers the best opportunity for spiritual healing. Here Taylor recalls the generally held Puritan notion that one cannot be fully healed by Christ without first becoming very sick. Disease of the body leads in some cases to death and redemption or to conversion and salvation, both cures for all sickness.

In "Meditation 2.67B," one of the many diseases that plagues the speaker is "Turns," a brain disease causing dizziness. Given the Puritan concept of physical disease as possibly leading to spiritual salvation, one can see that Taylor's punctuation of line twenty-four and his placement of the word "turns" therein suggests that all diseases lead up to "Turns": "Consumptions, Fevers, Head pains: Turns." That is, all diseases, with their spiritual origins, amount to "dizziness" or postlapsarian disorientation. But they might also lead to "turns" of the heart, the most significant step in the Puritan conversion process. Disease thus provides an opportunity for salvation, as suggested in *Christ Revealed*; one "turn" cures another, just as in the Paracelsian tradition, an adeptly administered poison heals the sickness caused by that poison. God, the ultimate Adept, administers physical "Turns" that produce "turns of the heart."

Some of Taylor's most fascinating poems in the *Preparatory Meditations* are those in which he draws together biblical types and Paracelsian medicine. His Rose of Sharon poems provide examples ("Meditation 1.4" and "The Reflexion," particularly),[38] as does "Meditation 2.61," a poem in which the central emblem or conceit is at once the hermetical symbol of the physician—the caduceus—the brazen serpent staff of Moses in *Numbers,* the crucifix upon which Christ-suffered, and the seventeenth-century place of physical healing, the surgery or "Doctors Shop."

> My Mights too mean, lend your Angelick might
>   Ye mighty Angells, brightly to define.
> A piece of burnisht brass, formd Serpent like
>   To Countermand all poison Serpentine.
>   No Remedie could cure the Serpents Bite
>   But One: to wit, The brazen Serpent's Sight.
>
> Shall brass the bosoms poison in't Contain
>   A Counter poison, better than what beds
> In Creatures bosoms? Nay, But its vertue came
>   Through that brass Shapt from God that healing sheds.
>   Its Vertue rode in th' golden Coach of th' eyes
>   Into the Soule, and Serpents Sting defies.
>
> So that a Sight of the brazen Serpent hung
>   Up in the Banner Standard of the Camp
> Was made a Charet wherein rode and run
>   A Healing vertue to the Serpents Cramp.
>   But that's not all. Christ in this Snake shapt brass
>   Raist on the Standard, Crucified was.
>
> As in this Serpent lay the only Cure
>   Unto the fiery Serpents burning bite,
> Not by its Physick Vertue, (that is sure)
>   But by a Beam Divine of Grace's might
>   Whose Vertue onely is the plaster 'plide
>   Unto the Wound, by Faith in Christs blood di'de.
>
> A Sight of th' Artificiall Serpent heales
>   The venom wound the naturall Serpent made.

A Spirituall Sight of Christ, from Christ down steals.
  A Cure against the Hellish Serpents trade.
  Not that the Springhead of the Cure was found
  In Christs humanity with sharp thorns Crownd.

This Brazen Serpent is a Doctors Shop.
  On ev'ry Shelfe's a Sovereign remedy.
The Serpents Flesh the Sovereign Salve is got
  Against the Serpents bite, gaind by the eye.
  The Eyebeames agents are that forth do bring
  The Sovereign Counter poison, and let't in.

I by the fiery Serpent bitt be here.
  Be thou my brazen Serpent me to Cure.
My Sight, Lord, make thy golden Charet cleare
  To bring thy remedy unto my Sore.
  If this thou dost I shall be heald: My wound
  Shall sing thy praises: and thy glory sound.

Taylor bases "Meditation 2.61" on the story of Moses who, in Numbers 21:6-8, must deal with his ungrateful charges in the desert. They have complained of having only manna to eat, and their lack of faith and gratitude has brought upon them a pestilence of stinging insects. God instructs Moses to raise a brazen serpent upon a wooden pole. This serpent, looked upon with the eye of faith, is the only cure for the painful stings, which are the earthly manifestations of the original "sting" of Satan. Both Samuel Mather in *The Figures or Types* and Thomas Taylor in *Christ Revealed* devote considerable space to an exegesis of this brazen serpent type, and Edward Taylor's poem is clearly predicated upon their interpretation, especially Thomas Taylor's.

In stanza one, Taylor refers to the brass of which the brazen serpent is made, and begins to suggest a Paracelsian remedy for affliction that is also the scriptural prescription. The cure for the bite of Satan, the real serpent, is the sight of the brass serpent coiled around the wooden pole. Thus one serpent heals the ailment caused by another; moreover, this Old Testament brazen serpent, in addition to being the type for Christ who hangs upon the wooden cross to "cure" sin, is a version of the caduceus, the hermetical sign of the physician.

Taylor's next four stanzas account for how the cure works. The poem equates brass, a strong alloy of tin and copper, with Christ, God's stronger alloy of divinity and humanity. Brass in itself contains no "Counter poison, better than what beds / In Creatures bosoms" (grace is the counter poison in the heart, which can turn toward God); neither does Christ in his human form contain any such remedy: "Not that the Springhead of the Cure was found / In Christs humanity with sharp thorns Crownd." Moreover, just as Christ is free of sin, the "Artificiall Serpent" is likewise free of the real serpent's venom. Both Christ and the brazen serpent are conduits of God's grace. God chooses to send "vertue" or healing power through brass rather than gold, and through his Son incarnate rather than through a purely divine being, because "lowly" instruments prevent idolatry; they focus human attention properly upon the source of grace. (Emphasizing this same notion in "Meditation 1.39," Taylor refers to Christ as "Nails made of heavenly Steel," an alloy "more Choice than gold.") God's "vertues" are Paracelsian, for they are remedies made of the same substance as that which causes the disease: one serpent cures the ills caused by another, and Christ's assuming a lowly human form redeems humanity from its fallen state. God's cure is also the "Sovereign remedy," for it ministers at once to body and soul. The "brass shapt from God" is the brazen serpent that healed Moses' charges in the desert and also is Christ, the "Sovereign" healer of all humanity.

Through a pun on the word "Beam" in the fourth stanza, Taylor yokes Old Testament, New Testament, and Paracelsian references. The "Beam Divine" is grace, the wooden pole on which the brazen serpent hangs and the wooden cross on which Christ hangs. Just as conventional seventeen-century religious poets often depict God's grace as descending upon "beams" from heaven, Paracelsians likewise regard the rays and beams of light from stars and heavenly bodies as bearing God's "breath,"[39] or healing power. In the sixth stanza, this grace flows through the "eyebeams" into the physician-poet and his "Doctors Shop." Here Taylor breaks the closed hermeneutic circle of conservative typology to suggest that, allegorically at least, earthly phenomena fulfill the typal foreshadowings in the Bible: "This Brazen Serpent is a Doctors Shop."[40] That is to say, the "beams" of grace descending through Christ, and figuratively through the caduceus that signifies the "Doctors Shop," can heal the physician-poet's "wound" and reflect back to glorify their sources in the ultimate Physician. Thus is the microcosmic earthly realm uplifted and transformed through a heavenly alchemy.

Taylor's Paracelsian poems show us how his medical and theological visions coalesce. Moreover, they demonstrate his vision of himself as an instrument in the healing and redemptive process; his conception of himself as poet (user of words) and as reader-interpreter (of the Word) is synonymous with his sense of himself as physician, as reader-interpreter of the Book of Nature who looks for the earthly signifiers of spiritual conditions and cures. For Taylor, all signifiers (words and phenomena of nature) are contained within the Logos, which is Christ, who is both the ultimate Physician and the ultimate Interpreter.[41] Consequently, language becomes one of the poet-physician's essential tools, since it can be another conduit of grace. Doubtless following Samuel Mather's advice to biblical exegetes to seek "Spiritual Wisdom to accommodate and apply Things rationally and spiritually,"[42] Taylor begins "Meditation 2.61" with a request that the "mighty Angells" help him "brightly to define" the type of the brazen serpent. The speaker considers his "Mights too mean," that is, inferior; however, he also makes a pun here on the word "mean." He asks help "to mean," that is, to define, to signify properly, in the manner that Mather advocates. One effect of the cure the speaker seeks is the brightening of his poetic powers, for according to Puritan convention, the language of sermons and religious meditation can at any time be "Wealded" to bear Christ's "disposing Influences."[43] Poet, physician, and minister, Taylor intends his words to act as conduits for the Word as healing grace.

"Meditation 1.7," another of Taylor's Paracelsian poems, even more emphatically stresses the connection between Logos and medicine. Here Taylor depicts Christ as a distillery of "Heavenly Choice drugs" and requests grace and redemption from fallen speech to flow to him from Christ's Word:

> Thy Speech the Liquor in thy Vessel stands,
>   Well ting'd with Grace a blessed Tincture, Loe,
> Thy Words distilld, Grace in thy Lips pourd, and,
>   Give Graces Tinctur in them where they go.
>   Thy words in graces tincture stilld, Lord, may
>   The Tincture of thy Grace in me Convay.

In the final stanza, the physician-poet depicts himself as a medicine "bottle" to hold the heavenly remedy for postlapsarian speech. Moreover, he asks God to effect the final alchemical transformation by filling him with "Liquid Gold":

And Dub with Gold dug out of Graces mine
    That they [the poet's words] thine Image might have in them foild.
    Grace in thy Lips pourd out's as Liquid Gold.
    Thy Bottle make my Soule, Lord, it to hold.

Though he is probably the last in the Paracelsian tradition, Taylor is one of the first of American literary figures who is also a physician. After Taylor and his writer-physician contemporaries such as John Winthrop, Jr., and Cotton Mather, among others, there are in the eighteenth century Benjamin Rush and two Connecticut Wits, Mason Fitch Cogswell and Lemuel Hopkins; in the nineteenth century, physician-writers include Oliver Wendell Holmes and James Gates Percival (obscure now, but honored in the 1820s as America's chief poet);[44] and in the twentieth century, the number of writers who are also medical doctors is even greater: William Carlos Williams, Walker Percy, Lewis Thomas, Oliver Sacks, Richard Selzer, and Gerald Weismann. Poet Robinson Jeffers attended medical school. Of all these personalities, Richard Selzer perhaps most eloquently expressed the affinities between writing and healing. He speaks of the "rich, alliterative language of medicine" and remarks upon the similarities between surgery and writing, both delicate searches for what is elusive and ineffable. He sees the surgeon as a kind of "reader" of the "self-absorbed" and "revelatory" language of the body, and he believes, like the holistic physicians of the Renaissance, in something resembling an "essence" beyond the symptoms. For the physician-as-reader, "comprehension [of this essence] is instantaneous, despite the absence of what we call words to clarify it." For the "reader" of the body, the body's language becomes "a detonation in the mind until the reader feels" what the other feels.[45]

Though separated by hundreds of years and different scientific traditions, both Selzer's essays and Taylor's poems share a mutual sense of the sacramental dimension of healing that is also a dimension of the writer's art. Such resonance suggests that despite the persistent efforts of empirical science to abandon the metaphysical territories that science once occupied, some central mystery of speech and existence prevents any such absolute separation. Exploring some of the overlapping concerns of religion, science, and art, well-known literary critic and theologian Walter J. Ong declares that all three of these disciplines attempt to "'open up,' or to 'open out,' to explicate and unfold" this central mystery.[46] The tradition of writer-physicians who variously perceive this metaphysical link corroborates Ong's insight and suggests that despite the positivist and empiricist heritage of the twentieth century, "a physitian cureth not only the body but the mind in some manner."

Notes

1. *A New Method of Physick; or, A Short View of Paracelsus and Galen's Practice; In 3 Treatises* (London, 1654) is Culpeper's translation of Simeon Partlitz's Latin text. It is reprinted in part in F.L. Poynter's "Nicholas Culpeper and the Paracelsians," in Allen G. Debus, ed., *Science, Medicine and Society in the Renaissance*, vol. 1 (New York: Science History Publications, 1972), 201-20. Culpeper's text appears as item number 147 in Thomas Johnson's inventory of Taylor's library; see *The Poetical Works of Edward Taylor* (New York: Rockland, 1939).

2. See Samuel Eliot Morison's *Harvard in the Seventeenth Century*, 2 vols. (Cambridge: Harvard Univ. Press, 1956).

3. See Francis Murphy, ed., *The Diary of Edward Taylor* (Springfield: Springfield Library and Museum Association, 1964), 37.

4. Morison, *Harvard in the Seventeenth Century*, 1:215.

5. Herbert Butterfield, *The Origins of Modern Science: 1300-1800* (New York: Free Press, 1965), 7.

6. See Morison's *Harvard in the Seventeenth Century* and my "Edward Taylor's Reluctant Revolution: The 'New Astronomy' and the *Preparatory Meditations*," *American Poetry* 1 (Winter 1984): 4-17.

7. See John Donne's "The First Anniversary," in John T. Shawcross, ed., *The Complete Poetry of John Donne* (Garden City: Anchor, 1967), 279.

8. Cited in Butterfield, *Origins*, 119.

9. The following texts contain discussions of the Scientific Revolution of the Renaissance: I. Bernard Cohen's *Revolution in Science* (Cambridge: Harvard University Press, 1985); Thomas Kuhn's *The Structure of Scientific Revolutions* (Chicago: Chicago Univ. Press, 1962), and *The Essential Tension: Selected Studies in Scientific Tradition and Change* (Chicago: Univ. of Chicago Press, 1977).

10. Butterfield, *Origins*, 14.

11. Michel Foucault, *The Birth of the Clinic: An Archaeology of Medical Perception* (New York: Vintage, 1975), xii-xiii.

12. Foucault, *Birth*, 91.

13. Authoritative sources on these medical disputes of the Renaissance include Debus's "The Paracelsian Compromise in Elizabethan England," *Ambix* 8 (June 1960): 71-97; "Paracelsus and the Neoplatonic and Gnostic Tradition," *Ambix* 8 (Oct. 1960): 125-66; *The English Paracelsians* (London: Oldbourne, 1965); *Science, Medicine, and Society in the Sixteenth and Seventeenth Centuries*, 2 vols. (New York: Science History Publications, 1977); *Man and Nature in the Renaissance* (Cambridge: Cambridge University Press, 1978); Walter Pagel's *The Religious and Philosophical Aspects of Van Helmont's Science and Medicine* (Baltimore: Johns Hopkins Univ. Press, 1944); *Jean Baptista Van Helmont: Reformer of Science and Medicine* (Cambridge: Cambridge Univ. Press, 1982); *Paracelsus: An Introduction to the Philosophical Medicine in the Era of the Renaissance* (Basel: Karger, 1982).

14. On Edward Taylor's "personal Platonism" and the influence of the Cambridge Platonists, see Willie T. Weathers's "Edward Taylor and the Cambridge Platonists," *American Literature* 26 (Mar. 1954): 1-31. Butterfield remarks upon the Cambridge Platonists' resistance to the mechanical model of the universe (137).

15. See Karl Keller's *The Example of Edward Taylor* (Amherst: Univ. of Massachusetts

Press, 1975), 161-68. Among those making the case for Taylor's controlled artistry are Jeffrey A. Hammond, "Reading Taylor Exegetically: The *Preparatory Meditations* and the Commentary Tradition," *Texas Studies in Literature and Language* 24 (Winter 1982): 347-71; William J. Scheick, "'The Inward Tacles and the Outward Traces': Edward Taylor's Elusive Transitions," *Early American Literature* 12 (Fall 1977): 163-76; and "Order and Disorder in Taylor's Poetry: Meditation 1.8," *American Poetry* 5 (Winter 1988): 2-11.

16. Ronald Sterne Wilkinson, "'Hermes Christianus': John Winthrop, Jr. and Chemical Medicine in Seventeenth-Century New England," in Debus, *Science, Medicine, and Society,* 224.

17. Cheryl Z. Oreovicz observes this in "Investigating 'the America of nature': Alchemy in Early American Poetry," in Peter White, ed., *Puritan Poets and Poetics: Seventeenth-Century American Poetry in Theory and Practice* (University Park: Pennsylvania State Univ. Press, 1985), 99-110.

18. Morison, *Harvard in the Seventeenth Century,* 1:283.

19. According to Johnson, Taylor's personal documents include copied passages from Lazare Riviere's *The Practice of Physick* (London, 1672), translated as Culpeper's *Dispensatory;* and William Salmon's *Pharmacopoeia Londinensis* (London, 1685). Morison's *The Intellectual Life of Colonial New England* lists the many texts generally available in Taylor's era; William J. Scheick's "'That Blazing Star in Joshua': Edward Taylor's 'Meditation 2.10' and Increase Mather's Kometographia," *Seventeenth-Century News* 34 (Summer/Fall 1976): 36-37, documents Taylor's exchange of ideas with the Mathers; and Theodore Hornberger's "Samuel Lee: A Clerical Channel for the Flow of New Ideas to Seventeenth-Century New England," *Osiris* 1 (Jan. 1936), documents the Lee contribution.

20. Articles on Taylor and science are these (and others cited above): Sister M. Theresa Clare's "Taylor's 'Meditation Sixty-Two'," *Explicator* 19 (Dec. 1960): 16; Joan Del Fattore's "John Webster's Metallographia: A Source for Alchemical Imagery in the Preparatory Meditations," *Early American Literature* 18 (Winter 1983-84): 233-41; Joel R. Kehler's "Physiology and Metaphor in Edward Taylor's 'Meditation. Can. 1.3,'" *Early American Literature* 9 (Winter 1975): 315-20; Cheryl Z. Oreovicz's "Edward Taylor and the Alchemy of Grace," *Seventeenth-Century News* 34 (Summer/Fall 1976): 33-36; William J. Scheick's "Edward Taylor's Herbalism in Preparatory Meditations," *American Poetry* 1 (Fall 1983): 64-71; "Edward Taylor's Optics," *American Literature* 55 (May 1983): 234-40; and Lawrence Lan Sluder's "God in the Background: Edward Taylor as Naturalist," *Early American Literature* 7 (Winter 1973): 265-71.

21. Robert Middlecoff, *The Mathers: Three Generations of Puritan Intellectuals, 1596-1728* (London: Oxford Univ. Press, 1971), 9, 11.

22. See Morison's *The Intellectual Life of Colonial New England,* 269, and Mason Lowance, Jr.'s *The Language of Canaan: Metaphor and Symbol in New England from the Puritans to the Transcendentalists* (Cambridge: Harvard Univ. Press, 1980), 163-69.

23. Karen Rowe has established Taylor's close familiarity with both these sources. See *Saint and Singer: Edward Taylor's Typology and the Poetics of Meditation* (Cambridge: Cambridge Univ. Press, 1986), 28-29.

24. Debus, *Man and Nature in the Renaissance,* 32.

25. See Marjorie Hope Nicolson's *The Breaking of the Circle: Studies in the Effect of the 'New Science' upon Seventeenth-Century Poetry* (Evanston: Northwestern Univ. Press, 1950).

26. "Meditation 1.4" refers to the "flowers of Garzia Horti," which is doubtless a Latinized reference to Garcia D'Orta. Debus, in *Man and Nature in the Renaissance*, remarks that a Latin text of D'Orta's work existed (47).

27. Debus, *Man and Nature*, 47.

28. Debus, *Man and Nature*, 31-32.

29. Debus, *English Paracelsians*, 99. Taylor's library items 10 and 52.

30. Debus, *English Paracelsians*. See especially chapter 1.

31. On Augustinian traits of Paracelsian thought, see P. Diepgen, "Was wissen wir von Paracelsus sicher und was bedeutet er uns heute?" *Gesundheitsfuhrung* 9 (Sept. 1941).

32. See Pagel's *Religious and Philosophical Aspects*, 17-22, and *Jean Baptista Van Helmont*, 96-102.

33. See William J. Scheick's *The Will and the Word: The Poetry of Edward Taylor* (Athens: Univ. of Georgia Press, 1974). He discusses the Augustinian backgrounds of Taylor's thought.

34. The "aqua vitae" poems include "Meditation 1.10," "2.60B," and "2.75." All references to Edward Taylor's poems are to Donald Stanford's *The Poems of Edward Taylor* (New Haven: Yale Univ. Press, 1960).

35. Edward Taylor, *Christographia*, ed. Norman S. Grabo (New Haven: Yale Univ. Press, 1962), 215.

36. See Debus, *English Paracelsians*, 96-98.

37. See Pagel, *Paracelsus*, 138.

38. Cheryl Z. Oreovicz discusses the alchemical traits of Taylor's Rose of Sharon poems in "Investigating 'the America of nature.'"

39. See Pagel's *Religious and Philosophical Aspects*, 20.

40. Among those who argue that Taylor opens out or personalizes his typological system to include historical events and phenomena are Thomas M. Davis, "Edward Taylor and the Traditions of Puritan Typology," *Early American Literature* 4 (Winter 1970): 24-47, and Lowance, *Language of Canaan*.

41. See Scheick, *Will and the Word*, Chapter 4.

42. Samuel Mather, *The Figures or Types of the Old Testament* (New York: Johnson Reprint Corporation, 1969), 145.

43. For the latest expression of this conventional Puritan notion of language in sermons, see Jonathan Edwards's "A Divine and Supernatural Light," in Clarence H. Faust and Thomas H. Johnson, eds., *Jonathan Edwards: Selections* (New York: Hill and Wang, 1962), 102-11.

44. See Robert E. Spiller, *Literary History of the United States* (New York: Macmillan, 1966), 288.

45. Richard Selzer, in Diane Allen, ed., "NCTE To You: Information, News, Announcements" *College English* 49 (Feb. 1987): 184-86.

46. Walter J. Ong, S.J., "A Dialectic of Aural and Objective Correlatives," in *The Barbarian Within And Other Fugitive Essays and Studies* (New York: Macmillan, 1962), 31.

Catherine Rainwater's essay has also appeared in *Studies in Puritan American Spirituality* 2 (1991): 51-76, and is reprinted with permission.

3

Benjamin Franklin: The Fusion of Science and Letters

A. OWEN ALDRIDGE

The eighteenth-century mind made very little distinction between science and the imagination. This is the reason that one may find every scientific theory of importance in the Enlightenment described somewhere or other in verse. Well-known mathematician Edmund Halley, the same who charted the famous comet, contributed a poetic preface to Newton's *Principia,* and Richard Glover, who was to become author of the most important British epic of the century, *Leonidas,* introduced a popular book with an elegant "Poem on Sir Isaac Newton," containing a well-known phrase, "NEWTON demands the muse." This book by Henry Pemberton, entitled *View of Sir Isaac Newton's Philosophy,* which explains Newton's theories for the layman, was one of the most prestigious publications of the eighteenth century. Its subscription list included the poets Christopher Anstey, John Byrom, John Gay, Lord Hervey, Alexander Pope, and Edward Young. In keeping with this interdisciplinary spirit, the minor English poet Mark Akenside, in a "Hymn to Science," called upon memory, fancy, and reason to join in exploring "great Nature's scenes." Ezra Stiles of Yale even joined literature and science together as representing a common intellectual endeavor. In 1762 while enlisting Franklin's aid in proposing the mathematician John Winthrop for membership in the Royal Society, Stiles wrote that a service such as this would contribute not a little to transmitting Franklin's own name "with honor to distant Posterity, as a Patron of Literature and instrumental in deriving Rewards to learned Merit."[1]

Relatively speaking, the word *science* itself was rarely used in the eighteenth century to refer to the objective study of natural phenomena. The most common expression for this activity was "natural philosophy" in contrast to "moral philosophy." Pemberton's title, for example, refers to "Newton's Philosophy," not to his science.

Johnson's *Dictionary* gives five different definitions of science: "1) knowledge; 2) certainty grounded on demonstration; 3) art attained by precepts, or built on principles; 4) any art or species of knowledge; and 5) one of the seven liberal arts: grammar, rhetoric, logic, arithmetic, music, geometry, [and] astronomy." The second definition, "certainty grounded on demonstration," is the only one that approaches the modern conception and the only one that stresses methodology.

The authoritative but controversial *Encyclopedia* of Diderot and d'Alembert defines science as a "system of rules or facts relating to a certain object" but also indicates that the sister discipline *art* may comprise "any system of knowledge which can be reduced to positive and invariable rules independent of caprice or opinion." In this sense there is little difference between science and art. Indeed, the *Encyclopedia* speaks of the "science of communication of ideas." Following a classification originated by Bacon, the *Encyclopedia* recognizes three separate republics of letters, those of memory, wisdom, and pleasure, essentially the same grouping as Akenside's memory, reason, and fancy. The *Encyclopedia* in another tripartite division classifies knowledge into the sciences, liberal arts, and mechanical arts. According to this system, there is a science of man, a science of God, and a science of nature.[2] The inclusion of theology as a branch of science is extremely important in regard to Franklin and most eighteenth-century Newtonians. The author of *Principia* specifically included the existence of God as part of his system.[3] Franklin began his scientific investigations with abstract theories concerning a master geometer. A major doctrine of the *Encyclopedia* is that of continuity or the interrelationship of all knowledge. If human understanding is conceived in terms of memory, reason, and imagination—or of scholarship, wisdom and intellectual pleasure—there is small likelihood of conflict between science and literature or between speculation and experiment. Franklin in his early years devoted considerable attention to metaphysics but in middle age turned his attention to physical experiment, the earliest source of his worldwide reputation.

In the eighteenth century, the term "Newtonian philosophy," as I. Bernard Cohen has pointed out, had five distinct aspects: the corpuscular theory of matter, the structure of the universe, the powers of gravity controlling the sun and planets, the motion of planets and comets, and the theory of the moon and tides.[4] Although contrasting "true philosophy" with "conjectures and suppositions," Franklin did not hesitate to engage in both observation and speculation on the structure of the universe. His own experiments he sometimes called "philosophical amusements."

In order to place Franklin in the hierarchy of eighteenth-century science, a distinction should be maintained between conjecture and theory. Newton set forth a number of theories in his *Principia* based in large measure on mathematical proofs. Conjectures lack this mathematical foundation. In the eighteenth century, experiments such as those by Franklin on electricity not based on mathematical theory were considered by some authorities as belonging to a subsidiary level of investigation. This attitude was expressed by John Sargent late in the seventeenth century in a book entitled *The Method to Science* (London, 1696). In his preface, Sargent remarked that "however the Experimental Man may be highly Commendable in other Respects, yet onely those who can lay just Claim to *true* Principles, and make out their Title to them, can be truly held Natural PHILOSOPHERS, which sufficiently shows that the way of Experiments cannot be a True METHOD TO SCIENCE." Long after Franklin's election to the Royal Society, an anonymous pamphleteer considered his "Pretensions to the title of NATURAL PHILOSOPHER." In this pamphleteer's opinion, "Every one who observes facts and records them faithfully, has a right to our thanks and esteem: but to consider such as Natural Philosophers, can have no other consequence than to bring science into contempt."[5]

According to this adverse critic, "God hath made every thing in the material world by weight and measure; and whoever pretends to comprehend any part of his works, must be well skilled in the science of magnitude and number," that is, the discipline of mathematics, in which Franklin was notably deficient. In his *Experiments and Observations on Electricity,* however, Franklin used almost identical words about God as a geometer. The existence of electric phenomena together with gravitational attraction, in Franklin's words, "affords another occasion of adoring that wisdom which has made all things by weight and measure!"[6]

Franklin has been compared to Newton in both the eighteenth century and the twentieth, but by the standards of the anonymous critic I have just quoted, he does not deserve even to be considered a scientist. Comparison with his contemporary Voltaire may help to clarify this point. Voltaire is ordinarily not looked upon as a scientist at all in the twentieth century, but he certainly would have easily met the anonymous critic's criteria. He had received an extensive training in mathematics at the exclusive Jesuit Lycée, Louis le Grand, in Paris. He corresponded on mathematical aspects of Newtonianism with Pierre Louis Maupertuis, one of the most eminent French mathematicians of the time, whose book on the curvature of the earth in large measure introduced Franklin to the practical application of Newtonianism. In at least one of his letters, Voltaire showed a knowledge of the original text of Newton's *Principia.* Also, he became along with Pemberton and Maclaurin one of the three foremost popularizers of Newton in the eighteenth century. Although Voltaire modestly indicated to one of his friends that he based his book *Elements of the Philosophy of Newton* on the little he knew about the great scientist for the benefit of his countrymen who knew nothing at all, he maintains in the body of the work that his major concern was to provide clear ideas concerning the fundamental laws of nature that Newton had discovered.[7] Nothing approaching this comprehensive aim is to be found anywhere in Franklin's writings.

There is considerable significance, moreover, in the circumstance that Franklin wrote no extended treatment of a scientific subject. His mind apparently responded more readily to individual situations or particular problems than to synoptic perspectives. In this way he was just the opposite of Voltaire, who portrayed various general relationships of phenomena in the Newtonian universe. A much broader panorama of scientific principles is reflected in the totality of Voltaire's works, moreover, than in Franklin's. Even in the nonscientific area, Franklin wrote only one extensive work, his *Memoirs,* and that is fragmentary, repetitious, and episodic despite the efforts of old-fashioned formalists and less antiquated but equally transient structuralists to give it the appearance of unity. In his autobiography, Franklin devotes only eight paragraphs to his electrical experiments, from his introduction to the subject in 1746 to his receiving the Copley Medal of the Royal Society in 1753. The only other topic in the *Memoirs* related to science is an account of Franklin on his first visit to England visiting Hans Sloane of the Royal Society and showing him a purse made of asbestos and, therefore, resistant to fire. Otherwise science did not intrude into his *Memoirs,* not even indirectly through metaphors or other figures of speech. In the reverse direction, however, Franklin made use of literary devices, particularly wit and humor, in making his letters on electricity appealing. I. B. Cohen has pointed out, for example, that when Franklin received the Copley gold medal, he remarked in his letter of acknowledgment, "I know not whether any of your learned Body have attain'd the ancient boasted Art of *multiplying* Gold; but you have certainly found the Art of making it infinitely *more valuable.*"[8] Voltaire affirms in his

Elements that "it is indeed indecent to indulge in pleasantries when one pretends to speak about philosophy,"[9] but he engages in persiflage, nevertheless, just as freely as Franklin. Voltaire also remarked that he would have liked Newton better if the latter had possessed a sense of humor.[10]

Perhaps modesty as much as anything else kept Franklin from weighting his autobiography with his scientific interests, but a better reason is that he was writing a personal memoir, not a history of science. Indeed his scientific writings provide a valuable supplement to his autobiography as a reflection of his psychological history. During the course of his correspondence with Collinson on his electrical experiments, Franklin admitted that some of the phenomena he had observed did not correspond with the general principles he had adopted. The "many pretty systems" erected by himself and other scientists, he realized, were doomed to destruction by new discoveries. "If there is no other Use discover'd of Electricity," Franklin declared, this "is something considerable, that it may *help to make a vain Man humble.*"[11] Like his contemporary Rousseau, Franklin admitted his own vanity and made no apologies for it. Indeed in his autobiography he classifies vanity as one of the comforts of life.[12]

Jacques Barbeu Dubourg, Franklin's French friend and editor, remarked that "those who see merely an electrician in M. Franklin know him only halfway." The multitude of other subjects on which he wrote "reveals the extent of his knowledge and the fecundity of his genius."[13]

Franklin did not, like Newton, attempt to survey broad relationships in an effort to discover new scientific laws. He was concerned merely to investigate particular phenomena, and the new laws came more or less as by-products. This does not mean, however, that Franklin was not interested in general principles or in hypotheses. He sometimes began with principles (as in his investigation of the Gulf Stream) in order to understand particular phenomena. A remark of Franklin's concerning utility has received considerable attention: "What signifies Philosophy that does not apply to some Use?"[14] A later remark, made in France verbally but twice recorded, however, reflects the opposite opinion that the utilitarian purpose need not be immediate or apparent. It grew out of the first balloon ascensions in history. A number of people observing them asked, "To what use do they expect to put these experiments?" Franklin replied, "What good is a new-born baby?"[15]

He soon recognized, moreover, a very practical possible application of aerial navigation—warfare. Five thousand invading balloons, he speculated, would lead to the surrender of almost any empire. Convincing sovereigns of the folly of conducting war in this manner, he suggested, "might give a new turn to human affairs," that is, to the abolishing of war altogether.[16] Franklin's phrase "Father of Lights" in his famous motion advocating prayers in the Constitutional Convention, moreover, was probably inspired by the sight of balloons flying over Paris.[17]

If it is important to notice that Franklin contributed his electrical discoveries in the form of letters, it is equally important to notice that, except for political subjects, he wrote on nearly every other major topic also in epistolary form. Many of these letters on subjects of general interest were printed during his lifetime and reprinted over and over throughout the nineteenth century. By means of these letters Franklin merged the realms of science and imaginative literature. This represents another parallel with Voltaire. One of Voltaire's earliest publications was a series of essays concerning English manners, literature, and philosophy, originally entitled *English Letters* and later changed to *Philosophical Letters*. Although ostensibly private epistles, they were actually written for the public and never addressed to individuals. Four of these letters concern Newton: the first, a contrast between systems of the Englishman Newton and the Frenchman Descartes; the second, a summary of Newton's concept of gravitation; the third, a summary of Newton's theory of light; and the fourth, a summary of Newton's theories of infinity and the chronology of the world. Although these chapters were undoubtedly the most difficult to understand of all those published in Voltaire's *Philosophical Letters* and may, therefore, have contributed little to the enormous popularity that the work as a whole eventually attained, they helped to acquire for Voltaire a reputation as a serious thinker.

Similar letters of Franklin, written to an actual correspondent, were instigated by the curiosity of a young English girl, Polly Stevenson, daughter of his London landlady, who begged him to engage in a correspondence concerning moral and natural philosophy.[18] Further to justify the parallel with Voltaire, it is relevant to notice that some of these letters were later printed in the 1769 edition of Franklin's *Experiments and Observations*. Barbeu Dubourg, the translator of a French edition in which these letters were reprinted, remarked "that many fathers would like to have a similar mentor for their daughters" and referred to proofs in his own hands "of the progress she has made under such a great teacher."[19]

Although Franklin was probably second to none in his admiration and public praise of Newton, he felt an uncomfortable reserve concerning two of the major elements of Newtonian philosophy, its mathematical basis and its use in metaphysical speculation.[20] In 1746, the year he began his electrical experiments, Franklin expressed regret to his friend Cadwallader Colden that he lacked "Mathematics enough" to work out the problem of why an eastern voyage across the Atlantic was shorter than a western one.[21] But in his *Memoirs* Franklin attempted, perhaps subconsciously, to minimize the importance of mathematics. After revealing that he had twice failed to acquire a grasp of figures while at school, he affirmed with apparent satisfaction that at the age of sixteen he took a widely used textbook, "Cocker's book of Arithmetick, & went thru' the whole by my self with great Ease."[22] At another point he characterized "Great Mathematicians" as expecting "unusual Precision in everything said" or "forever denying or distinguishing upon Trifles, to the Disturbance of all Conversation."[23] As we have seen, he lightly disparaged "dry Mathematics" in writing to Polly Stevenson, and he took pride in one of his meterological papers for not having "with some of our learned Moderns disguis'd my Nonsense in Greek, cloth'd it in Algebra, or adorn' it with Fluxions."[24] Parenthetically, although Franklin never attained the higher reaches of abstract mathematics, he derived great pleasure from devising so-called magic squares and circles—that is, numbers arranged in such a manner as to add up to the same sum from several different directions. These mathematical bagatelles were published in his *Experiments* along with his electrical discoveries.

Although it was a recognized convention in the eighteenth century to refer to the supposed regularity and order of the external universe as a proof of the existence of an intelligent creator, Franklin had an ambivalent attitude toward the union of science and metaphysics. He protested strongly against the combination in connection with the publication in 1745 of a treatise by his friend Cadwallader Colden entitled *An Explication of the First Causes of Action in Matter, and, of the Cause of Gravitation.* In this work Colden pretended to have succeeded where Newton failed in discovering the cause of gravitation, a claim to intellectual eminence that has been considered the "most audacious" ever made in colonial America.[25] Colden's friends, unable to a man to follow his reasoning, urged him to do further reading in such European forerunners as Descartes, Malebranche, Boerhaave, Leibniz, Bernoulli, and Berkeley, but surprisingly enough, as Raymond Stearns has pointed out, none "appear to have been led to Newton's *Principia* and *Optics*, where they would have found the keys to Colden's baffling work."[26]

A group of Franklin's friends urged him to read as background for

Collinson's treatise a work by a Scotsman, Andrew Baxter, entitled *An Inquiry into the Nature of the Human Soul, wherein Its Immateriality is evinced* (2nd ed., 1737). This was of no greater help to Franklin than the advice of Colden's friends had been to Colden. Baxter had drawn upon a fundamental Newtonian principle, but it does not appear that at this time Franklin recognized the principle as Newton's. In a letter to one of his friends Franklin complained: "The Author's *Vis Inertiae essential to Matter,* upon which the whole Work is founded, I have not been able to comprehend. And I do not think he demonstrates at all clearly (at least to me he does not) that there is really any such Property in Matter."[27] A corollary of Newton's first law of motion, the *Vis Inertiae* of matter, is described in Pemberton's *View* as that "quality in bodies, whereby they preserve their present state, with regard to motion or rest, till some active force disturb them." Apparently not recognizing the difference between velocity and acceleration, Franklin argued against Baxter and—although not aware of it—against Newton that "there is no Mass or Matter how great soever, but may be moved by any Force how small soever (taking Friction out of the Question) and this small Force continued will in Time bring the Mass to move with any Velocity whatsoever." By the last decade of his life, however, Franklin had come to accept the concept of *Vis Inertiae* as commonplace. In connection with a device of Bernoulli designed to increase the speed of a boat by funneling water through a tube with an intake above the surface of the river and the discharge below, a precursor of the modern hovercraft, Franklin remarked "it is to be considered, that every bucket-full pumped or dipped up into the boat, from its side or through its bottom, must have its *vis inertiae* overcome so as to receive the motion of the boat, before it can come to give motion by its descent; and that will be a deduction from the moving power."[28]

In his comments on Baxter, Franklin also treated a metaphysical problem that figures prominently in the works of Locke and Samuel Clarke and in the correspondence of Voltaire and Frederick the Great: whether matter has the power to think. Franklin settled it to his own satisfaction by referring to the intention of the creator. "If any Part of Matter does not at present act and think, 'tis not from an Incapacity in its Nature [but from] a positive Restraint."[29] This opinion did not by any means conflict with the principles of Newton, who, as we have seen, specifically included the existence of God as part of his system. Franklin concluded his critique of Baxter by affirming "some Reluctance" to "the metaphysical Way" because of "the great Uncertainty . . . in that Science;

the wide Contradictions and endless Disputes it affords; and the horrible Errors I led myself into when a young Man." This was written in 1746 just before Franklin began his electrical experiments. He did not completely abandon metaphysical conjectures and speculation but certainly devoted thereafter the major part of his scientific efforts to experimental investigation.

Franklin's notion of the "positive Restraint" of the creator represents a close parallel with Voltaire's solution to the question of why the earth rotates from west to east. Voltaire maintained that the direction might just as well have been the opposite, that "this Rotation from West to East is an Effect of the Free-will of the Creator, and that this Free-will is the only sufficient Reason that can be assigned for it."[30] Franklin makes no comment on the reasons behind the direction of rotation, but speculated on its effects upon navigation, particularly why the eastward voyage across the Atlantic is faster than the westward. As I have already indicated, he broached the subject to Cadwallader Colden in 1746. In his words, "Ships in a Calm at the Equator move with the Sea at 15 Miles per Minute and at our Capes suppose 12 Miles per Minute."[31] Franklin was literally saying that ships at the Equator move at a speed of 900 miles an hour, although he knew very well that in actuality it is the earth itself that moves at this rate and becalmed ships move no faster than stationary houses on land. Franklin, nevertheless, wondered whether ships traveled at different speeds at different latitudes because of the differences in velocity at these various latitudes and the resulting great resistance of the water at the equator and proportionately less in those approaching the North Pole. Colden replied that in his opinion the latitude would have no effect whatsoever because the minor difference in the force that the ship acquires from the diurnal rotation of the earth would be negated by the resistance of the water, and there would be no difference in the time coming and going.[32] Colden believed that the difference between the east and the west passage was caused by the tides. High water on the American coast is followed by high water in England six hours later. A boat leaving America at high tide could count on the ebb in her favor in America and the flow in England. A ship going in the westward direction, however, would have one tide against her in England and one in her favor in America. If the voyage from England to America takes thirty days, the tide would decrease $\frac{1}{30}$ each day. I confess that Colden's explanation is as confusing to me as was his theory of gravitation to his contemporaries. Distinguished mathematicians I have consulted have had no greater success in understanding it. The editors of an early volume of Franklin's writings suggested that Franklin in 1746 solved the problem of the speedier eastward voyage by indicating the influence of the Gulf Stream.[33] This is no answer, however, since it must be decided to what degree the Gulf Stream itself is affected by the diurnal rotation of the earth. Franklin himself never regarded the Gulf Stream as a solution to his problem, and he continued to measure the Gulf Stream and speculate on the motion of the earth for many years.[34] Eventually a fellow member of the American Philosophical Society convinced him—Franklin does not say how—that his theory of relating different speeds to different latitudes has nothing to do with the speed of ships.[35]

Franklin's theories on rainfall and rivers are related to the modern science of meteorology as are his theories on thunderstorms, which are in turn linked to his electrical experiments. In the eighteenth century, all of these subjects were ranked under the rubric "Natural History," which also embraced another of Franklin's primary interests, geology. Although little scholarly investigation of Franklin's geological studies has taken place until very recently, the topic was almost as important in Franklin's intellectual life as it was in Voltaire's. Nearly all Voltaire scholars have had their say on the subject because of his highly publicized refusal to accept the received opinion that marine fossils on the top of high mountains were the result of a universal deluge. Franklin, in treating the same circumstances, accepted the notion of Christian apologists that a universal catastrophe was responsible for mountain chains and their fossil remains. He has received, perhaps for that reason, none of the derision directed against Voltaire because of the latter's explanation that oyster shells may have been deposited on the mountains by pilgrims or other human agents.

An early illustration of Franklin's interest in theories of the earth combines literature and science. He published an essay in his newspaper, the *Pennsylvania Gazette*, December 15, 1757, concerning lightning as one of the causes of earthquakes. The concepts in this essay have been compared to almost identical ones in the diary of Jonathan Edwards. The essay, however, is largely a reprint from Ephraim Chambers's *Encyclopedia*, and so it cannot be considered as evidence of original scientific thinking on the part of either Edwards or Franklin. Ten years after this *Gazette* essay, Franklin wrote to a New England clergyman-scientist, Jaret Eliot, about storms and the origins of springs.[36] In this letter he alluded to places in the Appalachian Mountains revealing strata of seashells, including some in the solid rocks. Perhaps referring to the Biblical notion of a catastrophic deluge or perhaps indulging in a humorous reflection on it, he added, "'Tis certainly the *Wreck* of a World we live on!" Obviously in a light-hearted mood, he prefaced a description of pillar-like formations in mountains with the agricultural metaphor, "Ideas will string themselves like Ropes of Onions." In another letter of the same period written to John Mitchell of Virginia and eventually published in his *Experiments,* he set forth a "new hypothesis for explaining the several Phaenomena of Thunder Gusts."[37] The explanation in brief is that clouds bear in them electrical fire, which when driven by winds against mountains or against other clouds give off electricity in the form of lightning. In this paper he also attributes the origin of rivers to rain rather than to underground sources, essentially the same explanation he would offer to his London correspondent Polly Stevenson some years later. Incidentally, in his letter to Mitchell he denies stories that "a Sword can be melted in the Scabbard, and Money in a Man's Pocket, by Lightning, without burning either."[38] This may be a stroke of humor comparable to a reference in the French poet Du Bartas to a flash of lightning burning off a woman's pubic hair in an electrical flash and doing no other harm whatsoever.[39]

In commenting on a paper presented to the Royal Society by John Mitchell of Cambridge, England, Franklin revised his earlier interpretation of the origin of mountains. He was now "reconciled . . . to those convulsions which all naturalists agree this globe has suffered." And instead of considering the earth a "wreck," as he had previously, he regarded the exposure of formerly deep-lying strata as a benefit, since such exposure placed "a great variety of useful materials . . . into our power." "So that what has been usually looked upon as a *ruin* suffered by this part of the universe, was in reality, only a preparation, or means of rendering the earth more fit for use, more capable of being to mankind a convenient and comfortable habitation."[40] This was conventional natural theology, adopted by orthodox Christians and deists alike. While in England in 1759, Franklin visited salt mines in Norwich and renewed his speculation on the changes that may have occurred on the surface of the earth. There is no indication that Franklin at this time or at all throughout his life disagreed with the notion of a universal deluge. In a letter to his brother Peter, he affirmed his opinion that "all water on this globe was originally salt, and that the fresh water we find in springs and rivers, is the produce of distillation."[41] The rock salt found in mines was originally drawn from the sea, an effect of "Nature's distillery." Referring again to seashells and fossil remains of fish on high lands, he suggested that "either the sea has been higher than it now is, and has fallen away from those high lands; or they have been lower than they are, and were lifted to their present height by some internal mighty force, such as we still feel some remains of, when whole continents are moved by earthquakes."

Voltaire, unlike Franklin, refused to accept the hypothesis of a universal inundation. In a *Discourse on the Changes Which Have Occurred on Our Globe*, he rejected all theories that the world was at one time covered with water, expressed the concept of axial tilt, (that the earth has turned around completely so that what is now the North Pole was once the South Pole), explained the presence of maritime fossils on mountains as the refuse of pilgrims or other travelers, and affirmed that nothing in animated or vegetable life has changed since it was originally created. Voltaire had developed his theory of axial tilt at length in his *Elements*. It was based on the measurement by a French astronomer, who discovered the angle formed by the axis of the equator and the axis of the ecliptic to be twenty minutes less than it had been when measured by Pytheas more than two thousand years previously. Voltaire concluded that a single revolution by which the globe turns successively to the east, the south, the west, and the north would require a period of 1,944,000 years and would be accompanied by drastic changes in all the climates of the earth. It was not this daring hypothesis that brought upon Voltaire general ridicule of his capacity as a geologist, however, but rather his insistence that human agency was responsible for seashells on the mountaintops. He steadfastly maintained his opposition to the theory of a universal inundation but eventually modified his hypothesis of the origin of seashells. He did not stop with speculation but made objective observations of actual conditions. From the time of the printing of his *Discourse* until almost the end of his life he painstakingly examined fossil shells around Lake Geneva in Switzerland and came to the conclusion, now corroborated by modern geologists, that these were of freshwater rather than saltwater origin. In other words, he repudiated scientifically the seashell argument as evidence for a universal deluge. On this subject at least, Voltaire was the pragmatic observer and Franklin the theorist.

There is some indication that Franklin also adopted the notion of axial tilt or shifting of the poles but no evidence concerning the source from which he may have derived it. Some American naturalists at one time sent him specimens of the "great Bones at the Ohio," remains of a prehistoric animal just discovered there. Franklin observed that elephants in his day inhabited only hot countries with no winter, whereas the bones in question had been discovered in the winter country of Ohio, and elephant tusks had been found in Siberia, an even more wintry environment. This made him suspect, therefore, that "the earth had anciently been in another position, and the climates differently placed from what they are at present."[42] Franklin expanded his theory of the axial tilt in conversations with a French geologist, the abbé Soulavie. According to Soulavie's recollection, Franklin remarked in a parallel between political and geographical revolutions, "One continent becomes old, another rises into youth and perfection. But the perfected continent will in turn correct the other."[43] Franklin later asked Soulavie for his evidence in French geography to support the notion of a major *bouleversement* of the earth and sent to Soulavie his own observations on the coal mines of England. He later read his letter to the American Philosophical Society, and it was eventually published. The presence of oyster shells in the mountains Franklin accepted as proof of the great *bouleversement* or overturning of the earth. Indulging freely in imagination, he observed "superior beings smile at our theories, and at our presumption in making them." One of his own theories, eventually presented in a paper for the American Philosophical Society, was the one he shared with Voltaire of an axial tilt. In his own words,

> present polar and equatorial diameters differing from each other near ten leagues, it is easy to conceive, in case some power should shift the axis gradually, and place it in the present equator, and make the new equator pass through the present poles, what a sinking of the waters would happen in the present equatorial regions, and what a rising in the polar regions; so that vast tracts would be discovered, that now are under water, and others covered, that are now dry, the water rising and sinking in the different extremes near five leagues. Such an operation as this possibly occasioned much of Europe, and among the rest this mountain of Passy on which I live, and which is composed of limestone, rock and sea-shells, to be abandoned by the sea, and to change its ancient climate, which seems to have been a hot one.[44]

It should be noted that whereas Voltaire described a complete shifting of the poles, that is, a complete revolution of the globe, Franklin imagined merely half of the process, or the poles taking the place of the equator. Shortly before his death, Franklin supplied a cause for this axial tilt in a letter to James Bowdoin in 1788. Voltaire had supposed that the process was extremely gradual, taking more than a million years; Franklin assumed a sudden or catastrophic process. He wondered whether "in ancient times, the near passing of some large comet of greater magnetic power than this globe of ours have been a means of changing its poles, and thereby wrecking and deranging its surface." The reference to changing poles may suggest either a complete revolution or a partial one. This supposition, Franklin felt, is "the easiest way of accounting for the deluge, by getting rid of the old difficulty how to dispose of its water after it was over."[45]

In his letters to Soulavie and Bowdoin, Franklin indulged his imagination to such a degree that he wondered whether there might be a magnetical north and south of the entire universe as well as of the earth. From here he went on to imagine space flight. If such a universal magnetism existed and if it were possible for a man to fly from star to star, Franklin suggested, the spaceman might even "govern his course by the compass."[46] Franklin wrote this in 1782 at the age of seventy-five. Over fifty years previously at the age of nineteen, Franklin had also allowed his mind to conceive the possibility of penetrating outer space. At that time he wrote, "If we could take a Trip to the Moon and back again, as frequently and with as much Ease as we can go and come from Market, the Satisfaction would be just the same."[47] Voltaire is generally considered to be the more imaginative and Franklin the more practical of the two, but here is an example of Franklin's greater imaginative excursion into the unknown. To be sure, Voltaire wrote Micromegas about a visitor from another planet, but this was a satire on life in this world, and this kind of interplanetary travel as pure fantasy belonged to a recognized literary convention of human satire. Franklin conceived of space travel in terms of Newtonian philosophy, however, and as an eventual scientific possibility.

Three years after his speculation about travel to the moon, Franklin devised for his private use a creed and system of worship to which he gave the name "Articles of Belief and Acts of Religion." He conceived of "many Beings or Gods, vastly superior to Man" and that "each has made for himself, one glorious Sun, attended with a beautiful and admirable System of Planets."[48] A few years later in Poor Richard's Almanac, he further speculated on the higher reaches of the chain of being, turning into prose Alexander Pope's lines concerning the contrast between mere mortals and superior beings. According to Franklin, if angels observe "our actions, and are acquainted with our affairs, our whole body of science must appear to them as little better than ignorance."[49] He also quoted Pope's original lines concerning these superior beings, who "Admir'd such wisdom in a human shape, / And shew'd a Newton, as we shew an ape." In the same issue of Poor Richard, he showed a certain scepticism toward the notion of the inhabitability of plural worlds. "It is the opinion of all the modern philosophers and mathematicians," he observed, "that the planets are habitable worlds. If so, what sort of constitutions must those people have who live in the planet Mercury? where, says Sir Isaac Newton, the heat of the sun is seven times as great as it is with us; and would make our Water boil away. For the same person found by experiments, that an heat seven times as great as the heat of the sun in summer, is sufficient to set water a boiling."[50]

Voltaire included in his *Elements* a similarly cynical attitude toward the theory of the plurality of inhabited worlds. "We may suspect," he says, "that planets similar to ours are populated by animals; but we have on this subject no other degree of probability, to speak exactly, than a man with fleas would have, who would conclude that everyone he sees passing on the street would have fleas as well as he."

Franklin in his "Articles of Belief" affirmed his opinion "that Man is not the most perfect Being but One, rather that as there are many Degrees of Beings his Inferiors, so there are many Degrees of Beings superior to him." He also incorporated the notion of the Great Chain of Being in an oriental tale of unknown date. He called upon his readers to contemplate "the scale of beings, from an elephant down to an oyster," as well as a similar gradation "from an elephant to the infinitely Great, Good, and Wise."[51] Franklin and other eighteenth-century thinkers, with the apparent exception of Voltaire alone, who treated the chain of being were concerned exclusively with animated and organic creatures. Voltaire proposed the scientific relevance of the concept of the chain in his *Elements*, suggesting that it should be enlarged to include nonorganic matter. "Everything tends to make us believe," he affirmed, "that there is a chain of beings who elevate themselves by degrees. We are acquainted only imperfectly with some links in this immense chain, and we little men, with our puny eyes and puny brain, we boldly divide all of nature into matter and spirit, including God, and not knowing, moreover, a word about what is basically spirit and matter." In his *Dissertation on the Nature and Propagation of Fire*, moreover, Voltaire suggested that fire itself should be considered as part of a chain of beings midway between those substances that are more solid and those that are rarer than itself. It would resemble in this sense "those substances which seem to mark the limits of those species which are neither absolute animals nor absolute vegetables and which seem to be the degrees by which nature passes from one genre to another." Franklin also talked about a missing link in the chain of being, specifically an organism between an animal and a vegetable, but did so in the form of a hoax. He several times told the French physician Cabanis about an American bird carrying two tubercles at the joints of its wings. At the death of the bird these tubercles "become the sprouts of two vegetable stalks which grow at first in sucking the juice from its cadavre and which subsequently attach themselves to the earth in order to live in the manner of plants and trees."[52] Voltaire eventually rejected the notion of a chain of being entirely—primarily because of the disappearance of various species from the earth and the consequent interruption of the pretended continuous gradation among vegetables and animals.[53] Franklin, however, presumably never abandoned faith in the chain.

Much as Franklin prized scientific research and conjecture, he felt that social service and community leadership were vastly more important, a principle that he exemplified in his own life. Writing to Cadwallader Colden on the latter's "Retirement from Publick Business," he urged him not to let the "Love of Philosophical Amusements have more than its due Weight."[54] "Had Newton been Pilot but of a single common Ship, the finest of his Discoveries would scarce have excus'd, or atton'd for his abandoning the Helm one Hour in Time of Danger: how much less if she had carried the Fate of the Commonwealth." In a similar vein, Franklin reminded Polly Stevenson seriously that "there is no Rank in Natural Knowledge of equal Dignity and Importance" with that of being a responsible member of one's family, community, and country.[55] Franklin also unequivocally placed morality over scientific activities. The person who could discover a means of inculcating lasting virtue, he wrote to the evangelist George Whitefield, would "deserve more, ten thousand times, than the inventor of the longitude."[56]

But when social and political duties did not interfere, Franklin could not imagine a more worthy and pleasant style of life than that of pursuing philosophical knowledge. At a crucial stage in the career of his physician friend John Fothergill, Franklin advised him to "retire to your Villa, give your self Repose, delight in Viewing the Operations of Nature in the vegetable Creation, assist her in her Works, get your ingenious Friends at times about you, . . . or, if alone, amuse yourself with your Books and elegant Collection."[57] Franklin therefore ironically condemned the practice of medicine, or, as he put it, "the Impiety of being in constant Warfare against the Plan of Providence." He admonished Fothergill, perhaps partly seriously, "Disease was intended as the Punishment of Intemperance, Sloth, and other Vices." In effect, Franklin concluded, by curing the sick Fothergill performed the same service to society "as some favourite first Minister, who out of the great Benevolence of his Heart should procure Pardons for all Criminals that apply'd to him."

In just the opposite frame of mind, Franklin wrote to Joseph Priestley a famous letter predicting the absolute triumph of science over the forces of nature. In the midst of the American Revolution, he rhapsodically predicted the advances that what he termed "*true* Science" would make, including "the Power of Man over Matter."[58] "We may perhaps learn to deprive large Masses of their Gravity, and give them absolute Levity, for the sake of easy Transport. Agriculture may diminish its Labour and double its Produce: all Diseases may by sure means be prevented or cured, not excepting even that of Old Age." This is obviously hyperbole, and Franklin used similar exaggeration in the same letter in order to contrast the deplorable condition of contemporary ethics. In a serious paper written four years later and presented to the American Philosophical Society in 1788, Franklin gave a more realistic picture of scientific progress. "The power of man relative to matter," he declared, "seems limited to the separating or mixing the various kinds of it, or changing its form and appearance by different compositions of it; but does not extend to the making or creating new matter, or annihilating the old. . . . We cannot destroy any part of it, or make addition to it."[59]

Franklin is also the author of a scatological satire on the scientific community, a parody of the prizes offered by such learned societies, as the French Academy of Sciences, for which Voltaire wrote his *Dissertation on Fire*. Franklin suggested the offering of a prize for the discovery of a drug "that shall render the Natural Discharge of Wind from our Bodies, not only inoffensive, but agreeable as Perfumes."[60]

Franklin was a scientist with a sense of humor. He hoped to understand and to control the natural universe to the highest degree possible, but he placed human relations on a higher plane. Like most thinkers of his age, Franklin found in the natural universe much more of a geometrical plan than has been revealed by the research of later scientists. Franklin is known by his phrase "Let the experiment be made"[61] and Voltaire by the adage "Beware of systems," but in actuality both carried on serious experiments and both speculated about all conceivable aspects of the natural universe. Franklin did not, like Voltaire and the editors of the *Encyclopedia*, inveigh against systems, possibly because he was not personally involved with any. He was a Newtonian in the broad sense but carried his interests far beyond the range of Newton's physics and optics. Although he wrote on agriculture, he was, like Voltaire, relatively unacquainted with the life sciences. Despite his practical experiments, his deficiency in abstract mathematics, and his distaste for metaphysical reasoning, elements of his Newtonianism consisted in conjectures concerning unexplored space and the distant

future. He thus had great success in reconciling the world of experiment
with the world of imagination.

Notes

1. Leonard W. Labaree et al. eds., *Papers of Benjamin Franklin* (New Haven: Yale
Univ. Press, 1959 and continuing), X, 31.

2. Jean LeRond d'Alembert, *Preliminary Discourse to the Encyclopedia of Diderot.*
Translated Richard N. Schwab with Walter E. Rex. With an introduction and notes by
Richard N. Schwab. (Indianapolis, In.: Bobbs-Merrill, 1963), 32, 40, 116, 117, 144-45.

3. I. Bernard Cohen, *Franklin and Newton* (Philadelphia: American Philosophical
Society, 1956), 140.

4. Ibid., 180-81.

5. I. Bernard Cohen ed., *Benjamin Franklin's Experiments; A New Edition of Franklin's
Experiments and Observations on Electricity.* (Cambridge, Mass.: Harvard Univ. Press,
1943), 426.

6. Ibid., 215.

7. Theodore Besterman, ed., *Correspondence* (Paris: Gallimard, 1963), i, 980; Louis
Moland, ed., *Oeuvres Completes* (Paris: Garnier Freres, 1877-85), XXII, 438.

8. *Franklin and Newton,* 79.

9. Moland, *Oeuvres,* 22:455.

10. Besterman, *Correspondence,* 2:568.

11. Cohen, *Experiments,* 63.

12. J.A. Leo Lemay and P.M. Zall, eds., *The Autobiography of Benjamin Franklin: A
Genetic Text.* (Knoxville: Univ. of Tennessee Press, 1981), 2.

13. Barbeu-Dubourg, ed., *Oeuvres de M. Franklin* (1773), in vol. 20 of William B.
Willcox, ed., *The Papers of Benjamin Franklin* (New Haven: Yale Univ. Press, 1976), 427.

14. Labaree et al., *Papers,* IX, 251.

15. A. Owen Aldridge, *Franklin and His French Contemporaries* (New York: New York
Univ. Press, 1957), 188.

16. Albert Henry Smyth, ed., *The Writings of Benjamin Franklin* (New York: Macmillan, 1905-7), IX, 155-6.

17. A. Owen Aldridge, *Benjamin Franklin and Nature's God* (Durham, N.C.: Duke
Univ. Press, 1967), 32.

18. Labaree et al., *Papers,* IX, 102.

19. Dubourg, *Oeuvres,* II, 311.

20. Cohen, *Franklin and Newton,* 310.

21. Labaree et al., *Papers,* III, 67.

22. Lemay and Zall, *Autobiography,* 15.

23. Ibid., 61.

24. Labaree et al., *Papers,* IV, 442.

25. Brooke Hindle, quoted in Raymond Phineas Stearns, *Science in the British Colonies
of America* (Urbana: Univ. of Illinois Press, 1970), 568.

26. Stearns, *Science in the British Colonies,* 570.

27. Labaree et al., *Papers,* III, 85.

28. *Transactions of the American Philosophical Society,* Philadelphia American Philosophical Society, 2:308.

29. Labaree et al., *Papers,* III, 88.

30. Moland, *Oeuvres,* XXII, 542-43.

31. Labaree et al., *Papers,* III, 28.

32. Ibid., III, 69.

33. Ibid., III, 67n.

34. Ibid., XIX, 110n; XXIII, 23.

35. *Transactions of the American Philosophical Society,* II, 317n.

36. Labaree et al., *Papers,* III, 147-50.

37. Ibid., III, 365-76.

38. Ibid., III, 376.

39. A. Owen Aldridge, *Early American Literature: A Comparatist Approach* (Princeton: Princeton Univ. Press, 1982), 50.

40. Labaree et al., *Papers,* VII, 357.

41. Ibid., IX, 106-7.

42. Ibid., XIV, 221-22.

43. Aldridge, *Franklin and His French Contemporaries,* 68.

44. William Duane, ed., *Life and Writings of Benjamin Franklin* (New York: H.W. Derby, 1861), II, 386.

45. Ibid., II, 388.

46. Ibid., II, 386.

47. Aldridge, *Franklin and Nature's God,* 20.

48. Labaree et al., *Papers,* I, 102-4.

49. Ibid., III, 348.

50. Ibid., III, 345.

51. Smyth, *Writings,* X, 123-24.

52. Aldridge, *Franklin and His French Contemporaries,* 204.

53. "Chaine des etres crees," in *Dictionaire Philosophique,* vol. 18.2 of *Oeuvres completes de Voltaire,* 52 vols. (Paris: Garnier, Freres, Libraires-Editeurs, 1878), 123-25.

54. Labaree et al., *Papers,* IV, 68.

55. Ibid., IX, 121.

56. Ibid., III, 383.

57. Ibid., XI, 101.

58. Smyth, *Writings,* IX, 10.

59. Duane, *Life and Writings,* II, 387.

60. A. Owen Aldridge, *Benjamin Franklin: Philosopher and Man* (Philadelphia: Lippincott, 1965), 326.

61. Labaree et al., *Papers,* V, 524.

4

Thomas Jefferson

JOSEPH W. SLADE

> Mr. Jefferson came into Congress in June 1775, and brought with him
> a reputation for literature, science, and a happy talent of composition.
> —John Adams to Timothy Pickering
> 6 August 1822[1]

Thomas Jefferson gloried in his reputation as a scientist but did not seek
recognition as a writer of literature. To be sure, he listed his *authorship* of
the Declaration of Independence and the Statute of Virginia for Religious
Freedom as two of his greatest achievements on the inscription he wrote for
his tombstone, and Americans revere him for having invented their nation
with his pen, in a primal literary act. Aside from these documents, some
unsigned articles, and his political pamphlets, however, Jefferson did not
generally write for publication;[2] the dozens of volumes bearing his name
are compilations of his private papers, some of them—the *Anas*, his diary
of his mature political years—being gossipy if not downright scurrilous.
Under pressure, he did cobble together an *Autobiography* of astonishing
dullness, fortunately never finished. His only book, on which serious consideration of him as a writer of literature must ultimately depend, is his
Notes on the State of Virginia (written in 1780-81, published in 1785), which
Jefferson first published anonymously in France, not the United States.

His modesty about *Notes on the State of Virginia*, the first natural history of America, was extreme. He told a friend that it added "nothing new"
to literature.[3] Historians and biographers have too easily dismissed Jefferson's assessment of his own talents; studies of Jefferson the scientist
markedly outnumber those of the man of letters.[4] Of course, almost all of
the books treating him as a philosopher, a statesman, a founding father, a
tormented slaveholder, a conflicted lover, a canny politician, or a sage of
Monticello,[5] include praise for the Declaration of Independence as "great
literature," a term that acknowledges its ravishing rhetoric rather than its

imaginative elements. And almost all of them note that the mighty chords of the second paragraph of the Declaration vibrate with the harmonies of Newtonian physics. But this cliché suggests that it is easier to calculate Jefferson's place in American science than it is to establish his rank in American letters, particularly if the historian concentrates on the Declaration of Independence. By now, that document has attained a *supra*-literary status, partly because—as Garry Wills has observed in his magisterial analysis of its composition—there are actually three Declarations: the one written by Jefferson, the one revised by Congress, and the one that has come down to us misted in legend.[6] In any version, the Declaration overshadows everything else in the Jefferson canon, but its political nature muddles its status as a literary text. It demonstrates Jefferson's familiarity with the science of his day, to be sure, but no more than anything else in his career. By contrast, *Notes on the State of Virginia* proves that his literary talents exceeded his scientific accomplishments.

One of the ironies of that career is that while he fostered American science to the extent that he is regarded as one of its founders, he was himself not very distinguished as a scientist in any particular field—precisely because he resisted the specialization that was required. Although professional writers like Washington Irving, William Cullen Bryant, and Charles Brockton Brown sneered at his science as evidence of his literary failings,[7] Jefferson's contributions to literature—even leaving aside the Declaration of Independence—were quite specific. The democratic impulses that prevented his becoming a great scientist enhanced his writing, but he would himself not have believed that possible. He conceived of science and literature as moral activities: both were forms of experience, tools for understanding, and, more important, patterns for living. He wrote Hector St. John de Crèvecoeur that American farmers could read Homer,[8] and he advised astronomer David Rittenhouse to live, not just study, his discipline.[9] In any case, Jefferson wedded scientific exploration to literary sensibility in his own life,[10] and he did so only partly because his contemporaries did also.

John Adams used the word *literature* in the loose eighteenth-century sense. The term was applied haphazardly to almost any written or printed page on any subject. Benjamin Franklin's 1743 charter for the American Philosophical Society, which Jefferson served as president for seventeen years, gave equal weight to science and literature, as if a fluent pen were the natural extension of a curious mind. Indeed, the terms *literary* and *scientific* were virtually interchangeable as descriptions of the society's activities.[11] Obviously, eighteenth-century Americans did not use the word *science* in its modern meaning, either; it was only gradually losing the connotations of *scientia,* or general knowledge, and taking on the hard-edged virtues of close observations and rigorous experimentation. That does not mean that nobody knew the difference. Jefferson's most scathing criticism of a scientist was to call him a "romancer,"[12] and one of his own colleagues gently reproved Jefferson's paleontology as "fiction."[13] But this semantic confusion—perhaps still not entirely resolved—was compounded by the professionalization that was transforming many intellectual activities at the end of the eighteenth century. Professionalization is very important in assessing the relationship of science and literature for Thomas Jefferson, for it is the wedge that splits culture into the two traditions identified by C.P. Snow. If we simply enumerate all of the man's talents, as so many historians have understandably been tempted to do, we risk not noticing that both realms were undergoing intense change and that the changes undermined Jefferson's efforts to domesticate both literature and science.

Like Dr. Johnson and Goethe, like Voltaire and the French encyclopedists—all contemporaries of catholic interests—Jefferson was familiar with virtually every type of intellectual discourse. He had "a canine appetite for reading,"[14] he said, and it is just this ability to comprehend an entire universe through texts that we admire in the great figures of the eighteenth century—before various revolutions fractured knowledge and experience into specialized disciplines. Unlike those other polymaths, however, Jefferson was foremost a pragmatic egalitarian. He resisted the divisions deepened by the professionalization of both science and literature not just because he was an amateur scientist and an amateur writer, but also because he thought those transformations undemocratic and ultimately harmful to a fully realized life. His orientation was shaped by Francis Bacon, Issac Newton, and John Locke; these three, he told Alexander Hamilton, made up his personal pantheon.[15] What that meant was that all knowledge (or "knolege," as he consistently and charmingly misspelled it) must have utility, must be rational, and must be accessible to any educated person, since political equality rested on understanding applied to statecraft. Again and again he emphasized these points; his correspondence is studded with assertions that wide knowledge is crucial to a republican form of government, especially America's.

The progress of science and literature during the eighteenth century thwarted Jefferson's hopes. Daniel Boorstin has struck an elegiac note in

The Lost World of Thomas Jefferson,[16] which deals with the attempts of Jefferson's circle to circumscribe the world through knowledge, but few historians have quite grasped the mutations that professionalization wrought on intellectual traditions. Jefferson could dabble in anthropology, linguistics, physics, agriculture, theology, anatomy, biology, medicine, architecture, engineering, political science, and meteorology—the list is not exhaustive—because people in those disciplines still all spoke the same language. More important, they all subscribed to the same cosmology, whose outlines were knowable through reason and research. Their universe was uniform and fixed in design, driven by balanced Newtonian forces operating along a chain of being, the whole set in motion by some creative principle. As Howard Mumford Jones has said, "the natural philosopher thought God's thoughts after Him," and "from the point of view of developing science, it made little difference whether the deity was the god of the Christians or the God of the deists."[17] Another way of putting it would be to say that the science of Jefferson's time was largely deductive and descriptive narrative, one reason why so many of Jefferson's friends could refer to scientists as *literati.* At the same time, literature, in the person of writers like Pope and others—like Jefferson himself—who relied on Newton for their model of reality, was at its most scientific. Science had presence chiefly as writing, while literature was preoccupied with social and ethical symmetries. Eighteenth-century intellectuals read the universe like a book and unfolded its beauties on pages of their own composition.

So comfortable a worldview often made for poor science. Because the design of the universe was immutable, for example, Jefferson thought geology, or the study of the earth's evolution, "not worth an hour" of a man's time. This and other mistakes were the consequence of an age disposed toward what Brooke Hindle has called "synthesis based on inadequate data."[18] Even so, Jefferson helped not only to gather but also to organize better data. Experimental methods were still crude, but researchers invented new—and almost literary—tools for dealing with discoveries, chiefly systems of nomenclature and precise, descriptive languages. At the same time, as scientists refined their languages, they found that their goal of unified knowledge receded, through data too enormous for one man to grasp. When Jefferson was born, the sciences and some forms of literature were still subsumed by philosophy (divided, according to far from universal practice, into categories like "natural," "moral," and "political"). By the time of his death, they had rigidified into distinct endeavors. Jefferson had always planned to spend his retirement in scientific research. When he finally escaped public office, however, he realized that his favorite disciplines had advanced beyond his ability to catch up, and he devoted considerable time instead to reading literature at Monticello. Advances in taxonomy—the search for pattern—led to new ways of categorizing knowledge and experience. Far from restricted to science, this impulse affected writers like Jonathan Edwards, whose excursions into typology have been explored by Ursula Brumm,[19] and a succession of poets and novelists before and after Whitman, for whom only catalogs and types could contain the diversity of American experience. New systems of nomenclature caused great excitement, as when the classifications by Georges Louis Leclerc, Count Buffon, "actually received more popular attention than the literary classics of Voltaire and Rousseau."[20]

Devising systems of classification was an extension of the age of reason, the agenda set as much by the encylopedists as by Newton. In France, the Physiocrats identified the elements of economics, and in Britain, Adam Smith, in *The Wealth of Nations,* a work almost as important for America's future as the Declaration (both were published in 1776), dealt with the division of labor. Jefferson's fondness for classification is evident in the Declaration; after its early invocation of laws of nature comes a classification of grievances that spells out violations of those laws. It is even more visible in his *Notes on the State of Virginia,* which relies heavily on nomenclature. Since that work was in many ways seminal for various sciences in America, Jefferson thus stimulated professionalization of those sciences unintentionally. Professionalization involved formulating languages appropriate to different disciplines, but the scientists who invented specialized terms inevitably closed those disciplines to outsiders. (Thomas Kuhn has suggested that a science is on its way to maturity when it becomes incomprehensible to amateurs.[21]) The process is as irreversible—and perhaps as disturbing—as the progress of rationalization outlined by Max Weber. A great many disciplines made strides toward professionalization during Jefferson's lifetime, but the most obvious revolutions occurred in the revisions of nomenclature and classification in biology and chemistry, both of which he thought important, and about both of which he was ambivalent.

As he asserted often, the ideal American was a literate, scientific farmer, partly because Jefferson had absorbed his economic principles from the French Physiocrats, who believed that a country's agriculture was its only real source of wealth. Better agriculture might produce better citizens, and in that hope Jefferson rotated his crops, collected new seeds, and kept fastidious records.[22] Botany was probably Jefferson's greatest love, though he was fascinated by all living things. He embraced Linnaeus's classification of flora and fauna into genera and species and did what he could to improve these systems of comparison by describing plants and animals meticulously and sending specimens to specialists for official recording. In fact, wary of innovation, he clung to the Linnaean zoological classifications even after they had proved less useful than those for botany.[23] Jefferson not only recognized the need for nomenclature, he also invented notational schemes for meteorology and classification systems of Indian languages for comparative linguistics, while his efforts to catalog prehistoric animal bones earned him the title "Founder of American Paleontology."[24] But he knew that labels were artificial. As he told one correspondent in 1814, using terminology appropriate to a democrat, "Nature has, in truth, produced units only through all her works. Classes, orders, genera, species, are not of her work. Her creation is of individuals. No two animals are exactly alike; no two plants, nor even two leaves or blades of grass; no two crystallizations."[25] He was as suspicious of language as only a master writer can be. "I do not pretend that language is science. It is only an instrument for the attainment of science," he wrote in *Notes on the State of Virginia.*[26]

Jefferson's ambivalence toward nomenclature increased when he confronted chemistry, which he liked best when it improved beer or cheese. Perhaps the greatest single achievement of science during Jefferson's period was the reform of chemical nomenclature carried out by Lavoisier. Lavoisier suspected that behind matter lay a coherent arrangement of chemical elements, the basis for the periodicity of atomic weights that would be articulated by Mendeléyev in 1871. With Guyton de Morveau, Berthollet, and Fourcroy, Lavoisier published *Méthode de nomenclature chimique* in 1787, and in 1789 refined the method with greater clarity in his own *Traité élémentaire de Chimie* (translated into three American editions by 1805). Ironically, Lavoisier had been powerfully influenced by Condillac, a political philosopher whom Jefferson respected. Condillac had condemned antiquated jargon in all fields on the grounds that it led people astray. Lavoisier included this passage from Condillac, which should have been well received by the author of the Declaration of Independence: "We only reason well or reason badly in so far as our language is well or badly constructed . . . the whole art of reasoning can be reduced to the art of speaking well."[27] Condillac was more specific: "the progress of the sciences depends entirely on the progress of their languages." But the oxygen theory pioneered by Jefferson's close friend Joseph Priestley, which formed the basis of Lavoisier's system (though Priestley himself was unconvinced), was not yet fully established, so Jefferson thought the French scientist's reforms "premature."[28] "Chemists seem to write only for one another," the great layman complained.[29]

In addition to his objections to the increasing inaccessibility of science to the amateur, Jefferson had patriotic and political reasons for opposing specialization. A young nation could not afford that luxury. As Jefferson's close friend and fellow generalist Benjamin Rush remarked, a whole continent lay awaiting investigation; it would have been foolish for American scientists "to turn our backs upon a gold mine, in order to amuse ourselves catching butterflies."[30] However urgent the need to catch up to European science, Jefferson believed, specialization would have to be left to later generations. Although he could promote science, could build educational institutions, could send out expeditions, could keep the information flowing—indeed, his famous writing desk was a virtual clearinghouse of scientific news—he did not himself have time to devote to detailed investigation. For the time being, knowledge had to be judged by its immediate utility.

Jefferson understood that the process of discovery follows no man's timetable, of course. "No discovery is barren," he remarked in 1802; "it always serves as a step to something else."[31] Jefferson's pragmatism derived from his conviction that American culture was immature and vulnerable, while its needs were urgent. Rightly or wrongly, he emphasized practicality to offset what he saw as widespread American antipathy to European decadence, which often seemed to celebrate the intellect for purely aesthetic reasons. Practicality was a test of necessity, just as a determination to remain an amateur was an index of sincerity. Pragmatism certainly shaped his attitude toward literature, which he ranked below science in its utility. Although he wanted to domesticate both literature and science into American vernaculars, he may have felt that he could impose his prejudices on literature more easily. At any rate, in devising programs of education, he suggested reading literature in the evening, after a full day devoted to more important subjects.[32]

Jefferson often read literature through the lenses of science. A scholar of Greek and Latin, he parsed Homer and Virgil—in his view the only great poets, because they had withstood the test of time and because all educated men shared their experience.[33] In their works he found what he called "stores of real science" relevant to the astronomy, mathematics, and natural history of his own period.[34] But he was just as convinced that a familiarity with imaginative literature was essential to a full education. After his first library burned, he composed a list of books to be included in an ideal collection. Prominent among them, he wrote to Robert Skipwith, should be novels, poetry, and drama.[35] The list contained many great names of literature, including Shakespeare, Smollet, Richardson, and Sterne. Sterne's works, he said, "form the best course of morality that ever was written," and *King Lear* was better than "all the dry volumes of ethics and divinity that ever were written." Imaginative fiction evoked an interest in the lives of other people and encouraged "moral" responses like sympathy and altruism. He told Skipwith that readers were "wisely framed to be as warmly interested for a fictitious as for a real personage." The ethicality he demanded of literature he also demanded of science, which he thought had only truth as its end. Science for Jefferson was quite literally a replacement for religion: if it was skeptical, chaste, and rigorous, it was also complete and self-sustaining. More important, it was a fraternal and humanistic endeavor, the source of sensibilities common to those found in literature. To read and write literature, in turn, was to enter a republic of letters. Despite his celebrated mistrust of religion, he was sufficiently a Puritan to accept the notion that Americans are a people of the book and to share the conviction that every man could read and interpret that book for himself. So powerful an empirical tradition shaped his writing.

So did formal literary models, mostly classical, a preference that owed something to his father, who had insisted that young Thomas's education emphasize Tacitus and Livy rather than English essayists. But Jefferson schooled his own formidable powers of expression. That is evident from his commonplace books, one of which was published as *The Literary Bible of Thomas Jefferson* by Gilbert Chinard.[36] As a young man, Jefferson wrote poetry but recognized his lack of facility. Many years later, he responded to a gift of Joel Barlow's "American" epic, *The Columbiad,* with the statement, "Of all men living, I am the last who should undertake to decide as to the merits of poetry,"[37] but his reluctance to comment was probably occasioned by diplomacy, for Barlow's composition was unreadable. Actually he had pronounced opinions about poetry and about writing in general. Jefferson wrote the first American essay on prosody (which remained unpublished until 1903). Among reflections on style, he offered a preference for blank verse, which he thought was superior to jingling rhyme.[38] Throughout his life he honed his own prose into a gleaming instrument, an American "plainstyle," bereft of ornamentation, equally adaptable to cool observation or passionate enthusiasm.[39]

The dimensions of the republic of letters, like those of the fraternity of science, were determined by the principles of an orderly universe. Both scientists and writers could discover these principles and express them as observation and imagination. Scientific power derived from comprehending nature, not by achieving control over her, just as political power stemmed from understanding man, not by commanding. Literature acquired its force through expression, without which there could be no understanding, and it was powerful to the degree that it accurately mirrored nature. Since nature was there to be expressed, no one could claim that the ideas nature generated were original, and no one could claim property rights to them. This belief was the bedrock of Jeffersonian democracy, and it has offended the elitist sensibilities of professional writers—which might explain why Jefferson's literary reputation has languished.

Susan Sontag has noticed that literature as "a secular calling"—i.e., as a professionalized activity—separates from other forms of writing like journalism, belles lettres, hack fiction, and history in the eighteenth century,[40] but Caesar Grana has linked this splitting away to the rise of industrialization, when writers lost the patronage of church, crown, and aristocracy. Patronage had not entirely disappeared during Jefferson's time, of course; Goethe, to mention just one example, still drew subsidies from Weimar princes. The loss of patronage meant that the writer, like other artists, had to compete in a cultural marketplace as an independent agent as he saw fit. What the writer could sell was originality. The "absence of obligation to the standards of a specific social environment had made originality not only possible but also, in a sense, the sole point and foundation of literary creation."[41] Originality arose, as it did in the sciences, from experimentation, but in addition—as was not at all the case with science—from the kind of self-discovery historians would later call Romanticism. The very precariousness of the writer's economic position, says Grana, "bred in many writers a tendency to grow touchy concerning the momentousness and dignity of their trade, and one after another fell to speaking reverentially of the natural gap between the creator and the layman."[42] That was reflex, a defensive posture designed to offset the difficulty of making a living at authorship. The hardheaded Dr. Johnson put things less mysteriously: "No man but a blockhead," he said, "ever wrote for anything but money."

Jefferson disliked the Romantic writers as a group, although at the close of his life he enjoyed the poems of Ossian (the fictional persona created by James McPherson), whom he described as the greatest of poets.[43] Jefferson did not object to writers making money, although like Benjamin Rush he seems to have thought fame the chief "stimulus" to "difficult and laborious literary pursuits."[44] In fact, the small American population during the Revolutionary period could not support many professional writers, nor was original literature as a commodity adequately protected by copyright for many years. Jefferson was just as skeptical of copyright as he was of patent monopolies.[45] As the nation's first secretary of state, Jefferson did not administer the first Federal Copyright statute of 1790 as he did the first Federal Patent Act of that year, but his feeling about copyright was probably similar to his views on patents. The moment an idea "is divulged," said Jefferson, "it forces itself into the possession of everyone, and the receiver cannot dispossess himself of it."[46] The outrage occasioned by Jefferson's refusal to grant more than sixty-seven patents in three years led Congress to create a new patent office to take over his duties. So far as writing was concerned, he seemed to think that what the culture would lose in sophistication by keeping literature as the leisure pursuit of amateurs would be made up for in intellectual suppleness—an attitude, needless to say, that retarded the growth of a professional writing class in America.

Jefferson did not patent his famous moldboard plow nor did he copyright *Notes on the State of Virginia*.[47] Nor did he claim originality in the Declaration. At the height of his political battles with Jefferson, John Adams told Timothy Pickering that scarcely any of the ideas in the Declaration of Independence had been original. Jefferson was bewildered by the charge: "Pickering's observations, and Mr. Adams' in addition, that [the Declaration] contained no new ideas, that it is a commonplace compilation, its sentiments hacknied in Congress for two years before . . . may be all true. Of that I am not judge. Richard H. Lee charged it as copied from Locke's treatise on Government. . . . I only know that I turned to neither book nor pamphlet while writing it. I did not consider it as any part of my charge to invent new ideas altogether and to offer no sentiment which had never been expressed before."[48] In 1825, a year before his death, Jefferson responded to Lee more elaborately: he had provided readers of *The Declaration* with arguments of such common sense as would "command their assent": "Neither aiming at originality of principles or sentiments, nor yet copied from any particular and previous writing, it was intended to be an expression of the American mind. . . . All its authority rests on the harmonizing sentiments of the day, whether expressed in conversation, in letters, printed essays, on the elementary books of public right, as Aristotle, Cicero, Locke, Sidney, etc."[49]

What would have been the good, he implied, in springing new ideas on his audience? Revolutions were not made of novelty but of ideas that had been seething. The whole point was to make sure that nobody missed the point, that the expression be accessible to all. The *expression* of "the American mind" in the Declaration certainly made it as much a literary as a political document. Like so many of our native classics, including the Preamble to the Constitution, the Declaration is a first-person narrative,[50] and one could in fact argue that American literature itself grew slowly in part because that masterpiece said everything that the age required about the American mind.

Rather than add to the vast comment on that document, however, we might more profitably look at *Notes on the State of Virginia,* a work that does *not* express "the harmonizing sentiments of the day," as an example of Jefferson's ability to transform his scientific principles into literary statement that *is* clearly original. Written as a series of answers to scientific questions posed by François Marbois, secretary of the French legation at Philadelphia while Jefferson was wartime Governor of Virginia, *Notes on the State of Virginia* began in 1780 as a statistical survey, an outgrowth of the author's obsessive habit of note-taking, and over several months swelled into a full-scale manuscript complete with bibliography of works on the state. He arranged for an edition of two hundred copies to be printed privately five years later in France, without his name on the title page, for limited distribution to his friends, and then in 1787 for an English edition bearing his name to counter the threat of inaccurate pirated editions (the complicated publishing history has been best traced by William Peden[51]). The delay in acknowledging it can be attributed to Jefferson's worries that the chapters on religion, Indians, and slavery contained remarks that were not simply unharmonious but explosive. Fawn Brodie suggests that he first printed it anonymously because he knew that it was a work of emotion (which it is) and that its content violated his sense of scientific objectivity (which it does).[52] However factual he thought it, his treatment of the facts transformed them into literature. And whatever anxieties the book caused him, he revised and polished it for the rest of his life, doubtless because he secretly cherished its literary excellences.

Notes on the State of Virginia is the complement to the Declaration and the Virginia Statute for Religious Freedom, for it reveals the emotional turmoil behind those bold statements of idealism. Here is the originality smelted out of principles that appear now to have been engraved in empiric, metallic permanence. Most of what subsequent generations have called Jeffersonianism derives from this work, in which the man noted his thoughts on America in sustained form rather than in snippets of letters. Here is the glorification of farmers ("the chosen people of God, if ever he had a chosen people, whose breasts he has made his peculiar deposit for substantial and genuine virtue" [165]), the mistrust of manufacturing (although Jefferson would change his mind about factories after the Napoleonic Wars demonstrated the vulnerability of an economy dependent on imports), the fear of cities, and the worries about the democratic loyalties of future immigrants that would be echoed in the poetry and fiction of subsequent generations. But where later American writers adopt these themes as critiques of society, Jefferson's concern is with the fragility of culture in the new land. His antipathy to large-scale manufacturing in the United States arises from the desire to preserve the innocence of the scientific and democratic experiment, just as his resistance to the professionalization of both science and literature—what might be called the self-conscious creation of culture—grows out of a belief in the integrity of simpler intellectual cottage industries.

Notes is a personal vision by turns utopian and sober. It is a narrative of America: a chronicle of unfolding drama told in the languages of botany and zoology, meteorology and geography, ethnology and paleontology. These were, as we have noted earlier, languages that he helped to invent. *Notes* draws on Jefferson's scientific predecessors, builds upon and disputes their ideas. Its patriotism is most evident in its responses to Buffon, "the pope of eighteenth-century zoologists"[53]: Jefferson dismissed the Frenchman's patronizing pronouncements on American topography, meteoreology, and biology, which were easily refuted by direct observation. Among other things, Buffon had claimed that American mammals were smaller than their European counterparts. Jefferson simply cataloged animals by classes, using the Linnaean nomenclature, and ranked species according to continent by weight and size; little else needed be said. As this method indicates, scattered throughout *Notes* are tables of all sorts—on rainfall, on Indian tribes, on birds, on trees, on population—composed by a naturalist pleased at his ability to validate his chauvinism with figures.

The narrative voice charms, its ingenuousness neither smug nor naive, untainted by assumptions of great learning—convinced, rather, that any area of knowledge requires only reason to grasp. Jefferson is just an amateur, he implies, while Buffon is a professional zoologist whose errors are literary: the result of "his vivid imagination and bewitching language" (64). The strategy is effective; because Jefferson seems to aim only at fact, his own seductive style persuades. In its epistolary form *Notes* bears some resemblance to *Letters From an American Farmer* (1782), which was composed about the same time, although neither Crèvecoeur nor Jefferson, despite a later friendship, seems to have influenced the other. A more apt comparison would focus on a later work. *Notes on the State of Virginia* is as much about the character of Thomas Jefferson as *Walden* is about the mental "state" of Henry David Thoreau. They are similar personalities: Jefferson driven by a faith in objectivity but tugged also by his love of expression. Thoreau (in the words of Dirk Struik) spoiled by Emerson as a scientist, spoiled by Agassiz as a poet.[54] Thoreau and Jefferson are kindred naturalists, their penchant for careful observation wedded to a predilection for pithy comment. For example, in the section on religion, after reviewing the pressures for orthodoxy in Virginia, Jefferson makes the Thoreauvian remark, one of dozens of possible instances: "But it does me no injury for my neighbor to say there are twenty gods, or no god. It neither picks my pocket nor breaks my leg" (159). *Notes on the State of Virginia* is thus the first example of an American genre of naturalism as substratum for opinions and imagination that runs through Thoreau, Burroughs, and Muir to Annie Dillard and John McPhee in the present.

More significant, Jefferson in this work emerges as the psychic and visual geographer of America, her cartographer of the future. Howard Mumford Jones has singled out "the full panoramic landscape originated in aesthetic principles [as] . . . the special creation of Thomas Jefferson in his *Notes on Virginia*. In this book he did it twice: once in describing the Natural Bridge, and once in describing the confluence of the Shenandoah and the Potomac."[55] "For the mountain being cloven asunder," says Jefferson in the second instance, "she presents to your eye, through the cleft, a small catch of smooth blue horizon, at an infinite distance in the plain country, inviting you, as it were, from the riot and tumult roaring around, to pass through the breach and participate of the calm below" (19). According to Jones, Jefferson's "painterly" descriptions influenced the Hudson River School and also writers like James Fenimore Cooper and William Cullen Bryant.[56] That visual sense persists. Nearly two centuries later, Edmund Wilson would be amused by his own tendency to write "still . . . in the vein of old-fashioned landscape description."[57] It is the expression of an American consciousness aware of space rather than time, as befitted a national identity without much past or history. Jefferson's images fixed the parameters of America's visual landscape as much as his later Louisiana Purchase established the physical boundaries of the nation.

It is important to remember that Virginia then claimed territory in enormous excess of her present boundaries, so that in a genuine sense Jefferson's eye traverses at least a third of the continent. But though the vastness of the region is one of the subjects of Jefferson's narrative, it is limited, psychically, by the consciousness of a wider cosmos. Where the Declaration is confident, even aggressive in its nationalism, *Notes* seems more aware of the rest of the world's scrutiny of the new democracy, more doubtful of the moral superiority of its small population. In fact, virtually all of the memorable passages are the consequence of Jefferson's encounters with aberrations in the Newtonian universe whose principles he thinks so orderly and self-evident.

That does not mean that the work's literary characteristics are augmented by its author's scientific mistakes, only some of which are attributable to the ignorance of the time. Jefferson speculated absurdly on geology, essayed into areas of physiology he knew nothing about, reproduced questionable data from physics, allowed his prejudices to intrude. The mistakes do not make him a bad scientist, although they make him a less than first-rate one, at the same time that they make the man himself more human. Nor can we call *Notes on the State of Virginia* one of the fountainheads of American literature simply because it announces major national themes, or because it establishes a genre, or because it fixes a landscape. It is a triumph of our literature because of its ethicality (the quality Jefferson so readily praised in the poetry, drama, and fiction of others). Its honesty consists in its acknowledgment that Jefferson's attempt to domesticate his science has failed, a failure rendered all the more poignant by his evident longing. That is the real difference between the Declaration of Independence and *Notes on the State of Virginia.* If the former is a masterpiece because it finds in Newtonian mechanics a model whose rationality can inform the politics of a nation, the latter is a masterpiece because it discovers that the Newtonian model lacks humanity sufficient to guide the ethics of its citizens.

The cracks in the eighteenth-century cosmos of the *Notes* appear gradually, as Jefferson recognizes America's failings. For example, when he describes Virginia houses, he laments that "the genius of architecture seems to have shed its maledictions over this land. . . . The private buildings are very rarely constructed of stone or brick; much the greatest proportion being of scantling and boards, plaistered with lime. It is impossible to devise things more ugly, uncomfortable, and happily more perishable" (152-53). At a more important extreme, he marks injustices to Indians. He lists the major tribes, praises their virtues, refutes European myths of Indian inferiority. Forty years before Cooper, he asserts the nobility of native Americans and includes in the *Notes* a transcription of a speech by the Indian chieftain Logan, whose family was massacred by whites: "There runs not a drop of my blood in the veins of any living creature. This called on me for revenge. I have sought it: I have killed many: I have fully glutted my vengeance. For my country, I rejoice at the beams of peace. But do not harbor a thought that mine is the joy of fear. Logan never felt fear. He will not turn on his heel to save his life. Who is there to mourn for Logan?—Not one" (63). The reproduction of that speech, almost as eloquent as anything Jefferson himself ever wrote, caused outrage among many Americans and led to charges that Jefferson was betraying his white brethren when the book's authorship became known. As Jefferson handles it, Logan's is a story within the larger story of the nation, part of her chronicle, never told better. Not exactly small matters, these acknowledgments of blight in paradise are preludes to treatment of a more basic evil. Besides, Jefferson did his part to improve his state's architecture, and to redress injuries to the Indian. He spent years compiling Indian vocabularies that materially contributed to the study of Indian origins through philology.[58] The moral fault line in the book originates in the contrast between the personal and social inertia that permitted Jefferson to own two hundred slaves and the conscience that tormented him. When toward the end of *Notes* he confronts the institution made peculiar by democratic principles that he himself had derived from a scientific reading of the cosmos, the schism shakes his world.

Jefferson himself traces the crack in his Newtonian universe in the section innocuously titled "Manners," which is entirely concerned with slavery. The crack deepens sentence by sentence, from references to the "unhappy influence" of slavery upon America's citizens, to the infection of white children by this canker in the body politic, to deepening depravity, to the utter destruction of the country's morality. The litany is capped by epiphany, as the Newtonian architect of the world's greatest experiment in scientific statehood exclaims, "I tremble for my country when I reflect that God is just: that his justice cannot sleep for ever" (163). The mea culpa emerges as the hidden "expression of the American mind" behind the sublime cadences of the Declaration. The author embellishes the epiphany only to the extent that his rationality balks at blaming the power of darkness: the crime is a failure of light.

Jefferson's heirs, having ceded the responsibilities of the amateur to professional scientists, may view his eighteenth-century consciousness with a cynicism sharpened by the awesome discoveries that science has made in almost two centuries. Veteran readers of texts overwrought by generations of professional writers, they may find in his directness an imagination without artifice and a sensibility unaware of its own originality. Reading *Notes on the State of Virginia*, however, Americans perhaps may acknowledge Thomas Jefferson's paternity of their literature, just as they already call him father to their science.

Notes

1. John Adams to Timothy Pickering, Aug. 6, 1822, in John Adams, *Works*, ed. Charles Francis Adams, 10 vols. (Boston: Massachusetts Historical Society, 1856), vol. 2, 513-14.

2. As additional examples, even Jefferson's *A Summary View of the Rights of British Americans*, a work of which he was proud, was at first anonymously published as a pamphlet (Williamsburg: Clementin Arind, 1774); his *Manual of Parliamentary Practice* (1789) was just a hand-bound pocket compilation for his own use, though he showed it to people who asked; and his *An Essay Towards Facilitating Instruction in the Anglo-Saxon and Modern Dialects of the English Language* languished among his papers until the trustees of his university published it (Charlottesville: Univ. of Virginia, 1851). Anonymous pieces are still coming to light. As George B. Watts has pointed out, Jefferson contributed an unsigned essay on the United States to volume two of the four-volume dictionary called *Économie politique et diplomatique* (Paris: Panckoucke et Plomteux, 1784-88) published by Jean-Nicholas Démeunier, and material on Virginia and other states to François Soulés's *Histoire des troubles de l'Amérique anglaise* (Paris: Panckouke et Plomteux, 1786). George B. Watts, "Thomas Jefferson, the 'Encyclopédie' and the 'Encyclopédie méthodique,'" *French Review* 38 (Jan. 1965): 321-24.

3. Thomas Jefferson to Charles Thomson, July 21, 1875, in Julian Boyd et al., eds., *The Papers of Thomas Jefferson*, 19 vols. (Princeton: Princeton Univ. Press, 1950-1974), vol. 8, 245.

4. The most illuminating accounts of Jefferson as a scientist against the science of his period are Edwin T. Martin's *Thomas Jefferson, Scientist* (New York: Schuman, 1952); John C. Greene's *American Science in the Age of Jefferson* (Ames: Iowa State Univ. Press, 1984); Brooke Hindle's *The Pursuit of Science in Revolutionary America* (Chapel Hill: Univ. of North Carolina Press, 1956); and Dirk J. Struik's *Yankee Science in the Making* (Boston: Little, Brown, 1948). The best works on Jefferson as a writer are two similarly titled essays: Edd Winfield Parks, "Jefferson as a Man of Letters," *Georgia Review* 6 (Winter 1952), 450-461; and Max J. Herzberg, "Thomas Jefferson as a Man of Letters," *South Atlantic Quarterly* 13 (Oct. 1914), 310-27.

5. The works on Jefferson, are, of course, legion. The standard biography is Dumas Malone's *Jefferson and His Time*, 6 vols. (Boston: Little, Brown, 1948-1981). Adrienne Koch treats his political philosophy in *Jefferson and Madison: The Great Collaboration* (New York: Knopf, 1950) and in *The Philosophy of Thomas Jefferson* (1943; rpt., Gloucester, Mass.: Peter Smith, 1957). Fawn Brodie's *Thomas Jefferson: An Intimate History* (New York: W.W. Norton, 1974) treats his alleged affairs with his slave. John Dos Passos reviews contradictions in Jefferson's personality in *The Head and Heart of Thomas Jefferson* (Garden City, N.Y.: Doubleday, 1954). The most recent biography is Noble E. Cunningham's *In Pursuit of Reason: The Life of Thomas Jefferson* (Baton Rouge: Louisiana State Univ. Press, 1987). Various other works are cited in the notes to follow.

6. Garry Wills, *Inventing America: Jefferson's Declaration of Independence* (Garden City, N.Y.: Doubleday, 1978); that there are three Declarations is the premise of the book.

7. See Martin, *Thomas Jefferson, Scientist*, chapter 9, for an account of these attacks.

8. Thomas Jefferson to Monsieur de Crève Coeur, Jan. 15, 1787, in Albert Ellery Bergh, ed., *The Writings of Thomas Jefferson*, 20 vols. (Washington, D.C.: Thomas Jefferson Memorial Association, 1907), vol. 6, 55.

9. Quoted in Wills, *Inventing America*, 102.

10. Jefferson thought of the abortive André Michaux expedition and the more successful Lewis and Clark explorations quite literally as "literary enterprises," presumably because they were to produce written accounts. See Gilbert Chinard, "Jefferson and the American Philosophical Society," *Proceedings of the American Philosophical Society* 87 (1943), 266.

11. Chinard, "Jefferson and the American Philosophical Society," 263-76, esp. 266.

12. Martin, *Thomas Jefferson, Scientist*, 331.

13. Chinard, "Jefferson and the American Philosophical Society," 273.

14. Quoted in Karl Lehmann, *Thomas Jefferson: American Humanist* (New York: Macmillan, 1947), 13.

15. "Conversation with Washington," Feb. 28, 1792, in *Anas*, Writing L and B, vol. 1, 286; see also Brodie, *Thomas Jefferson*, 267.

16. Daniel Boorstin, *The Lost World of Thomas Jefferon* (Boston: Beacon Press, 1960).

17. Howard Mumford Jones, *O Strange New World! American Culture: The Formative Years* (New York: Viking, 1964), 343.

18. Hindle, *Pursuit of Science*, 44.

19. Ursula Brumm, *American Thought and Religious Typology*, trans. John Hoaglund (New Brunswick, N.J.: Rutgers Univ. Press, 1970), 86-102. Charles H. Faust, however, dismisses the thesis that Edwards himself was a scientist of some note in "Jonathan Edwards as a Scientist," *American Literature* 1 (Jan. 1930): 393-404.

20. Hindle, *Pursuit of Science*, 12.

21. Thomas Kuhn, *The Structure of Scientific Revolution*, 2nd ed. (Chicago: Univ. of Chicago, 1970), 20-22.

22. Interested readers should consult Jefferson's *Garden Book* (pub. 1944) and *Farm Book* (pub. 1953).

23. Thomas Jefferson to Dr. John Manners, Feb. 22, 1814, Bergh, *Writings of Thomas Jefferson*, vol. 14, 97.

24. For his systems of notation, see his letter to his son-in-law Thomas Mann Randolph in 1790, *The Works of Thomas Jefferson*, ed. Paul Leicester Ford, 10 vols. (New

York: Putnam's, 1892-1899), vol. 5, 159-60. For the reference to his paleontology, see Harlow Shapley, "Notes on Thomas Jefferson as a Natural Philosopher," *Proceedings of the American Philosophical Society* 87 (1943), 235.

25. Thomas Jefferson to Dr. John Manners, Feb. 22, 1814, in Bergh, *Writings of Thomas Jefferson,* 97-98.

26. Thomas Jefferson, *Notes on the State of Virginia,* ed. William Peden (Chapel Hill: Univ. of North Carolina Press, 1955), 148. This edition of the *Notes* is the standard and will be cited hereafter textually.

27. Quoted in M.P. Crosland, *Historical Studies in the Language of Chemistry* (1962; rpt., New York: Dover, 1978), 171.

28. Thomas Jefferson to James Currie, in Boyd, *Papers of Thomas Jefferson,* vol. 14, 366.

29. Still more ironically, from the standpoint of Jefferson's conviction that science was essential to democracy, the aristocratic Lavoisier was guillotined during the Terror in France because "the Revolution has no need of scientists."

30. Quoted by Boorstin, *Lost World,* 5.

31. Quoted in Martin, *Thomas Jefferson, Scientist,* 38.

32. Cited in Martin, *Thomas Jefferson, Scientist,* 27.

33. See Jefferson, *Notes,* 276, note 100.

34. Aug. 24, 1819, Bergh, *Writings of Thomas Jefferson,* vol. 15, 208. See also George T. Surface, "Investigations into the Character of Jefferson as a Scientist," *Journal of American History* 4 (1910): 214-20, esp. 216.

35. Thomas Jefferson to Robert Skipwith [1771], Bergh, *Writings of Thomas Jefferson,* vol. 4, 237-39.

36. Thomas Jefferson, *The Literary Bible of Thomas Jefferson: His Commonplace Book of Philosophers and Poets,* ed. Gilbert Chinard (Baltimore: 1928; rpt., New York: Greenwood, 1969); an earlier volume, not to be confused with *The Literary Bible,* but also edited by Chinard, was simply *The Commonplace Book of Thomas Jefferson* (Baltimore: Johns Hopkins Univ. Press, 1926).

37. Quoted in Jefferson, *Literary Bible,* 28.

38. Jefferson, *Literary Bible,* 27.

39. An example of his writing theory: "I readily sacrifice the niceties of syntax to euphony and strength. It is by boldly neglecting the rigorisms of grammar, that Tacitus has made himself the strongest writer in the world." Thomas Jefferson to Edward Everett, Feb. 24, 1823, quoted in Lehmann, *Thomas Jefferson,* 81.

40. Susan Sontag, "When Writers Talk Among Themselves," *New York Times Book Review,* Jan. 5, 1986, 22.

41. Caesar Grana, *Modernity and Its Discontents* (Glencoe, Ill.: Free Press, 1967), 41.

42. Grana, *Modernity,* 41-42.

43. Thomas Jefferson to Charles McPherson, Feb. 25, 1773, in Ford, *Works of Thomas Jefferson,* vol. 1, 413.

44. Quoted in Greene, *American Science,* 11-12.

45. For an account of Jefferson's duties as a patent commissioner, see Hugo A. Meier, "Thomas Jefferson and a Democratic Technology," *Technology in America: A History of Individuals and Ideas,* ed. Carroll W. Pursell (Cambridge: MIT Press, 1981), 17-33. The first Federal Copyright statute was almost wholly ineffectual because it merely protected pub-

lications from exact duplication; all a publisher had to do was add a paragraph to a work, then publish it with impunity.

46. Thomas Jefferson to Isaac McPherson, Aug. 13, 1813, Bergh, *Writings of Thomas Jefferson*, vol. 13, 333. Despite his reputation as a gadgeteer, Jefferson rarely invented; he improved. The device so often linked with Jefferson, the polygraph, or writing duplicator, was actually invented by a Philadelphian and merely refined by Jefferson.

47. Jefferson freely offered the plow to anyone who wished to copy its design. Jefferson arranged for the first public printing of *Notes* simply to prevent mutilations of his text, which a publisher had obtained.

48. Thomas Jefferson, quoted by Gilbert Chinard, *Thomas Jefferson: The Apostle of Americanism*, 2nd ed. rev. (Boston: Little, Brown, 1948), 71.

49. Quoted in Chinard, *Thomas Jefferson*, 72.

50. An observation for which I am indebted to Judith Yaross Lee.

51. William Peden, "Introduction" to Jefferson, *Notes*, xi-xxi.

52. Brodie, 152.

53. George Gaylord Simpson, "The Beginnings of Vertebrate Paleontology in North America," *Proceedings of the American Philosophical Society* 80 (Sept. 1942) , 130-88, 145.

54. Struik, *Yankee Science*, 218.

55. Jones, *O Strange New World!* 359-60.

56. Ibid., 359-66.

57. Edmund Wilson, *Upstate: Records and Recollections of Northern New York* (New York: Farrar, Straus and Giroux, 1971), 189.

58. See Greene, *American Science*, chapter 14, on "Comparative Linguistics and the Problems of Indian Origins," esp. 400-408.

5

An Intrinsic Luminosity: Poe's Use of Platonic and Newtonian Optics

WILLIAM J. SCHEICK

The place of science in Poe's thought and imagination can be easily misassessed if we judge it on the basis of his poetry. Such verse as "Sonnet—to Science" (1829), with its identification of the poet with the defiant but doomed mythological figures of Prometheus and Icarus, represents a clear assault on science as a force preying on the poet's heart, as a force inimical to creative imagination (Promethean fire) and mythic or metaphoric language (Icarian flight). This poem, however, appeared early in Poe's career, and although he later revised and continued to republish it together with much of his other early verse, this work remains a testament to the author's youthful, possibly exaggerated reaction to science. The true place of science in Poe's thought is manifest in his prose, where in various forms it plays significant roles in his layering of meanings in these writings.

In the 1840s—in fact, on no less than five separate occasions—Poe remarked the common ground between the scientist and the artist. This relationship is implied in the introductory remarks to "The Murders in the Rue Morgue" (1841), and in "A Chapter of Suggestions" (1845) Poe specifically wrote: "Some of the most profound knowledge—perhaps all *very* profound knowledge—has originated from a highly stimulated imagination. Great intellects *guess* well. The laws of Kepler were, professedly, *guesses.*" This same comment, in somewhat different words, is made in "Mellonta Tauta" (1849) and *Eureka* (1848), emphasizing that "Kepler *guessed,*" "*imagined,*" "*grasped* . . . with [his] *soul*" laws he surmised "through mere dint of *intuition.*" And in a letter (September 20, 1848) to Charles Fenno Hoffman he explained his position more fully: "There is no absolute *certainty,* either in the Aristotelian or Baconian process . . .

neither Philosophy is so profound as it fancies itself—and . . . neither has a right to sneer as that seemingly imaginative process called Intuition (by which Kepler attained his laws;) since 'Intuition,' after all is but the conviction arising from those *inductions* or *deductions* of which the processes are so shadowy as to escape our consciousness, elude our reason or defy our capacity of expression."[1]

At the outset of any attempt to assess the place of science in Poe's prose, however, one needs to express a cautionary note. Poe did in fact know much about science, but this knowledge came to him in various ways. Some scientific information came to him while he was a student, whereas much came to him from reading as an adult. But this reading is difficult to trace sometimes. Poe's scientific information came to him from primary and secondary, even sometimes journalistic, sources. As a result, when Poe cites a scientific source, we might be tempted to think he read the work containing the reference, when in fact he might well have read some other book or magazine article and might only be repeating something cited in this other source. This is certainly the case when in "Marginalia" (1844-49) he seems to quote from Newton's *Opticks* (1704), but in fact the misattributed remark derives from an article Poe had read (*Writ*, 2:176). This problem does not delimit a study of the function of science in Poe's writings, where traces of scientific information are in abundant evidence;[2] it does delimit any attempt at concluding with ease whether he had a first-hand familiarity with and a thorough knowledge of a specific scientific treatise. So a quotation from Sir Isaac Newton's *Principia* (1687) in "Marginalia" or a reference to it in "Mesmeric Revelation" (1844; *W*, 3:1035) and *Eureka* (*CW*, 16:223) does not necessarily mean that Poe read an edition of this late seventeenth-century work; it does mean that Poe was interested in the scientific observation made in the quotation or reference.

Perhaps the scientific field that most fascinated Poe was astronomy.[3] For his account of Hans Pfaal's trip to the moon, Poe relied on Sir John Herschel's *Treatise on Astronomy* (1833), which is quoted from and paraphrased in Poe's story. *Eureka* abounds in astronomical information, with reference to John Pringle Nichol's *Views of the Architecture of the Heavens* (1837) and some reliance upon David Brewster's notes to James Ferguson's *Astronomy* (1811). Poe's astronomical lore sometimes coalesced with his interest in physics,[4] especially the principle of gravity in *Eureka*, where he contrasts gravity's power of attraction to electricity's power of repulsion; if, Poe explains, "the principle of Newtonian Gravity" exhibits "the tendency of the diffused atoms to return into Unity," in contrast, electricity always is produced when the bodies that meet differ appreciably from one another in the character of their atoms (*CW*, 16:212-13).

The word *sums* alerts us to another scientific field of great interest to Poe: mathematics. Poe seems to have known the writings on mathematics and meteors by the Newtonian editor of *Principia*, Roger Cotes, among others. On mathematics and light, in particular, Poe notes in one place that "the diffusion—the scattering—the irradiation [of light], in a word—is *directly* proportional with the squares of the distances" (*CW*, 16:226). The pyrotechnical display of mathematical learning in some of Poe's works has led several critics to express a high regard for Poe's ability in this subject, although there has been dissent to that opinion.[5] Less evident than mathematics are traces of Poe's knowledge of chemistry (particularly the nature of phosphorescence and the use of bichloride of mercury in preservation), geology (primarily earthquakes), aeronautics (especially in ballooning), biology (specifically plants such as the sugar beet), and animal magnetism (preeminently in the pseudoscience of mesmerism, in which Poe *seems* to have believed).[6] Poe knew a little about paleontology and was familiar with Jacques-Henri Bernardin de Saint-Pierre's *Studies of Nature* (1808). Sometimes he could use technical terms drawn from biology, such as his reference in "Marginalia" (*Writ*, 2:122) to some people as *Epizoae* (parasites). He also had a hand in the revised *The Conchologist's First Book* (1839) and might have played a role in the production of *A Synopsis of Natural History with Human and General Physiology and Biology* (1839).[7]

More influential than all of these interests is Poe's information on psychology and medicine. In his fiction Poe delved into the subjects of mind, memory, dreams, hallucinations, insanity, fear, hysteria, personal identity, sexuality, and phrenology (the study of the shape of a skull as an index to a person's emotional, intellectual, and imaginative predispositions).[8] Poe was also an avid reader of medical journals, which in the nineteenth century were not so technical that the average literate person would find them inaccessible, and he even reviewed medical journals. He possibly wrote an article on *A Dissertation on the Importance of Physical Signs in the Various Diseases of the Abdomen and Thorax* (*CW*, 9:164-66). Pertinently, in his stories one finds frequent references to catalepsy, fevers, pestilence, consumption, synaesthesia, and hypochondria.[9]

Poe's interest in human psychology and biology, particularly as they correspond to his knowledge of physics, is manifest as well in a critically neglected feature of his work: how his notions about human perception relate to his ideas about optics. Even a cursory exposure to Poe's fiction leaves a strong impression of his recurrent emphasis on the eye, whether it be a horse's human-looking eye in "Metzengerstein" (1832), the seemingly pupilless eye of the subject of "Berenice" (1835), the deep well-like eyes of the heroine of "Ligeia" (1838), the luminous eyes of Roderick in "The Fall of the House of Usher" (1839), the entrancing eye of the artist's dying bride and model in "The Oval Portrait" (1842), the fiery feline eye in "The Black Cat" (1843) or the veiled, pale eye of the victim in "The Tell-Tale Heart" (1843). In Poe's time there was, among philosophers and scientists, a consensus that sight was the most comprehensive and engaged of the five senses.[10] In detailing the relationship between Poe's ideas about human perception and his understanding of optics, the depth of his knowledge of certain scientific information and the role of this knowledge in his fiction can be better appreciated. To date, the function of optics in Poe's works has not been immediately self-evident. Coming to terms with his thought about perception discloses features of his symbolism and shows how he found scientific authority to support his aesthetic management of optical concepts.

Classical Optics

An exploration of Poe's use of knowledge about the physics and physiology of human optics should begin with a consideration of his reliance in some instances upon optical theory derived from classical tradition. Concerning light and vision, there were two classical notions, the Platonic and the Aristotelian. These two notions differed over the source of light in the process of vision. The Platonic concept, which appears in *Meno* (76C), *Timaeus* (45), and *Thentetus* (153), held that the eye is the source of light, that vision results from the impact on objects of ocular beams emanating from the eye. Opposed to this concept—perpetuated as well by Euclid, Lucretius, and even Roger Bacon—is the Aristotelian notion set forth in *De Anima* (Pt. 2, ch. 7), *Parva naturalia* (ch. 2), and *Meteorologica* (372b), a belief perpetuated by Johannes Kepler (*Dioptrik*, ch. 61). The Aristotelian concept of optics maintained that light rays derive from luminous objects and that vision is the result of the reflection of the images of these objects upon the watery surface of the eye.

Poe knew well Plato's work, which echoes not only in, say, the word *Eidolon* in "Dream-Land" (1844), but also in all of Poe's works concerning the play between an essential Unity and its fragmentation into the phenomenological world of shadowy forms. "The Colloquy of Monos and Una" (1841), the second of Poe's trilogy of dialogues by heavenly creatures, refers to "the pure contemplative spirit and majestic intuition of Plato," whose teachings are "most desperately needed" now when they are "most entirely forgotten or despised" (W, 2:610-11). And it is not only the notion apparently fictitiously attributed to Plato by the devil in "Bon-Bon" (1835) that the mind is light (W, 2:108) but also the Platonic notion of vision, of light originating from the eye, that Poe sometimes adapts to symbolize the sight of a character who represents ideality, especially the artist in possession of an intense imagination recalling primal Unity.

This is the case with Augustus Bedloe in "A Tale of the Ragged Mountains" (1844) and Roderick Usher in "The Fall of the House of Usher." The narrator of "A Tale" reports that "in moments of excitement" Augustus's "abnormally large" eyes "grew bright to a degree almost inconceivable; seeming to emit luminous rays, not of a reflected, but of an intrinsic lustre, as does a candle or the sun" (W, 3:940). In "The Fall of the House of Usher" Roderick also possesses eyes "large, liquid, and luminous," a description repeated in "The Haunted Palace" (1839), the poem reprinted in this story that refers to "two luminous windows" representing Roderick's two eyes (W, 2:401, 407). At first one might be inclined to think that this luminosity in Usher's eyes is reflected light, but it is important to recall two facts. First, in Eureka Poe follows David Brewster's example in restricting the word luminous to a source of issuing light (CW, 16:225). Second, we need to recall how little light exists in the home of Roderick, whose eyes we are told "were tortured by even a faint light" (W, 2:403). Then, too, the narrator refers to the "miraculous lustre" of Roderick's eyes (W, 2:402). Roderick is an artist who pulls away from the world of sensation—he suffers, as in the instance of natural light, from "a morbid acuteness of the senses" (W, 2:403)—and through his art tries to retreat into the realm of the imagination. Augustus too possesses an "imagination . . . singularly vigorous and creative" (W, 3:942). The feverish light in their luminous eyes comes from within, as if Platonically defined, and it represents the interior light of the imagination shining outwardly through their eyes upon the world.

That this luminosity represents the Platonic interior light of the imagination is suggested as well in "Ligeia." Throughout the story, Ligeia is associated with art, mysticism, and imagination. Like Roderick, she has an inordinate swelling at the temples, which in phrenological studies (a pseudoscience in which Poe believed for a while) is said to suggest ideality, a frame of mind that strives toward Platonic essence beyond the material realm. Like Roderick and Augustus, her eyes are "large and luminous orbs," eyes of "radiant lustre" seemingly lit from within (W, 2:314, 316). Her very presence, the narrator reports (as he struggles to regain an *imaginary* vision of her), "rendered vividly luminous the many mysteries of the transcendentalism in which we were immersed" (W, 2:316).

Poe, as we shall see, was fundamentally Newtonian in his optical theory, and so this recourse to the classical Platonic optical concept that the eye emits light from within might seem odd, even if Poe used much from Plato and even if his symbolism is well served by these appropriations. But surprisingly he may have found some support for the Platonic concept among the Newtonian optical theoreticians, who make a sharp distinction between a luminous object (one that emits rays) and an illuminated object (one that reflects rays). Poe knew, for instance, David Brewster's *Letters on Natural Magic* (1832), which appeared six years before the publication of "Ligeia," seven years before the publication of "The Fall of the House of Usher," and twelve years before "A Tale of the Ragged Mountains." In this work, Brewster, who is the last great champion of Newtonian optics, writes, "When the retina is compressed in total darkness, it gives out light" because there exists a "phosphorescence of the retina." [11]

This might seem strange coming from a Newtonian, but there it is stated; and it might have given Poe scientific authority to use Platonic optical theory for symbolic purposes. Brewster resorts to this idea when he tries to explain why a blow to the eye or head produces a bright flash of light; Brewster concluded that the light is generated by the phosphorescence of the retina. Brewster did not know, as we do today, that the flash of light perceived from a blow to the head is the result of the stimulation of the optic nerve, which sends the only message it can to the brain which in turn translates all optic nerve messages as light. As Brewster's observation stands, however, it could have given particular authority to Poe's artistic predisposition to depict the eye as innately luminous, as if in accord with Platonic optical theory, to symbolize the imaginative orientation of the artist's vision toward ideality, essential Unity.

Newtonian Optics

Both Platonic and Aristotelian concepts assumed that light was only a means of sight and so was nothing itself, and this belief is precisely what Newton's rainbow disproved in the first quarter of the eighteenth century.

In *Opticks,* which Poe knew at least secondhand through the writings of subsequent Newtonian optical theoretians such as Robert Smith and David Brewster (both of whom he specifically cites), Newton demonstrated how a prism reveals the several components of the particles of light, bands of colors (particles of light differing in mass) that cannot be further reduced. Smith took Newton's idea, advanced in *Principia,* of attraction as a primary quality of all physical bodies—this is the Newtonian notion underlying Poe's belief in the imagination's intuitive sense of the return of matter to essential Unity—and Smith applied this concept to the corpuscular nature of light, the rays of which were thought to be attracted by material bodies.[12]

Apparently Newton was aware that the corpuscular theory did not explain every behavior of light, and there are moments in *Opticks,* especially in reference to the transmission of the stimulus of light to the brain, when he intimates that some properties of light might be undulatory rather than corpuscular. During the eighteenth century, however, Newton's corpuscular theory held sway among his followers (such as Smith) as if there were no questions about light left unanswered by Newton's concept of particles. In the first decade of the nineteenth century Thomas Young published an essay challenging the corpuscular theory and advancing a wave theory of light. Poe, who is fundamentally Newtonian in his optics theory, did in fact know something about this emergent undulatory theory. His knowledge of it may have come from a first-hand reading of Young's essay, for Poe did read issues of *Philosophical Transactions,* which published Young's article; but Poe more certainly encountered the concept in Brewster's writings, possibly in Brewster's otherwise fully Newtonian *Treatise on Optics* (1831), for example.[13]

In "Mesmeric Revelation" Poe gives a Newtonic account of how the eye sees: "A luminous body imparts vibration to the luminiferous ether. The vibrations generate similar ones within the retina; these again communicate similar ones to the optic nerve. The nerve conveys similar ones to the brain; the brain, also, similar ones to the unparticled matter which permeates it. The motion of this latter is thought, of which perception is the first undulation" (W, 3:1038). This reference to undulation aside, however, Poe here is esentially Newtonian. In this instance the eye seems passive, a view typical of the eighteenth-century Newtonists, who tended to stress the objective reality of an object. Although this sense of the fundamental passivity of the eye would be revised in the early nineteenth century by Brewster, the last Newtonian, it tended to be reinforced by nineteenth-century medical texts of the sort Poe read. In a review (*Southern Literary Messenger* 2 [November 1836], 784-86) of several volumes of *The British and Foreign Medical Review* Poe includes extensive praise of Andrew Combe's *The Principles of Physiology* (1834). In such works as this, he read about the passivity of the eye. In Andrew Combe's *Observations on Mental Derangement* (1831) we are typically told that the eye is "a passive instrument," with no "vital properties," and it only obeys "the ordinary laws of matter."[14] In this book, as in George Combe's *A System of Phrenology* (1825) and *Lectures on Phrenology* (1838), both of which Poe knew very well, the enlargement of size of this passive treatment increases its function.[15] Recall that Augustus Bedloe, Roderick Usher, and Ligeia each is characterized by especially large eyes.

But, as we have seen, the eyes of these three characters are far more active than the passive instrument described in many eighteenth-century treatises on optics and early nineteenth-century medical books. Besides Brewster's notion of the phosphorescence of the retina, was there any other authority for Poe's attention to the eye as an active agent in vision? Besides the possible authority provided by Brewster's idea, Poe's description of the eyes of Augustus, Roderick, and Ligeia as Platonic emitting luminosities could have also been authorized by medical and optical studies that intimated the subtle capacity of the eye to be a shaper, even a creator of perception well beyond the usual sense of that organ as a passive instrument.

A clue surfaces in George Combe's *A System of Phrenology*, which argues that "the eye only receives, modifies, and transmits the impressions of light," but also in another place states: "So little power has experience to alter the nature of our perceptions, that even in some cases where we discover, by other senses, that the visible appearance of objects is illusive, we still continue to see that appearance the same as before."[16] Combe does not speculate whether this problem of illusion, emphasizing the passivity of the organ of the eye, is the result of the objective limits of the eye or the subjective power of the mind. Whatever the implications of Combe's observation, Poe understood well the nature of illusions of sight. In "The Spectacles" (1844), "The Sphinx" (1846), and *Eureka*, for example, Poe specifically noted that a gap can exist between material reality and human perception.[17]

Optics and Perception

In Poe's prose this lacuna between phenomena and the perception of the human eye has five sources: technical problems with the eye, contextual influences on vision, innate capacities for indirect sight, conceptual deter-minations of vision, and powerful mental images informing perception. These features range from difficulties of an objective nature to difficulties of a subjective nature, and in reviewing them we shall see finally where Poe found scientific, late-Newtonic authority for his symbolic use of Platonic optics.

The first of these explanations, technical problems with the organ of sight such as myopia, receive ample coverage from nineteenth-century optical and medical studies. Poe, in fact, had fun with such technical problems in "The Spectacles." In this narrative, Simpson, who is badly nearsighted and who refuses to wear eyeglasses, falls in love with and almost marries his great-great grandmother. In an unfolding of plot that seems in part a parody of Poe's earlier detective fiction, Simpson's misper-ceptions are eventually revealed at the end of Poe's satire on "love at first sight," apparently (Poe suggests) an always myopic perception.

More fascinating is a second feature of human sight: contextual influ-ences on vision. Context introduces complexity to perception, and what one sees depends not only on what occurs but also on the situation, or the ensemble of events, or the relation of the seer to the thing seen. Poe, for instance, knows that a mirage is, as Brewster explains in *Letters,* an unusual refraction of light through strata of air of different densities. A mirage is a matter of context, the physical relation of light to atmosphere and the spatial relation of viewer to image.

Contextual problems pertaining to spatial relationships especially fas-cinated Poe. He hints at them when in *Eureka* he refers to "the wiseacre who fancies he must necessarily see an object the more distinctly, the more closely he holds it to his eyes" (CW, 16:190). Indeed, Poe's "The Sphinx" concerns just this problem, a story in which the narrator mistakes a butterfly for a "monster of hideous conformation" (W, 3:1247). The combi-nation of evening light and the narrator's proximity to the insect—it is one-sixteenth of an inch long and one-sixteenth of an inch from his face—creates a contextual distortion, as Poe's narrative raises the question of whether we can always trust "the evidence of [our] own eyes" (W, 3:1247).

Still more interesting to Poe is a third feature of sight: the eye's capacity for indirect perception. Brewster and Herschel refer to it as oblique vision, which they say is inferior to direct vision in both the distinctness of image and the preservation of a sustained view of an object; yet, Brewster explains, "it might give us a more perfect view of minute objects, such as small stars not seen by direct vision," a conclusion argued as well in modern-day textbooks on human perception.[18] Poe applies this concept in

"Murders in the Rue Morgue," in which Dupin points out that one can "impair . . . vision by holding the object too close. He might see, perhaps, one or two points with unusual clearness, but in so doing he, necessarily, lost sight of the matter as a whole." Dupin continues:

> The modes and sources of this kind of error are well typified in the con-
> templation of the heavenly bodies. To look at a star by glances—to view it in a
> side-long way, by turning toward it the exterior portions of the *retina* (more
> susceptible of feeble impressions of light than the interior), is to behold the
> star distinctly—a lustre which grows dim just in proportion as we turn our
> vision *fully* upon it. A greater number of rays actually fall upon the eye in the
> latter case, but, in the former, there is the more refined capacity for com-
> prehension. By undue profundity we perplex and enfeeble thought; and it is
> possible to make even Venus herself vanish from the firmament by a scrutiny
> too sustained, too concentrated, or too direct. [W, 2:545-46]

To an extent, furthermore, Poe maintained that beauty, truly supernal beauty, could not be apprehended by direct vision, but only obliquely, and this idea doubtless found reinforcement in the Newtonian recognition of indirect vision.

All three of the preceding characteristics of vision are for the New-tonian objectively definable. They have to do with the objective phys-iological makeup of the complex organ of sight, with its abilities and limitations, as well as with the context of the object perceived. In the nineteenth century the physical malfunction of the apparatus of the eye was not very mysterious and could sometimes be corrected by the use of glasses. The contextual influences on the eye seemed somewhat more mysterious, but in learning about them Poe's contemporaries could accom-modate the limitations these influences suggest. The capacity for oblique vision—the function of the rod cells of the retina—was even more mysterious in Poe's day, and it was accepted as a surprising, unusual, posi-tive attribute of the eye.

This increasing sense of mysteriousness compounds in the last two traits of human perception: conceptual determinations of vision and powerful mental images informing sight; and these two concerns are subjective in nature rather than objective, as in the instance of the first three features. These remaining two problems really stress the gap between perceiver and perceived, and Poe was especially fascinated by them. It is in light of these two problems particularly that we can appreciate Brewster's and Poe's early nineteenth-century sense of the abiding enigma of human perception: a sense of mystery that characterizes the eighteenth-century poetic reponse to Newtonic optics, appears in early nineteenth-century treatises like Brewster's, and still at times is explicitly expressed in today's studies of human sight.[19]

Conceptual determinations of perception interested nineteenth-century scientists, doctors, and artists. As we noted in passing earlier, in *A System of Phrenology* George Combe mentions the "illusions of optics" in terms that leaves uncertain whether they are the result of objective limitations of the eye or of the subjective powers of the mind. Specifically he remarks on those illusions associated with perspective in pictures: "The picture appears to us to represent objects at different distances, and the most determined resolution to see them all equally near is of no avail, although we know that, in point of fact, they are so."[20] That pictures, or art, can delude viewer perspective by illusions that are paradoxically complex is a theme of Poe's landscape tales: "The Landscape Garden" (1842), "The Domain of Arnheim" (1846) and "Landor's Cottage" (1849).[21] Moreover, in these works, as elsewhere, Poe allows for the possibility that conceptual influences can be active determinators of perception.

Perhaps Poe's most outspoken remarks on this point about how concepts shape vision occur in "Marginalia." In item 38 of "Marginalia" Poe attacks Dionysius Lardner, who tried to explain "the apparent difference in size between the setting and the noon-day sun." He believed that in looking at the setting sun we mentally, "by a process of the mind so subtle and instinctive" that we are "unconscious of it," compare the sun with the objects seen between it and ourselves; since we know that the intervening objects are smaller than the sun, we adjust our actual vision in terms of our conceptual knowledge of the larger size of the sun, a comparison we do not make when the sun rises to the meridian and consequently looks smaller than the setting sun. Poe objects, noting that even on a smooth sea, where there are no intervening objects, the setting sun on the horizon seems larger than usual. Poe then goes on through some difficult reasoning to argue that objects do not have to be actually present, for the viewer posits them there "mentally" and, rather than their size, abstractly senses their distances; he concludes that when distance increases or diminishes, "the mind instantaneously" increases or diminishes the size of a perceived object (CW, 143-46).

Lest we hastily conclude that both Lardner and Poe were mistaken that the setting sun appears larger at sunset than at meridian because of the greater amount of atmosphere and atmospheric particles at that angle to the viewer, we might consider that a modern-day textbook on this experi-ence of human perception suggests that the apparent difference in size "is not produced by factors such as the scattering of light by atmospheric conditions or disparities in the relative luminance . . . in different sky locations," for photographs do not show any size difference; and today, this text continues, arguments about the illusion are still made on the basis of real or apparent size, distance, and angle of regard—the last having to do with the belief that what is seen may differ depending on whether the viewer's eyes are looking straight ahead at the horizon or raised toward the zenith.[22] This text concludes "that there may be no single answer to the ancient puzzle of [this] illusion." Finally, of course, the rightness or wrongness of Poe's notion is less important than the fact that he was fully aware of how, mysteriously, interior conceptions in the mind can influence and even determine what is seen, thereby reflecting an enormous gap between the subject's mind and the object's corporeal reality.

This division between mind and world is even more radically enig-matic in the fifth feature of vision recognized by Poe and some nineteenth-century scientists: the effect on perception of powerful mental images. In *A System of Phrenology* George Combe, without focusing on the mind as an active agent in actual vision, speaks of the imagination as "the *impassioned representation* of . . . things—not merely in the forms and arrangements of nature, but in new combinations formed in the mind itself."[23] *Representa-tion:* this process involves the depiction of imagery, but just how are these images depicted so that they enter the mind? Andrew Combe, in *The Principles of Physiology* (a Poe favorite), remarks that "the mind cannot see without the intervention of the eye"; "the eye is the mind."[24] Neither of the Combe brothers quite closes with the relation of the imagination and the mind, nor does either of them quite suggest that subjective mental images can determine sight. But Poe could have found support in David Brewster's *Letters on Natural Magic* (another Poe favorite), which argues explicitly that spectral apparitions, recollected images, or imagined forms are pictures in the mind's eye that can be more vivid than those of the body's eye. Brewster asserts that the mind's eye *is* the body's eye, that imagination and memory generate actual impressions upon the retina, from whence they travel through the optic nerve to the brain. These impressions are *actual,* and they can be *more vivid* than what the retina perceives of the world through the eyeball.[25] Brewster's concept might inform Poe's presentation of obsessed characters, who perhaps do not merely hallucinate but possibly actually see what their heated imagination projects upon their retinas.

Moreover, Brewster could have provided Poe with late-Newtonic scientific authority for resorting to Platonic optics in order to symbolize how the fiery imagination seems to cause the emanation of an inward light from the eyes of an artist (like Roderick) or of a personification of the artist's ideal of beauty (like Ligeia). Even in "The Spectacles," which principally concerns a technical deficiency of Simpson's eyes, there is a clue that his imagination informed the impressions he had of the woman with whom he fell in "love at first sight," a woman not fully seen by his myopic eyes but a woman envisioned "rather of the imagination"—"the *beau idéal* of [his] wildest and most enthusiastic visions," who (in a self-parodic move by Poe) seems to possess Ligeia-like "large, luminous eyes"[26]; thus seen in his imagination, this lady is nonetheless apparently retinally perceived by Simpson.

Not only did Brewster assert that the retina of the eye was phosphorescent, thereby unwittingly preserving something of Platonic optics, but, more important, he also asserted the physiological realness of sense impressions on the retina that derive solely from imagination and memory. In a way Brewster was reaffirming the belief attributed to Plato in "Bon-Bon," that the mind is light (CW, 16:108). The imagination has the power to emit light-like stimuli, and these subjectively generated stimuli record on the retina and then travel to the brain.

Of course Poe knew that Platonic optics, with its concept of an inward light emitting from the eye outwardly upon the world, was mistaken. But in treatises like Brewster's he could have found scientific authority to resort to Platonic optics, not as literal fact, but as symbolic of the person with a very active imagination, an imagination that generates images that are literally perceived by the retina. In this sense the imagination generates something like an interior luminosity behind the eyeball, and so Poe depicts the highly imaginative person as someone who evinces this interior light in large luminous eyes, eyes that therefore *seem* to emanate light from within.

This meeting of scientific belief and aesthetic symbol in Poe's work has as one of its foundations Poe's firm belief that the *true* scientist is akin to the artist. As we noted as the start of this essay, Poe emphasized at least four times Kepler's use of the inner light of imagination or intuition (Poe's words) in combination with sense impressions of the corporeal eye in order to arrive at an understanding of the laws of nature. In Poe's opinion, Kepler was not merely responding to sense impressions from the physical world; he was, like an artist, also responding to impressions derived from within his imagination. Kepler was interested not only in physics but also in "physico-metaphysics" (CW, 16:223). As Kepler's example suggested to Poe, "true Science . . . makes its most important advances . . . by seemingly intuitive *leaps*" (W, 16:189). Only a complete perception by means of both the light of imagination and the light of nature can bridge the gap between viewer (subject) and viewed (object), the gap otherwise manifest in the behavior of the human eye. And, as we see in *Eureka*, this complete perception from within as well as from without, so apparent in a true scientist like Kepler or a visionary artist like Usher, suggests in microcosm something macrocosmic: Poe's belief finally in an essential Unity (an intrinsically luminous cosmic imagination, as it were) behind the phenomenological fragmentation that is the natural universe.[27]

Notes

1. These remarks on Kepler appear in "A Chapter of Suggestions," Burton R. Pollin, ed., *Collected Writings of Edgar Allan Poe, Vol. 2, The Brevities: Pinakidia, Marginalia, Fifty Suggestions, and Other Works* (New York: Gordian, 1985), 468; "Mellonta Tauta," in Thomas Ollive Mabbott, ed., *The Collected Works of Edgar Allan Poe* (Cambridge: Harvard Univ. Press, 1978), 3:1297; James A. Harrison, ed., *Eureka: The Complete Works of Edgar Allan Poe*, (New York: Fred de Fau: 1902), 16:197; and a letter to Charles F. Hoffman in John W. Ostrom, ed., *The Letters of Edgar Allan Poe* (Cambridge: Harvard Univ. Press, 1948), 380. Subsequent references to Pollin's edition are cited parenthetically in the text and identified as *Writ*; subsequent references to Mabbott's edition are cited parenthetically in the text and identified as *W*; and subsequent references to Harrison's seventeen-volume edition are cited parenthetically in the text and identified as *CW*. In light of Joseph Moldenhauer's "Mabbott's Poe and the Question of Copy-Text," *Poe Studies* (Dec. 11, 1978) 41-46, I have used Mabbott's edition of the tales cautiously, and I always checked passages against Harrison's edition to watch for any important variants.

2. Poe's interest in science has been generally acknowledged; see, for instance, Killis Campbell, "The Relation of Poe to His Times," *Studies in Philology* 20 (July 1923), 293-301; Clarke Olney, "Edgar Allan Poe—Science Fiction Pioneer," *Georgia Review* 12 (Winter 1958), 416-21; Carol Hopkins Maddison, "Poe's *Eureka*," *Texas Studies in Literature and Language* 2 (Autumn 1960), 350-67; Carroll D. Laverty, "Poe in His Place—In His Time," *Emerson Society Quarterly*, No. 31 (2nd Quarter 1963), 23-25; Harold Beaver, "Introduction" to *The Science-Fiction of Edgar Allan Poe* (New York: Penguin, 1976); and Ronald T. Curran, "The Fashionable Thirties: Poe's Satire in 'The Man That Was Used Up,'" *Markham Review* 8 (Oct. 1978), 14-20. Concerning Poe's preference for intuition or imagination over scientific reasoning, see particularly George Monteiro, "Edgar Poe and

the New Knowledge," *Southern Literary Journal* 4 (Spring 1972), 34-40; Gerard M. Sweeney, "'Beauty and Truth': Poe's 'Descent into the Maelstrom,'" *Poe Studies* 6 (Jan. 1973), 22-25; and Benjamin Franklin Fisher, "'That Daughter of Old Time': Science in the Writings of Edgar Allan Poe," *Publications of the Arkansas Philological Association* 9 (1983), 36-41. Most recently, in *The Place of Fiction in the Time of Science: A Disciplinary History of American Writing* (Cambridge: Cambridge Univ. Press, 1990), 70-120, John Limon has argued that Poe translated the gap between Baconianism and science into the gap between science and art, thereby creating a straw man to justify poetry; but, Limon continues, this maneuver merely disguised Poe's disgust with Jacksonian life and fear of the divine and the vital represented by art.

3. On Poe's knowledge of astronomy, see William H. Gravely, Jr., "New Sources for Poe's 'Hans Pfaall,'" *Tennessee Studies in Literature* 17 (1972), 139-49; and Maurice H. Bennet, "Edgar Allan Poe and the Literary Tradition of Lunar Speculation," *Science-Fiction Studies* 10 (June 1983), 137-47.

4. On Poe's knowledge of physics, see William H. Browne, "Poe's 'Eureka' and Recent Scientific Speculations," *New Eclectic Magazine* 5 (Aug. 1869), 190-99.

5. See, for example, Clarence P. Wylie, Jr., "Mathematical Allusions in Poe," *Science Monthly* 63 (Sept. 1946), 227-35; and Harry R. Warfel, "The Mathematics of Poe's Poetry," *CEA Critic* 21 (May 1959), 5-6.

6. Consider, as illustrative, Herbert F. Smith, "Usher's Madness and Poe's Organicism: A Source," *American Literature* 39 (Nov. 1967), 379-89; and Doris V. Falk, "Poe and the Power of Animal Magnetism," *PMLA* 84 (May 1969), 536-46.

7. Joseph J. Moldenhauer, "Beyond the Tamarind Tree: A New Poe Letter," *American Literature* 42 (Jan. 1971), 468-77.

8. Typical studies on this subject include Edward Hungerford, "Poe and Phrenology," *American Literature* 2 (Nov. 1930), 209-31; Madeleine B. Stern, "Poe: 'The Mental Temperament' for Phrenologists," *American Literature* 40 (May 1968), 155-63; John E. Reilly, "The Lesser Death Watch and 'The Tell-Tale Heart,'" *American Transcendental Quarterly* 2 (2nd Quarter 1969), 3-9; Jules Zanger, "Poe and the Theme of Forbidden Knowledge," *American Literature* 49 (Jan. 1978), 533-43; Edward W. Pitcher, "The Physiognomical Meaning of Poe's 'The Tell-Tale Heart,'" *Studies in Short Fiction* 16 (1979), 23-33; and J. Lasley Dameron, *Popular Literature: Poe's Not-so-soon Forgotten Lore* (Baltimore: Enoch Pratt Free Library, 1980).

9. See, for example, Allan Smith, "The Psychological Context of Three Tales by Poe," *Journal of American Studies* 7 (Dec. 1974), 279-92; David W. Butler, "Usher's Hypochondriasis: Mental Alienation and Romantic Idealism in Poe's Gothic Tales," *American Literature* 48 (Mar. 1976), 1-12; Elizabeth Phillips, *Edgar Allan Poe, An American Imagination: Three Essays* (Port Washington, N.Y.: Kennikat, 1979); and George R. Uba, "Malady and Motive: Medical History and 'The Fall of the House of Usher,'" *South Atlantic Quarterly* 85 (Winter 1986), 10-22.

10. Andrew Combe, *Observations on Mental Derangement* (Boston: Capen and Lyon, 1834), 101, 183.

11. David Brewster, *Letters on Natural Magic* (London: Murray, 1832), 19. Poe knew this work well, as he did Brewster's *A Treatise on Optics* (1833), both of which he cites. Brewster's *Letters* was a source for "Maelzel's Chess Player," a point made by W.K. Wimsatt, Jr., in "Poe and the Chess Automaton," *American Literature* 11 (May 1939), 138-51; and by

Carroll D. Laverty in an unpublished dissertation entitled "Science and Pseudo-Science in the Writings of Edgar Allan Poe" (Duke, 1951), the best overview available on the subject of Poe's scientific knowledge.

12. Smith's *Complete System of Opticks* (1738) is cited by Poe in some notes he might have intended for a revision of *Eureka* (*W*, 16:350-51). On Smith's relation to Newton's teachings, see Henry John Steffens, *The Development of Newtonian Optics in England* (New York: Science History Publications, 1977), 34-43. This work also discusses David Brewster's position as the last Newtonian.

13. Brewster mentions the wave theory of light in *A Treatise on Optics* (Philadelphia, 1843), 118-19. On Newton's hesitation over the corpuscular theory of light and on Young's argument for the wave theory, see Vasco Ronchi, *The Nature of Light: An Historical Survey*, trans. V. Barocas (Cambridge: Harvard Univ. Press, 1970), 194-213; 236-59.

14. *Observations*, 59. Since Poe greatly admired Combe's *The Principles of Physiology*, it is altogether likely that he knew this work by Combe as well. But even if he did not, the point about the objective limits of the passive eye is an idea that Poe would have encountered in the medical literature of the period.

15. On the significance of the largeness of the eyes, see George Combe's *A System of Phrenology* (New York: Harper, 1849), 44-45; and Combe's *Lectures on Phrenology* (New York: Fowler and Wells, 1851), 107-8. On Poe's first-hand knowledge of these two books, see Hungerford, "Poe and Phrenology," 212-14.

16. *System of Phrenology*, 276, 274.

17. In "The Distorted Perception of Poe's Comic Narrators," *Tropic 30* 16 (1976) 23-34, James W. Gargano notes the unreliability and malfunction of human perception in some of Poe's fiction.

18. *Treatise on Optics*, 248-50. Compare Brewster's *Letters*, 14-15. That Poe was interested in oblique vision was first noted in Laverty's "Science and Pseudo-Science," 190-210, and was later repeated in Walter Shear's "Poe's Use of an Idea about Perception," *American Notes and Queries* 21 (May/June 1983), 134-36.

19. The eighteenth-century literary response is documented in Marjorie Hope Nicolson's *Newton Demands the Muse: Newton's "Opticks" and the Eighteenth-Century Poets* (Princeton: Princeton Univ. Press, 1945). In the nineteenth century Brewster writes: "In what manner the retina conveys to the brain the impressions it receives from the rays of light is a mystery" (*Treatise on Optics*, 243). Today, that "our current knowledge in physiology is not sufficiently developed to account fully for perception" is a point made in William N. Dember and Joel S. Warm's *Psychology of Perception* (New York: Holt, Rinehart and Winston, 1979), 17.

20. *System of Phrenology*, 267.

21. See, especially, Catherine Rainwater, "Poe's Landscape Tales and the 'Picturesque' Tradition," *Southern Literary Journal*, 16 (Spring 1984), 30-43.

22. Dember and Warm, *Psychology*, 204-9.

23. *System of Phrenology*, 366.

24. Andrew Combe, *The Principles of Physiology* (New York: Harper, 1835), 211.

25. *Letters on Natural Magic*, 48-55.

26. Joseph J. Moldenhauer, "Poe's 'The Spectacles': A New Text from Manuscript," *Studies in the American Renaissance: 1977*, 210, 202, 215. That the ocular deception in this story might be the result of the protagonist's abnormally depressive mind and his affliction

by a contagious disease is argued by Elmar Schenkel, "Disease and Vision: Perspectives on Poe's 'The Sphinx,'" *Studies in American Fiction* 13 (Spring 1985), 97-102.

27. A shorter version of this essay was read at a session of the Poe Studies Association held during the Modern Language Association convention, December 28, 1989. I would like to express a special note of thanks to Joseph Moldenhauer and Catherine Rainwater for sharing thoughts and books.

6

Fields of Investigation: Emerson and Natural History

DAVID M. ROBINSON

> For poetry is science, and the poet a truer logician.
> —"Poetry and Imagination," *The Complete Works*
> *of Ralph Waldo Emerson*, VIII, 39

In an 1830 sermon at Boston's Second Church, Emerson singled out "the love of the natural sciences . . . beginning to spread among us the study of plants, of minerals, the history of beasts, birds, and insects" as a particularly hopeful sign of a shift in American society. Emerson praised this growing emphasis on natural science because he felt it was part of a general reorientation of American religious life that would result in a new focus on the cultivation of the self. The rise of interest in natural history "may have the effect to supplant in some degree the absorbing passion for wealth by supplying new measures of happiness & simpler and more spiritual pleasures" (CS, 2:230). Emerson lived long enough into the Gilded Age to recognize that with regard to a fading love of wealth in America, he was no social prophet. But his conviction of the centrality of scientific thinking to any reconception of the religious and moral life was prophetic. Emerson came to intellectual maturity during the period when intellectual culture would begin to be torn away from religious culture. The development of the natural sciences, which he unreservedly commended as one of the means of spiritual improvement, would in large part dictate that split. Yet the Victorian crisis of faith, at least insofar as it concerned the perceived threat of scientific naturalism to religious belief, left Emerson untouched. He found in the rise of science no threat to the religious sensibility, but a new source of its nurture. Emerson remains valuable to us in part because of his exemplary faith in the congruence of scientific and religious knowledge. Because of the state of science in his age, and because of his own craving to understand nature in every possible sense, his scientific and philosophical quests work in a broad harmony. This chapter will therefore sketch the outlines of Emerson's principal statements on science and nature, and the key comments of later critics on them. As I hope the chapter will suggest, the subject is a rich one, and the possibilities for extended research are great.

Scientific change was accelerating in the first decades of the nineteenth century, fueled by the continuing work of botanical and zoological classi- fication that had characterized the major advances of the century before. This process of classification continually raised questions about nature's order, development, and origin, which were, of course, crucial theological questions as well. While most scientists and theologians hoped and trusted that there was no conflict in the two enterprises, existing theories and boundaries of belief were constantly being pressed by the generation of new information. Moreover, the science of geology was adding new infor- mation on the age and history of the earth, thereby demanding a new theological accounting. To many like Emerson, there was an unmistakable excitement in the air, as the secrets of nature seemed to be opening. To those who shared his orientation, scientific work was no threat but was in fact helping to advance metaphysical and speculative thinking. Emerson recorded his interest in science with his first public discourses, the sermons preached during his career in the Unitarian ministry from 1826 through 1832. As a supply preacher, and then minister of the Second Church in Boston, he turned on a number of occasions to the study of nature as a support for his stance of moral aspiration. "Religion will become purer and truer by the progress of science" (YES, 171), he preached, and his develop- ing theology of the culture of the soul was closely tied to his attention to the development of a theory of nature. In language reflective of his developing poetic gift, Emerson explained the religious value of the love of nature: "Yet the song of the morning stars was really the first hymn of praise and will be the last; the face of nature, the breath of the hills, the lights of the skies, are to a simple heart the real occasions of devout feeling more than vestries and sermon hearings" (YES, 171).

The initial scientific assumptions underlying Emerson's praise of na- ture were those of natural theology, which saw the natural world as a centerpiece of the revelation of religious truth to humanity. From this perspective, the knowledge of God was attainable through the careful observation and analysis of nature. In his groundbreaking study of 1931, still the preeminent treatment of Emerson and science, Harry Hayden Clark showed how this tradition of natural theology, represented by Joseph Butler's *The Analogy of Religion* (1736) and William Paley's *Natural Religion* (1802), had a formative effect on Emerson's project of establishing the natural world as a spiritual and ethical analogy to the human soul.[1] Emerson's engagement with science centered upon his development of the implications of this analogy between nature and the soul. His absorption in science was not principally motivated by its methodologies; he formulated scientific questions in theological and philosophical terms, as part of a larger metaphysical and ethical speculation.

Carl F. Strauch has noted that Goethe was Emerson's primary scientific model, suggesting to him the goal of a "poet-scientist who traverses the kingdoms of nature, science, and art." Emerson regarded Goethe, in the words of Gustaaf Van Cromphout, as "the major force behind the revolt against the eighteenth-century mechanistic worldview."[2] The importance of Goethe as a model for Emerson is an important reminder that his scientific interests and approach were speculative and holistic rather than empirical. As Clark explained, Emerson's approach to natural history was "essentially *a priori,* ethical, and deductive, like that of Plato, Schelling, Goethe, Kant, and Coleridge."[3] His frequent return to scientific sources, which he studied at some depth in the early 1830s, was always motivated by the cosmic concerns of his initial acquaintance with natural theology.

Emerson had been steeped in natural theology in his Harvard training, and it was reinforced by the generation of Unitarian ministers who preceded him and who extended a long line of Christian speculation by arguing that the works of the natural world, including humanity itself, were evidences of the existence of a benevolent God. Emerson not only breathed this air as a Harvard student and Unitarian minister but also found a chord within himself that responded deeply to nature. For him, the experience of nature and of religion could be almost interchangeable. In one sermon, he speculated that the union of the soul with God might result in an omniscience about nature itself: "It has been maintained by some Christians, that, as the soul became united to God, it would learn all the sciences, not by the tedious analysis now in use but by consciousness, because God is the source of all; all exist in him, and as the mind became participant of his nature, it would read them by its knowledge of him. These speculations are too sublime for the reach of our knowledge. But though they ought to be carefully limited, they have a foundation in truth" (CS, 2:36). The young poet, enamored of the pleasures of such imaginative flights, here struggles with the more soberly responsible minister. The young poet, though, is clearly ascendant. The passage tells us much about Emerson's penchant for speculation, his high valuation of scientific knowledge, and his impatience with the "tedious analysis" involved in the work of close observation, classification, and ordering. The passage also suggests one important form of his developing discourse on nature. If we can finally understand nature by understanding God, can we not understand God by understanding nature?

In 1829, Emerson preached that "objects of sense" are best seen as "occasions and materials of thought," as the expansion of our knowledge leads us to look beyond the object to the truth it represents. "Every object, besides that it is large, or soft, or of one or another color or taste, we find is a symbol of something else" (CS, 1:244-45). When the mind focused on the entire system of physical relations that we call nature, the result was the perception of nature itself as a vast symbol of divinity. This suggested to him that the whole existence of nature might be explained in terms of its role in the religious cultivation of the self. In an 1832 sermon that anticipates his first book *Nature* (1836), Emerson preached that "the whole course of Providence" was to "assist in the work of self-cultivation," that the whole world was adapted "to the formation & education of the human soul."[4] Thus nature's religious value was manifold. Rationally considered, it suggested the presence of the creator. Experienced in its beauty and harmony, it provided a spiritual uplift closely akin to, and causative of, religious ecstasy. And considered as the symbol of an underlying ideal, it stood as an educator in the moral culture of the soul.

Emerson resigned his pulpit in 1832 and traveled to Europe. It was a literary and religious pilgrimage, but a scientific pilgrimage as well. The trip was marked by an important visit to the Jardin des Plantes and the Cabinet of Natural History in Paris, where Emerson encountered the botanical garden arranged by Antoine-Laurent de Jussieu. The visit had a powerful impact on Emerson.[5] Jussieu's work proposed to demonstrate a natural order of plant species in a continuous, harmonious chain. Emerson responded to the visit strongly in his journal: "I feel the centipede in me— cayman, carp, eagle, & fox. I am moved by strange sympathies, I say continually 'I will be a naturalist'" (JMN, 4:200). Emerson's resolution was serious, as his immediate future showed. He returned to America and made brief forays into botanical classification, pursuing the scientific activity that had impressed him the most. As Elizabeth A. Dant has recently explained, the cabinet of natural history seemed to promise Emerson an "ordering principle" for his thought, and his desire to create a "world-encompassing encyclopedic genre" was shared in the entire culture as the nineteenth century attempted to assimilate the explosion of facts generated by modern scientific investigation. Jonathan Bishop has pointed out that Emerson was attracted to scientific classification because its intellectual process suggested a translation of "facts into the language of law," an essential example of how the particular, rightly seen, could become the universal.[6]

The series of four lectures on science that Emerson undertook in 1833-34 (see *EL*, 1:1-83) are crucial texts in his long speculation on natural history. His fresh enthusiasm for science permeates the tone of "The Uses of Natural History," in which he pursued at length the advantages of scientific study and made public the declaration of his journal, "I will be a naturalist" (*EL*, 1:10). "The Relation of Man to the Globe" and "Water" are further immersions in the details of scientific study. "The Naturalist," however, marks a turn in Emerson's thinking, typified by his realization that he, like many others interested in science, can hope to attain only "quite superficial knowledge" (*EL*, 1:70). Emerson was admitting, of course, what has been an increasingly worrisome problem in the modern world, the recession of scientific expertise from the public mind in an increasing necessity of specialization. He had discerned by then that it might be a "waste of time to study a new and tedious classification" (*EL*, 1:70), and had begun to make peace with the fact that his own skills and inclinations were not those of an investigative, experimental, and empirical scientist.[7] But the controlling purpose of his intellectual commitment to science emerged in that lecture more clearly than anywhere in his career. His intellectual agenda was increasingly centered on the conception of the unfolding of the innate power of the human soul, a power that was at once divine and natural. He found in his study of nature, with its continual recurrence to theories of development, a powerful confirming analogy to his conception of human nature. In particular, the preevolutionary theories of natural development, as suggested by Goethe and Lamarck, which were then laying the groundwork for the Darwinian revolution, were of enormous importance to his self-culture project. The dynamism of nature cohered with his sense of the dynamism of the soul.

Emerson's early exploration of science eventuated in a very speculative book, *Nature*.[8] Yet that book could not have been what it was without

Emerson's immersion in science. The book seems to undermine the empiricism of scientific procedure by pointedly questioning "whether nature outwardly exists." Does this not deny science its very subject? But far from threatening nature as a field of investigation, Emerson argues that his idealism vitalizes it: "It is the uniform effect of culture on the human mind, not to shake our faith in the stability of particular phenomena, as of heat, water, azote; but to lead us to regard nature as a phenomenon, not a substance; to attribute necessary existence to spirit; to esteem nature as an accident and an effect" (CW, 1:30). The whole book pivots on the distinction Emerson makes between nature as phenomenon and nature as substance. Seen as substance, nature was inflexible and dead. Seen as phenomenon, it was mutable and alive. To think of nature in terms of phenomena emphasized its quality of constant change, making it a model of growth and development. That mutability was for Emerson an essential part of its moral purpose.

The idealism that Emerson propounded in Nature thus synthesized his stance of moral aspiration with his predilection for the study of natural history. Nature thus suggests the principal mode of analysis that he would bring to natural history and the principal avenue through which science would continue to affect him. He saw the laws of science—natural laws— as analogies to the law of intellect, or of the spirit. As Sherman Paul noted, science "supplied him the terrestrial map for his spiritual explorations," helping him to generate "the material of new symbols and therefore the vehicles of perception" that would aid him in his philosophical specula- tion.[9] What Emerson called "the great analogical value of most of our natural science" (JMN, 5:384), explained his principal reason for pursuing it. In Nature, Emerson expounded "this radical correspondence between visible things and human thoughts" (CW, 1:19), finding in it the Platonic and neo-Platonic basis of his ethical and literary assumptions: "There seems to be a necessity in spirit to manifest itself in material forms; and day and night, river and storm, beast and bird, acid and alkali, preexist in necessary Ideas in the mind of God, and are what they are by virtue of preceding affections, in the world of spirit. A Fact is the end or last issue of spirit. The visible creation is the terminus or the circumference of the invisible world" (CW, 1:22). While this doctrine relegates physical nature to a secondary status, Emerson felt that the highest lesson of science was always the precedence of theory, or the ideal, over observation, or the empirical. "Thus even in physics, the material is ever degraded before the spiritual. The astronomer, the geometer, rely on their irrefragable analysis, and disdain the results of observation" (*CW*, 1:34). The essential fact, however, was that idealism connected nature to spirit inextricably. It thus provided an imperative for observing nature minutely.

That Emerson meant the analogy of nature quite literally at this moment in his career has been recently confirmed in an important interpretation of *Nature* by Barbara Packer.[10] Emerson's reading in science, Packer explained, was linked to his theological speculation in quite precise ways. Packer finds Emerson's odd but arresting description of the fall of man crucial to an understanding of his appropriation of scientific speculation for broader issues. "The axis of vision is not coincident with the axis of things" (*CW*, 1:43), he wrote. Working from Newton's theory of the polarity of particles, descriptions of Newton's theories of light and color as explained and amplified by David Brewster, and theories of the symbolic properties of light from Guillaume Oegger, Emerson came to an account of spiritual "vision" derived very closely from his understanding of physical "vision." As Packer put it, "Emerson conceived the startling idea of treating the 'inner light' of the radical Protestant tradition as though it behaved according to Newton's laws" (78). Emerson's working principle that "every natural fact is a symbol of some spiritual fact" (*CW*, 1:18) was not hyperbole.

A later lecture, "Humanity of Science," part of Emerson's "Philosophy of History" lecture series of 1836-37, introduced no new innovations into Emerson's scientific thinking, but the lecture does help us to see more clearly the way science fit into his developing intellectual project. The lecture series intended to demonstrate by history the common nature of humanity and was an important precursor to "The American Scholar" and *Essays: First Series*. "We are compelled in the first essays of thought to separate the idea of Man from any particular men. We arrive early at the great discovery that there is one Mind common to all individual men" (*EL*, 2:11). To this end, the history of science was powerful evidence. Through its stress on the classification of various phenomena into more general categories, science demonstrated the fundamental unity of things, and the mind's constant tendency to search for that unity. Unity was exemplified in the discovery of scientific laws that showed through the predictability of events that there were properties common to different things. "This reduction to a few laws, to one law," he wrote, "is not a choice of the individual. It is the tyrannical instinct of the mind" (*EL*, 2:23). He argued that "the great moments of scientific history, have been the perception of these relations," citing Newton's analysis of gravity and Goethe's theory of the universality of the leaf as instances (*EL*, 2:23). But such classifying was not the exclusive property of science, as the history of religion showed. "Calvinism, Romanism, and the Church of Swedenborg, are three striking examples of coherent systems which each organize the best-known facts of the world's history, and the qualities of character into an order that reacts directly on the will of the individual" (*EL*, 2:25). To understand science was to understand the act of classification or, in its broadest terms, the search of the intellect for unity. To understand classification was to understand religion, philosophy, and other fundamental attempts of the mind to order the world.

The particular appeal of science, however, was the ready confirmability of its discoveries, which validated the mind's generalizing tendencies. Science was not the projection of an order onto things, as Emerson saw it, but the discovery of an existing order. Science was possible because "there is in nature a parallel unity, which corresponds to this unity in the mind, and makes it available" (*EL*, 2:25). Emerson's analysis of scientific classification thus reconfirmed his doctrine of the correspondence of nature and the mind. The unity-seeking intellect and the unity-in-diversity of nature cohered, confirming the monistic unity at the basis of Emerson's vision. All his scientific investigation can be said to be crystallized in this definition: "Science is the arrangement of the phenomena of the world after their essential relations. It is the reconstruction of nature in the mind" (*EL*, 2:27).

Emerson emphasized these essentially religious and metaphysical conclusions in his lecture, finding essential unity in the cycle of life and death that nature reveals: "The permanence and at the same time endless variety of spiritual nature finds its fit symbol in the durable world, which never preserves the same face for two moments. All things change; moon and star stand still never a moment. Heaven, earth, sea, air, and man are in a perpetual flux, yet all motion is circular, so that, whist all parts move the All is still" (*EL*, 2:32). Emerson's language strains to encompass the paradox of movement within stillness, but his emphasis is clearly on the pervasiveness of change. He thus describes nature as one substance in a continual state of metamorphosis. That substance is related on the one hand to the human intellect, to which it corresponds, and on the other to an originating spirit. "Nature proceeds from a mind analogous to our own" (*EL*, 2:33), Emerson concludes. "Humanity of Science" thus summarized positions that Emerson had worked toward in the early 1830s and set forth the agenda for later work, in which he searched the literature of science for analogies to a theory of the spirit.

By the early 1840s Emerson's initial enthusiasm for science was overshadowed by two other aspects of his intellectual life. He felt a gradual, worrying diminishment of the religious or ecstatic experience that had been a significant part of his vision. That such experiences had often been connected with the natural world helped to render scientific thought secondary. He also felt a rising pressure for political commitment, as the antislavery cause and other reform movements increasingly controlled the discourse of New England's intellectuals. Emerson did not lose his sense of the metaphysical possibilities of science, but it would be his friend Henry David Thoreau who continued most profoundly Emerson's impulse to investigate nature. [11]

Essays: First Series (1841) gives some indication of the ways in which science was being absorbed into broader philosophical questions for Emerson. In "Compensation," for example, Emerson used the analogy of the natural law of compensating physical reactions to indicate a parallel moral law. The polar quality of nature was universal, manifesting itself in both the physical and intellectual realms. The range of physical phenomema that exhibit this dualism is wide: "in the inspiration and expiration of plants and animals; in the equation of quantity and quality in the fluids of the animal body; in the systole and diastole of the heart; in the undulations of fluids, and of sound; in the centrifugal and centripetal gravity; in electricity, galvanism, and chemical affinity" (CW, 2:57). These are the physical analogues of the moral principle that "every act rewards itself" (CW, 2:60), creating an appropriate reaction, positive or negative, on the moral nature of the actor.

A later address of 1841, The Method of Nature, showed the influence of a new scientific source, John Pringle Nichol's Views of the Architecture of the Heavens (1840). [12] Astronomy had always held a special place among the sciences for Emerson, and he had acquaintance with the writings of a range of astronomers from the beginning of his career. [13] Nichol's work, which extended Emerson's acquaintance with current theories of astronomy, led him to speculate on the vastness and energy of an endlessly changing cosmos. His initial reaction to Nichol's account of the enormity of the universe is not unlike Ishmael's warning of the danger of the mast-head in Moby Dick. The "immense parade of arithmetic" of astronomy induces the same dizzying wish as "that dreadful GIRO at the top of the interior of the

Cupola of St. Peter's," to "throw [oneself] over the balustrade." But Emerson eventually comes to find in the unsettling fear of vastness also a promise of the energy of the universe: "We can point nowhere to anything final, but distinct tendency appears on all hands; the planet, the system, the firmament, the nebula, the total appearance is growing like a field of maize, or a human embryo, or the grub of a moth; is becoming somewhat else; is in the most rapid & active state of metamorphosis" (JMN, 7:427-28).

The confirmation that Nichol offered of this principle of metamorphosis was crucial to Emerson. In Nature, his "Orphic poet" had preached a concluding sermon on the "fluid" and "volatile" aspect of nature when perceived spiritually (CW, 1:44). "Circles" (1841) had been a prolonged meditation on flux or process in nature and thought, and on its connection with growth or progress. In "Experience" (1844), Emerson would call "Succession" one of the "lords of life" (CW, 3:47), a principle of rapid change or flux that was in some ways unsettling and in others salvific. But whether seen as inspiriting, as it usually was, or unsettling and chaotic, as he sometimes feared, this law of metamorphosis dominated Emerson's thinking in the 1840s. In fact, a conception of a cosmos of change and process was a widely held doctrine of Romanticism, arguably one by which Romanticism can be defined.[14] In The Method of Nature Emerson examined the possibility that natural processes, metamorphic in their essence, could be consciously seized upon as a guide for intellectual processes. He urged his audience to explore "the method of nature . . . and try how far it is transferable to the literary life" (CW, 1:123). He found that method to be metamorphosis, which he defined essentially as an active and vital tendency. He went on to argue that this law or essence of nature had, by way of analogy, moral applications, flowing from the conception of nature as an open field of energy, organized by a tendency, or direction.[15]

Thus in the trajectory of Emerson's thinking, Nature's quality of metamorphosis, reinforced by the scientific indications of the vast energies of the universe, had increasingly become the focus of its analogical link to the soul. Certainly this explains his ready, even impatient, acceptance of developmental and evolutionary scientific theses. Joseph Warren Beach has argued that Emerson moved "by insensible degrees" toward the theory of natural evolution, proceeding from earlier "scale-of-being" theories of nature to modern "evolutionary" ones. Beach's analysis of Emerson's acceptance of evolutionary theory is modified in important ways by Strauch, who emphasized how closely intertwined scientific "evolution" and neo-Platonic "emanation" were for Emerson.[16] Both Beach and Strauch find important clues to Emerson's conception of evolution in his reaction to Robert Chambers's controversial pre-Darwinian work of 1844, *Vestiges of the Natural History of Creation*—"the most elaborate statement and most plausible defense of the evolution theory that Emerson had ever encountered" (Beach, 339). Chambers's theories, like those of Darwin after him, were perceived in many quarters as a threat to the traditional idea of the creator God.[17] But as his journals reveal, Emerson was instead bothered by what he called Chambers's "polite bows to God," which seemed to mar the "courage" of the book. "Everything in this Vestiges of Creation is good except the theology, which is civil, timid, & dull" (*JMN*, 9:211). For Emerson, the concept of the evolutionary development of nature was itself a profound theological statement, giving powerful support to the conception of the creation as a field of dynamic energy. That energy reflected the dynamism of the soul.

But final and stable conclusions are rare in Emerson's work. He himself had enunciated the law of perpetually breaking the bounds of past achievement by inscribing another "circle" of expansion. The very doctrine of metamorphosis itself, if applied to the process of thought, required that one attempt to push beyond it. And, with an extraordinary frankness, Emerson was prone to confess his doubts even of his own doctrines. Thus in his 1844 essay "Nature," he extended the idea of nature's metamorphosis into the realm of doubt. "Nature" must be read not only in the context of Emerson's previous speculation on science and nature, but as part of a book marked with a worrying but intellectually invigorating skepticism. "Experience" is the best known of these skeptical departures, but "Nature" also shares this doubt, making it a fertile extension of Emerson's work on natural history.

The essay begins with an extended praise of the beauty of the natural world.[18] "It seems as if the day was not wholly profane, in which we have given heed to some natural object" (*CW*, 3:100-101). This worshipful praise is eventually explicated in terms of correspondence: "Nature is loved by what is best in us" (*CW*, III, 104). Indeed the landscape has an Edenic call: "Man is fallen; nature is erect, and serves as a differential thermometer, detecting the presence or absence of the divine sentiment in man" (*CW*, 3:104). Ultimately, Emerson moves from praise of what he calls "nature passive" or "*natura naturata*" to "Efficient Nature" or "*natura naturans*" (*CW*, 3:103-4), a principle of motion or energy that is the causative and creative force in nature.[19] "It publishes itself in creatures,

reaching from particles and spicula, through transformation on transformation to the highest symmetries, arriving at consummate results without a shock or a leap" (CW, 3:104). Obviously, this creative force is the fuel
of natural evolution, and Emerson relies on geology's record of natural
change as evidence of this vast, lengthy, but inevitable process of development. "Geology has initiated us into the secularity of nature," he notes,
teaching us much vaster measures of time, space, and change. "It is a long
way from granite to the oyster; farther yet to Plato, and the preaching of
the immortality of the soul. Yet all must come, as surely as the first atom
has two sides" (CW, 3:104-5).

But the assurance here is prelude to an eroding doubt. Emerson has
portrayed nature as progressive power but now also finds "something
mocking" in nature, "something that leads us on and on, but arrives
nowhere, keeps no faith with us" (CW, 3:110). Nature's very energy
destroys the present by perpetually promising the future. In this sense, the
metamorphic energy that Emerson has celebrated becomes demoralizing
and destructive. "Every end is prospective of some other end, which is also
temporary; a round and final success nowhere" (CW, 3:110). Even Emerson's beloved landscape has become unfulfilling. Surely the following
confession of disappointment in nature, from one of the preeminent
American nature writers, is one of the most surprising reversals in the
history of American literature: "There is in woods and waters a certain
enticement and flattery, together with a failure to yield a present satisfaction. This disappointment is felt in every landscape" (CW, 3:111). Nature's
metamorphic energy leads to a kind of estrangement, in which the individual is distanced from the reality of nature. Emerson explains that "the
poet finds himself not near enough the object," and nature becomes a
forever receding goal: "The pine-tree, the river, the bank of flowers before
him, does not seem to be nature. Nature is still elsewhere" (CW, 3:111).
The estrangement from nature, the failure to grasp reality, is consonant
with the report of numbed emptiness that begins "Experience." If Emerson
had found a sense of power in his conception of evolutionary nature, a
sense confirmed by the increasing evidence of evolutionary theories, he
also realized that the energy of metamorphosis had an alienating side as
well.

Emerson recognizes that this "uneasiness . . . results from looking too
much at one condition of nature, namely, Motion" (CW, 3:112-13). In a
philosophical move characteristic of his later thought, he plays on the
polarities of reality, urging that the opposite of nature's motion be per-

ceived as an answer to the experiential problems generated by metamorphosis. "But the drag is never taken from the wheel. Wherever the
impulse exceeds, the Rest or Identity insinuates its compensation" (CW,
3:113). The "checks and impossibilities" are advantageous to us, as is
nature's energy or motion, if they are used to balance the dizzying motion of
the perpetual quest. "Let the victory fall where it will," Emerson suggests
shrewdly, "we are on that side" (CW, 3:113). The question thus becomes
one of perspective—and the pragmatic problem of making use of what we
perceive. "Every moment instructs, and every object: for wisdom is infused
into every form" (CW, 3:113-14). So even in modifying his identification of
nature's energy as its chief analogical and educative factor, he maintains
his belief that nature's forms are infused with wisdom. The contribution of
nature to the soul's culture can thus continue even despite the alienating
qualities of its energy.

While Emerson did not lose interest in science in his later work, the shape
of his response to it had been formed and would not change substantially.
There are interesting references to Swedenborg's scientific background in
Representative Men (1850), and two later works, "Poetry and Imagination"
and *Natural History of Intellect*—both of which reached final form in the
1870s—contain substantial discussions of scientific issues. Beach cites the
early section of "Poetry and Imagination" as the place at which Emerson
expresses most clearly his understanding of evolutionary theories. [20] There
Emerson does cite the phrase *"arrested and progressive development"* as "the
poetic key to Natural Science, of which the theories of Geoffroy Saint-
Hilaire, of Oken, of Goethe, of Agassiz and Owen and Darwin in zoology
and botany, are the fruits" (W, 8:7). That phrase suggests "the way upward
from the invisible protoplasm to the highest organisms," an evolutionary
vision that is important in the perception of the unity of nature and its link
to intellect. *The Natural History of Intellect,* which was in some ways
Emerson's failed or uncompleted masterwork, was ultimately a sketch of a
plan to do for the mind and mental processes what the great classifying
scientists of the eighteenth and nineteenth century had done for botany,
geology, and the other sciences. [21]

Emerson's later attention was, however, attracted to that beautiful but
difficult child of science, technology. Leonard Neufeldt's detailed discussion of Emerson's reaction to the problems that technology posed to the
human spirit reminds us of how contemporary Emerson can seem. Although positive in general about the possibilities of technological progress,

Emerson sounded important warnings later in his career about the combined threat of commercial and industrial society. Neufeldt suggests that his second tour of England in 1847-48 was important in bringing him to check "his enthusiasm" for technological progress, eventuating in his attempt to accommodate technology to appropriate intellectual control.[22] Neufeldt's treatment suggests many possibilities for further research and analysis, especially when we realize that it bears directly on Emerson's accommodation to modern American culture generally. Surely his view of technological progress is an important aspect of the question of the extent of his adversarial relationship to nineteenth-century American culture.

Despite his sustained inquiries into science, Emerson's place is ultimately with the poets and religious thinkers, as he himself knew. "Science was false by being unpoetical," he said in "Poetry and Imagination." And, with some prophetic sense of the intellectual rift that would separate science and imaginative thought so decisively in our century, he warned that "Science does not know its debt to imagination" (W, 8:10). Emerson could speak with authority of such debts, being himself a lifelong debtor to science. The example of his intellectual project that integrated scientific knowledge with metaphysical curiosity stands as the principal value of our renewed and deepened understanding of Emerson's debt to natural history. He had the advantage of living at a moment when the worlds of science and literature were not separate ones, and he used that advantage fully. But he also witnessed the beginnings of that very rift. While his focus on nature as a metamorphic field of energy continues to be instructive, his own motivation as a thinker about science is as valuable. He turned to science because he needed its facts and its vision, and he was unafraid of any truth he might discover there.

Notes

I would like to acknowledge support from the Center for the Humanities, Oregon State University, and the American Philosophical Society in completing this essay.

The following abbreviations will be used: CS for Albert J. von Frank, et al., eds., *The Complete Sermons of Ralph Waldo Emerson* (Columbia: Univ. of Missouri Press, 1989-); *CW* for Robert E. Spiller, et al., eds., *The Collected Works of Ralph Waldo Emerson* (Cambridge: Harvard Univ. Press, 1971-); *EL* for Robert E. Spiller, Stephen E. Whicher, and Wallace E. Williams, eds., *The Early Lectures of Ralph Waldo Emerson* (Cambridge: Harvard Univ. Press, 1959-72); *JMN* for William H. Gilman, et al., eds., *The Journals and Miscellaneous Notebooks of Ralph Waldo Emerson* (Cambridge: Harvard Univ. Press, 1960-82); *W* for Edward Waldo Emerson, ed., *The Complete Works of Ralph Waldo Emerson*, Centenary

Edition (Boston: Houghton Mifflin, 1903-04); YES for Arthur C. McGiffert, Jr., ed., *Young Emerson Speaks: Unpublished Discourses on Many Subjects* (Boston: Houghton Mifflin, 1938).

1. Harry Hayden Clark, "Emerson and Science," *Philological Quarterly* 10 (July 1931): 225-60. See especially notes 10 and 11, pp. 226-27.

2. Carl F. Strauch, "Emerson's Sacred Science," *PMLA* 73 (June 1958): 237-50, quote from p. 238. The source of much of Emerson's knowledge of Goethe as a scientist was Sarah Austin's *Characteristics of Goethe* (1834). Gustaaf Van Cromphout, *Emerson's Modernity and the Example of Goethe* (Columbia: Univ. of Missouri Press, 1990), 26.

3. Clark, 228. While I concur with Clark in general on this point, I have argued that Emerson's visit to the Jardin des Plantes in Paris in 1833 ushered in a brief period in which he moved in the direction of investigative rather than speculative science. See David Robinson, "Emerson's Natural Theology and the Paris Naturalists: Toward a 'Theory of Animated Nature,'" *Journal of the History of Ideas* 41 (Jan.-Mar. 1980): 69-88; also abbreviated in *Apostle of Culture: Emerson as Preacher and Lecturer* (Philadelphia: Univ. of Pennsylvania Press, 1982), 71-94.

4. Ralph Waldo Emerson, Manuscript Sermon #146, Houghton Library, Harvard University, quoted by permission of the Ralph Waldo Emerson Memorial Association and the Houghton Library.

5. See a full discussion in Robinson, "Emerson's Natural Theology and the Paris Naturalists." For Emerson's own account of his visit, see *JMN*, IV, 198-200.

6. Elizabeth A. Dant, "Composing the World: Emerson and the Cabinet of Natural History," *Nineteenth-Century Literature* 44 (1989): 18-44; and Jonathan Bishop, *Emerson on the Soul* (Cambridge: Harvard Univ. Press, 1964), 54.

7. As Van Cromphout notes, "The Naturalist" also suggests Emerson's view of the scientists' "being obsessed with scientific method and losing sight of the real aim of science" (24).

8. There has been extensive exploration of the background of Emerson's *Nature*. See in particular Kenneth Walter Cameron, *Emerson the Essayist*, 2 vols. (Raleigh, N.C.: Thistle Press, 1945); Sherman Paul, *Emerson's Angle of Vision: Man and Nature in American Experience* (Cambridge: Harvard Univ. Press, 1952); Joel Porte, *Emerson and Thoreau: Transcendentalists in Conflict* (Middletown: Wesleyan Univ. Press, 1966); Merton M. Sealts, Jr., *Emerson's Nature—Origin, Growth, Meaning*, 2nd ed. (Carbondale: Southern Illinois Univ. Press, 1979); Warner Berthoff, "Introduction," *Nature: A Facsimile of the First Edition* (San Francisco: Chandler, 1968); and Jaroslav Pelikan, "*Nature* as Natural History and as Human History," in *Nature: A Facsimile of the First Edition* (Boston: Beacon, 1985).

9. Paul, 209 and 212. See Paul's general discussion of Emerson's symbolic use of scientific facts, 207-24.

10. *Emerson's Fall: A New Interpretation of the Major Essays* (New York: Continuum, 1982), 63-82.

11. For two excellent recent discussions of the profound impact of science on Thoreau's intellectual life, see Robert D. Richardson, Jr., *Henry David Thoreau: A Life of the Mind* (Berkeley: Univ. of California Press, 1987); and William Rossi, "Roots, Leaves, and Method: Henry Thoreau and Nineteenth-Century Science," *Journal of the American Studies Association of Texas* 19 (Oct. 1988): 1-22.

12. For a fuller discussion, see David Robinson, *"The Method of Nature* and Emerson's Period of Crisis," in Joel Myerson, ed., *Emerson Centenary Essays* (Carbondale: Southern Illinois Univ. Press, 1982), 74-92.

13. See Clark, 230-34.

14. For more detailed discussions of the doctrine of metamorphosis in Emerson, see Daniel B. Shea, "Emerson and the American Metamorphosis," in David Levin, ed., *Emerson: Prophecy, Metamorphosis, and Influence* (New York: Columbia Univ. Press, 1975), 29-56; and Leonard Neufeldt, *The House of Emerson* (Lincoln: Univ. of Nebraska Press, 1982), 47-71. On the question of process or dynamism as a defining characteristic of the Romantic world view, see Morse Peckham, "Toward a Theory of Romanticism," *PMLA* 66 (Mar. 1951): 5-23.

15. Emerson's endorsement of energy or metamorphosis in the essay is complicated by his attraction to mystical "ecstasy." See Robinson, *"The Method of Nature* and Emerson's Period of Crisis."

16. Joseph Warren Beach, *The Concept of Nature in Nineteenth Century English Poetry* (New York: MacMillan, 1936), 336-45. Strauch, 239; and Strauch, "Emerson's Sacred Science."

17. For information on Chambers, see Milton Millhauser, *Just Before Darwin: Robert Chambers and Vestiges* (Middletown: Wesleyan Univ. Press, 1959); Gavin de Beer, "Introduction" to Chambers, *Vestiges of the Natural History of Creation* (New York: Humanities Press, 1969); and Robert J. Scholnick, "'The Password Primeval': Whitman's Use of Science in 'Song of Myself,'" in Joel Myerson, ed. *Studies in the American Renaissance 1986* (Charlottesville: Univ. Press of Virginia, 1986), 392-401.

18. Kenneth Marc Harris has commented that Emerson's lengthy description of nature, in which "the author gets carried away by his own prose," is in fact a "clever strategy" that illustrates our tendency to lose ourselves in the natural world. See "Emerson's Second Nature," in Joel Porte, ed., *Emerson: Prospect and Retrospect, Harvard English Studies 10* (Cambridge: Harvard Univ. Press, 1982), 42.

19. Harris discusses Emerson's probable use of Spinoza for this distinction, 43-45.

20. Beach, 341-43.

21. See Neufeldt's discussion of this text, 66-69.

22. Neufeldt, 75-92.

7

Thoreau and Science

ROBERT D. RICHARDSON, Jr.

Thoreau's early zest for science is bright and uncomplicated. Three and a half months out of college, he writes in his new journal, "How indispensable to a correct study of Nature is a perception of her true meaning—The fact will one day flower out into a truth."[1] Thoreau's lifelong engagement with science begins early, with this positive and hopeful asserting of the connection between fact and meaning. Thoreau goes on in this entry to emphasize the difference between the "master workmen" of science and the "mere accumulators of facts." The young Thoreau begins with an immense respect for fact, an attitude that is always notched to his account, especially when he is compared to Emerson. But he also has a long-running skirmish with the idea of fact as sufficient or sole truth. Facts could mirror truths, could lead to truths, could assemble into truths, could be irreducibly true as facts. But for most of his life, fact was mainly valuable to Thoreau when it led him on to greater things, to general truths about nature, to human truths, to laws, or to ideas. Facts, especially scientific facts, were always indispensable to Thoreau, but they were always means and never ends in themselves. And his frank self-questioning about the nature and use of fact does not, finally, represent major doubts about the value of science. It indicates rather the depth of Thoreau's interest in science and its claims.[2]

At the beginning of his intellectual life, Thoreau has an attitude of confident enthusiasm and openness to science. This is not surprising, as Transcendentalism in general and Emerson in particular were keenly and approvingly interested in science. Goethe, whose ethic of self-cultivation underlies so much of Concord thought, was also active in science, challenging Newton in optics, and making a still-valuable contribution to plant morphology. Kant, who is above all the intellectual founder of modern Idealism, of which Transcendentalism is the American branch, devoted his major work to revitalizing modern philosophy by trying to gain for it the care for detail and the rigor that had made modern science so successful. Schelling's later development of Kantian principles results in a "naturphilosophie," a theory of nature's ultimate unity that still has currency in the search for a single basic underlying unit of matter or energy.[3] For the German Idealists (excepting Schleiermacher) and for their American counterparts, the Transcendentalists, science had essentially replaced theology as the key to the nature of things. The Book of Nature now took precedence over the Bible as the true revelation, the true word of God. For Emerson and Thoreau both, the new interest in natural science had genuine religious urgency.

For the young Thoreau, science is heroic. His early experimental essay on "Bravery," which he drafted in 1839, has a paragraph beginning "Science is always brave, for to know is to know good: doubt and danger quail before her eye. . . . Cowardice is unscientific—for there cannot be a science of ignorance." He is interested in the qualities of the "true man of science" and concludes that he "will have a rare Indian wisdom—and will know nature better by his finer organization. He will smell, taste, see, hear, feel, better than other men. . . . The most scientific should be the healthiest man." Later, in his first important essay review for the *Dial*, "The Natural History of Massachusetts" (1842), Thoreau will gather up and redirect these comments to the reader, adding others in his exclamatory enthusiasm. "What an admirable training is science for the more active warfare of life!" "The Natural History of Massachusetts" is, fittingly for a review of state-sponsored scientific surveys of local "resources," characterized by such exclamations, representing science not only as simple, modern, and good, but also as a heroic battleground, a field for noble striving.[4]

In 1845, while he is working on the first draft of what will become *A Week on the Concord and Merrimack Rivers*, Thoreau turns again to the subject of science. His train of thought, toward the end of the "Thursday" chapter, leads from human art to nature's "more perfect art," to nature's perfect adaptation of means to ends ("She supplies to the bee only so much wax as is necessary for its cell") to the laws by which Nature operates. This last is indeed a major theme of the book as a whole. Thoreau goes on in this passage to explore the connection between these natural or scientific laws, and the moral law that should direct our lives. Thoreau argues that while natural laws, such as gravity, are "to the indifferent and casual observer . . . mere science—to the enlightened and spiritual they are not only facts but actions—the purest morality—or modes of divine life."[5]

This is the characteristic Idealist or Transcendental position, that the facts and laws of external nature have discoverable bearing on our moral lives, taking the word "moral" in its large Arnoldian sense: that is moral that teaches us how to live. Yet it is characteristic of the young Transcendental Thoreau to lay his emphasis on the scientific or fact-respecting side, on the intelligibility of the natural world, and on the disciplined gathering and observing of facts. Echoing Emerson's comment in *Nature* that "undoubtedly we have no questions to ask which are unanswerable," Thoreau insists, "all nature invites to further acquaintance and abets the efforts of the honest inquirer—for by the visible form or shell truth is simply contained not withheld."[6]

Thoreau's respect for what William James calls "stubborn and irreducible fact" is very high indeed in 1845. He insists that facts "must be learned directly and personally." He praises the collector of facts as possessing "a perfect physical organization." By comparison, the philosopher possesses a "perfect intellectual one." But it is, predictably, the poet, or as we would say, the writer, who now represents for Thoreau the evenly but mysteriously balanced combination of these two. In other words, Thoreau's current respect for fact and fact-collecting is so high in 1845 that he takes it as half of the mental process of the writer.

During the winter and spring of 1846-47 Thoreau is revising and expanding his manuscript of *A Week*. In this draft, which is the one he published in 1849, the "Friday" or last chapter contains an expanded reworking of his earlier comments on science and fact. It is, in effect, a short essay, running to about five printed pages and constituting Thoreau's most extended and in some ways his most important comments on science. His own life is beginning, but only beginning, to turn toward scientific pursuits. In February 1847, he starts the first of what are to be many statistical studies of Concord's natural phenomena. In May 1847 he will be collecting specimens for the great scientist Louis Agassiz recently arrived from Switzerland. Thoreau's most thoughtful, certainly his most method-conscious, meditation on science stands on the threshhold of his own serious involvement in doing science, not just reading about it.

He begins the science section of "Friday" with what is, for a moralist, a startling claim: "The eye which can appreciate the naked and absolute beauty of a scientific truth is far more rare than that which is attracted by a moral one." The comment underscores the importance science now plays in Thoreau's mature thought. He loves the clean, economical beauty of physical law or principle and the elegance of mathematical proof. He says, and it reminds one of Poe, "the most distinct and beautiful statement of any truth must at last take the mathematical form." This is not just his customary hyperbole or paradox, it is the conceptual center of his lifelong interest in statistics that give us access to patterns or "laws" that are not apparent in individual cases. [7]

Thoreau continues to pursue the connection between the natural and the moral worlds. Indeed, he presses the connection now, phrasing it in his best assertive style as self-evident axioms: "All the moral laws are readily translated into natural philosophy. . . . The whole body of what is now called moral or ethical truth existed in the golden age as abstract science." He explicates this by reference to Stoic thought. "Or, if we prefer, we may say that the laws of Nature are the purest morality." He is not now troubled by the moral problem of nature's voraciousness, by the nature "red in tooth and claw," which will seem to the generations after Darwin a license for predatory violence. The point of his assertion about the link between natural (or scientific) truth and moral truth is not to play down science but to protest the separation of science from morals. [8]

Similarly, Thoreau will not separate science from the person doing the science. "The fact which interests us most," Thoreau writes, "is the life of the naturalist. The purest science is still biographical." Thoreau will remain interested in the personal, the biographical, the human approach to science. Like Goethe, he is concerned with how things strike us, not just how things are, apart from human observation. This is an interest in the subjective aspect of science, but it is not therefore whimsical or idiosyncratic. Strictly speaking, the sky is not blue. Space is black—the blue is short wavelengths of light colliding with and dissipating into the atmosphere—but it is a universal subjective experience that the sky is blue. It is a subjective truth. Geography or astronomy teach us to regard the earth and the stars as apart from us. But there is enabling power, perhaps even for the scientist, in Emerson's observation that it is our own eye that makes the horizon, or in Thoreau's comment that "man's eye is the true star-finder, the comet-seeker." [9]

But even as he tracks science back to the scientist and recalls his earlier, Baconian belief that the "poet uses the results of science and philosophy, and generalizes their widest deductions," he goes on now to formulate his clearest understanding of the importance of method. Method is, in Thoreau's eyes, a behavioral manifestation of the rule of law so evident in, say, physics or botany or astronomy. Thoreau is interested in the *process* of scientific discovery, which he says, with customary and maddening coolness, "is very simple." The way it works, he explains, is that "an unwearied and systematic application of known laws to nature, causes the unknown to reveal themselves." With remarkable clearsightedness, Thoreau the lifelong observer now notes that what matters most, even in observation, is method or system. "Almost any *mode* of observation will be successful at last, for what is most wanted is method. Only let something be determined and fixed around which observation may rally." As he will say elsewhere, we all look at the same things, but some see more than others. How to direct attention, focus observation, find and learn to trust a fixed point against which other things may be set for comparison, these are aspects of the process of discovery that now fascinate Thoreau.[10]

Thoreau maintains a steady, indeed a constantly deepening, interest in fact or data. Yet he can be dismayed at the prospect of the passive or mindless accumulation of data and is generally more interested in the process by which general laws emerge from facts. Thoreau's grasp of science and its procedures during the years 1846 and 1847 is very much like Darwin's when the latter says that "science consists in grouping facts so that general laws or conclusions may be drawn from them." It is not quite so easy, of course. Thoreau is keenly aware of how "the power to perceive a law is equally rare in all ages of the world."[11]

He goes on to make a remarkably useful distinction about just what we mean when we talk about the advance of science. "Much is said about the progress of science," he observes, adding, "I should say that the useful results of science had accumulated, but that there had been no accumulation of knowledge." The reason for this, he explains, is that knowledge "is to be acquired only by a corresponding experience." It does not count as knowledge when we do not experience it ourselves. "How can we *know*" he asks, "what we are *told* merely?" This central question, which occurs to anyone who finds himself obliged to accept on faith the results of a predecessor's work, has a special urgency for Thoreau. For science deals with what we know, and literature deals with what can be told. At present, Thoreau seems more inclined to trust experience than other people's accounts of experience. There is of course a limit to how much one can learn for oneself, but Thoreau's insistence on getting things at firsthand will serve him both in his science and in his writing.[12]

For he can also always see the value in the telling, the describing, of nature. It is a characteristic of his way of working that, whenever he becomes interested in a subject, such as botany or zoology, he will start with current scientific work, fanning out quickly to read related current books and, at the same time, reading backwards toward the beginnings of the subject, coming ultimately to the classics. Thus he will study a subject and the history of that subject simultaneously. As he does this, he thereby gains a balanced outlook that can simultaneously appreciate (in this case) the modern scientist and the ancient naturalist. "Our books of science," he says, "as they improve in accuracy, are in danger of losing the freshness and vigor and readiness to appreciate the real laws of Nature, which is a marked merit in the oft-times false theories of the ancients." He observes—and it is true of his own work in relation to *our* modern science—that "the older naturalists are better qualified to appreciate than to discriminate the facts." As it is true of Aristotle, Aelian, Pliny, and others, so it is still true of Thoreau that "their assertions are not without value when disproved. If they are not facts, they are suggestions for Nature herself to act upon." More interesting than mere facts are the laws that arise from observed facts, and more interesting than either is the peculiar quality of focused attention that can find the process by which those laws arise.[13]

In retrospect, it is notable that these years from 1839 to 1842, marking Thoreau's most straightforward, least qualified admiration for science, are the years in which Thoreau least identifies his life and work with science. As he becomes more and more involved in science itself, his view of it will become correspondingly more complex. Still, his brave view of science remains essentially the same throughout the mid 1840s, as Thoreau passes through his late twenties and as he writes both drafts of A Week.

In the spring of 1847, just before his thirtieth birthday, Thoreau becomes involved in collecting local specimens for the classifying labors of Louis Agassiz, the great Harvard professor who is the single person most responsible for the professionalization of American science during the middle of the nineteenth century.[14] Agassiz was an ebullient, energetic, entrepreneurial scientist who built and maintained a network of collectors all over the globe. There is some irony in Thoreau's working as a specimen collector for Agassiz. By Thoreau's own distinction, Agassiz would be the "master craftsman," the person seeking laws, synthesis, and ideas, while he, Thoreau, was the mere collector or accumulator. He can hardly have thought of himself at this time as seriously engaged in science. Indeed, at the end of September 1847, when asked what his profession was, he answered by listing thirteen occupations, not one of which makes any mention of science or natural history. Yet his enthusiasm for science is as high as ever. In a long paragraph of a letter to Emerson in November 1847, Thoreau talks about the new astronomical discoveries and the powerful new telescope at Harvard. "It is true enough," he tells Emerson, in a rare burst of approval of his alma mater, "Cambridge college is really beginning to wake up and redeem its character and overtake the age. I see by the catalogue that they are about establishing a scientific school in connection with the University."[15]

During the late 1840s Thoreau's general interest in science was leading him ever more deeply into doing science itself. He begins now to keep detailed data on such things as the height of the Concord River. He takes a minute interest in identifying species accurately. In December of 1850, he is elected a corresponding member of the new and energetic Boston Society of Natural History, and on most of his future trips to Boston he will make a stop at the society's rooms to consult their collections or their library. In January 1851, he reads Darwin's *Voyage of the Beagle*, taking notes that show he is beginning to share Darwin's interests in how plants and animals are dispersed over the earth, in the relation of geology to botany and zoology, and in such marvels of adaptation as the Tierra del Fuegians who sweat, naked, even when they are further from the fire than the clothed, shivering Europeans.

The more serious Thoreau's involvement in science becomes, the more intense his questionings become. This January (1851) he notes that "Science does not embody all that men know, only what is for men of science." (It should be remembered that the word "scientist" was only coined in 1840. "Man of science" still did duty for several decades. Darwin calls himself not scientist but "a person interested in natural history.") After noting that a woodman "can relate his facts to human life," Thoreau continues with an elaborate image that is remarkably evenhanded. He writes, "The knowledge of an unlearned man is living and luxuriant like a forest, but covered with mosses and lichens and for the most part inaccesible and going to waste: the knowledge of the man of science is like timber collected in yards for public works, which still supports a green sprout here and there, but even this is liable to dry rot."[16]

In 1851, Thoreau reads a good deal of botany, including, of course, the history of botany. He reads Bartram, Agassiz and Gould, Kalm (a disciple of Linnaeus), Cuvier (the teacher of Aggasiz), Loudon (apostle of the Linnean "artificial" system of botanical classification), Stoever (the biographer of Linnaeus), Pultenay (another Linnaean), and, eventually, in February 1852, Linnaeus. (Later, Thoreau will read Lindley, Alphonse de

Candolle, and other defenders of the "natural" system.) By comparison with these scientific writers whom he openly admired and learned from, Thoreau finds the "Annual of Scientific Discovery" a "poor, dry compilation," and he complains that "one sentence of perennial poetry would make me forget, would atone for, volumes of mere science." But he perseveres past the ill-natured comment to try to fix the source of the difference between interesting and dull science. "The astronomer is as blind to the significant phenomena, or the significance of phenomena, as the wood-sawyer who wears glasses to defend his eyes from sawdust. The question is not what you look at but what you see." A Darwin, a Cuvier, a Linnaeus looked at the same things everyone else did, but they saw more. [17]

This same August 1851, he notes the changes in his own thinking that had resulted from his renewed scientific interests. "I fear," he begins, "that the character of my knowledge is from year to year becoming more distinct and scientific; that in exchange for views as wide as heaven's cope, I am being narrowed down to the field of the microscope. I see details, not wholes nor the shadow of the whole. I count some parts and say 'I know.'" This is not a deprecation of scientific knowledge. It is more an acknowledgement that scientific knowledge comes only at some considerable cost in other areas. And the next day sees Thoreau's enthusiasm back at its usual pitch. Now it is the language of botany which attracts him. "How copious and precise the botanical language to describe the leaves, as well as the other parts of a plant! Botany is worth studying if only for the precision of its terms—to learn the value of words and of system." [18]

Thoreau is delighted with the language for describing leaves. The special vocabulary extends the range of one's ability to translate the natural world into language, plant by plant, leaf by leaf, and down to the smallest detail. "The situation of leaves," says Sir J.E. Smith, author of an attractive, Linnaean *Grammar of Botany,*

> is either at the root, or on the stem, or branches; alternate, scattered, opposite, crowded, whorled, or tufted. Their *insertion* is either sessile or stalked; peltate, clasping, connate, perfoliate, sheathing, equitant, or decurrent. The *margin* of leaves or leaflets is either entire, wavy, serrated, jagged, toothed, or notched, in a simple or compound manner; naked, fringed, spinous, cartilaginous, glandular; flat, revolute (rolled backward) or involute (the reverse). Their *surface* is smooth, naked, glaucous, downy, hairy, woolly, warty, glandular, or prickly; even, rugged, or blistery; veiny, ribbed, or veinless; coloured, variegated, opaque or polished. Some leaves are fleshy,

cylindrical, semi-cylindrical, awlshaped, tumid, channelled, keeled, two-
edged, hatchet-shaped, solid or hollow. Others are membranous, leathery,
rigid or almost woody. With respect to *division*, simple leaves are either
cloven, lobed, sinuated, deeply divided, laciniated, or cut; palmate, pin-
natifid, pectinate, unequal (as in Begonia) lyrate, runcinate, fiddle-shaped,
hastate, arrow-shaped.[19]

As Emerson notes in "The Poet," there is a liberating exhilaration
when "the world is thus put under the mind for verb and noun." The power
of precision to specify is not lost on Thoreau. He notes that Linnaeus
thought that precise and adequate terms "have preserved anatomy, mathematics, and chemistry from idiots; but the want of them has ruined
medicine." Though he will later come to articulate a similar view of the
function of scientific language, Thoreau now sees it as a great enriching of
verbal expressiveness. Speaking about the writing of earlier naturalists, he
writes, "Evelyn and others wrote when the language was in a tender,
nascent state and could be moulded to express the shades of meaning;
when sesquipedalian words, long since cut and apparently dried and drawn
to mill—not yet to the dictionary lumber-yard, put forth a fringe of green
sprouts here and there along in the angles of their rugged bank, their very
bulk insuring some sap remaining; some florid suckers they sustain at least;
which words, split into shingles and laths, will supply poets for ages to
come."[20]

Eighteen fifty-two is a peak year for Thoreau. He is reading deeply in
modern science and old naturalists (during an era in which this modern
clarity of distinction is only dimly emerging). He has discovered William
Gilpin and the power of the picturesque to educate the outdoor eye. He is
working on the fifth revision of *Walden*, a major creative reshaping, and his
journal is at its richest and fullest. His mood is up. He exults in the world.
"This is my year of observation," he writes.

In his botanical reading, he is caught up in the controversy between
the natural and artificial systems of botanical classification. The artificial
system was championed by Linnaeus; the natural by, among others, John
Lindley. Over time, as he compares the systems, Thoreau comes to prefer
the natural, which is particularly worth noting because Darwin later says,
in *The Origin of Species*, in a reference to his view that speciation is the
result of "descent with modification": "I believe this element of descent is
the hidden bond of connexion which naturalists have sought under the
term of the Natural System."[21]

Thoreau in the early 1850s is naturally drawn to science, but he voices hesitancies. "The actual bee hunter and pigeon catcher is familiar with facts in the natural history of bees and pigeons which Huber and even Audubon are totally ignorant of. I love best the unscientific man's knowledge; there is so much more humanity in it." In a journal entry for June 30, 1852, he goes much further: "Nature must be viewed humanly to be viewed at all; that is, her scenes must be associated with humane affections, such as are associated with one's native place, for instance. She is most significant to a lover. A lover of Nature is pre-eminently a lover of man. If I have no friend, what is Nature to me? She ceases to be morally significant." There would seem to be an unbridgeable gap between this way of viewing nature and the scientific approach, as we understand the latter now. Thoreau articulates both approaches, the moral and the scientific, and it would be a mistake to regard this last cited comment, and others like it, as reflecting a growing hostility to science. The problem is that Thoreau has, near the center of his thought, a strongly held idealist position. Idealism held, in Schelling's fine summary, that nature is externalized spirit (read "mind") and spirit is internalized nature. A.N. Whitehead observes in *Science and the Modern World* that idealism "has conspicuously failed to connect, in any organic fashion, the fact of nature with their idealist philosophies." This conflict is particularly severe for Thoreau during 1852 and 1853. Just after his birthday in July of 1852 he writes to his sister Sophia a listless dispirited letter in which he complains, "I am not on the trail of any elephants or mastodons, but have succeeded in trapping only a few ridiculous mice, which can not feed my imagination. I have become sadly scientific."[22]

We should not put too much weight on that word "sadly," because it is contradicted by the fact, noted by every reader of Thoreau's journal, that Thoreau becomes increasingly *interested* in science as time goes on, taking pleasure in exactness and precision. His attitude toward science is now quite complex, indeed two-sided, because he is, from this time in his life onward, both a person interested in science and scientific methods— interested in knowing nature—and a writer or artist whose main aim is to express, describe, or tell nature. The two aims are, strictly speaking, incompatible. That is, they cannot be exercised on the same material at the same time. The incompatibility of these views is an affront to the orderly mind, and Thoreau acknowledges the dilemma fully in a journal entry on March 5, 1853, in which he discusses a questionnaire he was asked to fill out for the Association for the Advancement of Science. The key question had to do with "What branch of science I was specially interested in." His reflections on this deserve quotation in full:

> Now, though I could state to a select few that department of human inquiry which engages me, and should be rejoiced at an opportunity to do so, I felt that it would be to make myself the laughing-stock of the scientific community to describe or attempt to describe to them that branch of science which specially interests me, inasmuch as they do not believe in a science which deals with the higher law. So I was obliged to speak to their condition and describe to them that poor part of me which alone they can understand. The fact is I am a mystic, a transcendentalist, and a natural philosopher to boot. Now I think of it, I should have told them at once that I was a transcendentalist. . . . How absurd that though I probably stand as near to nature as any of them, and am by constitution as good an observer as most, yet a true account of my relation to nature should excite their ridicule only.[23]

If we discount the slightly forced tone of disdain, Thoreau can be seen wanting it both ways. His transcendental aims are different (he suggests they are better) than those of science, but Thoreau is the first to poke fun at the opposite mentality, the overly transcendental approach, at the poor philosopher "grown insane with too large views," or the "sublimo-slipshod" style of his walking friend Channing, who was a careless observer and almost completely impervious to fact.

It had been Thoreau's early hope that the results of science would give the writer new material, that the facts so basic to science would also be illuminating to the poet. In "The Natural History of Massachusetts," and in his journal and letters down through the late 1840s, Thoreau seems to assume that Transcendentalism and science will both serve the writer. But, increasingly in his notes for the early 1850s, Thoreau writes as though scientific methods and aims were antithetical to and subversive of literary aims. Where he once rejoiced at the gain of descriptive power from the use of scientific language, he now complains that "one studies books of science merely to learn the language of naturalists,—to be able to communicate with them." Here Thoreau seems to agree with Linnaeus's view that technical scientific language serves to keep the uninitiated out. Further, when Thoreau now writes about expression, he does not talk about expressing what the scientist has found. He no longer assumes that the writer draws equally on fact-gathering and generalizing. He now thinks that the kind of writing he is interested in and the kind of work he understands as science are fundamentally opposed.[24]

In an often-quoted passage, Thoreau writes on May 10, 1853, "He is the richest who has most use for nature as raw material of tropes and symbols with which to describe his life. If these gates of golden willows affect me, they correspond to the beauty and promise of some experience on which I am entering. If I am overflowing with life, am rich in experience for which I lack expression, then nature will be my language full of poetry—all nature will be a fable, and every natural phenomenon be a myth." By ominous contrast, nature now yields the scientist something quite different. Thoreau goes on to insist that "the man of science, who is not seeking for expression but for a fact to be expressed merely, studies nature as a dead language." To some extent, Thoreau is reacting to the immense bustle of fact and specimen-gathering touched off by Agassiz, and perhaps to Agassiz's own swelling self-importance and relentless promotion of science, self, and fact. To some extent Thoreau's unhappiness with science is a displaced impatience with himself. But beyond all that can be said in extenuation, the above passage and others like it point to Thoreau's growing and unsettling awareness that the science to which he was so drawn was antithetical to the writer-transcendentalist-naturalist for whom nature is the raw material of expression. "I pray," he concludes, "for such inward experience as will make nature significant."[25]

From this time until his death ten years later, Thoreau never gives up looking for a way to resolve this dilemma, to combine the respect for fact of the scientist with the idealist conviction that there are important, indeed determining connections between inner nature and outer, between the human spirit and the phenomena of the world. But now, during 1852 and 1853, in the white heat of a major reshaping of *Walden*, Thoreau records some of his sharpest, if not his best-reasoned, criticisms of science. Five years later, he is *still* voicing similar reservations. "I think that the man of science makes this mistake," Thoreau writes, "and the mass of mankind along with him: that you should coolly give your chief attention to the phenomenon which excites you as something independent of you, and not as it is related to you. The important fact is its effect on me." This is hardly a fair criticism, faulting science for what science doesn't try to do, but it does describe the writer's approach to the same material. Thoreau goes on, "He [the scientist] thinks that I have no business to see anything else but just what he defines the rainbow to be, but I care not whether my vision of truth is a waking thought or dream remembered, whether it is seen in the light or in the dark. It is the subject of the vision, the truth alone, that concerns me." And trying now to fix the focal point with scientific precision, Thoreau concludes, "with regard to such objects, I find that it is not they themselves (with which men of science deal) that concern me: the point of interest is somewhere *between* me and them (i.e. the objects)."[26]

As his journals are filled increasingly with precise botanical nomenclature, Thoreau also comes increasingly to see what such language does *not* do. "Our scientific names convey a very partial information only: they suggest certain thoughts only," he writes in 1858. "It does not occur to me that there are other names for most of these objects, given by a people who stood between me and them, who had better senses than our race. How little I know of that *arbor-vitae* when I have learned only what science can tell me! It is but a word. It is not a *tree* of *life*. But there are twenty words for the tree and its different parts which the Indian gave, which are not in our botanies, which imply a more practical and vital science. He used it every day. He was well acquainted with its wood, and its bark, and its leaves. No science does more than arrange what knowledge we have of any class of objects."[27]

Thoreau is no longer looking for the bravery of science, or scientist, no longer open to the scientist's new methods, new languages, and new discoveries. Instead he asserts that scientific language actually gets in the way of our understanding how the world relates to us. Thoreau has here pushed his characteristic fondness for paradox too far. Whatever one may say of the American Indian, he did not have a "more practical and vital science" than the European. Not even Thoreau's intimidating way with exaggeration and extravagance can carry that off. Even his closing generalization about science is a serious underestimate, though perhaps partly it is a reaction against an age then so obsessed with "mere" fact-gathering that the *Scientific American* could say, in 1852, "Science is but a collection of well-arranged facts."[28]

Even these occasional, quotable denigrations of science, untenable or excessive as they appear to us, are the cavils of a man whose own enterprise was becoming ever more scientific, as he himself was well aware. In 1856, two years after the publication of *Walden,* he spots a plant on May 21, noting, "I am still in doubt whether it is a stellaria or cerastium. This is quite smooth, four to five inches high, spreading and forking, with a single flower each fork, on a long peduncle; square stemmed, oblong-lanceolate leaves, slightly ciliate and connate," and on the same day he writes a letter to decline a lecture, saying "what I have is either too scattered or loosely arranged, or too light, or else is too scientific and matter of fact"; and he added, "I run a good deal into that of late." [29]

In the late 1850s, Thoreau's scientific interests are still growing actively. He fills an entire notebook with natural history extracts and notes; in 1859 he is appointed a member of the Harvard Visiting Committee in Natural History, charged with the annual evaluation of the college curriculum. Even if the committee is largely a pro forma affair (though there is lively evidence that some of the visiting committees were active and influential groups who forced changes), Thoreau's presence on the committee suggests that he is by now considered a member of the science establishment. The committee includes six doctors, and such notables as Samuel Cabot (who befriended Edward Desor, who broke with Agassiz after 1848), Theodore Lyman (a former student of Agassiz's who raised money for him), James Eliot Cabot (who worked with Agassiz, corresponded with Thoreau, and later wrote a life of Emerson), and Augustus Gould, who coauthored with Agassiz an important text called *Principles of Zoology.*

The year 1859 is an active one for science in Boston and Cambridge, and Thoreau is taking an active part in it. It is the year in which Agassiz's new museum of Comparative Zoology opens, with considerable fanfare and a grant from the Massachusetts legislature. The natural history department of the college, over which Thoreau is supposed to watch, is, on the other hand, under the direction of Asa Gray, the major American ally of Darwin's in the soon-to-come struggle with Agassiz over evolution. There is no direct proof that Thoreau is deeply involved in the work of the visiting committee, but we should remember that Thoreau undertakes nothing pro forma and that he allows himself to be reappointed the following year. It may also not be entirely a coincidence that Gray is teaching a course in vegetable physiology to the sophomores and a course in geographical and systematic botany to the juniors while Thoreau's reading for these years includes a great deal in these exact areas. [30]

On January 1, 1860, Charles Brace, a New York social worker and general intellectual, arrives in Concord with a copy of Darwin's *Origin of Species,* which he had picked up from Asa Gray. The book has only been out for a month, and Brace, Sanborn, Alcott, and Thoreau have dinner and discuss the book, which Thoreau soon gets hold of, reads, and makes notes from. (By contrast, John Torrey, a professional botanist and a colleague of

Gray's, waits more than three years to get around to reading Darwin.) As has been noted by several writers, Thoreau quickly picks up several of Darwin's main ideas, and these play an important part in Thoreau's late unpublished work. Thoreau even comes by himself, to accept Darwin's "developmental" hypothesis over Agassiz's theory of "special creation." It is difficult to escape the conclusion that by 1860, Thoreau has become the very "man of science" he had at first so admired, then later had so many doubts about. Though he might continue to say that such essays as "Autumnal Tints" are "not scientific," he no longer says it with hostility. Quite the contrary, when he delivers the talk on "The Succession of Forest Trees," in 1860, he describes it frankly at the outset as "a purely scientific subject."[31]

It would be rash to assert that Thoreau ever fully reconciled his interests in science and Transcendentalism. For one thing, the manuscript materials needed for a full assessment of Thoreau's late papers have never been published and have only recently been transcribed. Thoreau's Natural History Extract Notebook, and his two long manuscripts on "Wild Fruits" and "The Dispersion of Seeds" are not only not published, they are in such a rough state as manuscripts that they have so far defeated all efforts to understand them. Only in the last decade have a few essays and chapters appeared concerning the late work, but even these must be considered as tentative and exploratory. There is, then, a mass of unarranged, undigested manuscript, incorporating much of Thoreau's best energies after *Walden* and bearing directly on his involvement in science, that has never been taken adequately into account.[32]

Yet a few points about the late papers seem clear enough to emphasize. The "Dispersion of Seeds" and the "Wild Fruits" and the hundreds of meticulous charts Thoreau assembled to plot annual occurences of many hundreds of separate natural phenomena over ten years—these projects are the work of an energetic, disciplined, scientific mind. In a letter written on March 21, 1862, when Thoreau knows he is dying, he writes, "I have not been engaged in any particular work on Botany or the like, though, if I were to live, I would have much to report on Natural History generally." For all his interest in and sympathy with Darwin's work, Thoreau's own late work shows no real interest in the problem of speciation, which is the problem at the heart of *The Origin of Species*. Thoreau is much more interested in how plants are dispersed, how one kind of plant succeeds another, and in applying this knowledge to forest management. Thoreau's "The Succession of Forest Trees" is rightly considered an early founding text of modern technical ecology.[33]

At the end of the first chapter of *Walden*, Thoreau quotes the Persian poet Saadi saying, "they call none azad, or free, excepting the cypress, which bears no fruit." As the central issue of *Walden* is personal liberation, so the central issue in the late work is interconnectedness. The manuscript of "The Dispersion of Seeds" begins by citing the cypress again. But this time it is the Roman writer Pliny whom Thoreau quotes approvingly, saying that such trees as the cypress that bear no fruit are considered unlucky or unhappy.

As Thoreau moves from the economy of individual freedom to the detailed study of New England field and forest, his methods become more and more those of the scientist. And perhaps the late projects try, once again, to bridge the chasm between scientist and Transcendentalist, for Thoreau's *methods* pay attention to observation and detail, while his *aim* is nothing less than comprehensive: to describe the natural world, in a typical cross section called Concord. It is a world in which everything is interrelated, a world of change and process, a world that is above all and in all respects, alive. "The very earth is a granary," he says in the unpublished "Dispersion of Seeds," and by some people, including Thoreau himself, "its surface is regarded as the cuticle of one great living creature."

Notes

1. Henry D. Thoreau, *Journal*, vol. 1, ed. John C. Broderick et al. (Princeton: Princeton Univ. Press, 1981), 19. Hereafter cited as *PJ*.

2. Significant treatments of Thoreau and Science include Raymond Adams, "Thoreau's Science," *Scientific Monthly* 60 (1945): 379-82; Nina Baym's excellent "Thoreau's View of Science," *Journal of the History of Ideas* 26 (1964): 221-34; Loren Eiseley's "The Golden Alphabet," which is chapter 6 of *The Unexpected Universe* (New York: Harcourt Brace, 1969); Kichung Kim, "Thoreau's Involvement with Nature, Thoreau and the Naturalist Tradition," (Ph.D. diss., University of California, Berkeley, 1969); James McIntosh, *Thoreau as Romantic Naturalist* (Ithaca: Cornell Univ. Press, 1974), which has an excellent discussion of Thoreau's science as compared with that of Goethe. Basic to any study of the subject is Donald Worster, "The Subversive Science: Thoreau's Romantic Ecology," which is part 2 of his *Nature's Economy: A History of Ecological Ideas* (1977; rpt., Cambridge: Cambridge Univ. Press, 1985). John Hildebidle's *Thoreau: A Naturalist's Liberty* (Cambridge, Mass.: Harvard Univ. Press, 1983) makes a substantial contribution to our understanding of Thoreau's effort to reconcile science with writing.

3. On Schelling, see *Encounter* (Sept. 1981): 74-75.

4. *PJ*, vol. 1, 91-92, 187; Henry D. Thoreau, *The Natural History Essays*, ed. R. Sattelmeyer (Salt Lake City: Peregrine Smith, 1980), 4.

5. Linck C. Johnson, *Thoreau's Complex Weave: The Writing of the Week on the Concord and Merrimack Rivers, with the Text of the First Draft* (Charlottesville: Univ. Press of Virginia, 1986), 374-75.

6. Ibid., 375.

7. Henry D. Thoreau, *A Week on the Concord and Merrimack Rivers*, ed. Carl F. Hovde, William L. Howarth, and Elizabeth H. Witherell (Princeton: Princeton Univ. Press, 1980), 361-62.

8. Ibid., 362.

9. Ibid., 362; Bradford Torrey and Frances H. Allen, eds. *The Journal of Henry D. Thoreau* (Boston: Houghton Mifflin, 1906), vol. 4, 471. Hereafter cited as *J*.

10. Thoreau, *Week*, 363.

11. Ibid., 364.

12. Ibid., 365.

13. Ibid., 364.

14. For Agassiz, see Edward Lurie, *Louis Agassiz: A Life in Science* (Chicago: Univ. of Chicago Press, 1960). For the development of American science during the mid-nineteenth century, see Robert V. Bruce, *The Launching of American Science 1846–1876* (New York: Knopf, 1987).

15. Walter Harding and Carl Bode, eds., *The Correspondence of Henry D. Thoreau* (New York: New York Univ. Press, 1958), 190.

16. *J*, vol. 2, 138; on the new coinage "scientist," see Bruce, *Launching*, 80.

17. *J*, vol 2, 373.

18. Ibid., 406, 409.

19. Sir James E. Smith, *A Grammar of Botany*, (New York: 1822), 25-26.

20. *J*, vol. 3, 326; vol. 5, 43.

21. Ibid., vol. 4, 174; Charles Darwin, *The Origin of Species* (1859; rpt., New York: Penguin, 1968), 414.

22. *J*, vol. 3, 299; vol. 4, 163; A.N. Whitehead, *Science and the Modern World* (New York: MacMillan, 1925), 64. Whitehead's usual magisterial command does not seem here to do justice to the work of Schelling in particular. *Correspondence*, 283.

23. *J*, vol. 5, 4-5.

24. Ibid., 42.

25. Ibid., 135.

26. Ibid., vol. 10, 164-65.

27. Ibid., 294.

28. Bruce, *Launching*, 68.

29. *J*, vol. 8, 351; *Correspondence*, 423.

30. For Thoreau's appointment to the Harvard Visiting Committee in Natural History, see the Harvard Archives, "Reports of the Overseers, vol. 1, 1859–64, Academical Series I, call no. UA II 10.6.1." On Gray's instruction, see the "Thirty-Fourth Annual Report of the President of Harvard College to the Overseers for 1858–59" (Cambridge: Welch Bigelow and Co., 1960), 29-30.

31. On Torrey's delay in reading Darwin, see Bruce, *Launching*, 67. On Thoreau's

acceptance of Darwin's developmental hypothesis, see my *Henry Thoreau: A Life of the Mind* (Berkeley: University of California Press, 1986), esp. sections 96, 98, and 99. Thoreau, *Natural History Essays,* 73.

32. See especially William Howarth, *The Book of Concord* (New York: Viking, 1982), and John Hildebidle, *Thoreau, A Naturalist's Liberty* (Cambridge: Harvard Univ. Press, 1983).

33. *Correspondence,* 641.

8

(Pseudo-) Scientific Humor

JUDITH YAROSS LEE

Scientific humor in America is older than the Republic. When Washington Irving lampooned Thomas Jefferson's scientific activities in Book IV of *A History of New York . . . By Diedrich Knickerbocker* (1809),[1] he followed the example of Connecticut Wits David Humphreys, Joel Barlow, John Trumbull, and Lemuel Hopkins, who had already ridiculed Jefferson in *The Anarchiad* (1786-87). When Samuel Clemens published his spoof of fossil finds "Petrified Man" (1862) a few months before becoming Mark Twain,[2] he joined the journalistic tradition of Richard Adams Locke, whose infamous moon hoax in the New York *Sun* of August 25-28, 1835, presented science fiction as fact. Near the end of his career, when Twain wrote "Three Thousand Years among the Microbes" (composed 1905), he had still not exhausted science as a subject for humor.[3] Nor have his successors. When he burlesqued the scientific report in "Oya Life These Days" (1975),[4] Garrison Keillor probably did not see his work of mock-anthropology as part of a distinguished tradition, but in fact scientific issues and topics have attracted all our major comic writers since colonial days.

Their humor offers an index to the spread of scientific ideas and a window on popular thinking about them. Shortly after Darwin's *Origin of Species* was published in 1859, for example, an old joke drew new life from an emerging scientific theory: "FACT IN NATURAL HISTORY. Passing up Carson street the other evening, we saw a donkey pick up a newspaper and deliberately swallow same, editorial, correspondence, items and all, without bolting a single statement. The circumstances clearly demonstrated to our mind the identity of the two and four legged specimens of the species donkey."[5] Among the several reasons for singling out this bit of mock-biology, including its comic respect for science (rather than ridicule), not the least is its source, the Virginia City *Territorial Enterprise*, Mark Twain's literary birthplace. When the item appeared, the emergence of Mark Twain was still three years away, and the paper yet awaited the arrival of editor William Wright, who not only tutored Sam Clemens but also wrote humor himself and was for thirty years Nevada's premier editor and journalist.[6] But the joke hints at why the fledgling *Enterprise* eventually became the largest paper in the West of the gold and silver rushes: miners depended on scientific knowledge, and even the humor of the paper treated that knowledge with respect.

Such affection has been in short supply in American humor because writers have lacked the expertise for the task. Genres of scientific humor reflect the writer's own learning and his or her assessment of the audience's knowledge. Writers with technical expertise tend to parody scientific discourse, play with scientific ideas, or experiment with science fiction. Their humor may debunk individual scientists or projects, but learning itself retains its positive value. By contrast, humorists without technical backgrounds—that is, amateurs—tend to ridicule science and the scientist as one.

Many more writers belong to the second group than to the first. Indeed, until Thomas Pynchon and Don DeLillo began writing comic fiction in the 1960s and 1970s,[7] only two major American humorists based their scientific humor on professional-level knowledge: George Horatio Derby (1823-1861), a U.S. Army engineer trained at West Point, and William Wright (1829-1898), editor of the Virginia City *Territorial Enterprise* and the West's most able writer on mining. Derby and Wright both belong to the tradition known as Literary Comedy, which embraced a large number of mid-nineteenth-century pseudonymous humorists. Along with the fame of the other so-called Phunny Phellows, the reputations of "John Phoenix" (Derby) and "Dan De Quille" (Wright) were rapidly surpassed by the success of their student "Mark Twain"; yet for a time Phoenix and De Quille were also stars. Twain himself called Phoenix the father of American humor[8] and wrote a laudatory preface to De Quille's *History of the Big Bonanza* (1876), composed in Twain's Hartford home and issued by his publisher.[9] Sales of *Phoenixiana* (1855), Derby's first collection of sketches, exhausted eleven printings in its first year and remained in print throughout the nineteenth century; a new edition in 1903 was important enough to include illustrations by E.W. Kemble and an introduction by John Kendrick Bangs.[10] For his part, De Quille reached newspaper readers from San Francisco to New York for more than thirty years (1859-1895), but because he never collected his humorous sketches into a book he is almost unknown today;[11] what reputation he has rests on *The Big Bonanza*, the

definitive though not particularly comic history of Nevada's Comstock
Lode. Many of Phoenix's and De Quille's works deserve obscurity as
ephemera of the past. But for their scientific sketches, Phoenix and De
Quille merit resurrection as progenitors of two affectionate traditions of
scientific humor—learned wit and the hoax—and they stand together as
nineteenth-century exceptions to the dominant anti-intellectual tradition, the vernacular humor of the amateur.

This familiar scientific humor exploits the conventional democratic
values of the American vernacular tradition, which lumps science with
other learned targets of comic ridicule (such as theology and grammar) and
takes particular pleasure in knocking down authorities from their positions
of respect. The usual charge is irrelevance, as in the anonymous report on
"*Meleagris Gallopavo*—The American Turkey" (1872): "Audubon and
other scientific bushwackers having discribed [sic] the habits, manners and
personal appearance of this distinguished fowl, as it exists in native
thickets, I shall say little or nothing of the Wild Turkey of the Plateau and
the cover; but confine my remarks mainly to the Tame Turkey of the
Platter and the Dish. In this connection, I will take leave to say, that the
untraveled barnyard Ornithologist enjoys better opportunities for studying
and digesting the subject than usually falls to the lot of his peripatetic
confreres."[12] Fifty years later even so momentous a scientific contribution
as Einstein's theory of relativity evoked from an amateur much the same
comic condescension. The hero of *archy and mehitabel* (1927), a poet
reincarnated as a cockroach who communicated with Don Marquis by
hopping on typewriter keys, observed that the physicist's discovery
changed nothing on earth:

> old doc einstein has
> abolished time but they
> haven t got the news at
> sing sing yet[13]

Nor are these isolated examples. The topicality of scientific subjects
continues to attract the mainstream of American humorists, always ready
to deflate the nearest controversy.[14] Among contemporary humorists, Jim
Davis's comic strip "Garfield" gives the pugilistic cat the last word on
creationism ("I stay out of drafts"),[15] while James Stevenson's "Fossil
News" (1987) burlesques the quandary over hominid evolution as embodied in the conflict between Richard E. Leakey's *Homo erectus* skull and

Donald C. Johanson's "Lucy" find, *Australopithecus afarensis*.[16] Topical jokes like these generally subordinate science to other rhetorical concerns—Garfield's self-possession, for instance, or the indignity of scholars beating each other, smashing their specimens, and then sustaining the dispute in "a private race to see which one might obtain the larger grant for research into orthodonic reconstruction of australopithecine jaw and molar fragments."[17] Similar ridicule dots the history of American comic writing, portraying scientists and scientific issues as a lot of sound and fury over nothing.

Mark Twain's "Some Learned Fables for Good Old Boys and Girls" (1875) provides an ideal example of the vernacular assumptions behind this anti-intellectual tradition of scientific humor. The narrative conventions of vernacular humor developed to celebrate American democratic values.[18] Just as the volunteer militiamen of the American colonies outfought the professional soldiers of their British fatherland, so in American humor vulgar young men have consistently outwitted their elders, public authorities, and social superiors. Time and again in American comic narratives, British and American traits come into symbolic conflict, and democratic virtues trounce aristocratic pride: common sense proves wiser than book learning, for in this context the vernacular speech of common men and women signals their innate sincerity, virtue, and heroism. These durable comic conventions shape the scientific humor of Twain's "Learned Fables" and its description of "How the Animals of the Wood Sent Out a Scientific Expedition." The tale consistently elevates the lowly Tumble-Bug from the dung heap that he normally inhabits and makes him the hero of the tale. Hired to pitch camp and dig specimens, the Tumble-Bug proves that a little common sense is worth a great deal more than the erudition of the all the expedition's professors combined. So of course Twain grants him the privilege of evaluating every episode in the tale and announcing the moral at the end: "science only [needs] a spoonful of supposition to build a mountain of demonstrated fact out of."[19]

Usually seen as an example of Twain's literary debt to Phoenix,[20] the story actually satirizes contemporary scientific activities,[21] especially the Yale Scientific Expeditions of 1870-1874 led by Othniel Charles Marsh (1831-1899). The burlesque reduces "the very greatest among the learned" (MT 127) to Professor Woodlouse, Professor Snail, and Professor Mud Turtle, in addition to the leader, Professor Bull Frog, a caricature of the pug-faced and notoriously tenacious Marsh. The professors' knowledge of "the Mastodon, the Dodo, and other dead languages" (*MT* 130) does not help them decipher mysterious inscriptions like "Boats for Hire Cheap," much less prevent them from interpreting railroad tracks as "parallels of latitude" (and revising all astronomical tables accordingly), nor from mistaking the headlight of the midnight express for the transit of Venus (a major event of 1874). The Duke's insistence *"for we have SEEN it!"* (*MT* 131) sums up the story's attack on empiricism, not so much because the remark stops all dissent within the expedition about whether Venus crosses the earth or the sun as because this tale equates professors with dukes and, with typical democratic prejudice, attacks the aristocracy of intellect.

Throughout the tale, Twain takes up vernacular values first and science second—a tendency typical of scientific humor by the scientifically inexpert. His comic targets, including the allusions to contemporary scientific activities, suggest that he cared more about making jokes than about evaluating scientific ideas. For instance, instead of implying any particular opposition to evolutionary theory or Darwin's four-year-old *The Descent of Man* (1871),[22] Twain simply has fun with his reversal of "the mysterious law of Development of Species" (*MT* 138), especially the animals' discovery of "the long extinct species of reptile called MAN," formerly considered "a myth and a superstition" (*MT* 141).

So well sustained is this reversal that it has obscured the tale's most pointed satire. Involving the group's discoveries in paleontology, the satire aims straight at O.C. Marsh, who in 1871 discovered the pteranodon, America's first specimen of the flying reptile pterodactyl. The humorist, who moved to Hartford that same year, was well aware of the Yale paleontologist, who first won notoriety in 1869 for his exposure of the fossil fraud known as the Cardiff Giant. Years later, in the first chapter of "A Horse's Tale" (1906), Twain poked fun at Marsh quite explicitly, as Buffalo Bill's horse recalls,

> When Professor Marsh was out here hunting bones for the chapel of Yale University he found skeletons of horses no bigger than a fox, bedded in the rocks, and he said they were ancestors of the father. My mother heard him say it; and he said those skeletons were two million years old . . . Professor Marsh said those skeletons were fossils. So that makes me part blue grass and part fossil; if there is any older or better stock, you will have to look for it among the Four Hundred, I reckon. I am satisfied with it. And am a happy horse, too, though born out of wedlock.[23]

This little joke demonstrates that Twain knew at least the bare outlines of Marsh's great work on fossil horses in the 1870s; the paleontologist's reports appeared in 1874 when the humorist was at work on his "Learned Fables."[24] Twain satirizes Marsh more indirectly in "Learned Fables" than in "A Horse's Tale," however. Professor Bull Frog sends Engineer Spider up a telegraph "tree" on reconnaissance, and the spider identifies the telegraph wires as "a web hung there by some colossal member of his own species": "for he could see its prey dangling here and there from the strands, in the shape of mighty shreds and rags that had a woven look about their texture and were no doubt the discarded skins of prodigious insects which had been caught and eaten" (MT 136). As Marsh had reconstructed the pteranodon's twenty-foot wingspan on the basis of a single six-inch fossil bone, so the naturalist of the animal expedition "built a beautiful model of the colossal spider, having no need to see it in order to do this, because he had picked up a fragment of its vertebrae by the tree, and so knew exactly what the creature looked like and what its habits and its preferences were, by this simple evidence alone. He built it with a tail, teeth [like Marsh's toothed birds[25]], fourteen legs and a snout, and said it ate grass, cattle, pebbles and dirt with equal enthusiasm. . . . The conference ended with the naming [of] the monster after the naturalist, since he, after God, had created it" (MT 136). Twain could hardly be more contemptuous of the naturalist, but the grudging praise for his godlike creativity is also telling. The inconsistency between this irreverent reference to God and the Tumble-Bug's devout resolution "not [to] go prying into the august secrets of the Deity" (MT 148) suggests that in the "Learned Fables" Twain cared more about satirizing Marsh than about examining scientific principles.

Indeed, Twain's scientific humor is most notable for the convenience and conventionality of its targets: true to vernacular values, he would ridicule whatever learned authority he could and apparently trusted his audience to take pleasure in the iconoclasm along with him. Ten years before "Learned Fables," Twain's "A Full and Reliable Account of the Extraordinary Meteoric Shower of Last Saturday Night" (1864) lampoons his own scientific pretensions along with those of the noted Yale scientist Benjamin Silliman, Jr., (1816-1885) and his influential American Journal of Science. Adopting the comic pose of the Simpleton, Twain offers ("for the good of Science") the observations he made "with the very best apparatus I could find wherewith to facilitate my labors": "I got a telescopic glass tumbler, and two costly decanters, (containing eau de vie and Veuve Clicquot to wash out the instrument with whenever it should become clouded,) . . . I then poured about a gill of liquid from each decanter into the telescopic tumbler and slowly elevated it to an angle of about ninety degrees. I did not see anything. The second trial was also a failure, but I had faith in that wash."[26] Twain's weakness for the easy attack on science also shows in *Roughing It* (1872), although it proclaims quite different attitudes toward scientific knowledge. The semiautobiographical story of his life in the West has a structure often described as "the transformation of a tenderfoot,"[27] a variation of the *Bildungsroman* in which the Mark Twain character throws off useless kinds of booklearning (aptly symbolized by his unabridged dictionary, which doesn't even make a good pillow and eventually becomes a dangerous projectile on the stagecoach); then he can immerse himself in the science of mining, among other necessary facts of western life. Despite this implicit approval of science, the humorist devotes the entire preface to debunking knowledge anyway. He adopts a comic pose of weary resignation as he apologizes for putting so much information into the book, which, he assures his audience, aims "rather to help the resting reader while away an idle hour than afflict him with metaphysics, or goad him with science."[28]

Multiplied in one example after the next, this tropelike condemnation of science and abstract philosophy shows Twain's reliance on conventions of vernacular humor. Twain ridicules science as he debunks other aspects of genteel culture: with the irreverence and the distance of an outsider. That remained his preferred comic perspective for most of his career, though the point of view occasionally showed some signs of strain after literary success brought the wild westerner of *The Innocents Abroad* to the eastern inner circle of William Dean Howells. But no matter how ambivalent his relation to the American cultural establishment, the largely self-taught Clemens would always remain an outsider to science, dependent for his knowledge on the popularizers of the lecture circuit and reports in the press. To be sure, as Sherwood Cummings demonstrated in *Mark Twain and Science,* fairly sophisticated ideas about science emerge in Twain's more serious writing,[29] and his scientific sketches certainly show the humorist keeping abreast of the issues of his day; in fact, his "Brace of Brief Lectures on Science" (1870) originally appeared over quotations from the scientific volume he parodied in it.[30] But over the course of Twain's career, from "Petrified Man" (1862) to "Three Thousand Years Among the Microbes" (1905), his humor looks askance at science from the secure perspective of the amateur, the same perspective behind most scientific humor today.

Among nineteenth-century American humorists, however, none stands in stronger contrast to this amateur scientific comic tradition than George Horatio Derby, whose expertise shaped a very different humor based on learned wit. A member of the exceptionally distinguished West Point class of 1846, Derby enjoyed perhaps the finest technical education available in pre–Civil War America. He studied chemistry, natural philosophy, astronomy, calculus, and civil engineering, and he graduated seventh in his class—just three places behind George B. McClellan of Pennsylvania and well ahead of two future military giants from Virginia, Stonewall Jackson (seventeenth) and George E. Pickett (fifty-ninth, the bottom of the class).[31] For his outstanding record, Derby received a commission in the Topographical Engineers, which eventually took him to California. There he began in 1850 to publish the comic cartoons and witticisms for which he was already notorious among his fellows, whose education allowed them to appreciate even the more erudite examples of his scientific humor.

Derby is barely known today, but Americans in the mid-nineteenth century doted on his japes on astronomy, paleontology, dentistry, and surveying, in addition to his spoofs of inventions and the patent process. Signed first with the pseudonym "John P. Squibob" and then (after Squibob's "death and spirit resurrection") as "John Phoenix," Derby's literary sketches appeared in major upper-class periodicals on both coasts—including the *Knickerbocker*, the *Spirit of the Times*, and the *[California] Pioneer*. Illness forced him to stop writing in 1857, two years after the publication of *Phoenixiana*, his major collection; he died in 1861, before his second, *The Squibob Papers* (1865),[32] was published. Even after his death, Derby's humor remained so well known that in 1864 Ulysses S. Grant, worried that his Union troops might not get through Georgia, grumbled that "they can keep the enemy off General Sherman a little, as Derby held the editor of the San Diego *Herald*"[33]—that is, with his own nose between the adversary's teeth. The image conveys the audacity of John Phoenix, Derby's comic persona. Among his other distinctions, including a gentleman's distaste for vernacular values, Phoenix took pride in displaying his technical expertise.

Nonetheless, even his scientific humor does not always avoid anti-intellectual tropes. In fact, Twain almost certainly derived part of the anti-intellectualism of "Some Learned Fables" from Derby's "Official Report" (1855), which satirizes contemporary government surveys as mainly benefiting the reputation and purse of the leader, in this case, the zany John

Phoenix, A.M., Chief Engineer and Astronomer, S.F.A.M.D.C.R. For this survey of the proposed central route for a railroad between San Francisco and Mission Dolores (a distance of a mere two and a half miles), Phoenix has assembled a "scientific corps" including a geologist, naturalist, botanist, ethnologist, and a dentist, as well as two assistant astronomers, seven other members of the Phoenix family, and nearly two hundred laborers—the whole lot equipped with sidearms and a mountain howitzer in addition to the regulation load of technical apparatus. All these resources notwithstanding, the expedition has one failure after another in the ten-day survey of Kearney Street and environs. The chainmen forget to measure the sidewalk. The precaution of attaching a "Go-it-ometer," a pedometer that Phoenix invented,[34] turns to naught when its bearer detours to a saloon and (after five beers) performs a four-mile jig. Scientific research fares little better. The geologist observes "that red-headed children appear to grow spontaneously" (P 25), while the specimens accumulated by the botanist's party after a day of independent exploration number "a box of sardines, a tin can of preserved whortleberries, and a bottle of whisky" (P 29). John Phoenix, A.M., and his assistant are the direct ancestors of Twain's pompous incompetents.

But although both Twain and Phoenix mock the pretensions of scientific expeditions by emphasizing the participants' intellectual incompetence,[35] the two stories depend on different comic and narrative techniques expressing very different attitudes toward science. Whereas Twain belittles science and scientific methods, Phoenix inflates his scientists' dubious accomplishments, described in great technical detail. This comic technique effectively praises science even while ridiculing the scientists, who in this case is none other than Phoenix himself.

The first-person narration of "Official Report" focuses attention on the eccentricities and vested interests of an engineer who has nothing respectable to show for ten days and $40,000 of work—and who wouldn't show it if he could, since the supporters of a competing route have offered to buy his silence. In contrast to Twain's third-person fable, in which the humorist smirks at contemporary figures from above and the Tumble-Bug sneers at learned fools from below, Phoenix's first-person narrative exudes good cheer throughout, thereby defusing his critique. Self-congratulation and self-interest dominate the burlesque report, which opens with a brash "Having notified that Honorable Body of my acceptance of the important trust confided to me, in a letter, wherein I also took occasion to congratulate them on the good judgment they had evinced" (P 14) and closes with a breezy "I remain, with the highest respect and esteem for myself and every body else" (*P* 30). In between, the engineer's bravado reveals abuse of funds—"I drew . . . the amount ($40,000) appropriated for my peculiar route, and . . . invested it securely in loans at three per cent a month (made, to avoid accident, in my own name)" (*P* 14)—and parades his professional ineptitude. First-person narration and indeterminate satiric targets give this earlier story a much more slapstick, much less negative tone than Twain's. Making fun of oneself precludes the sort of nasty reproof possible when ridiculing someone else. Phoenix's theme is widespread incompetence and madcap corruption in government as well as in science and technology—without any sobering moral whatsoever.

As a result, the satire in "Official Report" takes a backseat to the scientific imagination creating it. Chief Engineer Phoenix calculates the distance between Fort Point and Saucelito (sic) according to his own "entire new system of triangulation": the mean of 1,867,434,926,465 triangles defined by spreading the feet of a tripod (to be exact, the feet of 184 tripods) as widely as possible. A mathematical solution of exactly 324 feet, instead of a number approximating ten miles, cannot upset his confidence: "I will stake my professional reputation on the accuracy of our work," he insists in a moment of delicious irony, "and there can, of course, be no disputing the elucidations of science, or facts demonstrated by mathematical process, however incredible they may appear *per se*" (*P* 18). The procedure is so ridiculous that we can overlook its burlesque of Simeon Borden (1798-1856), the Massachusetts engineer who devised the standard method of triangulation for surveyors and who had recently written *A System of Useful Formulae, Adapted to the Practical Operations of Locating and Constructing Railroads* (1851).[36] Nor do we care about the assistant's faulty solution to a problem of byzantine complexity when solved by pencil and trigonometric table. These elements of satire become irrelevant because the rhetoric of this sketch calls for displays of learning, not attacks on it.

Therefore, rather than debunk science itself, Phoenix prefers to lampoon scientific language, in the manner of the Literary Comedians, whose preference for verbal wit distinguishes their tradition. A very large group of pseudonymous comic writers flourishing mainly between 1860 and 1900, the Literary Comedians, or Phunny Phellows, included Artemus Ward (Charles F. Browne), Petroleum V. Nasby (David Ross Locke), and Mark Twain (Samuel L. Clemens), as well as John Phoenix and Dan De Quille. These writers alternated poses of superiority and inferiority depending on the subject at hand; their pseudonyms stood as comic signatures, not coherent literary personae.[37] As a result, they wrote fewer tall tales and mock-oral yarns, devices of an earlier humor of character, and wrought more verbal and literary jokes instead. Infamous as misspellers, the Phunny Phellows played with language, tone, and scene as they burlesqued literary and oratorical forms. They delighted in misquotation and illogic and adored deadpan narration by an "amiable idiot"[38]—like Chief Engineer and Astronomer John Phoenix.

Derby's burlesques involving scientific language range from the strained to the inspired. In a humorous book review, for example, the Literary Comedian seizes upon an infelicity in an explanation of the gyroscope's motion ("by developing and neglecting the powers of u superior to the square") with the sort of literalism that made S.J. Perelman famous a century later: "Allow us to inquire the object of developing the powers of u provided they are to be subsequently neglected? . . . Or, how do we know that u, or its powers, *are* superior to the square, which, as every school-boy knows, is next to the sphere, the most perfect of figures?"[39] The puns in this passage are exceptionally erudite, one reason for the disputed authorship of the sketch, but a similar impulse to promote mathematics over words also lies behind "A New System of English Grammar" (1854), which Phoenix promises will make its users "at once an exact, precise, mathematical, truth-telling people" (P 39). His example of how literature should benefit from his new grammar proves the point: "As a 19 young and 76 beautiful lady was 52 gaily tripping down the sidewalk of our 84 frequented street, she accidentally come [sic] in contact—100 (this shows that she came in close contact) with a 73 fat, but 87 good-humored looking gentleman, who was 93 (i.e. intently) gazing into the window of a toyshop" (P 39). The humor of this sketch exploits the presumed incompatibility of numbers and words, that is, of quantitative and qualitative language. But the joke here falls equally on mathematics and language. It's just as silly to presume that language lacks precision as to consider numbers incompatible with words. Even more to the point, considering how this sketch acts out what would later become the controversy between C.P. Snow and F.R. Leavis over the so-called "Two Cultures," the comic incongruities prove that numbers and words can combine productively, if unconventionally. Certainly it is no coincidence that the sketch also illustrates Phoenix's characteristic portrayal of science and technology as benevolent activities: generally useful, definitely not harmful, and fun, to boot.

That affection shows most clearly in Phoenix's absurd machines that nonetheless serve a useful function, occasionally even correcting the flaws in other machines. These stand in strong contrast to Rube Goldberg's unnecessarily complicated inventions, which criticize the technological imagination as high-blown and bombastic.[40] Derby was an accomplished cartoonist, and offered "Sewing Machine—Feline Attachment" (1857) as a mock-patent, complete with illustration. Probably the most inspired of Phoenix's inventions, the Feline Attachment runs the sewing machine on cat-and-mouse power, thereby avoiding any injury to the seamstress from operating the hand crank and foot treadle (S 62A). A similar comic respect extends to the scientific mind in the idea that triangulation by tripod can rescue a mission that has lost, misused, or broken all its other equipment. In this sense, even when he isn't proposing inventions, Phoenix celebrates intellectual inventiveness. Such attitudes form the cornerstone of a humor based on learned wit.

The two "Lectures on Astronomy" (1854) demonstrate not only Derby's own intellectual dexterity, but also the way his humor demands and flatters an equally educated audience. The relatively small size of that group, especially in comparison to the audience for the anti-intellectual humor of amateurs, may explain why learned wit receives less attention than vernacular scientific humor. Indeed, the "Lectures" make fun of the lay public and the debased science they acquired through the various public lecture series enjoying success in the 1840s and 1850s, when, following the discovery of several planets and satellites, public interest in astronomy ran high. In a postscript between the two installments of his burlesque, Phoenix indicates his contempt for the intellectual level of popularizers and their listeners as he describes how previous audiences had foiled his plan "to exhibit and explain to the audience an orrery, accompanying and interspersing his remarks by a choice selection of popular airs on the hand organ" (P 66): these folks just wanted to eat the planets and sun, represented by apples spaced on wires around an orange. His contempt for the ordinary citizens who flocked to such demonstrations indicates how far Derby's intellectual humor stood from the vernacular assumptions of Twain's scientific sketches, and what a different conception of his audience Phoenix held.

Derby may have considered himself the ideal reader of the "Lectures," which, instead of offering a narrative, invite the reader to untangle the facts, irrelevancies, and puns mingled in a sophomoric survey of the solar system:

Copernicus (who was a son of Daniel Pernicus, of the firm of Pernicus & Co., wool-dealers, and who was named Co. Pernicus, out of respect for his father's partners) . . . started the idea of the present Solar System. [P 54]

In consequence of the rapid movement of Jupiter upon his axis, his form is that of an oblate spheroid, very considerably flattened at its poles, and the immense centrifugal force resulting from this movement (26,554 miles per hour), would, undoubtedly, have long since caused him to fly asunder, were it not for a wise provision of nature, which has caused enormous belts or hoops, to encircle his entire surface.

These hoops, usually termed belts, are plainly visible through the telescope. They are eight in number, and are supposed to be made of gutta percha, with an outer edge of No. 1 boiler iron. [P 239][41]

These examples represent some of the more accessible details in the "Lectures," whose erudition must have puzzled more than a few readers. Of course, the audience of the *Pioneer,* an avowedly intellectual monthly that originally published the sketches, would have enjoyed the advice to "our old friend and former schoolmate, Mr. Agassiz, . . . [who] by closely observing one of these [sun]spots with a strong refracting telescope, . . . may discover a new species of fish" (P 58). Similarly, the section on Neptune could rest on residual publicity from the planet's discovery just eight years earlier, in 1846.[42] But other sections contain technical jokes that probably excited enthusiasm only among Lieutenant Derby's colleagues in the Topographical Engineers, who doubtless shared his opinion about "a light course of reading" including texts on "Deferential and Integral Calculus" [sic], optics, and astronomy (P 248).

The "Lectures" parade Derby's learning, but an earlier sketch, "The San Francisco Antiquarian Society, and California Academy of Arts and Sciences" (1851), stands even further from the anti-intellectual tradition by making fun of other people's ignorance.[43] Here, instead of serving vernacular values, the various misspellings, mispronunciations, grammatical errors, and malapropisms all ridicule the intellectual pretensions and philanthropy of the self-made and self-educated B.S. Bags (get it?), who volunteers to fund the new society: "He had not the advantage of an early education . . . but he read a good deal, and liked it; and he dare say now, that if the truth had been found out, he knowed a great deal more than some of those filosifers at the east. . . . By reading the papers daily, particularly the 'Alta California,' he found all sorts of new matters which he supposed give him considerable idea of 'New Mattix.'" (P 141). Phoenix's visual humor typically involves cartoons and comic typography, not illiterate misspellings,[44] although other Literary Comedians so exploited their love of cacography that they became known as the Misspellers. But here in "The San Francisco Antiquarian Society" he sneers unbecomingly at democratic ideas about education and self-improvement, since even the Society's more conventionally qualified leadership, including two doctors and M. Quelque Chose, fall below the humorist's intellectual standards. Assigned to write a constitution for the new San Francisco Antiquarian Society and California Academy of Arts and Sciences, the executive committee declares, "The objects of this Society shall comprise inquiries into every thing in the remotest degree scientific or artful" (*P* 143). Derby's disparagement of the scientific society follows the same procedure as his ridicule of the pamphlet on the gyroscope's motion: he deflates pretensions of learning while parading his own superior knowledge.

This tradition of wit continues today in the humor of *Journal of Irreproducible Results* (1962-), published quarterly by Blackwell Scientific Publications. For example, a 1991 research report, "Aging: A Contagious Disease," presents epidemiological data from nursery schools to support its hypothesis: both aging and slow viral diseases "show late onset," "[are] difficult to diagnose," and "have lethal outcome."[45] *Stress Analysis of a Strapless Evening Gown* (1963), which spoofs the technological imagination, and *The Journal of Polymorphous Perversity*, a quarterly lampoon of psychology and psychiatry,[46] also sustain Derby's brand of learned wit.

For the most part, however, Derby did not write the sort of scientific humor that aims directly at the audience's ignorance: the hoax. This third tradition of American scientific humor has a long, if not particularly honorable, history that continues today primarily in science fiction. Walter Blair and Hamlin Hill have traced the American comic hoax all the way back to tracts extolling the extraordinary flora and fauna of the new world,[47] but the genre received a boost from the nearly continuous stream of scientific discoveries in the mid-nineteenth century. The great moon hoax of Richard Adams Locke in 1835 featured British astronomer Sir John Herschel in a report, ostensibly reprinted from the *Edinburgh Journal of Science,* on the flora and fauna of the moon.[48] The gold rush and railway construction excited interest in rock-collecting and other forms of amateur geology and mineralogy, and descriptions of fictitious fossils began to constitute a subgenre.[49] For his only excursion into the genre, John Phoenix became Dr. Herman Ellenbogen, M.D., whose "Remarkable Discoveries in Oregon and Washington Territories" (1855) firmly established the guyascutus and the prock in the American bestiary.[50] Other tales offered greater astonishments. In a geological and mineralogical vein, for instance, Dr. Friedrich Lichtenberger's "Extraordinary Account of Human Petrifaction" (1858) detailed the geological action producing semiprecious gemstones from petrified blood and arteries.[51] Mark Twain's "Petrified Man" (1862) took similar advantage of contemporary interest in fossils, although it didn't imitate scientific journalism but simply gave proof to the folk myth that a foolish grimace can become permanent.[52] These and similar stories satisfied the hunger of readers from California to New York for tales of America's natural wonders. But for all their popularity, none of these reports took in both lay readers and professional scientists as did the various hoaxes perpetrated by William Wright (1829-1898).

Under his nom de plume Dan De Quille, Wright wrote hundreds of factual and imaginative newspaper sketches, expecting readers to distinguish truth from hoax. His stories about the Comstock, America's silver-mining capital, appeared nationwide. He wrote for the New York Sun (America's best-selling daily) and the New York Herald (as Nevada correspondent) in addition to the Virginia City Territorial Enterprise and its sister publication, San Francisco's Golden Era; his work also appeared regularly in a variety of smaller and more specialized publications, including the Overland Monthly, Engineering and Mining Journal, Mining and Scientific Press, and the journals of the Lorborn Publishing Company of Baltimore.[53] Most of his journalism falls into familiar categories: local news, popular science and technology, adventure narratives. His humorous sketches often recall the early works of Mark Twain, who seems to have taught the local editor as much as the editor taught him. De Quille contributed to the mid-century's conventional stock of petrification lore with "Petrified or the Stewed Chicken Monster" (1863), his first exaggerated tale, a dream of having eaten so much stewed chicken that his own body petrified as a result.[54] But beginning two years later with his first real tall tale, "A Silver Man" (1865), and continuing with other stretchers, De Quille exploited scientific subjects in a tone so authentic that some German scientists apparently resented the secrets withheld by "Herr Dan De Quille, the eminent physicist of Virginiastadt, Nevada."[55] That Wright could pass as a physicist (much less be accused of eminence) demonstrates not only how much he knew about science and how expertly scientific lies came from his pen but also how differently experts and amateurs have fun with science. The hoax takes humor beyond the inside jokes of learned wit and leads to the realm of the practical joke.

"Dan was a good deal of a geologist and something of a mineralogist," C.C. Goodwin recalled, and no less an authority than the zoologist and paleontologist Edward Drinker Cope (1840-1897), editor of the *American Naturalist,* sought De Quille's aid in describing the "mountain alligator."[56] But just where Wright acquired his expertise remains a mystery. In contrast to the extensive biographical material available for Derby, including records of his academic work at West Point, Wright's biography consists mainly of snippets in books by or about his more famous friends from the Comstock Lode, especially Mark Twain and Wells Drury.[57] Few facts exist about Wright's life before 1862, when he joined the staff of Virginia City's *Territorial Enterprise* a few months ahead of Samuel Clemens, and fewer still before 1857, when Wright left his wife and their three living children near what is now West Liberty, Iowa,.to begin prospecting in California.[58] Doubtless he learned much of his science on the job, since even unsuccessful miners like him acquired a rudimentary knowledge of mineralogy and geology; if he had any formal education in Knox County, Ohio (where he was born in 1829 and lived until 1849), it was probably fairly basic when he matriculated at the poor man's Harvard—that is, the newspaper office.

He had already published more than fifty sketches in *Golden Era* by the time Joe Goodman signed him up for the *Enterprise,*[59] but once there his opportunities for self-education, particularly in mineralogy, expanded greatly. While the western press followed the example of eastern sheets in reprinting public lectures and reporting scientific discoveries, editors in the mining districts knew that their readers had especially hearty appetites for science with a local angle: western geology and the newest procedures for locating, identifying, and purifying minerals. The weekly *Golden Era*—"the most important journal ever published on the Pacific slope," according to Franklin Walker[60]—set the formula. In the late 1850s and early 1860s, the *Golden Era* won readers well beyond San Francisco by running regular deparments on mining and agriculture alongside literary contributions by staff writer Bret Harte and Nevada correspondents De Quille and Twain. Following suit, the *Overland Monthly* (founded 1868) not only published local-color tales like Harte's sentimental "Luck of Roaring Camp" and De Quille's mining stories but also featured nonfictional writing like geologist Clarence King's harrowing accounts of mountain climbing in the Sierra Nevada and John Muir's speculations on glacial erosion.[61] The daily *Territorial Enterprise* enjoyed at least as much success with the formula as its two more literary city cousins: in his local news column, a feature rather like the *New Yorker's* "Talk of the Town," De

Quille covered the news of the mines, including new techniques and discoveries, and filled any remaining space with fiction, leaving it to his readers to separate fact from fancy. He had every reason to expect that they would. The *Territorial Enterprise* could joke about "two and four legged specimens of the species donkey" nearly a month before the American edition of *On the Origin of Species* appeared because its readers kept up with scientific news.

The newspaper clippings in De Quille's personal papers demonstrate that he followed technical publications as well as the popular press. But regardless of the source of his knowledge, his authority was widely respected. He contributed to mining journals, Myron Angel's *History of Nevada* (1881), and the *Encyclopedia Britannica* (10th ed., 1884). Although his reputation as a humorist has suffered because he did not publish a volume of comic sketches, his reputation as a science journalist has been well served by the two books he did write: *A History of the Comstock Silver Lode Mines* (1889), a volume of popular science and local lore aimed at rail travelers, and *The Big Bonanza* (1876), the authoritative history of mining science, technology, and society on the Comstock Lode.

De Quille exploits this expertise in his scientific humor quite differently from either Phoenix or Twain; he lacked Twain's irreverence for science as surely as he spurned Phoenix's contempt for the self-taught. Folklorist C. Grant Loomis, who judged De Quille's scientific tales "a departure from the usual tradition of lying,"[62] traced their unusual powers of deception to two factors: readers had become accustomed to astonishing tales of scientific discovery, while the writer had chosen topics within the range of the probable.[63] But the narratives themselves reveal two additional, perhaps more important factors. Dan De Quille knew enough science to fill his tales with incredible *facts* as well as convincing fantasies. In consequence, the stories conveyed an authentic respect for scientific knowledge in general and a persuasive pride in his own explanation of the "truth."

All these factors animate "A Silver Man" (1865), De Quille's most elaborate pseudo-scientific tale, although his first hoax. Headlined "The Wonder of the Age," the sketch masquerades as a news item describing a human body that became "a mass of sulphuret of silver, slightly mixed with copper and iron (in the shape of pyrites)" (Q 38). First, De Quille puts his yarn in the journalistic tradition of fossil-finds when he observes that the miners who discovered the body originally considered it "a most remarkable petrifaction" (Q 38) and only later realized that it was actually "mineralized." Then he carefully places it within the realm of the possible by detailing the practical aspects of its discovery and excavation. But both of these tactics, far from being unique either to De Quille's humor or to scientific yarns, fall within the standard narrative devices of the tall tale. A tall talker typically piles realistic details onto fantasy, offers irrelevant examples, and cites evidence unavailable for inspection; De Quille follows the formula. He details the excavation of the silver man (facts especially convincing to an audience of miners), proposing the "very reasonable" opinion of how the man got into the cave (he was looking for shelter) and glossing over the lack of hard evidence (the silver man is already disintegrating from contact with the atmosphere!). Like many another western yarnspinner who tricked his listeners a while and thus eventually brought them within the circle of the initiated, De Quille flatters his audience a bit when he describes his news source, one Peter Kuhlman, as "not only a good practical miner, but an excellent chemist and minerologist" (Q 38). Along with the miners who also came to accept the reality of the silver man, Kuhlman serves as a rhetorical role model for the audience.

More revealing of De Quille's originality, however, is the respect for science implicit in the appeal to his readers' vanity. He suggests that only the ignorant would reject the report as fantastic. "All who have the least knowledge of palaeontology," he admonishes, "know that all those wonderful remains of fishes, animals, etc., found in limestone and other rocks, and about which so much is said and written, are not the creatures themselves, but merely their shapes replaced by mineral substances" (Q 40). The boldness of this passage sustains a tone established in the first two sentences, which seem charmingly coy to the initiated but assert an intimidating authoritativeness to the naïve: "Everybody, no doubt, has heard of the discovery of the wonderful 'Silver Man,' found in a mine between Esmeralda and Owen's River. Everybody, however, has not heard the full particulars of the discovery, and many will hoot at the idea of any such discovery ever having been made. They will at once say that it is impossible for a human body to be changed to silver ore. Let them have their say!" (Q 37). Indeed, far from laughing at science and scientists, De Quille's hoax delights in learning and ridicules those too ignorant to enjoy his game. He does not resort to nonsense terms or neologisms, for example, when he wants comic jargon. On the contrary, he celebrates scientific learning by reaching for the highest available diction—real scientific terminology—to describe "the argentiferous homo . . . held by an accumulation of pyritous concretions" (Q 39).

Respect for science also influences the narrative structure of "The Silver Man." Rather than citing authorities and facts at the beginning of the story and then building upon them, as in a conventional yarn, De Quille reserves them for the end. Placed there, his appeals to authority not only gain strength from the rhetorical power of the ending but also distract the reader from the questionable silver man to verifiable scientific curiosities. In the process, De Quille shifts the focus of the tale from the imaginary to the real. To similar effect, he does not entirely populate the tale with fictitious experts like the miner Kuhlman but refers to genuine scientific authorities, as well. He cites the German mineralogist J.F.A. Breithaupt (1791-1873) and the French physicist Henri Hureau de Sénarmont (1808-1862) for evidence of related phenomena, a human body turned to iron and artificial crystal formation, respectively.[64]

Such mixing of the historical and the imaginary has become commonplace in American comic fiction, for example in Thomas Pynchon's *Gravity's Rainbow* (1973) and Philip Roth's *The Great American Novel* (1973), both of which construct what Roth has called "a passageway from the imaginary that comes to seem real to the real that comes to seem imaginary."[65] Compared to these twentieth-century writers and their self-conscious narration, De Quille uses the technique rather prosaically. His scientific explanation of the silver man comes only after all his various appeals for belief, and he reasons mainly from three facts: that fossils of mineral-rocks develop inside the earth, that mine gases have preserved human remains for up to sixty years and have even allowed iron pyrites to fossilize human form, and that under certain circumstances new mineral deposits continuously replace worked-out veins. But this blending of the real and the imaginary was rare for 1865.

So he must have taken great pleasure in the apparently universal belief in his story of "The Traveling Stones of Pahranagat Valley" (c. 1865-66)— at least before matters got out of hand. The sketch announced the discovery of round stones with such strong magnetic properties that they would travel to each other within a radius of five feet. In addition to the jealous German scientists, no less a skeptic than P.T. Barnum seems to have been taken in by the tale (rumor has it that he offered De Quille ten thousand dollars for a set),[66] and of course ordinary citizens fell for it too. In 1872, six years after the original story, a request for five pounds of the stones prompted De Quille to hint at the truth when he announced in the *Enterprise,* "We have none of said rolling stones in this city at present but would refer our Colorado speculator to Mark Twain, who probably still has on hand fifteen or twenty bushels of assorted sizes."[67] But the tale, reprinted a few years later in *The Big Bonanza,* continued spreading until 1879, when after fifteen years the humorist decided he'd had enough. Adopting the pose of the Sufferer familiar to readers of Mark Twain, De Quille complained that "this thing . . . is becoming a little monotonous":

> Letter after letter have we opened from foreign parts in the expectation of hearing something to our advantage—that half a million had been left us somewhere or that somebody was anxious to pay us four bits a column for sketches about the mountains and the mines—and have only found some other man wanting to know all about those traveling stones. . . . We are now growing old, and we want peace. We desire to throw up the sponge and acknowledge the corn; therefore we solemnly affirm that we never heard of any such diabolical cobbles as the traveling stones of Pahranagat—though we still think there ought to be something of the kind somewhere in the world. If this candid confession shall carry a pang to the heart of any true believer, we shall be glad of it, as the true believers have panged it to us, right and left, quite long enough."[68]

None of De Quille's other sketches had quite the same longevity as "The Traveling Stones of Pahranagat Valley," but one story did inspire similar belief, the tale of how inventor Jonathan Newhouse froze to death in the desert on the trial run of his air-conditioning apparatus. Generally known as "The Solar Armor," it was originally published in two stages in the *Territorial Enterprise,* first as a brief item headed "Sad Fate of an Inventor" (1874) and later as an elaborate sketch titled "A Mystery Explained" (1874).[69] The development of De Quille's tale demonstrates his pleasure both in displaying scientific knowledge and in blending fact with fantasy. The various second-hand versions of the tale, on the other hand, which caught the public imagination, clarify the difference between De Quille's affectionate humor of science and the anti-intellectual tradition of the amateurs.

The first version follows the formula of "A Silver Man": the *Territorial Enterprise* summarizes a report, ostensibly from a gentleman elsewhere in the state, of an unusual finding. With deadpan restraint, the one-paragraph item simply describes the apparatus devised by Jonathan Newhouse, "a man of considerable inventive genius" (Q 33). The armor consisted of a hooded jacket made of sponge that was connected by a tube to a rubber water-sack under one arm, and the contraption kept the wearer cool by bathing his skin with water, supplied when he squeezed the sack with his upper arm. "Thus, by the evaporation of the moisture in the armor," De Quille explains, "it was calculated might be produced any degree of cold" (Q 34). The nub of the story concerns the condition of the inventor when he was found dead two days after he left town for a trial in the desert: "He was dead and frozen stiff. His beard was covered with frost and—though the noonday sun poured down its fiercest rays—an icicle over a foot in length hung from his nose. There he had perished miserably, because his armor had worked too well, and because it was laced up behind where he could not reach the fastenings" (Q 34). With his typical respect for science, De Quille places the failure of the trial in the context of two successes: of the operation of the apparatus itself and, more important, of the underlying scientific principle of cooling by evaporation. Indeed, he implies that complete success requires only the minor matter of redesigned fastenings for the jacket.

The second version of the tale exploited public interest in the story, which in two months had spread to London, where to its credit the *Daily Telegraph* cautioned, "we should require some additional confirmation before we unhesitatingly accept it" (Q 35). After summarizing the original account and its treatment in the English press, De Quille begins an elaborate hoax with a tweak at the British: "glad that the *Telegraph* has given us the opportunity, long awaited, of publishing in detail the sequel to the curious affair," he immediately points to an error in the *Telegraph*, which placed Virginia City next to Death Valley, and only then proceeds with the full report of "one David Baxter . . . Justice of the Peace and ex-officio Coroner of Salt Wells, a station in Inyo County, California, situated at the head of the Sink of Amargosa River, at the north end of Death Valley" (Q 35). Such careful identification of geographical location, like the details of excavating the Silver Man, belies his other liberties with truth as he corrects "our first brief and imperfect account of the affair" (Q 35).

The water-cooled apparatus of the first version develops a more complex thermodynamics in the second. The site alongside the inventor's corpse is now revealed to have been littered with various vials—liquid ether and carbon bisulphide, and various salts of sodium and ammonium—and these chemicals are now believed to have produced extreme cold through various unspecified chemical reactions as well as simple evaporation. Very high diction enhances the pseudo-scientific explanation: "the frost and icicle found on the beard and depending from the nose of the deceased were formed from the water mingled with the more volatile fluids comprising the frigorific mixture" (Q 36). The evidence in this tale is as elusive, however, as it was fragile in "A Silver Man"— as scarce as a snowball in hell or ice in Death Valley. In addition to the testimony (secondhand) of the men who reported that their fingers nearly froze as they handled the corpse, the evidence in this case consists of the armor itself. But examining it will prove difficult: as the men struggled to load the corpse onto a horse, "the freezing moisture oozed out of the spongy armor upon their hands and gave them intense pain. Finally—after they found they could handle the body in no other way—they were obliged to cut the lacings to the armor. When, after an infinite deal of pain to their hands and fingers, the armor was peeled off the body and left lying in the desert, where it probably still remains" (Q 36). With the familiar coyness of the tall talker, De Quille feigns bewilderment at the failure of the San Francisco Academy of Sciences to comment on Newhouse's chemicals, but he does not joke about the meaning of the inventor's death: "he fell victim to a rash experiment with chemicals with the nature of which he was but imperfectly acquainted" (Q 37). In other words, Newhouse died because he knew too little about science.

Although De Quille consistently locates the solar armor in a context of respect for science, most of its secondary versions belong to the dominant anti-intellectual tradition. De Quille's near-contemporary Wells Drury comes close to the spirit of the original story when he reports, incorrectly, that the inventor had filled the apparatus with too much ammonia, "with the most unhappy results."[70] But DeLancey Ferguson's account, in which "the inventor froze to death . . . because a valve had stuck and he couldn't turn off the power,"[71] turns the simple apparatus into a dangerous, autonomous machine and illustrates in the process the Luddite assumptions of conventional American humor. These stand out even more sharply when Ivan Benson tells the tale in *Mark Twain's Western Years* (1938); the original sponge-and-sack apparatus of 1874 has metamorphosed into a portable air conditioner complete with "a small air compressor [!] and a battery," though the first practical dry cell was not invented until 1888, nearly fifteen years after De Quille's story. But more important than the technical improvements on the apparatus are the implications arising from them. The autonomous invention outwits its inventor, and a voracious science demands human sacrifice: "With his rubber suit on, the wearer could turn on the compressor, which was concealed within. One button started the compressor; another turned it off. . . . *The daring inventor had given his life for science.* He had started the compressor but had been unable to turn it off, and had frozen to death. The machine was still running when the body was found."[72] In the slightly more than half a century between De Quille's version and Benson's, a tale elevating scientific knowledge over ignorance became a fable of dangerous science and technology. Whatever the reason for the transformation—surely influenced by sources ranging from Twain's *A Connecticut Yankee in King Arthur's Court* (1889) to Mussolini's invasion of Abyssinia—the damage to De Quille's "quaint," as he termed this sort of yarn, underscores how fragile has been respect for science in American humorous literature.

The fragility offers a clue to the conflict between the enthusiasm for technology running through most of *Connecticut Yankee* and its apocalyptic, Luddite ending: Twain's admiration could not withstand the contempt implicit in his vernacular narrative conventions. Even more important, the transformation of "The Solar Armor" helps explain why the amusing and historically important proscientific humor of Dan De Quille and John Phoenix has receded from public view. The utter dominance of the anti-intellectual tradition has obscured it. The obscurity has proved doubly unfortunate for Dan De Quille, since his small place in American literary history already rests primarily on his silence. It was after all De Quille's *absence* from the *Territorial Enterprise,* whose local news department then fell to Clemens, that gave birth to Mark Twain. Yet Phoenix's reputation has fared only a little better. Attention has focused almost exclusively on the atypical "Official Report," the satire on government scientists that Twain easily turned into an attack on science itself. Indeed, so pervasive are America's anti-intellectual comic conventions that one critic recently asserted, despite all the evidence of Derby's intellectual snobbery, that Phoenix deserved greater attention because his "scientists' methods . . . provided an apt symbol for the tyranny of reason."[73] Such misunderstanding is not at all surprising, given the general prejudice against science in American humor. But it is disappointing nonetheless, for it cheats George Horatio Derby and William Wright of their genuine significance in American letters. In contrast to amateurs like Mark Twain, Phoenix and De Quille knew enough about science to laugh with it as friends.

Notes

1. See Henry Beckman, ed., *Washington Irving: Representative Sketches* (New York: American Book Company, 1934), esp. 57-58.

2. See Samuel Clemens, "Petrified Man," *Territorial Enterprise* n.d.; rpt. in *San Francisco Bulletin*, Oct. 15, 1862; text in Ivan Benson, *Mark Twain's Western Years* (New York: Russell and Russell, 1966), 175.

3. Mark Twain, "Three Thousand Years Among the Microbes" in John S. Tuckey, ed. *Mark Twain's "Which Was the Dream?" and Other Symbolic Writings of the Later Years* (Berkeley: Univ. of California Press, 1967), 433-553.

Twain's other works with significant references to science include "Silver Bars—How Assayed" (1863), rpt. in *Early Tales & Sketches*, vol. 1 1851-1864, of Edgar Marquess Branch and Robert H. Hirst, *The Works of Mark Twain* (Berkeley: Univ. of California Press for the Iowa Center for Textual Studies, 1979), 211-14; "A Full and Reliable Account of the Extraordinary Meteoric Shower of Last Saturday Night" (1864), rpt. in *Early Tales & Sketches*, Vol. 2, 1864-1865, (1981), 118-24; and "A Brace of Brief Lectures on Science," *The American Publisher*, Sept. 1870 and Oct. 1870, rpt. in Hamlin L. Hill, Jr., "Mark Twain's 'Brace of Brief Lectures on Science,'" *New England Quarterly* 34 (1961): 228-39. Among critical discussions of Twain's scientific interests and knowledge are Hyatt Howe Waggoner, "Science in the Thought of Mark Twain," *American Literature* 8 (Jan. 1937): 355-70; Stan Poole, "In Search of the Missing Link: Mark Twain and Darwinism," *Studies in American Fiction* 13 (Autumn 1985): 201-15; and Sherwood Cummings, *Mark Twain and Science* (Baton Rouge: Louisiana State Univ. Press, 1989).

4. Garrison Keillor, "Oya Life These Days," *New Yorker* 50 (Feb. 17, 1975): 31-32.

5. *Territorial Enterprise*, Dec. 17, 1859. The English edition of *Origin of Species* was published Nov. 24, 1859, and sold out immediately; the American edition appeared in January 1860.

6. Wright began reporting for the *Enterprise* in May, 1862; Clemens in August. "Mark Twain" as a pseudonym and comic persona emerged in February of 1863.

7. One might also include Kurt Vonnegut, although the scientific humor in *Cat's Cradle* (1963) and "Tom Edison's Shaggy Dog" (1953) mainly exploits the popularized science of science fiction. By contrast, the three novels of Thomas Pynchon—*V* (1963), *The Crying of Lot 49* (1969), and *Gravity's Rainbow* (1973)—display extraordinary expertise both in the history of science and in contemporary physics, making him the champion among comic novelists treating science; of the dozens of books on this important author, Joseph W. Slade's *Thomas Pynchon* (New York: Warner Paperback Library, 1974) remains the best introduction to Pynchon's thought and technique. As for Don DeLillo, an expert in the philosophy of mathematics who has written eight novels since 1971, *Ratner's Star* (1976) and *White Noise* (1984) are perhaps his most important works; useful introductions to DeLillo's themes and concerns are the entry in *The Chelsea House Library of Literary Criticism* (New York: Chelsea House, 1986), 2, 969-76; and Thomas LeClair's "Don DeLillo, *Ratner's Star*, and the Art of Excess, " *The Markham Review*, 14 (Spring-Summer 1985): 27-32.

8. Cited in David E.E. Sloane, *Mark Twain as a Literary Comedian* (Baton Rouge: Louisiana State Univ. Press, 1979), 19.

In Twain's Notebook 19 (July 1880-Jan. 1882), the name "John Phenix" [sic] tops a list of writers to be included in *Mark Twain's Library of Humor*. See Frederick Anderson, Lin Salamo, and Bernard Stein, eds., *Mark Twain's Notebooks & Journals*, vol. 2 (1877-1883) (Berkeley: Univ. of California Press, 1975), 429.

9. Dan de Quille, *History of the Big Bonanza* (Hartford: American Publishing, 1876; rpt., New York: Knopf, 1959). Some editions appear under the volume's best-known title, *The Big Bonanza*.

10. On the publishing history of *Phoenixiana*, see George R. Stewart, *John Phoenix, Esq., The Veritable Squibob: A Life of Captain George H. Derby, U.S.A.* (New York: Holt, 1937), 169-71 and 210-11.

For the Kemble illustrations, see John Phoenix, *Phoenixiana; or Sketches and Burlesques*, ed. John Kendrick Bangs (New York: Appleton, 1903).

All the citations in this paper come from John Phoenix, *Phoenixiana; or Sketches and Burlesques*, 7th ed. (New York: Appleton, 1856), abbreviated *P,* and are noted parenthetically in the text.

11. Forty-four of these are reprinted in C. Grant Loomis, "The Tall Tales of Dan De Quille," *California Folklore Quarterly* 5 (1946): 26-71. Quotations from the stories follow these texts, and are cited parentheticaly. Loomis notes that De Quille contributed fifty-four pieces to San Francisco's *Golden Era* between Nov. 25, 1860 and Aug. 24, 1862 (p. 28), the first two of his nearly thirty years on the Comstock. A series consisting of twelve of these pieces was issued in book form a century later. See Dan DeQuille [sic], *Washoe Rambles,* with an introduction by Richard E. Lingenfelter (Los Angeles: Westernlore, 1963).

The unavailability of De Quille's work probably explains why he was omitted from the recent volume on American humorists in the *Dictionary of Literary Biography* (1982).

12. Q.V.A., "*Meleagris Gallopavo*—The American Turkey," Street and Smith's *New York Weekly* (Jan. 15, 1872), 4; rpt. pp. 309-11 in David E.E. Sloane, ed., *The Literary Humor of the Urban Northeast, 1830-1890* (Baton Rouge: Louisiana State Univ. Press, 1983), 309.

13. "certain maxims of archy," *archy and mehitabel* (1927; rpt., Garden City, N.Y.: Doubleday, 1973), 54.

14. Of course, this phenomenon is not exclusively American—witness Jonathan Swift's satire of the Royal Society in *Gulliver's Travels*—but American humorists have Americanized it.

15. Jim Davis, "Garfield," *International Herald Tribune*, June 12, 1987, 18.

16. James Stevenson, "Fossil News," *New Yorker* 63 (May 11, 1987), 36-37.

17. Ibid., 37. Research funding offers another tempting target these days. Lest his readers fail to recognize that he is satirizing a real example of government funding for research of dubious merit, Roy Blount, Jr., quotes a news article at the beginning of "Yet Another True Study of Mankind," *Atlantic* 259 (April 1987): 34.

18. Classic descriptions of the vernacular tradition appear in Walter Blair's *Native American Humor* (1937; rpt., Scranton, Penn.: Chandler, 1960); and Henry Nash Smith, *Mark Twain: The Development of a Writer* (Cambridge, Mass.: Belknap Press of Harvard Univ. Press, 1962). A more recent discussion is in the early chapters of Walter Blair and Hamlin Hill's *America's Humor: From Poor Richard to Doonesbury* (New York: Oxford Univ. Press, 1978), especially 71-73.

19. Mark Twain, "Some Learned Fables for Good Old Boys and Girls: . . . How the Animals of the Wood Sent Out a Scientific Expedition," in *Mark Twain's Sketches, New and Old* (Hartford, Conn.: American Publishing Company, 1875), 126-48; quotation, 148. Further references to this tale follow this first edition, abbreviated *MT,* and are cited parenthetically in the text. Twain was apparently so pleased with this formulation that he

repeated it, slightly revised, in *Life on the Mississippi* (1883; rpt., New York: Harper and Row, 1951), 109: "There is something fascinating about science. One gets such wholesale returns of conjecture out of such a trifling investment of fact."

20. Gladys Carmen Bellamy, "Mark Twain's Indebtedness to John Phoenix," *American Literature* 3 (Mar. 1941): 29-43.

21. Though he underestimates the importance of O.C. Marsh, Howard Baetzhold traces many of the contemporary allusions in "Mark Twain on Scientific Investigation: Contemporary Allusions in 'Some Learned Fables for Good Old Boys and Girls,' " in Robert Falk, ed., *Literature and Ideas in America: Essays in Memory of Henry Hayden Clark* (Athens: Ohio Univ. Press, 1975), 128-54.

22. Sherwood Cummings notes that Twain read *The Descent of Man* in 1871 and "by the 1870s" accepted Darwin's view of nature. See "Mark Twain's Theory of Realism; or The Science of Piloting," *Studies in American Humor* 2 (Jan. 1976): 209-21; esp. 214 and 221, n. 17.

23. Mark Twain, "A Horse's Tale" (1906), rpt. in Charles Neider ed., *The Complete Short Stories of Mark Twain* (New York: Bantam, 1957), 527.

24. O.C. Marsh, "Fossil Horses in America," *American Naturalist* 8 (May 1874): 288-94; and O.C. Marsh, *The Horse in America: Discoveries in Fossils* in *Tribune Popular Science* (Boston, 1874).

25. One of Marsh's most notable contributions to the evidence for evolution involved positing connections between modern birds and extinct dinosaurs. He wrote "On a New Sub-class of Fossil Birds (Odontornithes)" in 1873.

26. Mark Twain, "A Full and Reliable Account of the Extraordinary Meteoric Shower of Last Saturday Night," *Californian*, Nov. 19, 1864; rpt. in *Early Tales & Sketches*, vol. 2, 1864-1865, 118-124; quotations on 124, 118-19.

27. Henry Nash Smith defined the pattern in *Mark Twain: The Development of a Writer* (Cambridge: Belknap Press of Harvard Univ. Press, 1962), 52-70.

28. Mark Twain, "Prefatory," *Roughing It*, in *The Works of Mark Twain*, 28.

29. Sherwood Cummings, *Mark Twain and Science: Adventures of a Mind* (Baton Rouge: Louisiana State Univ. Press, 1988).

30. According to Hill, "Mark Twain's 'Brace'," 229, the volume was Louis Figuier's *Primitive Man* (London, 1870), which Twain knew from the review, "Our Earliest Ancestors," *Chambers's Journal of Popular Literature, Science, and Arts* 4th Ser., 7 (Aug. 13, 1870): 521-24.

31. Stewart, *John Phoenix*, 33, 39.

32. John Phoenix, *The Squibob Papers* (New York: Carleton, 1865). All references follow this edition, probably the only printing, and are cited parenthetically in the text, prefaced S.

33. Cited in Stewart, *John Phoenix*, 3.

34. Phoenix invented his Go-it-ometer, but pedometers were commonly used as surveying equipment in eighteenth-century England. The *O.E.D.* traces *pedometer* to 1712 in French, 1723 in English.

35. Bellamy, "Indebtedness," 33-36, catalogues the correspondences between the accounts. These similar details make the rhetorical differences in the two stories all the more important and emphasize the distinction between Twain's attack on science and Phoenix's affection for it.

36. Simeon Borden, *A System of Useful Formulae, Adapted to the Practical Operations of Locating and Constructing Railroads* (Boston: Little, Brown, 1851). Borden triangulation was a standard method of measuring the base line in a topographical survey, a method Lieutenant Derby would have learned at West Point and applied in his work as an engineer with the U.S. Army. In the 1830s Borden devised a surveying apparatus with four compound microscopes that became the standard tool in the field, and from 1841-1851 the engineer was chief surveyor of railroads in Maine, New Hampshire, Massachusetts, and Connecticut. See Dirk Jan Struik, *Yankee Science in the Making* (Boston: Little, Brown, 1948), 194; and *Who Was Who in America*, Historical Vol., 1607-1896, rev. ed. (Chicago: Marquis Who's Who, Inc., 1967).

37. Twain used at least seven distinct poses, switching among them with great rapidity from paragraph to paragraph. According to John C. Gerber, four are poses of superiority (the Gentleman, the Sentimentalist, the Instructor, and the Moralist); three are poses of inferiority (the Sufferer, the Simpleton, and the Tenderfoot). See Gerber's "Mark Twain's Use of the Comic Pose," *PMLA* 77 (1962): 297-304. More recently Louis J. Budd has examined the commercial dimensions of Mark Twain's public persona in *Our Mark Twain: The Making of A Public Personality* (Philadelphia: Univ. of Pennsylvania Press, 1983).

38. Walter Blair, *Native American Humor* (Scranton, Pa.: Chandler, 1960), 121-24, describes the Literary Comedians in general; for description of "amiable idiot," see p. 116. Blair and Hill enlarge this basic description in *America's Humor*, 274-99. The ethical dimension of literary comedy is a major theme of Sloane's *Mark Twain as a Literary Comedian*.

39. John Phoenix, "The Gyroscope: A Review," in his *Squibob Papers*, 187. All further citations to this volume follow this first edition, abbreviated *S* and noted parenthetically in the text. Stewart, *John Phoenix*, 216, doubts that Derby wrote this sketch, which originally appeared unsigned in the *Knickerbocker*, July 1857.

40. For examples, see *Rube Goldberg: A Retrospective*, with introduction by Philip Garner (New York: Delilah, 1983).

41. The two lectures, separated by nearly two hundred pages, exemplify the dreadful editing of *Phoenixiana*. The first lecture runs pp. 51-66; the second, 236-53.

42. B.A. Gould's detailed *Report on the History and Discovery of Neptune*, still considered a classic, appeared in 1850.

43. Derby's earliest pieces were signed G. Squibob, as in this piece, or John P. Squibob. After the "Death and Spirit Resurrection of Squibob" on June 15, 1853 (P 176), Derby became John Phoenix.

44. Among the best examples of his visual humor is the parodic "Phoenix's Pictorial, and Second Story Front Room Companion" of "Illustrated Newspapers," (P 116-25).

45. See John A. Robbins and Jochen Schacht, "Aging: A Contagious Disease," *Journal of Irreproducible Results*, 36, no. 1 (Jan.-Feb. 1991): 8-9; quotations, 9.

46. See Robert A. Baker, ed. *Stress Analysis of a Strapless Evening Gown and Other Essays for a Scientific Age* (Englewood Cliffs, N.J.: Prentice-Hall, 1963). *The Journal of Polymorphous Perversity* (1984-) is published semiannually by the Wry-Bred Press.

47. For a survey of the hyperbolic claims, see Blair and Hill, *America's Humor*, 3-9.

48. Excerpts of the hoax, which originally appeared in the *New York Sun*, Aug. 25-28, 1835, are reprinted in Calder M. Pickett, ed., *Voices of the Past: Key Documents in the History of American Journalism* (New York: Macmillan, 1979), 88-89.

49. *Mark Twain's Early Tales & Sketches*, vol. I, 156-58, cites other examples of this mania over petrifaction.

50. Herman Ellenbogen, M.D. [George H. Derby], "Remarkable Discoveries in Oregon and Washington Territories," *San Francisco Herald*, Dec. 10, 1855; rpt. as "Discovery of Two Remarkable Animals in the Rocky Mountains," *The Spirit of the Times* 25 (1856): 617.

Norris W. Yates, *William T. Porter and "The Spirit of the Times"* (Baton Rouge: Louisiana State Univ. Press, 1957), notes that for a time the sketch may have taken in the staff of the *Spirit*, and that it spawned at least one imitation, "Forest Scenes and Sketches, Adventure with a Guyascutus," by "A. Strecher, U.S.A.," *Spirit of the Times* 27 (1857): 278; Derby himself probably borrowed from the anonymous "The Guyasticus," *Spirit of the Times* 20 (1851): 548. See Yates, *Porter and "Spirit,"* 166, 182.

51. Dr. Friedrich Lichtenberger, "Extraordinary and Shocking Death of Miner," *San Francisco Alta California* (1858), 1; rpt. as "Extraordinary Account of Human Petrifaction" (1858); quoted in *Mark Twain's Early Tales & Sketches*, vol. 1, 1851-1864, 157-58.

52. Sam. L. Clemens, "Petrified Man," *Territorial Enterprise*, [Oct. 5, 1862, according to Bellamy, "Indebtedness," 37]; rpt. in *San Francisco Bulletin*, Oct. 15, 1862; see Ivan Benson, *Mark Twain's Western Years* (New York: Russell and Russell, 1966), 175-76. Bellamy, "Indebtedness," 37, observes that Twain's petrified man has the same grimace as Squibob, from whose deathbed Phoenix emerged.

53. As evidenced by clippings and memorabilia in the William Wright Papers, Bancroft Library, University of California, Berkeley.

54. Dan De Quille, "Petrified or the Stewed Chicken Monster," *Golden Era*, Aug. 30, 1863; cited and described in Loomis, "Tall Tales," 29, who observes that Mark Twain's earlier story of petrification almost certainly influenced its composition.

55. Wells Drury, *An Editor on the Comstock Lode* (New York: Farrar and Rinehart, 1936), 212. Dan De Quille, "A Silver Man," *Golden Era*, Feb. 1865; rpt. in Loomis, "Tall Tales," 37-41.

56. Charles Carroll Goodwin, *As I Remember Them* (Salt Lake City: Salt Lake Commercial Club, 1913), 213; Edward Drinker Cope to Dan De Quille, Sept. 18, 1888, unpublished letter in the William Wright Papers.

57. See, for example, Paul Fatout, *Mark Twain in Virginia City* (Bloomington: Indiana Univ. Press, 1964), 35-37; Wells Drury, *An Editor on the Comstock Lode* (New York: Farrar and Rinehart, [1936]), 210-19; Goodwin, *As I Remember Them*, 213-17. The most accessible and reliable account of De Quille's life appears in Oscar Lewis's introduction to *The Big Bonanza*, esp. viii-xiii, which draws on material in the William Wright Papers.

58. The most comprehensive biography to date is Lawrence I. Berkove's introduction to Dan De Quille, *Dives and Lazarus: Their Wanderings and Adventures in the Infernal Regions* (Ann Arbor: Ardis, 1988).

59. Loomis, "Tall Tales," 28, reports that *Golden Era* carried fifty-four sketches by De Quille between Nov. 25, 1860, and Aug. 24, 1862. Richard G. Lillard surveys De Quille's work in "Dan De Quille, Comstock Reporter and Humorist," *Pacific Historical Review* 13 (1944): 251-59.

60. Franklin Walker, *San Francisco's Literary Frontier* (1939; rpt., Seattle: Univ. of Washington Press, 1970), 24; for extensive discussion of the *Golden Era*, see chapter V, 116-45. Bret Harte was a staff writer on the *Era* until the fall of 1863, when he and C.H. Webb founded the more self-consciously sophisticated *Californian* (132).

61. Walker, *Literary Frontier*, 288, 293. Muir published only a small percentage of his work in eastern publications, including *Scribner's* and the *New York Tribune*; all the rest appeared in the *Overland Monthly*. By contrast, King relied primarily on his articles for the *Atlantic Monthly* when he composed *Mountaineering in the Sierra Nevada* (1872).

62. Loomis, "Tall Tales," 30.

63. Ibid., 32, 31.

64. Johann Freidrich August Breithaupt wrote the nineteenth century's classic work of systematic mineralogy, *Vollständiges Handbuch der Mineralogie*, 3 vols. (Dresden-Leipzig, 1836-47). De Quille surely would have known the English edition of Gustav Bishoff's *Textbook of Chemical and Physical Geology* (1859), based on Breithaupt's work.

Henri Hureau de Sénarmont, a mineralogist and former mining engineer was noted for his synthesis of crystals as in nature. He held the chair in Physics at the École Polytechnique from 1856 until his death in 1862. The *Dictionary of Scientific Biography* contains biographies of Breithaupt and Sénarmont.

65. Roth, "On *The Great American Novel*" (1973); rpt. in *Reading Myself and Others* (New York: Farrar, Straus and Giroux, 1976), 91.

66. Drury, 212-13, mentions simply "the greatest circus-man of America."

67. Dan De Quille, [untitled in rpt.], *Territorial Enterprise*, Mar. 31, 1872; rpt. in Loomis, "Tall Tales," 32.

68. Dan De Quille, [untitled in rpt.], *Territorial Enterprise*, Nov. 11, 1879; rpt. in Loomis, "Tall Tales," 33.

69. Dan De Quille, "The Solar Armor," includes "Sad Fate of an Inventor," *Territorial Enterprise*, July 2, 1874, rpt. in Loomis, "Tall Tales," 33-34; and "A Mystery Explained," *Territorial Enterprise*, Aug. 30, 1874, rpt. in Loomis, "Tall Tales," 34-37.

70. Drury, 213.

71. DeLancey Ferguson, *Mark Twain, Man and Legend* (Indianapolis: Charter Books/Bobbs-Merrill, 1943), 83.

72. Ivan Benson, *Mark Twain's Western Years* (Stanford: Stanford Univ. Press, 1938), 69; my italics. The italicized sentence, with its romantic struggle for life and death, is Benson's only contribution to the lore: in fact, the rest of his account comes almost verbatim from Goodwin's *As I Remember Them*, 215-16. DeLancey Ferguson, "The Petrified Truth," *Colophon* n.s. 2 (Mar. 1937), 193-94, traces many of the violations to De Quille's tale—but not his own, of course.

73. John Lang, "George Horatio Derby," in Stanley Trachtenberg, ed., *American Humorists, 1800-1950*, vol. 11 of *Dictionary of Literary Biography* (Detroit: Gale Research, 1982), 199.

9

Traveling in Time with Mark Twain

H. BRUCE FRANKLIN

We all travel in time every day. The sun rises and sets, our bodies age, the world changes, and our minds move backward with memory and forward with anticipation. After a night's sleep, we wake into a different world. But time travel means something different from all these common experiences. Time travel is a peculiarly modern form of exploration.

Historical time, at least in Anglo-European culture, used to be mere chronology—a sequence that arranged genealogy, the reigns of kings, famous battles, natural disasters, and other notable events. But when science and technology began to induce changes in material existence so rapid that people could perceive them in a single lifetime, the fundamental conditions in other "times" began to seem qualitatively different from those of the present. These ever swifter changes effected by science and technology led inevitably to the remembrance of time past and the anticipation of future time when life was and would be different from the present—in ways determined by science and technology.

Indeed, "the future" is itself a modern concept. The first fictions set in a human (rather than religious) future appeared in the middle of the seventeenth century.[1] But it was not until the Industrial Revolution and the concurrent emergence of revolutionary ideology that fiction began to project a future changed radically by science and technology. Perhaps the earliest unequivocal example is Louis-Sebastian Mercier's 1770 *L'An 2440*, which dreams of a scientifically organized utopia eight centuries hence when youth receive their "first communion" through the telescope and the microscope.

During the nineteenth century, time was continually being redefined by new instruments of observation and measurement, new modes of industrial organization, and new means of transportation, communication, and even lighting. Industrial capitalism transmuted the units of time that mark the planet's rotation and history, substituting the workers' punch clock for the sun and extending the age of the earth back beyond the carbonaceous fossils consumed ever more voraciously by the fires of machines. Science conceptualized cosmic time, within which it located geological time, within which it established a macrohistory of organic species, within which it designed a history of the human species.

By the second half of the nineteenth century, the scientific design of that human history had become clear to the leading thinkers of Europe and the United States. It seemed sequential, linear, progressive, and defined by the level of science and technology. Historical time is thus arranged in a spatial hierarchy. Each age is categorized by its prevailing technology, and "ahead" in time means more technologically, and therefore more socially, advanced. (The Bronze Age is "ahead" of the Stone Age, but "behind" the Iron Age.) Forward and backward in time become directions with an unequivocal meaning.

Time travel literature could now have profound social significance. A striking example is Edward Bellamy's 1888 *Looking Backward,* which became an instant best-seller and changed the consciousness of Americans more than any other novel of the century except for *Uncle Tom's Cabin.* The following year appeared a true masterpiece of time travel fiction, Mark Twain's *A Connecticut Yankee in King Arthur's Court.*

When in 1906 Twain thinks back on what he was trying to do in *A Connecticut Yankee,* he draws upon the predominant model of historic time: "*A Connecticut Yankee in King Arthur's Court* was an attempt to imagine, and after a fashion set forth, the hard conditions of life for the laboring and defenseless poor in bygone times in England, and incidentally contrast these conditions with those under which the civil and ecclesiastical pets of privilege and high fortune lived in those times. . . . I was purposing to contrast that English life . . . of the whole of the Middle Ages, with the life of modern Christendom and modern civilization—to the advantage of the latter, of course."[2] But then he notes two anomalies in the conventional model of historical progress: "That advantage is still claimable and does creditably and handsomely exist everywhere in Christendom—if we leave out Russia and the royal palace of Belgium." The case of Belgium seems to refute the linkage between technological and moral progress, as Twain next dramatizes in an eloquent denunciation of King Leopold's genocidal imperialism in the Congo, which makes the miserable conditions of the poor in the Middle

Ages seem like "heaven itself as compared with those which have obtained in the Congo." Twain concludes his reflections on A *Connecticut Yankee* by using the conventional spatial directions of time to show how Russia under the czar radically distorts the whole structure of human history:

> I have mentioned Russia. Cruel and pitiful as was life throughout Christendom in the Middle Ages, it was not as cruel, not as pitiful, as is life in Russia today. In Russia, for three centuries, the vast population has been ground under the heels, and for the sole and sordid advantage, of a procession of crowned assassins and robbers who have all deserved the gallows. Russia's hundred and thirty millions of miserable subjects are much worse off today than were the poor of the Middle Ages whom we so pity. We are accustomed now to speak of Russia as medieval and as standing still in the Middle Ages, but that is flattery. Russia is way back of the Middle Ages; the Middle Ages are a long way in front of her and she is not likely to catch up with them so long as the Czardom continues to exist.

Historical time is also distorted by the time travel in A *Connecticut Yankee* itself, which leads to complexities and difficulties, often attributed by critics to Twain's carelessness. Of course Twain was not a neat and tidy artist, but some of the novel's most apparently problematic aspects in fact constitute part of its highest achievement. For A *Connecticut Yankee* is probably the first fiction to explore philosophical and political paradoxes inherent both in the very conception of time travel and in Anglo-European perceptions of time relationships in nineteenth- and twentieth-century history. To comprehend the novel's scope, it is helpful to approach it through a somewhat simpler time travel work by Twain, "From the 'London Times' of 1904."

In the spring of 1898, Mark Twain met Jan Szczepanik, the famous inventor from Cracow who had devised a "telelectroscope" for transmitting televised images by wire.[3] Twain referred to the invention in a brief essay about Szczepanik, published as "The Austrian Edison Keeping School Again" in the October *Century Magazine*. The following month, the *Century Magazine* somehow was able to reprint the subsequent history of the telelectroscope, originally published in the *London Times* of 1904 in the form of correspondence by Mark Twain, datelined Chicago, April 1, 5, and 23, 1904. Remember that this story, supposedly from 1904, actually appeared in November 1898, just as the United States was fulfilling its new "Manifest Destiny" of becoming a global empire.

On the surface, "From the 'London Times' of 1904"[4] is a rather ingenious but puzzling little squib. But compressed into its few pages are coiled mechanisms designed to make shocking connections. The story gives a small sample of Twain's innovative use of fictive time travel as a vehicle for dramatizing perceptions into the interplay among science, technology, the nature of time, causality, and social change.

The opening scene takes place after midnight on March 31, 1898. "War was at that time threatening between Spain and our country," the author reminds his 1904 readers. The inventor Szczepanik ends up in a fistfight with Lieutenant Clayton, a U.S. Army officer who had baited him with the taunt that the telelectroscope would never "do a farthing's worth of real service for any human being." The two men meet and fight again in the fall of 1901, after the telelectroscope has been connected with the "limitless-distance" telephone systems of the whole world, thus making the daily doings of the globe "visible to everybody."

Then Szczepanik vanishes. In December 1901 a corpse, "easily identified as Szczepanik's," is discovered in Clayton's cellar. The man had died by violence. Clayton is convicted of the murder and sentenced to be hanged. After all reprieves are exhausted, the execution time is fixed ineluctably for 4 A.M., March 31, 1904.

An hour before he is to go to the gallows on this stormy night, Clayton, wishing to see the sun once again, calls Peking. The fictive Mark Twain of 1904, who is sharing the doomed man's final hours, is "strangely stirred" and muses: "To think that it is a mere human being who does this unimaginable miracle—turns winter into summer, night into day, storm into calm, gives the freedom of the great globe to a prisoner in his cell, and the sun in his naked splendor to a man dying in Egyptian darkness!" This paean to the wonders of science seems to materialize in the image that floods into the cell, described by Clayton's exclamations in the telephone conversation:

"What light! what brilliancy! what radiance! . . . This is Peking?"
"Yes."
"The time?"
"Mid-afternoon."
"What is the great crowd for, and in such gorgeous costumes? What masses and masses of rich color and barbaric magnificence! And how they flash and glow and burn in the flooding sunlight! What *is* the occasion of it all?"

In the melodramatic context, with the bell tolling "another age" with each passing hour, it is easy to read right over the significance of the answer evoked by Clayton's excited question: "The coronation of our new emperor—the Czar."

The story hurries on to its melodramatic happy ending without lingering over this revelation. With the halter around Clayton's neck and only an instant before the fatal lever is to be pulled, "Mark Twain" sees Szczepanik's televised image at the Czar's Chinese coronation. Clayton is instantly pardoned and freed. "The kings and queens of many realms" buzz around Szczepanik, who explains that he had assumed a false identity so that he could "wander about the earth in peace" without being constantly lionized for his scientific miracle. So "Twain" concludes the tale that began on March 31, 1898, and "came near ending as a tragedy" on March 31, 1904. An April 5 sequel seems to be just a cute postscript that underscores the happy ending.

But on April 23, 1904, "Twain" communicates an alternative, very nasty, conclusion. People begin to murmur: "But *a man was killed,* and Clayton killed him." Others try to excuse this oversight by pointing out that "we have been led away by excitement" (here is a hint to readers about their own responses). Then, "under the new paragraph added to the Constitution in 1899," the prohibition against double jeopardy has been repealed and the case is heard by the Supreme Court of the United States. The new chief justice, named Lemaitre, points out: "By the decision of the French courts in the Dreyfus matter, it is established beyond cavil or question that the decisions of courts are permanent and cannot be revised." Since Clayton "has been fairly and righteously condemned to death for the murder of the man Szczepanik," he must be hanged. Addressed as "your Excellency"—another hint that more has changed in this 1904 America than inattentive readers might realize—Lemaitre dismisses the argument that Clayton has been pardoned for that murder: "The pardon is not valid, and cannot stand, because he was pardoned for killing a man whom he had not killed. A man cannot be pardoned for a crime which he has not committed; it would be an absurdity." Equally irrelevant is the fact that Clayton did kill another man: he must—and does—hang for killing Szczepanik. The final words of the tale are: "All America is vocal with scorn of 'French justice,' and of the malignant little soldiers who invented it and inflicted it upon the other Christian lands."

Some critics find "From the 'London Times' of 1904" to be "confused" or "chaotic," or ascribe puzzling details, such as the identification of the corpse as Szczepanik, to Twain's purported carelessness.[5] To be understood, this story must be read as a specimen of modern time travel literature, with some sense of the history, assumptions, and special paradoxes of this subgenre of science fiction.

Since travel into the future is travel "forward" into a time technologically ahead of the present, the future scenes projected in fiction from the late eighteenth century through Looking Backward were dominated by visions of social progress associated with the advance of science. Even the anti-utopian reactions to these optimistic scenarios tended to blame the unpleasant futures they foresaw not so much on present social or technological trends but on supposedly intractable human nature, as in Notes from the Underground, Dostoyevsky's 1864 response to the utopian socialism of Chernyshevsky's What Is To Be Done? Some future-scene fiction even imagined the world happily transformed by a single invention, especially one leading to swifter or broader communication (since, of course, all human problems come from a failure of communication). By the late 1880s, such wondrous inventions were commonplace in the most popular literary form in the United States—the dime novel.

On one level, "From the 'London Times' of 1904" is a response to such naive enthusiasm for technology. Within a mere six years, the entire planet has been linked together by the "limitless-distance" telephone network, wondrously enhanced by Szczepanik's telelectroscope. Yet Clayton wins his bet that the telelectroscope would never "do a farthing's worth of real service for any human being"; at the end, even his miraculous rescue by the marvelous invention is undone. Despite spectacular technological progress, the world of 1904 apparently has gone "backward" from the world familiar to the story's 1898 readers. American jurisprudence (headed by Chief Justice "Lemaitre") now slavishly follows the precedent set by France in the Dreyfus case. The Russian czar, regarded by Twain as the incarnation of everything evil and reactionary, is being crowned emperor of China.

As soon as Clayton learns what he is witnessing, this strange dialogue ensues:

"But I thought that that was to take place yesterday."
"This is yesterday—to you."

But according to our conception of time, this should be tomorrow, not yesterday, for the United States is a day behind the lands west of the

International Date Line. So in this alternative future, daily time, as well as historical time, actually seems somehow to be running backward.

But is this "backward"? That depends on the definition of temporal directions. If technological advance nourishes the growth of alien forces such as dictatorship and imperialism, then the tyranny encroaching on the nation and world in "Twain's" 1904 might be what is encountered when traveling *forward* in time, into the twentieth century.

"From the 'London Times' of 1904" envisions a possible future in which runaway technological progress offers diverting entertainment while the forces of empire are snuffing out the democratic and republican ideals of America. Although most of the story is set during April 1904, its subtext relates to events taking place during April 1898, in the days after its opening scene on March 31, when war was "threatening between Spain and our country." That war, declared in mid-April, ended in the triumph of imperialism and militarism. Though the corpse in Lieutenant—later Captain—Clayton's house may not be Szczepanik's, the representative of the U.S. Army officer corps has apparently killed, perhaps even more than the unidentified body in his basement. Readers who focus only on the personal melodrama miss the historical drama raging in the background.

The corpse may be Szczepanik's or not, Clayton may be reprieved or hanged, China may or may not be annexed by the Russian czardom, French protofascism may or may not master American jurisprudence, the telelectroscope and other exciting technology may or may not be of "real service" to human beings—for this story is a subtle example of alternative-future fiction. Any change in what *did* happen in the past—and Twain's March 31, 1898, is an alteration from the actual events—can logically produce any conceivable course of future events. By changing the past, the time traveler changes the present, which includes the actual history that led to it.

Modern science fiction is replete with stories and novels dancing through these paradoxes. What happens to the present if you journey into the past and accidentally snuff out a little prehistoric creature integral to the course of evolution (as in Ray Bradbury's "A Sound of Thunder")? Or kill Columbus before he discovers America (as in Alfred Bester's "The Men Who Murdered Mohammed")? Or conceive yourself (as in Robert A. Heinlein's "All You Zombies—")? Or introduce late-nineteenth-century technology and ideology into a preindustrial society—as in both *A Connecticut Yankee* and the world it mirrors?

The conventional model of historical time places the age of industrial capitalism *ahead* of all preindustrial ages. Therefore according to this model, time travel was actually occurring in the late nineteenth century, as industrial societies encountered, and colonized, feudal and prefeudal societies in Asia and Africa. Another form of time travel was the eruption of industrial capitalism within a preindustrial society—such as the transition taking place in nineteenth-century America. A man like Thomas Alva Edison, bearing the technology of the future, could then be considered "the Wizard of Menlo Park," single-handedly transforming the world with his genius. Or Jan Szczepanik, whom Twain labels "the Austrian Edison," might herald a strange new century. What might happen, Twain asks in *A Connecticut Yankee*, if a man embodying the latest technology and ideology of late-nineteenth-century America could instantly be transported to a feudal, slave society? And what if this preindustrial society were the ancestor of modern England, the dominant imperialist power of the nineteenth century, which was then ruthlessly colonizing as many preindustrialist societies as it could? And what if the time traveler's special area of expertise were the industrial development of modern weapons?

An erstwhile foreman of a modern Connecticut gun factory, Hank Morgan has command of the technology of his times. Dropped into sixth-century England, this knowledge makes him a lone genius, a "magician" single-handedly capable of organizing an industrial revolution that transforms a feudal society into the material semblance of a modern industrial society. In other words, he thus becomes the heroic archetype of late nineteenth-century capitalist culture.

Hank also incarnates the ideology of industrial capitalism. So in his mind there is no contradiction between his social and personal goals: remaking feudal England into a replica of late-nineteenth-century America while establishing himself as "the Boss." Although he hopes that changing society's technological base will lead to democratic culture and polity, he is by no means convinced that transforming the mode of production will automatically transform the cultural and political superstructure. Indeed, he recognizes that without a thoroughgoing political and cultural revolution, his industrial revolution may not take root, much less achieve the democracy supposedly generated by industrial capitalism.

In three separate passages (in chapters 13, 20, and 40), including one that coined the term "New Deal," Hank explains that his method of "peaceful revolution" would be unique in history. For "the ungetaroundable fact" is that "all gentle cant and philosophising to the contrary notwithstanding, no people in the world ever did achieve their freedom by goody-goody talk and moral suasion: it being immutable law that all revolutions that will succeed, must *begin* in blood, whatever may answer afterward. If history teaches anything, it teaches that. What this folk needed, then, was a Reign of Terror and a guillotine, and I was the wrong man for them."[6]

Thus Hank's voyage backward in time creates a double set of contrafactual paradoxes. The past he enters thereby becomes radically different from the actual past of the present: among other things, he introduces an industrial revolution twelve centuries before it took place. Furthermore, he brings about historical change in ways contrary to the apparent laws of history. Twain plays these paradoxes out to their logical conclusions with astonishing ingenuity and originality, creating within *A Connecticut Yankee* what may be the first fully-developed alternative-future fiction, and then having this alternative future self-destruct from its own internal contradictions.

In the alternative future, Hank does achieve his dream of a modern industrial political economy in the sixth century: "Slavery was dead and gone; all men were equal before the law; taxation had been equalized. The telegraph, the telephone, the phonograph, the type-writer, the sewing machine, and the thousand willing and handy servants of steam and electricity were working their way into favor. We had a steamboat or two on the Thames, we had steam war-ships and the beginnings of a steam commercial marine; I was getting ready to send out an expedition to discover America" (443-44). Then the actual past and the laws of history reassert themselves, leaving only these remnants of the sixth-century industrial republic: a bullet-hole in a suit of armor, the narrative itself, and Hank's dying dream, in which nineteenth-century America is only a dream.

Hank's industrial republic is destroyed by three main forces: the Church; finance capitalism; and modern warfare. Without a political and thorough cultural revolution, human nature remains shaped by feudalism. So the Church is able to mobilize the aristocracy and the commoners to overthrow the capitalist polity established by the Boss. But these organized forces of feudalism get their opportunity from the self-destructive contradictions of finance capitalism itself. When Hank returns from France, his youthful protégé Clarence explains how everything would have gone along fine if it hadn't been for "one of your modern improvements—the stockboard" (459). In other words, capitalism would follow its own ideals if it were not for capitalism. This paradox takes shape in an obvious satire on the contemporaneous robber barons. The feudal knights played their role as capitalists only too well, with Sir Launcelot driving his rivals to desperate measures:

> "When you left, three miles of the London, Canterbury & Dover were ready for the rails, and also ready and ripe for manipulation in the stock market. It was wildcat, and everybody knew it. The stock was for sale at a give-away. What does Sir Launcelot do, but—"
> "Yes, I know; he quietly picked up nearly all of it, for a song; then he bought about twice as much more, deliverable upon call." [459]

When Launcelot calls for delivery, the train of events leads to civil war and the unleashing of the Church. This in turn opens the gates for the most destructive of all forces—scientific, technological warfare.

Modern warfare—the war of the factories and machines and organization inevitably generated by the Industrial Revolution—had burst upon the actual world between 1861 and 1871 in the U.S. Civil War and the Franco-Prussian War. From the repeating rifle, primitive machine gun, observation balloon, submarine, and steam-powered ironclad warship of the Civil War would evolve the twentieth-century juggernaut capable of devastating the planet. In the final three decades of the nineteenth century, the great colonial empires—armed with ever more potent weapons, driven by the forces of their own economies, and increasingly equipped for global activities—were carving up all that remained of the preindustrial world. *A Connecticut Yankee in King Arthur's Court* presents this deepening historical crisis of the age as grimly comic and finally catastrophic.

As Twain wrote, American culture was generating a contradictory vision of the relations between industrial capitalism and modern warfare, one that exalted weapons technology as the path to peace and progress. American popular fiction was shaping the cult of the superweapon—an invincible product of American ingenuity that would defeat all the backward and evil forces of the planet, thereby ending war and bringing about a global Pax Americana.

Take, for example, Frank Stockton's *The Great War Syndicate*, published the same year as *A Connecticut Yankee*. When war breaks out between England and the United States, twenty-three "great capitalists" form themselves into a "Syndicate, with the object of taking entire charge of the war."[7] The Great War Syndicate develops and demonstrates the

"Motor Bomb," which has the explosive force of a thermonuclear warhead. When England surrenders without a fight, it is permitted to join as a junior partner in what becomes the "Anglo-American Syndicate of War" (180). Because warfare in the future would lead to "battles of annihilation" (191), the world submits to the enlightened rule of the Anglo-American Syndicate. In the final words of the novel: "all the nations of the world began to teach English in their schools, and the Spirit of Civilization raised her head with a confident smile."

It is in this spirit that Hank prepares for the final showdown between progressive Yankee capitalism and preindustrial darkness. Left with only fifty-three boys he personally has trained and indoctrinated to be technocratic lads of his own historic age, Hank intends to employ his "deadly scientific war material" to eradicate the dark forces of feudal superstition, ignorance, and oppression. As the embodiment of modern technological genius, Hank will use the most scientifically advanced weapons to inaugurate the reign of reason and progress.

The culmination of A Connecticut Yankee in "the Battle of the Sand Belt" has long been cited as an eerie forecast of the trench warfare of World War I. But it is an even more uncanny projection of the ultimate war, in which the victors end up as victims of the universal death they have sown. Beyond that, it probes to the very core the ideology of warfare that was emerging in the late nineteenth century, to cast its spreading shadow over the planet for at least more than the next hundred years—as we know all too well.

As brilliantly conceived by Twain, Hank and his young protégés are thorough pragmatists who hook "secret wires" to dynamite deposits under all their "vast factories, mills, workshops, magazines, etc." and connect them to a single command button. This is "a military necessity" so that nothing can stop them "when we want to blow up our civilization" (466). When Hank does finally initiate this instantaneous push-button war, his rationalization is appallingly ominous for late-twentieth-century readers: "In that explosion all our noble civilization-factories went up in the air and disappeared from the earth. It was a pity, but it was necessary" (476). For the readers of 1889, this devastating electric impulse had a different context.

Electricity—quasi-magical and usually invisible, used as thunderbolts by ancient gods and rapidly transforming daily life in the late nineteenth century—was bound to generate visions of dynamic weapons and lightning wars, with victory bestowed by electric submarines or electric airships or electric beams. The apotheosis of the religion of electrified warfare was Edison.

When it suited his purposes, Edison capitalized on this worship, frequently proclaiming his command of terrible electric superweapons. But in playing this role, he was mainly advancing and protecting his far-flung commercial enterprises. Neither the public nor various government bodies were convinced that electricity was safe, so any emphasis on its death-dealing capacities might interfere with sales, and Edison was nothing if not a master salesman. However, the main threat to sales of Edison's inventions and direct-current system was not public caution but a formidable rival—the alternating-current system largely devised by Nikola Tesla and being successfully marketed by George Westinghouse. Hence, Edison spent much energy trying to turn public apprehension about electricity into terror of alternating current.

The "war of the currents" broke out in 1886. Edison had staked all his investments in electric-power distribution on a direct-current system that was restricted by the available technology to low voltage incapable of transmission beyond a few miles. Tesla's polyphase alternating-current system, on the other hand, allowed for stepping up the voltage to very high levels for long-distance transmission and then stepping it down for safe use. Equipped with Tesla's inventions, Westinghouse was rapidly displacing Edison's DC with the AC system that was to become standard in the United States. Edison's response was a frenetic campaign to prove that alternating current is intrinsically lethal.

In addition to articles, pamphlets, and rumors, Edison and his agents staged public demonstrations in which cats, large dogs, and even horses were electrocuted with AC. Simultaneously, a powerful movement had developed in New York state against capital punishment, a movement that focused on the excruciating agony of hanging. Seizing this opportunity, Edison's lieutenants in 1889 bought three Westinghouse generators, resold them to three New York state prisons, and engineered the first use of the "electric chair." Edison also began proposing even more dreadful uses for alternating current, including an assortment of increasingly preposterous weapons.[8]

Twain was well aware of the war of the currents, and, unlike Edison, was unambiguous about the advantages of AC. On November 1, 1888, he recorded in his journal the belief that the alternating current "electrical machine lately patented by a Mr. Tesla & sold to the Westinghouse Company . . . will revolutionize the whole electric business of the world": "It is the most valuable patent since the telephone."[9]

The second grand electric weapon in A *Connecticut Yankee* seems to poke slyly at Edison's campaign against the dangers of AC. But its primary role is to dramatize Twain's insights into the relations between industrial capitalism and modern war. It is a fence designed in his absence by Hank's well-trained boys. Consisting of twelve large circles of wire powered by a direct-current generator, this death machine is designed to annihilate whole armies. (It may have inspired Edison in 1892 to conjure up an invincible alternating-current device that would allow a mere twenty-five men to defend a fort against an army.[10]) As Hank and his faithful lieutenant Clarence discuss technical improvements in their electric fence, they become vehicles for Twain's savage satire on the crass materialism and pragmatism of modern industrialized war:

> "The wires have no ground-connection outside of the cave. They go out from the positive brush of the dynamo; there is a ground-connection through the negative brush; the other ends of the wire return to the cave, and each is grounded independently."
>
> "No-no, that won't do!"
>
> "Why?"
>
> "It's too expensive—uses up force for nothing. You don't want any ground-connection except the one through the negative brush. The other end of every wire must be brought back into the cave and fastened independently, and *without* any ground connection. Now, then, observe the economy of it. A cavalry charge hurls itself against the fence; you are using no power, you are spending no money, for there is only one ground-connection till those horses come against the wire; the moment they touch it they form a connection with the negative brush *through the ground,* and drop dead. Don't you see—you are using no energy until it is needed; your lightning is there, and ready, like the load in a gun; but it isn't costing you a cent till you touch it off. Oh, yes, the single ground-connection—"
>
> "Of course! I don't know how I overlooked that. It's not only cheaper, but it's more effectual than the other way, for if wires break or get tangled, no harm is done." [467]

Beyond the electrified fence, these modern lads have prepared what Clarence rhapsodically calls "the prettiest garden that was ever planted," a belt forty feet wide entirely covered by concealed glass-cylinder dynamite torpedoes. When the first wave of many thousands of knights charges into this belt, the resulting explosion has disturbingly modern reverberations: "As to destruction of life, it was amazing. Moreover, it was beyond estimate. Of course we could not *count* the dead, because they did not exist as individuals, but merely as homogeneous protoplasm, with alloys of iron and buttons" (478).

But the most sensational part of the victory comes when Hank and his boys trap the rest of the feudal army inside the circles of their electric fence. Hank electrocutes the first batch: then a flood is released on the survivors as the boys man machine guns that "vomit death" into their ranks: "Within ten short minutes after we had opened fire, armed resistance was totally annihilated, the campaign was ended, we fifty-four were masters of England! Twenty-five thousand men lay dead around us" (486). The conquerors themselves are conquered by "the poisonous air bred by those dead thousands." All that remains of this first experiment in industrialized warfare is a scene of total desolation, devoid of human life and marked by gigantic craters.

Hank's apocalyptic weapons resolve the paradoxes of time travel by destroying everything that the nineteenth century has anachronistically introduced into the dark ages. But this resolution itself is paradoxical. The science and technology that mark progress, that distinguish forward from backward in time, become the means to annihilate all that humanity has created. Thus they display their potential to transform the future into the prehuman primeval past, that is mindless oblivion.

Notes

A small portion of this essay has been adapted from my *War Stars: The Superweapon and the American Imagination* (New York: Oxford Univ. Press, 1988). The most comprehensive account of Mark Twain's relations with science and technology is to be found in *The Science Fiction of Mark Twain*, edited with an introduction and notes by David Ketterer (Hamden, Conn.: Archon, 1984), which includes a useful bibliography. Hyatt H. Waggoner, "Science in the Thought of Mark Twain," *American Literature* 8 (Jan. 1937): 357-70, argues that Twain used contemporaneous scientific writings to corroborate his pessimism and determinism. Sherwood Cummings, "Mark Twain's Acceptance of Science," *Centennial Review* 6 (Spring 1962): 245-61, explains Twain's apparent ambivalence about science as characteristic of an intelligent amateur intellectual of his period. James D. Wilson, "'The Monumental Sarcasm of the Ages': Science and Pseudoscience in the Thought of Mark Twain," *South Atlantic Bulletin* 40 (May 1975): 72-82, sees Twain moving from an early celebration of science to condemning it for creating "a world bereft of meaning." Henry Nash Smith, *Mark Twain's Fable of Progress: Political and Economic Ideas in "A Connecticut Yankee"* (New Brunswick: Rutgers Univ. Press, 1964), offers a useful analysis of the ideological genesis of the novel but grants what seems to me far too little aesthetic control to Twain. The novel's innovative encounter with the paradoxes of time travel is discussed in my "Mark Twain and Science Fiction," *Future Perfect: American Science Fiction of the*

Nineteenth Century (1966; rpt., New York: Oxford Univ. Press, 1978), Philip Klass, "An Innocent in Time: Mark Twain in King Arthur's Court," *Extrapolation* 16 (Dec. 1974): 17-32, and William J. Collins, "Hank Morgan in the Garden of Forking Paths: A *Connecticut Yankee in King Arthur's Court* as Alternative History," *Modern Fiction Studies* 32 (Spring 1986): 109-14. Bud Foote's *The Connecticut Yankee in the Twentieth Century: Travel to the Past in Science Fiction* (Westport, Conn.: Greenwood, 1990) is an exceptionally imaginative and suggestive exploration of the novel as the headwaters of the river of twentieth-century science-fiction travel to the past.

1. Francis Cheynell's *Aulicus his dream of the king's sudden coming to London,* an antiroyalist pamphlet published in 1644, may be the very first fiction of the future, according to the leading work in the field, I.F. Clarke's *The Tale of the Future: From the Beginning to the Present Day* (London: Library Association, 1972), 2, 7.

2. Bernard De Voto, ed., *Mark Twain in Eruption: Hitherto Unpublished Pages about Men and Events* (New York: Grosset and Dunlap, 1922), 211-12; also in Charles Neider, ed., *The Autobiography of Mark Twain* (New York: Harper and Row, 1959), 271-72.

3. Tom Burnam, "Mark Twain and the Austrian Edison," *American Quarterly* 6 (Winter 1954): 365.

4. "From the 'London Times' of 1904," *Century Magazine* 57 (Nov. 1898): 100-104. Available in my *Future Perfect*, revised edition, 382-92, and Ketterer, *Science Fiction of Mark Twain,* 126-35.

5. Burnam, "Mark Twain," 370-71; Ketterer, *Science Fiction of Mark Twain,* 355.

6. Mark Twain, *A Connecticut Yankee in King Arthur's Court,* edited by Bernard L. Stein (Berkeley: Univ. of California Press, 1979), 229. Further references are by parenthetical citation to this edition.

7. Frank Stockton, *The Great War Syndicate* (New York: Dodd, Mead, 1889), 12; the novel was originally serialized in *Collier's Weekly* in 1889.

8. Edison's claimed superweapons were ridiculed as early as 1881 in Park Benjamin's short story, "The End of New York," *Fiction Magazine* (Oct. 31, 1881). See my discussion of Edison's mythic role as a wizard of war in "Thomas Edison and the Industrialization of War" in *War Stars.* Some of his fantastic electric weapons are cataloged in "Mr. Edison and Electricity in War," *Birmingham (England) Mercury,* Nov. 28, 1895.

9. Twain goes on to assert that Tesla's application of alternating current would have made James W. Paige's earlier electromagnetic motor successful: "The drawings & description show that this is the *very* machine, in every detail which Paige invented nearly 4 years ago. I furnished $1,000 for the experiments, & was to have half the invention. We tried a direct current—& failed. We wanted to try an alternating current, but we lacked the apparatus." Robert Pack Browning, Michael B. Frank, and Lin Salamo, eds., *Mark Twain's Notebooks & Journals: Volume III (1883–1891)* (Berkeley: Univ. of California Press), 1979, 431. Twain later became a personal admirer and good friend of Tesla.

10. Edison's bizarre AC weapon was an electric battlefield hose, described in "Edison Could Whip Chili. Or Any Other Country That Might Tackle This Fair Land. He Would Just Turn on a Hose with 20,000 Volts in It," *New York World,* Jan. 17, 1892; reprinted as "A Talk with Edison," *Scientific American* 66 (Apr. 2, 1892): 216-17.

10

Hart Crane and John Dos Passos

JOSEPH W. SLADE

> [Of post-World War I American writers] only Hart Crane, in his
> heroic cycle of poems *The Bridge,* and John Dos Passos, in
> the trilogy ending with *The Big Money,* tried to measure themselves
> against the great poets or novelists of other ages.
> —Malcolm Cowley, *After the Genteel Tradition*[1]

During the 1920s, America was mutating at speeds accelerated by rampant industrialization, political upheaval, revolutions in communication and transportation, population migrations, economic cycles, corporate reorganization, artistic ferment, and intellectual advance. All this activity generated new information of enormous volume and diversity; the question was not merely whether it could be comprehended, but when. One popular response was to defer interpretation, in the hope that the next generation would eventually sort matters out when still more information became available. The lingering trauma associated with the Great War and the hedonism of the Jazz Age that followed doubtless also encouraged procrastination. Political activists converted information into ideology, convinced that disorder in the present would soon produce a classless society in a rational utopia. Artists revelled in the chaos, some juxtaposing bits of information at random in Dada compositions, while others turned Futurist, hoping to anticipate meaning that was yet to emerge. The culture was on a roll toward the future.

The principal propellant was the growing authority of science, whose sources of knowledge and tools of interpretation held seductive promise for the years to come. Hart Crane and John Dos Passos both characterized science as the new religion of their time. Neither thought that faith in science was necessarily misplaced, but they were worried about its dimensions.[2] To construe science as a conjuring of imminent marvels, Crane said, was to avoid the responsibilities of the moment: "I think that this unmitigated concern with the Future is one of the most discouraging symptoms of the chaos of our age, however worthy the ethical concerns may be," he wrote; "it seems as though the imagination had ceased all attempts at any creative activity—and had become simply a great bulging eye ogling the foetus of the next century."[3] Dos Passos considered the tendency especially damaging to the writer. As "dependence on the future" displaced dependence on the past, he claimed, American literature had become "a rootless product."[4]

The accumulations of data were frightening because of the proliferation of terms and concepts, a babel at once existential and metalinguistic. In his essay "General Aims and Theories," Crane conceded the "terrific problem that faces the poet today—a world that is so in transition from a decayed culture toward a reorganization of human evaluations that there are few common terms, general denominations of speech that are solid enough or that ring with any vibration or spiritual conviction."[5] To his friend Waldo Frank, Crane wrote, "beginning with Spengler and Wells, this age seems too typically encyclopaedic. This may assist the artist in time—by erecting some kind of logos, or system of contact between the insulated departments of highly specialized knowledge and enquiry [sic] which characterize the times—God knows, some kind of substantial synthesis of opinion is needed before I can feel confident in writing about anything but my shoestrings."[6] The poet had to learn new vocabularies, master new images, fashion new metaphors; his Bridge would function as an "unfractioned idiom"[7] of his time.

Dos Passos shared Crane's anxiety concerning the explosion of information and like him deplored fragmentation: "Life in our changing industrial world has become so cut up into specialized departments and vocabularies, and has become so hard to understand and to see as a whole that most people won't even try."[8] The novelist had to describe the dynamics of an America reshaped by science, trace economic power along paths complicated by new technologies, annotate the rhythms of an environment whose artifice was increasing. For both Crane and Dos Passos the flood of new information had to be accomodated by expanded literary forms, difficult though that would be. They both aimed to assimilate and reshape, but their approaches differed. Crane attempted to narrow theories to images, to invest the physical character of the world with a secular numinosity. Dos Passos dealt with the flow of information itself, not its precise content, and revealed it as a public, collective phenomenon.

Behind the aesthetics of Crane and the sociology of Dos Passos, however, lies a common metaphysics. Crane believed that, in shifting the emphasis of Western civilization away from traditional religion, science had altered the nature of poetry as well: "Analysis and discovery, the two basic concerns of science, became conscious objectives of both painter and poet. A great deal of modern painting is as independent of any representational motive as a mathematical equation; while some of the most intense and eloquent current verse derives sheerly from acute psychological analysis, quite independent of dramatic motivation."[9] The poet could restore drama, and, more important, a sense of the spiritual to a secularized world, a world whose artificiality and rationality—whose humanness, in short— had to be acknowledged. Crane aspired to be "the *Pindar* for the dawn of the machine age,"[10] he wrote Gorham Munson, to whom he confessed two weeks earlier that he intended *The Bridge* to express "our scientific hopes."[11] Similarly, where for Crane the analysis and discovery associated with science had become the province of poets, for Dos Passos art and science were bound by "half-opposed ideals" that "overlapped": "One is the desire to create; the other the desire to fathom. Intangibly mixed up with them is a sense of beauty, quicksilver-like, three times dangerous to argue about, to dogmatize on, by which, somehow, we veneer the crudeness of the world and make it bearable—far more than bearable."[12]

While they minimized traditional cleavages, neither tried to gloss over crucial distinctions. Crane could be blunt: "Science (ergo all exact knowledge and its instruments of operation) is in perfect antithesis to poetry. (Painting, architecture, music as well.) It operates from an entirely opposite polarity, and it may equate with poetry, but when it does so its statement of such is in an entirely different terminology. I hope you get this difference between *inimical* and *antithetical,* intended here. It is not my interest to discredit science, it has been as inspired as poetry,—and if you could but recognize it, much more hypothetically motivated."[13] And Dos Passos wished to preserve for literature the writer's special values, despite their close resemblance to those rigorous virtues frequently associated with the scientist. The writer has to recognize, he said, that "the living material out of which his work is built must be what used to be known as the humanities: the need for clean truth and sharply whittled exactitudes, men's instincts and compulsions and hungers and thirsts."[14]

Even so, in their various manifestoes Crane and Dos Passos insisted that the writer had to map culture, the domain of meaning and the ground of literature, across the *entire* range of the present.[15] What made their assessments unique was the assumption that science was not merely an essential ingredient in national life but part of what it meant to be human and American. If Crane and Dos Passos were not quite certain that science was central to culture, they knew it was not alien. It is clear in retrospect, however, that they misjudged the reactions of their colleagues, especially those writers who thought of science as hostile to letters. Thirty years after the two wrote their masterpieces, the historian of science Gerald Holton suggested that one of the most urgent tasks *still* facing Americans was that of redefining culture so that "the sciences are not automatically thought to be a disturbing component."[16] Ironically, then, considering their mistrust of visions of the future, they were ahead of their time in their efforts to integrate science and the information it created.

To make a place for science, Crane's *The Bridge* and Dos Passos's three novels called *U.S.A.* used two overlapping strategies. The first was to fold the revelations of science smoothly into these works, to treat the information produced by investigation and discovery from a perspective that neither inflated nor diminished it. The second, more discretely literary, was to fabricate metaphors sufficient to encompass the vast quantities of information that were characteristic of every sector of American endeavor. Although these strategies were not revolutionary in themselves, the novelty with which they were executed has gone largely unremarked.

One reason is fairly obvious. For Crane and Dos Passos to invite comparison with great predecessors, as Cowley suggests in the statement quoted at the beginning of this essay, was to invite misunderstanding, particularly when so many of their contemporaries saw literature as embattled.[17] American writers in the third and fourth decades of this century faced cultural competition from industrial designers transforming automobiles and plumbing into objects of beauty, visual artists abstracting a modernist aesthetic from images of turbines and smokestacks, and physicists graphing field discontinuities that appeared to extend into consciousness itself.[18] The Poetic Renaissance, which began in 1912, reinvigorated American poetry to a certain extent but could not recapture territory lost over a quarter-century of creative sterility. Engineers had permanently displaced autocrats of the breakfast table in popular esteem, while scientists had acquired even greater standing. The authority of scientists appeared to rest on knowledge acquired by methods that—to some humanists, at least—appeared arrogant if not downright inhuman. Moreover, nearly everyone conflated science with technology and believed that scientific knowledge was readily convertible to materialism. Although neither Crane nor Dos Passos endorsed the worrisome social effects of the "bastard children" of science,[19] as Dos Passos called industrialization and mechanization, they knew that agendas for America were being set on blackboards and in laboratories as well as in factories. They thought that practical and artistic reasons compelled the writer to address that fact.

Thus, in one of the supreme acts of moral and aesthethic faith in American letters, Hart Crane asserted the fundamental unity of all forms of human creativity, whether manifest as science, technology, or art. More important, unlike other artists who might pay lip service to such asser-tions, Crane *meant* it. And in a radical revision of the American novel, John Dos Passos demonstrated that fictional narratives could code a culture's scientific messages despite their incomprehensibility to the lay-man. *U.S.A.* is perhaps the first novel of the information age. Yet when Crane and Dos Passos opened their literature to science, and to the technology they understood as allied to science, they opened themselves to accusations that still surface today. Put simply, their reputations have been undermined precisely by their attempts to incorporate in their work a science regarded by literary critics as either artistically foreign or politically suspect.

Even a sympathetic critic like Hyatt Waggoner, for example, while sure that Crane translated science into poetry more brilliantly than any other poet of his time, faults *The Bridge* because it suffers by comparison with "the great religious and mythic poems" of the past.[20] The standard view of Crane is that he was an untutored genius, the most junior in talent of the small group of modernists that includes Pound and Eliot. The latter's reactionary disdain for science and for the information explosion ("Where is the knowledge we have lost in information?" Eliot asks in *The Rock*) has long set the tone for criticism, so that Crane's lack of hostility toward science and his embrace of the virtues of machinery still make humanists uneasy. Because Crane himself emphasized his affinities with the Roman-tics, a connection reinforced by his fairly lurid personal life, some literary historians charge him with betraying that tradition when he exalted the aesthetics of technology. Typical is the sneer of Derek Savage: "Crane accepted without question the centralized, top-heavy industrial environ-ment, tagging along behind the racketeers and financiers whose creation it all was."[21]

Drawing that conclusion from *The Bridge* requires prejudices that the apolitical Crane lacked, and requires also a blindness to the poem's comic passages linking "SCIENCE—COMMERCE and the HOLYGHOST" in "The River" section. Culturally it was quite impossible to distinguish

science from technology, nor did Crane wish to. He did try to separate
technology from industrialization, not to free it from sin but to differenti-
ate tool-making as an aesthetic and moral activity from managerial,
commercial, and political contexts. He was socially naive perhaps, certainly by comparison with Dos Passos, and historically naive as well, but
he was consistent in his account of what was, after all, the spiritual
evolution not so much of a nation as a continent of consciousness, a
progression, moreover, set against a cosmic background. In the "Cape
Hatteras" section of *The Bridge,* he sketches the history of the American
continent in images of upwelling geological strata:

> Imponderable the dinosaur
> > sinks slow,
> > > the mammoth saurian
> > > > ghoul, the eastern
> > > > > Cape . . .
> While rises in the west the coastwise range,
> > slowly the hushed land—
> Combustion at the astral core—the dorsal change
> Of energy—convulsive shift of sand . . . [88]

That is cosmological time, not history, the precess of nature, not human
endeavor, observation as rapture, not analysis. Crane's vision of science is
mystical, beginning with "the immaculate sigh of stars" that opens the
poem.

Numerous critics have identified *The Bridge*'s theme as one common to all
great literature and science: the dynamic between order and chaos. But
despite the religious aspects of the poem, Crane chose to represent neither
natural chaos or urban confusion nor corporate order or political control as
evil. Knowledge is neither good nor evil; his is an exercise in physics rather
than social comment. Whatever else could be said of science, Crane knew,
it had changed the consciousness and the environment of Americans.
That was why he called for poetic "readjustments incident to science and
other shifting factors related to that consciousness"[22] of integrated experience.

Dos Passos's receptivity to science and technology has not helped his
standing either. Jean-Paul Sartre, aware that a fascination with science
permeates Dos Passos's work, says that the American's novels "are to the

classic works of Flaubert and Zola what the non-euclidian geometry is to the old geometry of Euclid."[23] But most critics, judging him inevitably by the predecessors Dos Passos himself sometimes invoked, think of him precisely as a failed Zola, convinced that he was a naturalist who lacked the courage to make his novels wholly deterministic. The stock view of Dos Passos is that he was really a journalist, the originator of several brilliant narrative techniques, but at base a closet conservative who dissipated his energies in writing patriotic histories of the nation's founding fathers. Worse, some critics will not forgive Dos Passos for what they believe is his betrayal of a different kind of "science," the Marxist historical analysis to which he was attracted in his youth, despite his mature arguments that such analysis was inadequate to deal with evolving capitalist structures.

Generally speaking, Dos Passos *was* sympathetic to social programs formulated on the political left, but he thought literature could be suborned by ideology: "At this particular moment in history, when machinery and institutions have so outgrown the ability of the mind to dominate them, we need bold and original thought more than ever. It is the business of writers to supply that thought, and not to make of themselves figureheads in political conflicts."[24] In another essay (in which he also said that "art is an adjective not a noun"), he claimed that becoming a socialist was like drinking near-beer.[25] Dos Passos came to believe that Marxism's pseudo-scientific "objective reality" was essentially a nineteenth-century anachronism. Far more sophisticated about economics than the average Marxist, Dos Passos realized that information was becoming the real capital of corporate America, and that the most valuable information was that derived from genuine scientific achievement. For Dos Passos, science interacted with culture chiefly in the marketplace, the reason that he said "it's about time that American writers showed up in the industrial field where something is really going on, instead of tackling the tattered strawmen of art and culture."[26] At the very least, literature had to enlarge its focus, even though this placed heavy demands on the writer.

The writer of the twenties and thirties who wished to acknowledge that science was an engine of culture faced several difficulties in translating scientific abstractions into literary representations. The first had to do with the legitimacy of his role. From the 1890s well into the 1930s, hundreds of books and essays interpreted the discoveries of science and their cultural impact for wide American audiences.[27] It is easy to find mainstream writers who joined in the popular enthusiasm. Even Edith Wharton, whose social terrain seems improbable ground for such ebullience, could burble about "the wonder-world of nineteenth century science" that overwhelmed "our little geocentric universe,"[28] but what made nineteenth-century science so wondrous to Wharton and others like her was their own unfamiliarity with it. Retrograde scientism actually precluded genuine consideration of what science was about in the twentieth century, or so it appeared to those impatient with writers of high literature. Perhaps the most explicit attack came from Max Eastman, whose *The Literary Mind: Its Place in an Age of Science* (1931) charged poets and novelists with deliberate misunderstanding of scientific developments. Yet literature had its defenders, sometimes on the opposite side of the aisle. The most articulate was Alfred North Whitehead, whose *Science and the Modern World* (1925) was extremely influential. That Hart Crane read it is certain;[29] Dos Passos doubtless knew it also. In that volume, Whitehead announced a thesis that has since become familiar: that the Romantic Movement had been essentially a reaction against overly rational concepts, especially their configuration into a mechanistic model of the universe, and that the new insights of physics had confirmed the writer's preference for more organic constructs. What Whitehead did, said Edmund Wilson in his gloss on the philospher's text in *Axel's Castle*, was to restore to the writer a metaphysical legitimacy, for it was clear that modern physics had rejected mechanical models as well. The Romantic poets stood validated as upholders of reality after all, heroes of intuition; to use a political term later employed by the left, William Blake and his colleagues had been "premature anti-fascists" of the metaphysical realm and were now rehabilitated by scientific orthodoxy. In short, Whitehead implied, poets and novelists were entitled to comment on the work of scientists.

A second difficulty facing the writer convinced that he must assimilate science involved expertise. Despite the imprimatur Whitehead gave to writers, neither Crane nor Dos Passos engaged science directly. Dos Passos, born three years earlier than Crane, lived three decades longer, and thus had more time to comprehend the changes that science wrought on America; one of the novelist's more astute essays was a 1952 interview with J. Robert Oppenheimer, "Science Under Siege," in which Dos Passos acknowledged that the process of discovery would always force the revaluation of culture itself.[30] Unlike Crane, who never went to college and envied acquaintances who had, Dos Passos attended Harvard, where he ranked a course in the history of science as highly as one on Chaucer.[31] Even so, his familiarity with scientific matters was essentially that of an undergraduate.

In this regard, Crane and Dos Passos can be contrasted with Henry Adams, who actually read scientific texts, conversed as an equal with Willard Gibbs, easily followed statistical arguments, and could apply the laws of thermodynamics to history. Yet the examples of Crane and Dos Passos are reminders that a writer, so long as he is sensitive to the total text of his culture, has no special obligation to read lab reports or scientific documents. That Crane and Dos Passos in their works drew conclusions of more enduring relevance than Adams may rest on the relative merits for the poet or novelist of broad cultural versus specific scientific literacy. Dos Passos could see, for instance, that Adams had overdramatized the cultural disruptions of science. In 1921, on board ship to Europe with e.e. cummings, Dos Passos read *The Degradation of the Democratic Dogma,* edited by Henry's brother, Brooks Adams, and, "because it went against the Walt Whitman-narodnik optimism about people I've never quite lived down," spent part of his voyage trying to refute the historian's thesis.[32] Dos Passos could be optimistic if only because it was clear that civilization had survived global catastrophe as well as the lesser types of entropy that Adams feared.

Dos Passos's reference to Whitman is a reminder of the constant consciousness of past masters that Malcolm Cowley discerned in the ambition of both Dos Passos and Crane. Again and again Crane apostrophizes Whitman ("My hand / in yours, / Walt Whitman— / so—") in *The Bridge,* invoking his syncretic vision. Like Crane and Dos Passos, the good gray poet had addressed the whole of American culture, had tried to reconcile science and religion, industrialization and idealism, Romanticism and rationality. The poetic polarities of order and chaos in *The Bridge* only superficially resemble those explored by Adams in *Mont St. Michel and Chartres* and *The Education*; Crane is far more indebted to Whitman's "Passage to India" and even to "Song of Myself" both of which coded enormous quantities of information in verse form. For all his scientific literacy, Adams could not anticipate the historical process by which the insights of thermodynamics would begin to flower into an information theory that would account for his multiplicities. Through experimentation with meter and with metaphor, Crane sought to expand the storage and display capacity of poetry to accomodate multiple bits of information, while Dos Passos would make similar multiplicities into the stuff of fiction.

A third difficulty had to do with what sort of subject matter, exactly, the writer sympathetic to science was supposed to try to assimilate! Here Crane and Dos Passos understood something important about science that most of their literary colleagues did not: that science is not monolithic. Although both often construed "science" in conventional generalized terms, more or less as objective method or hard-edged rationality, they were aware that scientific hierarchies were being realigned. The major disciplines were fluctuating against one another in terms of their relative standing within the scientific community and within the larger context of American culture.

For example, developments in physical chemistry held considerable relevance for a wide range of other sciences, but organic chemistry was almost entirely industry-driven, with American corporations frenetically competing with German combines to patent dye and polymer formulas. The industrialization of chemistry meant that Americans felt its effects chiefly as consumers. It was scarcely possible to speak of the discipline without reference to the physical technologies that created its compounds and the corporate technologies that distributed its products.[33] Such associations virtually ensured that no writer would deal with chemistry, for to do so meant that he had to dirty his hands with a tainted industrialism.[34] In other words, chemistry was basic and powerful, but its lack of theoretical glamour denied it high rank among scientists and the lay public.

Whitehead and other arbiters gave primacy among the sciences to the "new" physics, whose paradoxes were cosmologically intoxicating, especially since they were identified with the awesome intellect of Albert Einstein, who was to become one of the country's chief cultural deities. Einstein's public image was that of a loveable fuddy-duddy who just happened to be another Isaac Newton; Crane referred to him as the grandson of Spinoza,[35] wise and pantheistic.[36] But the cultural accession of physics took place at the expense of biology, whose influence on American literature over the last fifty years had been profound. Although he was friendly with the Harvard bacteriologist Hans Zinsser,[37] and although he wrote an exceptionally sympathetic review of James Whalen's *Green River*,[38] a narrative poem based on the career of the great naturalist Constantine Raffinesque, Crane made little use of biology in his own work. In fact, he construed modern science chiefly as physics. The fiction of Dos Passos, on the other hand, provides perspective on the shifting status of biology and physics. That different disciplines influenced the two men had something to do with their respective educations but even more with their choice of literary genres; poets as a group are probably less interested than novelists in biology.

Darwin's *The Origin of Species* (1859) was the last major scientific text fully accessible to the average man, a factor that explains not only the longevity of debate over evolution but also the popularity of Social Darwinism. Social Darwinism, in turn, grew out of the conflation of an evolutionary scheme extrapolated from Darwin with thermodynamic principles extrapolated from Joule, Helmholtz, and Kelvin. While biologists themselves usually sidestepped questions of determinism, Herbert Spencer and popularizers of Social Darwinism like John Fiske and Edward Youmans in America did not. Spencer applied deterministic schemes not only to biology but also to sociology and psychology,[39] and Freud would later enshrine thermodynamic concepts in his steam-engine model of the psyche, with a superego governor regulating the energies of the id. Ronald Martin has traced the outlines of what he calls "the universe of force" by studying the accretions of metaphor in the works of Herbert Spencer, Henry Adams, and various novelists. Metaphors of force fueled the fiction of Norris, London, and Dreiser in particular and American literary naturalism in general.[40] Naturalism waned, however, as animal morphology gave way to cytology and as thermodynamics lost ground to more glamourous particle research. By 1900, with the rediscovery of Mendel's work on genetics and its confirmation of evolutionary theory, biology became thoroughly professionalized, and the opinions of amateurs—writers or otherwise—soon ceased to affect the discipline. Geneticists closed their laboratory doors, and their research receded from public view, save for occasional bulletins from the Ernest Haeckels and J.B.S. Haldanes.[41] When not diverted by flamboyant ministers still fighting evolutionist-creationist battles already lost, Americans now thought of biology chiefly in terms of the succession of new botanical products that appeared from the greenhouses of Luther Burbank.

Luther Burbank figures (in one of the "biographies") in U.S.A., as does Rockefeller's funding for departments of anatomy, botany, neurology, physiology, and zoology at the University of Chicago. But Dos Passos did not fully grasp the significance of such developments. Rather, his narratives reflect the lessening influence of nineteenth-century models of social force: numerous critics have noted that his fiction seems informed by a residual literary naturalism rather pale beside Dreiser's or Farrell's. For Dos Passos, forces are the usual ones: childhood traumas and family obsessions, sexual drives, repressive educational and religious institutions, cleavages of class and disparities of income, politicized unions and greedy corporations. Those forces do influence the lives of the characters in U.S.A., but not in classically causal ways; they do not so much extrude personalities as add dimension to them.

Indeed, Dos Passos in the trilogy sketches biological and social forces crudely, even impatiently, because he is himself uncertain of their weight. When the inarticulate Joe Williams complains that the wealthy exploit the workers, or when Mac writes pamphlets for the I.W.W. attributing political and economic control to corrupt alliances between business and government, they are mouthing slogans that are largely reflex; the slogans hold truth, but constitute no platform for social change. In fact, most of the characters are aimless, alienated, their opinions impoverished by lack of conviction. They drift mentally as well because they are unable to locate the sources of power—for liberation·or oppression—in any concrete institution or agency; if anything, there are too many targets for their resentment. In their atomistic world, behavior is probable, not determined—statistically predictable, not certain. One critic has applied the term "Brownian motion" to the erratic behavior of Dos Passos's characters in *Manhattan Transfer*, [42] and it is an even more accurate description of the pathways in *U.S.A.*

In the early twentieth century, statistical methods, like those generated by study of Brownian motion and refined by their application to thermodynamic processes, proved even more useful in their application to particle research. As Planck, de Broglie, and Schrödinger quantized energy, their successors calculated probabilities. The emphasis on probability, in turn, undermined concepts of determinism, and—at a cultural distance—revised notions of character in fiction. If to the Greek dramatist character had been destiny, to the nineteenth-century novelist character was biology: personality was the product of heredity and an environment of measurable vectors. But to the twentieth-century novelist like Dos Passos, the individual was far more problematic, his consciousness more diffuse, his responses less dependent on specific stimuli, his actions more random. Gauged against older fictional standards, a modern character seems attenuated, his surfaces smoothed by the friction of a highly fragmented culture. Increasingly, he occupies multiple states. He will intersect with one character but deflect another because of their different masses and speeds. But the cultural ground is different too. Where classic literary naturalism constructs an environment out of forces, Dos Passos builds an environment of mediated messages. Corporations and institutions operate—and oppress—as much through their manipulation of information as through the traditional inequities of production. [43]

While Dos Passos could hardly have anticipated that thermodynamics would furnish the statistical tools for measuring information and for deciphering languages of all kinds (including the genetic code) in the forties and fifties, he was extraordinarily sensitive to the volume of messages carried by various media. Marshall McLuhan patronizes Dos Passos by accusing him (among other things) of holding a Frank Capra view of life, comes close to saying that the most noteworthy feature of *U.S.A.* is the sheer mass of information that no other "American had ever been able to master," and then, as might be expected, diverts his attention to the "cinematic velocity of images" in the novel.[44] McLuhan learned more than he knew from Dos Passos, especially from Dos Passos's use of "discontinuity as a means of enriching artistic effect."[45]

The discontinuities are brilliant and numerous—a dozen major narratives intercut with sixty-eight "Newsreels," twenty-seven "Biographies," and fifty-one "Camera Eye" segments. Aside from providing information as bits of jargon, ideologies, gossip, slogans, clichés, headline, pictures, radio broadcasts, recordings, comic strips, movies, and popular songs, they underline the pervasiveness of communication technologies as they filter messages, restructure the environment, and shape cultural and personal awareness. Dos Passos understood, as have few American writers before or since, that the surges of information through channels of mass media like radio, movies, and newspapers literally *rewrote* American culture every morning. Science was only one source of information, part of the flood conveyed by media that were becoming the new corporate structures of America. *Manhattan Transfer* deals at length with the prostitution of the press and the "making" of news.[46] Among the most important characters in *U.S.A.* are journalists whose idealism sours to cynicism, and J. Ward Moorehouse, a public relations agent for corporations who manipulates the media and deals in information as a commodity. This traffic becomes Dos Passos's metaphor for modern American capitalism, grafted onto and gradually replacing industrial models.

Biology, then, led Dos Passos by a circuitous route to information technologies. Crane followed a somewhat different path from physics. One effect of the new physics on novelists was to revise their conception of character and motion. The effect on poets was to force their confrontation with the nature of language and with metaphor. In a way, the influence of biology encourages a literary focus on inner, subjective experience, as a ground for the external forces operating outside the individual. By contrast, the influence of physics fosters an expressionistic concentration on external energies that are understood as correlatives of inner states, all of which are colored by semantics. To poets like Crane, William Carlos Williams, and Wallace Stevens, the paradoxes of Werner Heisenberg and

Niels Bohr restored a sense of mystery if not to the world then at least to language. Late-nineteenth-century positivists like Poincare, Mach, and Pearson had tried to purge language of metaphor; the Principles of Complementarity and Indeterminacy affirmed the indispensability of metaphor. Seeking precision, postivists measured phenomena on a gray scale of rationalism; balked by the limitations of measurement, quantum physicists demanded an electromagnetic spectrum of many shades. Poets like Williams chose to interpret these new priorities in physics as an endorsement of the poet's subjectivity. As Lisa Steinman has pointed out, however, Williams and other poets of Crane's period made only token efforts to assimilate science and seemed motivated more by an envy of the salaries of engineers and the glamour of the laboratory.[47]

Unlike them, Crane was attracted principally by the aesthetics of physics. Both Dos Passos and Crane were less interested in acquiring the sanction of science for what they wrote than they were of placing science itself in a proper context. Crane's goal in writing The Bridge, he told his patron Otto Kahn, was to "enunciate a new cultural synthesis of values in terms of our America,"[48] and he chose a technological symbol that represented "the conquest of space and knowledge."[49] Although at first the Bridge in its very spatiality seems to hearken back to Newtonian cosmology, it is clear from the "Cape Hatteras" section of the poem that Crane's allegiance is to Einstein, and that the Bridge is curved by the dynamics of a relativistic world:

> But that star-glistered salver of infinity,
> The circle, blind crucible of endless space,
> Is sluiced by motion,—subjugated never. [89]

That he also meant the Bridge to embody human knowledge can be understood from his discussion of the "logic of metaphor" included in his essay, "General Aims and Theories." Metaphor, he said there, is "the genetic basis of all speech, hence consciousness and thought-extension." The poet was especially equipped to deal with new knowledge because he was an expert in language, the most primal of all technologies and the one common to all arts and sciences: "New conditions of life germinate new forms of spiritual articulation. And while I feel that my work includes a more consistent extension of traditional literary elements than many contemporary poets are capable of appraising, I realize that I am utilizing the gifts of the past as instruments principally; and that the voice of the present, if it is to be known, must be caught at the risk of speaking in idioms and circumlocutions sometimes shocking to the scholar and historians of logic. Language has built towers and bridges, but itself is inevitably as fluid as always."[50]

Such passages are crucial to assessing the lasting value of *The Bridge* because they reflect Crane's understanding of language as a technology. It is easy to be diverted by the machine images of the poem. Somewhat ironically, Crane aspired to be "the Pindar of the machine age" just as the machine age was beginning to close, to be superseded by the information age.[51] Victor Ferkiss has described the transition from one age to another in terms that Crane would have found comprehensible:

> [In the new era] energy is still utilized, but increasingly it is used to affect states of consciousness rather than to move physical objects. Though machines abound, there is a sense, not clearly grasped by all prophets of the new, that the age of mechanization is over. Not levers and pulleys exerting force but sounds in the air, lights flashing on the dial of the computer, are the archetypal symbols of the new era, and electronics rather than mechanical physics is supreme. . . . For the instruments of the new technology are like the human body in having few rigid moving parts; as in the biological organism, what is most important is not forces but process.[52]

Another way of understanding that *process* is as energy—in this case, *energy* defined as communication within systems. It would be silly to claim that Crane fully foresaw the dimensions of that shift in metaphor. His notion of process and organicism, noted by many critics, was derived mostly from Whitehead, with significant additions from the mystic Ouspensky.[53] But his intuition was faultless. He conceptualized energy as language, as in this passage:

> The nasal whine of power whips a new universe . . .
> Where spouting pillars spoor the evening sky,
> Under the looming stacks of the gigantic power house
> Stars prick the eyes with sharp ammoniac proverbs,
> New verities, new inklings in the velvet hummed
> Of dynamos, where hearing's leash is strummed . . .
> Power's script—wound, bobbin-bound, refined—
> Is stropped to the slap of belts on booming spools,
>   spurred
> Into the bulging bouillon, harnessed jelly of the stars. [90]

For Crane, as Frederick Hoffman has remarked, "power's script" is a lower-case language.[54] In that respect, Crane's use of technological imagery seems to embody John Kouwenhoven's thesis that the design and fabrication of machines have traditionally constituted an American vernacular.[55] In any case, there is no question that Crane saw technology as did McLuhan a few decades later, as "the extensions of man," nor that he bestowed iconographic status upon machines. In *The Bridge*, technology serves as a demotic plane where art and science can meet, a vernacular where spirituality can converge with everyday secular life, a non-Latinate version of the Mass. Things can bear intellectual and emotional weight because they are elements in Crane's poetic language. Moreover, arching over the more prosaic acetylene torches, subways, elevators, jackhammers, steam engines, and so on is the great Bridge itself, which Crane conceived as a communications medium, a literal passageway and route of transportation, but also a symbol of human interchange, its linkages multiplied by other transmission technologies:

> The last bear, shot drinking in the Dakotas
> Loped under wires that span the mountain stream.
> Keen instruments, strung to a vast precision
> Bind town to town and dream to tickling dream. [64]

And messages are everywhere, forming an environment:

> I think of cinemas, panoramic sleights
> With multitudes bent toward some flashing scene
> Never disclosed, but hastened to again
> Foretold to other eyes on the same screen. [45]

In his introduction to *U.S.A.*, Dos Passos, like Crane, focused on metaphor and language, the tools of the writer and the stuff of his work:

U.S.A. is the slice of the continent. U.S.A. is a group of holding companies, some aggregations of trade unions, a set of laws bound in calf, a radio network, a chain of moving picture theatres, a column of stock-quotations rubbed out and written in by a Western Union boy on a blackboard, a public library full of old newspapers and dogeared historybooks with protests scrawled on the margins in pencil. U.S.A. is the world's greatest rivervalley fringed with mountains and hills. U.S.A. is a set of bigmouthed officials with too many bank accounts. U.S.A. is a lot of men buried in their uniforms in Arlington

Cemetery. U.S.A. is the letters at the end of an address when you are away from home. But mostly U.S.A. is the speech of the people.[56]

Dos Passos was even more explicit about the writer's technology. He drew parallels between the scientist and the writer, and suggested that both "produced" knowledge and interpretations that were commercial commodities as well as art or science: "The professional writer discovers some aspect of the world and invents out of the speech of his time some particularly apt and original way of putting it down on paper. If the product is compelling enough, it molds and influences ways of thinking to the point of changing and rebuilding the language, which canalizes the mind of the group. The process is not very different from that of scientific discovery and invention. The importance of a writer, as of a scientist, depends on his ability to influence thought."[57]

His acceptance of a technological role for the writer does not necessarily mean that Dos Passos construed his novels as machines, nor his characters as interchangeable parts, as Cecilia Tichi has recently maintained.[58] To call him an engineer-novelist, as Tichi does, is to overstate. A poet like William Carlos Williams could toss off a line such as "a poem is a machine made of words,"[59] but deep down, Williams hated technology, or what he thought of as technology, and he used the line in part because it was inappropriate; there is a vast difference between mechanical models and linguistic technologies. The structure of Dos Passos's narrative was metaphorically based on information-processing rather than industrial machinery. As we have seen, Dos Passos was intensely sympathetic to socialist critiques of corporate capitalism, but he was already impatient with the hackneyed cliches that charged industrialization with turning humans into "cogs in a machine" or making of them "interchangeable parts on an assembly line." Dos Passos understood that technology— defined as simple tool, complex machine, as management, production, distribution, advertising, or selling of products—essentially embodied knowledge. He had no quarrel with technology per se, but he chafed at the greed that transformed it: he reacted against privileged information, such as that held by corporations. His critique of capitalism was directed at proprietary knowledge as opposed to shared. That is why he could so admire the great inventor-scientist Steinmetz: Steinmetz's mathematics "was a closed garden, free from corruption and death as the New Jerusalem of the early Christians, where he was absolute god and master. If he'd been a less warm-blooded man, that would have been enough, but he wanted

real life, too. So it was inevitable that he should become a social revolu-
tionist. . . . He was of the race of those who do not cash in."[60] When he
translated this portrait into *The 42nd Parallel*, he added that "Steinmetz
was the most valuable piece of apparatus General Electric had / until he
wore out and died." General Electric had "let him be a Socialist and
believe that human society could be improved the way you can improve a
dynamo, and they let him be pro-German and write a letter offering his
services to Lenin because mathematicians are so impractical who make up
formulas by which you can build powerplants, factories, subway systems,
light air, sunshine, but not human relations that affect the stockholders'
money and the directors' salaries" (335, 334). But that did not make
Steinmetz a cog. If General Electric owned Steinmetz's research, still his
knowledge was "purer" than that of the company's founder, the inventor-
entrepreneur Thomas Edison (also the subject of "biography"); the two
were different. Similar corporate strategies had already turned literature,
including Dos Passos's own, into a commodity,[61] and he probably realized
that corporations in an information age tolerated his social ideas much as
they tolerated Steinmetz's, but Dos Passos, like the rest of us, discriminated
between messages and ideas, despite the ultimate commercialization of all
of them. Despise capitalism though he might, Dos Passos respected its art.
Not that he had much choice. After *U.S.A.*, Dos Passos spent much of his
career trying to unravel what had gone wrong, turning backward to
Jefferson and to Jefferson's hope that knowledge could be shared, not
patented or made profitable, in books like *The Head and Heart of Thomas
Jefferson* (1954) and his series of volumes on the Founding Fathers.

   Their grapplings with language and their perceptions that language *is*
reality do not make Crane and Dos Passos postmodernists, although they
were remarkably prescient. They understood not only that messages articulate an environment but also that the speed and the volume of channels
of communication mediate that environment.

   That environment was increasingly defined by the messages embodied
in science and technology, and to understand them was to understand the
culture. Crane articulated this point in a letter to Harriet Monroe: "Hasn't
it often occurred that instruments originally invented for record and
computation have inadvertently so extended the concepts of the entity
they were intended to measure (concepts of space, etc.) in the mind and
imagination that employed them, that they may metaphorically be said to
have extended the original boundaries of the entity measured? This little
bit of 'relativity' ought not to be discredited in poetry now that scientists

are proceeding to measure the universe on principles of pure *ratio,* quite as metaphorical, so far as previous standards of scientific methods extended, as some of the axioms in Job."[62] Crane's own instruments extended the curve of heaven. His is a universe beautiful in the knowledge that informs it, its outlines mirrored in the artificiality of a technological landscape, rendered by a technician of the sacred. For all that Dos Passos's symbolism seems more compelling, he remains a chronicler while Crane speaks as a prophet. The *U.S.A.* trilogy explores a spectrum of life in the United States fully three decades wide because he chose as his metaphor information technologies acting less over space than over time. Literary historians are only now beginning to understand just how severely a rapidly changing science challenged the literary and political assumptions of the twenties. What invests these two writers with lasting value is the urgency of their need to respond, to experiment, and to achieve in an age of cultural transition. Those qualities—and their honesty—make it possible for modern audiences to read their texts as documents for their own time, but also for the future they feared.

Notes

1. Malcolm Cowley, *After the Genteel Tradition: American Writers 1910-1930* (Carbondale: Southern Illinois Univ. Press, 1964), 182.

2. See, for example, John Dos Passos, "A Humble Protest," *Harvard Monthly* 62 (June 1916): 116; Crane's numerous references to science as religion require no citation.

3. Hart Crane to Isidor Schneider, Mar. 28, 1928, *The Letters of Hart Crane, 1916-1932,* ed. Brom Weber (Berkeley: Univ. of California Press, 1965), 222.

4. John Dos Passos, "Against American Literature," *New Republic* 8 (Oct. 14, 1916): 270.

5. Hart Crane, *The Complete Poems and Selected Letters and Prose of Hart Crane,* ed. Brom Weber (New York: Liveright, 1966), 218.

6. Hart Crane to Waldo Frank, Mar. 4, 1928, in *Letters,* 319.

7. Hart Crane, "The Bridge," in *Complete Poems,* 46; all subsequent references to this edition of *The Bridge* will be cited parenthetically in my text.

8. John Dos Passos, "A Question of Elbow Room," in *Occasions and Protests* (New York: Henry Regnery, 1964), 62.

9. Hart Crane, "Modern Poetry [1930]," in *Complete Poems,* 261. From time to time, Crane voiced fears that science would diminish the human spirit. As he wrote in a book review, "science, grown uncontrollable, has assumed a grin that has more than threatened the supposed civilization that fed it; science has brought light,—but it threatens to destroy the idea of reverence, the source of all light. Its despotism recognizes no limits" (Ibid., 201).

10. Hart Crane to Gorham Munson, Mar. 2, 1923, in *Letters,* 129.

11. Hart Crane to Gorham Munson, Feb. 18, 1923, in *Letters,* 124.

12. Dos Passos, "Humble Protest," 116.

13. Hart Crane to Gorham Munson, Mar. 17, 1926, in *Complete Poems*, 225-26.

14. John Dos Passos, "The Writer as Technician," in Henry Hart, ed., *American Writers Conference* (New York: International Publishers, 1935), 82. Crane said pretty much the same thing in his essay "Modern Poetry," when he remarked that "human values remain essentially immune from any of the so-called inroads of science," in *Complete Poems*, 261.

15. In the recent (Feb. 28, 1988) PBS broadcast of "Hart Crane," one of the series called "Voices and Visions," the poet Derek Walcott spoke of "'the conditional' of Eliot and Pound—the 'what should be,'" as opposed to Crane's practice of speaking "of what is now."

16. Gerald Holton, "Introduction," in Gerald Holton, ed., *Science and Culture: A Study of Cohesive and Disjunctive Forces* (Boston: Beacon, 1967), viii.

17. Alan Trachtenberg calls Crane "embattled" in his introduction to *Hart Crane: A Collection of Critical Essays*, ed. Alan Trachtenberg (Englewood Cliffs, N.J.: Prentice Hall, 1982), 12.

18. Recent works to address this cultural matrix are Cecelia Tichi's *Shifting Gears: Technology, Literature, Culture in Modernist America* (Chapel Hill: Univ. of North Carolina Press, 1987), and Lisa Steinman's *Made in America: Science, Technology, and American Modernist Poets* (New Haven: Yale Univ. Press, 1987). For general background, see also Stephen Kern's *The Culture of Time and Space, 1880-1918* (Cambridge, Mass.: Harvard Univ. Press, 1983). The influence of technology, and, to a lesser extent, science, on the culture at large was traced by the fall 1986 exhibit at the Brooklyn Museum called "The Machine Age in America 1918-1941"; for a review of that exhibit see Phil Patton, "How Art Geared Up to Face Industry in Modern America," *Smithsonian* 17 (Nov. 1986): 156-67.

19. Dos Passos, "Humble Protest," 119, and many other places.

20. Hyatt Howe Waggoner, *The Heel of Elohim: Science and Values in Modern American Poetry* (Norman: Univ. of Oklahoma Press, 1950), 190. The standard biography of Crane is John Unterecker's *Voyager: A Life of Hart Crane* (New York: Farrar, Straus and Giroux, 1969).

21. Derek Savage, "The Americanism of Hart Crane," in Trachtenberg, *Crane Collection*, 48; this collection offers a wide sampling of criticism.

22. Crane, "Modern Poetry," in *Complete Poems*, 260.

23. Jean-Paul Sartre, "American Novelists in French Eyes," *Atlantic Monthly* 178 (Aug. 1946): 117. The most recent book on Dos Passos, though one that scarcely considers his interest in science, is Linda Welshimer Wagner's *Dos Passos: Artist as American* (Austin: Univ. of Texas Press, 1979). Interesting is Robert C. Rosen's *John Dos Passos: Politics and the Writer* (Lincoln: Univ. of Nebraska Press, 1981). John D. Brantley's *The Fiction of John Dos Passos* (The Hague: Mouton, 1968) deals with machine imagery in the fiction.

24. Dos Passos, "Writer as Technician," 81.

25. Dos Passos, "Whither the American Writer? A Questionaire," *Modern Quarterly* 6 (Summer 1932): 11-12.

26. John Dos Passos, "Edison and Steinmetz: Medicine Men," *New Republic* 61 (Dec. 18, 1929): 105.

27. See Frederick J. Hoffman, "Science and the 'Precious Object,'" *The Twenties: American Writing in the Postwar Decade*, rev. ed. (New York: Free Press, 1965), 275-78.

28. Edith Wharton, *A Backward Glance* (New York: Appleton-Century 1934), 94.

29. Crane, *Letters*, 322; see also 235, where he says he is reading *Science and the Modern World* (New York: Macmillan, 1925).

30. The interview is reprinted in *Occasions and Protests*, 145-52.

31. John Dos Passos, "The Harvard Afterglow," in *Occasions and Protests*, 17.

32. John Dos Passos, *The Best of Times* (New York: Signet, 1966), 102.

33. For more on the developments in American chemistry, see Dean Stanley Tarbell and Ann Tracy Tarbell, *Essays on the History of Organic Chemistry in the United States, 1875-1955* (Nashville: Folio, 1986).

34. Nor would any American writer make significant use of chemistry until Thomas Pynchon, in *Gravity's Rainbow*.

35. Hart Crane to Solomon Grunberg, Jan. 10, 1931, in *Letters*, 363.

36. Even today this image persists. The memorial statue to Einstein in Washington depicts him in the attitude of Lewis Carroll. Children clamber on the form much as they swarm over the Alice in Wonderland sculpture in New York's Central Park.

37. Hart Crane to Samuel Lovemen, Apr. 12, 1931, in *Letters*, 368.

38. Hart Crane, "From Haunts of Proserpine," in *Complete Poems*, 264-66.

39. A list of Spencer's principal works illustrates the degree to which fledgling sciences were shaped by these notions: *The Principles of Psychology* (1855), *First Principles* (1862), *The Principles of Biology* (1864), *The Principles of Sociology*, 3 vols. (1876-1896), *The Principles of Ethics*, 2 vols. (1892, 1893).

40. Ronald Martin, *American Literature and the Universe of Force* (Durham, N.C.: Duke Univ. Press, 1981).

41. For a historical review of German biology, which casts some light on American developments, see Lynn Nyhart, "The Disciplinary Breakdown of German Morphology, 1870-1900," *Isis* 78 (Sept. 1987): 365-89.

42. Iain Colley, *Dos Passos and the Fiction of Despair* (Totowa, N.J.: Rowan and Littlefield, 1978), 49.

43. Dos Passos enjoyed a kind of insider's knowledge passed on by his father (1844-1917) of the workings of American capitalism; see the elder man's analysis in John Randolph Dos Passos, *Commercial Trusts: The Growth and Rights of Aggregated Capital, An Argument Delivered Before the Industrial Commission at Washington, D.C., December 12, 1899* (New York: Putnam's Sons, 1901).

44. Herbert Marshall McLuhan, "John Dos Passos: Technique Versus Sensibility," in Harold C. Gardiner, S.J., ed., *Fifty Years of the American Novel: A Christian Appraisal* (New York: Scribner's, 1951), 157, 154. The crack about Dos Passos and Capra is on p. 164. The essay is a by-product of McLuhan's most Catholic phase.

45. Ibid., 157.

46. See, for example, John Dos Passos, *Manhattan Transfer* (1925; rpt., New York: Houghton Mifflin, 1953), 195. An excellent study of the influence of journalism on Dos Passos's fiction is included in Shelley Fisher Fishkin, *From Fact to Fiction: Journalism and Imaginative Writing in America* (Baltimore: Johns Hopkins Univ. Press, 1985).

47. See Steinman, *Made in America*. She mentions essays by Williams on "The Poem as a Field of Activity" and digressions on the role of the variable foot in verse as suggested by the radium experiments of the Curies.

48. Hart Crane to Otto Kahn, Dec. 3, 1925, in *Letters*, 223.

49. Hart Crane to Otto Kahn, Mar. 18, 1926, in *Letters*, 241.

50. Hart Crane, "General Aims and Theories," in *Complete Poems*, 222-23.

51. See K.G. Pontus Hulten, *The Machine As Seen at the End of the Mechanical Age* (New York: Museum of Modern Art, 1968).

52. Victor C. Ferkiss, *Technological Man: The Myth and the Reality* (New York: New American Library, 1969), 75.

53. Waggoner, *Heel of Elohim*, 168-70.

54. Frederick J. Hoffman, "The Technological Fallacy in Contemporary Poetry: Hart Crane and MacKnight Black," *American Literature* 21 (1949): 94-107; and his *Twenties*, 257-74.

55. John A. Kouwenhoven, *The Arts in Modern American Civilization* (New York: Norton, 1967), 13-42.

56. John Dos Passos, *The 42nd Parallel* (New York: Signet, 1969), xx. Subsequent references to this edition are cited in my text.

57. John Dos Passos, "The Workman and His Tools" (1936), in *Occasions and Protests*, 8.

58. See Tichi, *Shifting Gears*, 194-216.

59. See Steinman's discussion of Williams in *Made in America*.

60. Dos Passos, "Edison and Steinmetz," 104.

61. For a discussion of the commercialization of literature and art, which began in earnest during the thirties, see Alice Goldfarb Marquis, *Hopes and Ashes: The Birth of Modern Times* (New York: Free Press, 1986), and Charles Newman, *The Post-Modern Aura: The Act of Fiction in an Age of Inflation* (Evanston: Northwestern Univ. Press, 1985).

62. Hart Crane to Harriet Monroe (1926), in *Complete Poems*, 239.

11

Fields of Spacetime and the "I" in Charles Olson's *The Maximus Poems*

STEVEN CARTER

> Or you can take an attitude, the creative vantage. . . . It involves a
> first act of physics. You can observe POTENTIAL and VELOCITY
> separately, have to, to measure THE THING. You get approximate
> results. They are usable enough if you include the Uncertainty
> Principle, Heisenberg's law that you learn the speed at the cost of
> exact knowledge of the energy and the energy at the loss of exact
> knowledge of the speed.
>
> —Charles Olson, *Call Me Ishmael*

The notorious eclecticism of Charles Olson's reading and scholarship owes
a great deal to his interest in scientific texts. Unlike Robert Frost, who
discovered after having written certain poems that he had intuitively
embroidered into them concepts of quantum physics,[1] Olson was apparently directly influenced as a thinker and a poet by the work of a select
group of scientists and mathematicians, including Bernard Riemann and
Norbert Wiener. Thomas F. Merrill has pointed out that, in his important
1957 essay, "Equal, That Is, To the Real Itself," Olson relied heavily on
Hermann Weyl's *The Philosophy of Mathematics and Natural Science*. It is
Weyl's influence, Merrill suggests, that contributes to the scientific bias of
Olson's argument, wherein "Olson spells out in remarkable detail, although in the confusing technical jargon of space-age physics, how he
regards projective writing as an inevitable consequence of the same non-
Euclidean 'redefinition of the Real' . . . that gave birth to relativity theory,
quantum physics, and the whole conception of a continuous, as opposed to
a classically discrete, universe." Merrill concludes his discussion of "Equal,

That Is, to the Real Itself," with an interesting observation: "An apt metaphor for such a continuous reality is the electromagnetic field in which interrelated transformations of energy points take place. In such a field discrete formulations, such as subject-object, cause-effect, and even mind-body, give way to the notion of flexible interplay between 'things among things.'"[2]

As we shall see, however, for the Charles Olson of *The Maximus Poems*, the quantum field heuristic represents less of a mere metaphor than it does a new poetics, or rhetoric of verse. At the conclusion of "Equal, That Is, to the Real Itself," Olson celebrates the flexibility of "the inertial field":

> Which it is [i.e., flexible], Einstein established, by the phenomena of gravitation, and the dependence of the field of inertia on matter. I take care to be inclusive, to enforce the point made at the start, that matter offers perils wider than man if he doesn't do what still today seems the hardest thing for him to do, outside of some art and science: to believe that things, and present ones, are the absolute conditions; but that they are so because the structures of the real are flexible, quanta do dissolve into vibrations, all does flow, and yet is there, to be made permanent, if the means are equal.

For Olson, "the structures of the real" may carry over from the physical universe, the worlds of matter, to what he calls in the title of another essay the "Human Universe," or the worlds of consciousness. The two systems of matter and mind are inextricably bound up with each other. Olson's inspiration for such a holistic view of nature and man is Alfred North Whitehead, whose theory of "eternal objects" as physical qualities Olson applied to the mind itself:

> . . . Whitehead's important corollary: that no event is not
> penetrated, in intersection or collision with, an eternal
> event
>   The poetics of such a situation
> are yet to be found out.[4]

Among other things, *The Maximus Poems* represents Olson's attempt to "find out" the poetics of a cross-pollination of scientific epistemologies and the language of verse.

Thomas F. Merrill is not alone in borrowing from the language of quantum field theory to describe the aesthetics of contemporary poets. A decade ago Joseph N. Riddell provided a thumbnail sketch of one variety of postmodern poem. For him it is "a field located within known things, like the periodic table of elements, which composes a space housing an unknown disturbance, a dissonance, an undiscovered element that indicates the dynamics of the field."[5] It is likely that Riddell had in mind Charles Olson's earlier prolegomenon to the poetics of open form, the familiar "Projective Verse," in which Olson too defines poetry in terms of "*Composition by field*, as opposed to inherited line, stanza, over-all form, what is the 'old' base of the non-projective." What Riddell called "dynamics" Olson called "the *kinetics* of the thing. A poem is energy transferred from where the poet got it (he will have some several causations), by way of the poem itself to, all the way over to, the reader. . . . From the moment he ventures into *Field Composition*—puts himself in the open—he can go by no track other than the one the poem under hand declares, for itself."[6] Olson's use of the word "kinetics" suggests that as early as 1950, when "Projective Verse" was written, he had a specific discipline in mind as a model for his theory of field, or open form. The discipline was, of course, physics, or, more accurately, post-Einsteinian physics. In a letter to his friend and publisher, Cid Corman, Olson insists that "the kinetics of contemporary physics [is] more healthful than"[7] the rigidities of either/or, man and world, psyche and cosmos, those separate categories inherited from the Greeks. The scientist Neils Bohr recalls the crucial distinction Olson is making when he suggests that for the contemporary quantum physicist as well, language markers inherited from the Greeks (cause and effect words like "because" and "therefore," for instance, which assume *a priori* a cause-and-effect cosmos) are inappropriate. For Bohr, "When it comes to atoms, the language that must be used is the language of poetry."[8] Both postmodern poetry and quantum physics, it would seem, have much to learn from each other.

Perhaps the most fertile epistemological common ground shared by the two disciplines is "the field concept," which, according to the scientist Donna Jean Haraway, "defined developments in dynamic instead of geographical terms. Every aspect of ontogeny had to be viewed in a double light, as the result of 'interactions between the material whole with its field properties on the one hand, and the material parts on the other.'"[9] The essence of Haraway's definition is to be found in the phrase "a double light." It is the doubleness of field which creates difficulty in understanding its ambiguities. As the physicist B.K. Ridley has observed, "The total energy of a moving particle, rest-mass plus kinetic, is . . . nothing but the total energy of its own electromagnetic field."[10] To say that a particle is both a particle *and* the field that it "inhabits" makes no sense in classical physics, which, as Charles Olson suggests, is epistemologically less "healthful" for the postmodern poet than quantum physics.

Projectivist verse is a poetry of relationships. As Karl Malkoff has written, "the domain of the Projectivist poem is the point of intersection between inner and outer realities."[11] *The Maximus Poems,* for example, is not a series of discrete, watertight expressions of Charles Olson's visions of Gloucester, Massachusetts, past and present; it expresses its meanings only in a focus of relationships among the poems. These foci, or "interactions," include the voice(s) of Maximus, who moves freely in space and time throughout the sequences of poems; the town and people of Gloucester, Massachusetts; and the historical personages who appear and disappear in the shimmering spacetime field of *Maximus.*

The epistemology which Malkoff uses to describe Projectivist verse is also used by physicists to define field. A subatomic particle is nothing but a focus of relationships between fields. As far as *Maximus* is concerned, the key feature of field poetics is the classical quantum paradox, or the non-Aristotelian habit of mind that suggests that reality can be two or more different things at the same time. The physicist Gary Zukav points out that "Quantum field theory is, of course, an outrageous contradiction in terms. A quantum is an indivisible whole. It is a small piece of something, while a field is a whole area of something. A 'quantum field' is the juxtaposition of two irreconcilable concepts. In other words, it is a paradox. It defies our categorical imperative that something be either *this* or *that.*"[12]

Three fields of action in *Maximus* create this paradox, defying Aristotelian logic and linearity by interacting with each other "*instantaneously* and at one single point in space instantaneously and locally."[13] The fields of *Maximus* may be defined as time, space, and the "I" of the sequence; *The Maximus Poems* represents the interactions of these three fields. Each of the three poems I will discuss exhibits all three fields of action: "Letter 15," however, emphasizes the field of time, whereas "On First Looking out through Juan de la Cosa's Eyes" emphasizes the field of space. In "The Twist," fields of spacetime coalesce around the "I," or the speaker (Maximus), who emerges as a fully articulated consciousness. Although three poems represent a necessarily small sampling of the considerable riches of *Maximus,* each poem included here fully expresses at least one of the three central themes of the work: the rapaciousness and waste that Olson assoociates with twentieth-century American capitalism; the close per-

sonal and mythical identification of the speaker with the fishing town of
Gloucester; and Maximus' wider identification with the past, wherein
Gloucester becomes not simply a city, or *polis*, to be discovered, but a
means of discovery of what it means to be Maximus, or man.

"Letter 15" from *Maximus* begins with a remembrance of things past, as
the speaker corrects the historical record concerning the fate of a ship
called the *Putnam*. The narrative dramatizes the difficulty of keeping the
truth alive through time: "The whole tale, as we have had it, from his son,
goes by the board. The son seems to have got it thirty-five years after the
event from a sailor who was with the father on that voyage (to Sumatra,
and Ile de France, cargo: shoes). This sailor apparently (he was twenty
years older than the captain) was the one who said, that night they did get
in, 'Our old man goes ahead as if it was noonday.' He must have been 85
when he added the rest of the tale."[14] The theme of the mutability of
memory—and therefore of history—is reinforced elsewhere in *Maximus*
when the speaker declares, "History is the memory of time" (*Maximus*,
116). This theme in the opening section of "Letter 15" also prefigures the
technique of many of the poems to come. Even as memory is slippery—an
old man's reminiscences of a ship in Gloucester—so time itself is slippery.
   Indeed, it is Olson's treatment of time as a narrative technique that
makes many of the poems in *Maximus* difficult. Sherman Paul elaborates:

> Maximus tells us that his poem will not make us comfortable because it does
> not follow a linear track to a foreseen destination. In addressing his method,
> he reminds us of his weaving and of the indivisibility of his concerns—and of
> his materials, since everything, as with the bird, everything (immediate
> observation, document, recollection, dream, myth) is the common real
> material of his poem. In the field there are no boundaries . . . the field he
> enters is not a subject but the reality he fronts, the place of his attentions. . . .
> His subject, if he may be said to have one, is man-within-the-field.[15]

In "Letter 15," what Paul refers to as the "indivisibility of [Maximus's]
concerns" is dramatized, not *in*, but *as*, a field of time. The adventure of
the *Putnam* cannot be described as a singularity in space or time, cannot be
reduced to an "event" that "happened." Instead, Olson distributes authority for the "truth" of the ship's fate among several narrators and audiences—Maximus himself, the "we" of the passage, the son, the sailor,
and the distant father. It is a technique that recalls the radical narrative

strategies of Joseph Conrad in *Heart of Darkness* and William Faulkner in *The Sound and the Fury*. For these writers, as for Olson, what used to be called "the heart of the matter" may not exist at all.

Significantly, Olson's technique in "Letter 15" recalls Einstein's definition of fields of energy: "Matter which we perceive is merely nothing but a great concentration of energy in very small regions. We may therefore regard matter as being constituted by the regions of space in which the field is extremely intense. . . . There is no place in this new kind of physics both for the field and matter for the field is the only reality."[16] For Olson the rhetorician of verse, Einstein's physical field represents more than a phenomenon that is restricted to the physical cosmos. Nor is field for Olson just a metaphor for postmodern poetics. Rather, in Olson's view, human consciousness itself is a field, whether it is expressed in a scientific or a poetical view of things: "At root (or stump) what *is*, is no longer THINGS but what happens BETWEEN things, these are the terms of the reality contemporary to us—and the terms of what we are."[17]

But if field as Einstein defines it here denotes a unity in space, it also denotes for Olson in "Letter 15" a unity in time. Olson's attempt to orchestrate a unity between time present and time past in the human cosmos of Gloucester becomes clearer if we examine a quantum model that theoretical physicist David Bohm uses to describe the "implicate order" of the physical cosmos: "each local clock of a given level exists in a certain region of space and time [i.e., the field] which is made up of still smaller regions, and so on without limit. We shall see that we can obtain the universality of the quantum of action, h, at all levels, if we assume that each of the above *sub-regions* contains an effective clock of a similar kind, related to the other effective clocks of its level in a similar way, and that this effective clock structure continues indefinitely with the analysis of space and time into subregions."[18] Bohm's thought-experiment with ideal clocks is meant to suggest the universality of the quantum of action: that is, a "truth" about space and time that exists in both micro- and macroscopic physical reality. I am arguing that Charles Olson's use of time in "Letter 15" and elsewhere in *Maximus* represents an attempt to devise a quantum of action in language. Olson's quantum of action will serve the same epistemological function of "reading" the experiences of generations of people in the region and sub-regions of Gloucester as Bohm's quantum of action, the physicist's rosetta stone for "reading" patterns of wholeness in regions and sub-regions of energy. Olson achieves his quantum of action ("h" in the physical cosmos) by searching out in *Maximus*—in the lives of men and women who populate the poems—what is common to all times and places, dividing time as he does so into conventional sub-regions (the seventeenth and twentieth centuries, say), and then using these universal human constants ("h" might well stand for "human") to erase the boundaries of the sub-regions, of time altogether, creating a sense of what in the physical cosmos Bohm simply calls "wholeness."

In Part II of "Letter 15," for example, Maximus leaps from the historical account of the *Putnam* to a conversation in the present with poet Paul Blackburn, who has accused Maximus/Olson of "twisting" the poem, i.e., beating around the bush, leaving the subject for bizarre tangents. Olson/Maximus agrees with Blackburn, and then replies cryptically, "I sd., Rhapsodia. . ." (*Maximus*, 72). Olson knew that the word "rhapsodist" comes from *rhaptein*, which, as Don Byrd points out, means "to sew, to stitch together, and *aidein*, to sing. The poet is a stitcher of songs."[19] The songs of Maximus in part comprise the "tangents" of the poem that Blackburn objects to; and yet the tangents are the poem also; it is Maximus who is singing them, even if they are written by someone else: John Smith, for example. Smith, as a historical personage, is part of the field of *Maximus*. Maximus, the "I" of the poem where intersecting fields of time and space meet, is also the field. That is to say, Maximus subsumes John Smith:

> The winters cold, the Summers heat
>   alternatively beat
> Upon my bruised sides, that rue
>   because too true
> That no releefe can ever come
>   But why should I despaire
>   being promised so faire
> That there shall be a day of Dome [*Maximus*, 74]

Smith's poem is a testament of self, but it is also another voice in the Greek chorus that is the testament of Maximus. Thus, historical time for Olson is an illusion; "Letter 15" ends in a sudden, bitter shift to the present age, a wrinkle *in* the intersecting fields of the poem, thanks to one word. "ADVERTISEMENTS" forms part of the title of a book by John Smith. In present-day American culture, ADVERTISEMENTS leads to this:

> o Republic, o
> Tell-A-Vision, the best

is soap. The true troubadors
are CBS. Melopoeia
    is for Cokes by Cokes out of
    Pause

  IV
(o Po-ets, you
should getta
job [*Maximus*, 75]

In "Letter 15," linear time is subsumed by the "universality" of the temporal
quantum of action: in this case, greed. In Section II of the poem, Maximus
points out that John Smith was rejected for the job of navigator by the
pilgrims in favor of Miles Standish. For Maximus, Smith is a man of
integrity, and yet, even in his time, the seeds of American corporate
venality can be detected; the decision to appoint Standish as navigator was
made "to save charges," as Smith himself wrote bitterly.[20]

Maximus is quick to dramatize equivalent examples of self-interest and
shortsightedness in the above references to both contemporary advertising
and pragmatic American attitudes toward "lazy" poets. From the point of
view of a crassly materialistic capitalist society, linear time, therefore, has
made little difference between Smith's day and our own. In other words, to
borrow Einstein's terminology above, greed appears in "Letter 15" as a
"region" of Maximus' consciousness where the field of time becomes
"extremely intense"; more than three centuries of chronological time melt
away in favor of a "concentration," not of physical, but of human psychic
energy, whose localized manifestations in the seventeenth and twentieth
centuries appear with an American twist, and are similarly perverse. Thus
a precise correspondence exists between the manner in which physicists
(Einstein and Bohm) perceive energy fields, and the manner in which a
poet (Olson) perceives the intricate orders of the human psyche, whose
representations in *Maximus* are interwoven with the tissues and textures of
post-Einsteinian spacetime.

In the poem, "On first Looking out through Juan de la Cosa's Eyes,"
the explorer la Cosa emerges as a hero of *Maximus* because, like Maximus
himself, he presents for the reader a "mythological present." But the true
value of la Cosa's voyages in *Maximus* is spatial: his "centrality" as a human
being is expressed by the poet in terms of literal fields of space. Literal,
because it is Juan de la Cosa's map of the world which makes of the world a
whole for the first time in history. La Cosa captained the *Niña* in 1492, but

is better known as "Chief Chart Maker" for Christopher Columbus. Eight years after the voyage to the New World, la Cosa produced his "mappenmunde" of the Old and New Worlds, inscribed "Juan de la cosa la fizo en el puerto de s:mjª en ano de 1500."[21] For Charles Olson, la Cosa's map is a mythological model for wholeness as well, for in it all men share the same space; the map is a spatial metaphor for human brotherhood in the poem. It is also a model for Maximus, the "I" who transcends space in "la Cosa's Eyes" in the same fashion as the "I" of "Letter 15" who transcends time. Maximus says ecstatically,

> . . . before la Cosa, nobody
> could have
> a mappenmunde [Maximus, 81]

Later in Maximus the "I" takes his place as a "settler" in la Cosa's mappenmunde, when he declares, "I am making a mappenmunde. It is to include my being" (Maximus, 201). The physical space of la Cosa's world thus dovetails with the spirituality of Maximus's being; in space now, as he does in time in "Letter 15," Maximus becomes the field and the man-within-the-field. As Olson says elsewhere, "The littlest [man-within-the-field of history] is the same as the very big [the field of history], if you look at it."[22] Put another way, the lineaments of physical space dwell within the psyche of each man who is "contained by" space, because physical space is also "contained" (i.e., perceived by) each man. La Cosa's mappenmunde is thus psychic and physical, a sort of Mercator's projection of inner and outer spaces that coexist as a simultaneous field.

In "la Cosa's Eyes," as always in Maximus, the fields of space, time, and the speaker's "I" overlap; as Don Byrd correctly observes, "Space and history [in] the post-Einsteinian cosmos of [Maximus] are only different manifestations of the same order."[23] For Einstein, of course, space and time are not separate quantities: they are both linked phenomena in a universal continuum called spacetime. For Maximus/la Cosa, the world is no longer flat, for the mappenmunde remakes the frightening world "out there," a world of "mermaids and monsters" (Maximus, 82), into curved space, a terrestial precursor of universal curved space:

> Respecting the earth, he sd,
> it is a pear, or,
> like a round ball upon a part of which there is a prominence

> like a woman's nipple, this protrusion
> is the highest & nearest to
> the sky [*Maximus*, 83]

La Cosa's space is a psychic/feminine discovery, therefore, for "My New-foundlanders/My Portuguese," and the people of Gloucester.

It is in "On first Looking out through Juan de la Cosa's Eyes" that a reader may understand, perhaps for the first time in *Maximus*, the literal uses of space on the page. Like a sculptor—Henry Moore, for instance—Olson uses blank (negative) space to create as much meaning as words create—or, as in Moore's case, bronze creates. There are entire pages of *Maximus* that Olson leaves purposefully blank. It is as if pure spacetime, pure becoming, takes over where words suddenly fail Maximus. The spaces between words create as much meaning as the words themselves: if the poem is a process, then the not-yet-there, or "future" space that words on the next page will embroider on, is just as much a part of the poem as the "present" words are. Thus, as the holes in Henry Moore's sculptures are meant by the artist to be seen, or as the silences in John Cage's musical compositions are meant by the composer to be heard, so the white spaces on the pages of *Maximus* are meant by the poet to be read. Put another way, Olson's white spaces represent future time which, like the past, is encysted by the Bergsonian perpetual *now* of *Maximus*.

Olson's syntax in *Maximus* also depends for its meaning upon the open spaces in the poems. It is a fractured syntax, a fractured typography, floating like jetsam in the sea off Gloucester, the sea of spacetime Olson observes through Maximus's colossal memory, which he defines as "the history of time" (*Maximus*, 256):

> No worms. Storms,
> Ladies &
>
> to the bottom of the,
>
> husbands, & wives,
>
> little children lost their [*Maximus*, 84]

Here, Maximus's syntax is perpetually in the process of becoming a sentence, i.e., a complete thought. Similarly, Olson's characterization of Maximus himself represents a process of becoming a sentient whole. Of course it is this process of becoming, of succeeding generations lost and found at sea off Gloucester, that is the subject of the passage. The

"becomingness" of the syntax is the subject as much as what the words
"floating" in the syntax say.

The subject of "On first Looking out through Juan de la Cosa's Eyes" is
therefore continuity: the continuity of the curved space of la Cosa's
"mappenmunde" which, in Gloucester's flower ceremony in August, translates thematically into the continuity between living and dead:

> . . . each summer, at the August full,
> they throw flowers, which, from the current there, at the Cut,
> reach the harbor channel, and go
>
> these bouquets (there are few, Gloucester, who can afford florists' prices)
> float out
>   you can watch them go out into,
> the Atlantic [Maximus, 84]

The field of the dead and the living in Maximus is meshed by the flower
ceremony, which, in "Letter 36" as well, exists to create continuity:

> the flowers
> turn
> the character of the sea   The sea jumps
> the fate of the flower   The drowned men are undrowned
> in the eddies
>
>   of the eyes
>   of the flowers
>   opening
>   the sea's eyes [Maximus, 157]

The syntactical mixing of flowers, eyes of the people, and the drowned
men of Gloucester, represents a direct attack in language on the illusion
of spatial and temporal separateness in the world. Indeed, the very concept
of field denies a reality of bits and pieces altogether. By embracing
Gloucester, the Cut, Dogtown, the sea, the drowned men, and flowers
tossed into the waves by huddled women and children stitching the field of
spacetime together with remembrance, la Cosa's mappenmunde ultimately
meshes the temporal field of "Letter 15" with the spatial field of "On first
looking out through Juan de la Cosa's Eyes."

"The Twist," the third major poem in the fields of Maximus, is also one
of the most personal poems. In it the "I" of Maximus, the "being" in la

Cosa's mappenmunde, takes his place in the spacetime field of "Letter 15"
and "On first Looking out through Juan de la Cosa's Eyes." "The Twist"
bears a striking contrast, however, to "la Cosa's Eyes" because it represents
la Cosa's mappenmunde turned inside out: now we have Maximus' naked
being, the "personal" Maximus, the man-in-the-field. In fact, as Don Byrd
has pointed out, Olson's flipover of world to man-in-the-world makes "The
Twist" resemble a kind of moebius strip of words[24] and reminds us again
that the Einsteinian space of *Maximus* is not linear but curves back on
itself. Thus la Cosa's stormy coast becomes, in "The Twist,"

> . . . my inland waters
> (Tatnuck Sq. and the walk
> from the end of the line
> to Paxton, for May-flowers
>
> or by the old road to Holden
> after English walnuts [*Maximus*, 86]

If a man departs from Gloucester in a straight line, following la Cosa's map,
he will curve his way backward to the "inland waters" where he began. The
discovery of a new world therefore becomes a discovery of self, of Maximus'
"being" which is suddenly incarnated among the May-flowers and walnut
trees of Gloucester. As we saw in the poem dedicated to him, the fact that
la Cosa, who saw these same May-flowers centuries ago, is dead, is
immaterial. For both time and space are dissolved in "The Twist," and
Maximus—who is an echo of la Cosa himself—is the locus of the two, the
intersection of the fields. "The Twist" is subjective: everywhere in the
poem, the "I" is fluid, not as one identity separate from the field of objects,
memories, and reflections, but as a kind of chorus:

> I went home
> as fast as I could,
>
> the whole Cut
> was a paper village my Aunt Vandla
> had given me, who gave me,
> each Christmas,
> such toys
>
> As dreams are, when the day
> encompasses. They tear down
> the Third Ave El. Mine stays,

as Boston does, inches up.
I run my trains
on a monorail, I am seized
—not so many nights ago—
by the site of the river
exactly there at the Bridge

where it goes out & in

I recognize
the country . . . [*Maximus*, 89]

The concept of "in" and "out" in "The Twist," both as the physiog-
nomy of the moebius strip, and also as a metaphor for Einsteinian curved
space, is fundamentally important for an understanding of *Maximus* as a
whole. The meandering of the river exists in time as well as space: "—not
so many nights ago—" unites the boy Maximus and the man Maximus
remembering, and suddenly spills into the spatial "out & in" of the river. In
Einsteinian space, the concept of "inness" as opposed to the concept of
"outness" makes no sense; like the surfaces of the moebius strip, both "in"
and "out" are made of what the particle physicist Fritjof Capra calls
"inseparable energy patterns."[25] For Olson as for the contemporary physicist, there can be no isolation of events in the universe of space and time.
Olson demonstrates this Einstein-inspired truism in both "la Cosa's Eyes"
and "The Twist." La Cosa's mappenmunde is the "out" of "The Twist,"
whose "in" is the map of Gloucester retraced in the personal memory of
Maximus. "La Cosa's Eyes" ends with the lines,

On ne doit aux morts nothing
else than
la verite [*Maximus*, 85]

which translate, "We owe the dead nothing else than the truth."
    "The Twist" ends with the lines,

    the whole of it
coming,
to this pin-point
to turn

    in this day's sun,
in this veracity

> there, the waters of several of them the roads
> here, a blackberry blossom [*Maximus*, 90]

"There/here": the historical veracity we owe to the memory of the dead, to la Cosa, structurally twists on the moebius strip of "The Twist" to become the "veracity" of personal observation and discovery, exemplified by the care with which the poem names Maximus's memories of flowers.

It is chimerical to ask of any epic narrative that it attain perfect unity; indeed, the concept of unity itself is anathema to postmodernism. As many critics have noticed, there are real differences between *The Maximus Poems* of 1960 and *Maximus IV, V, VI*, published in 1968.[26] Nonetheless, if seeing *The Maximus Poems* I-VI as all of a piece is a matter of infinite hope, unity may be perceived in certain elegant clusters of poems within the larger work. The "quantum poetics" of field offers a skeleton key to the interrelationships among the lyrics of at least one such cluster in *Maximus*. For in "The Twist," that little masterpiece of open form, the field of space, time, and the "I" of Maximus is complete; the passion of historical memory in "Letter 15" embraces the floating flowers of grieving women in "la Cosa's Eyes" and harmonizes in the moebius strip of "The Twist" with Maximus' sympathies for la Cosa, for Gloucester's own sailors, and for the "waters" of his own past in a village by the sea.

Notes

1. See Guy Rotella, "Comparing Conceptions: Frost and Eddington, Heisenberg, and Bohr," *American Literature* 59 (1987): 168-89.

2. Thomas F. Merrill, *The Poetry of Charles Olson: a Primer* (Newark: Univ. of Delaware Press, 1982), 57-58.

3. Charles Olson, *Selected Writings*, ed. Robert Creeley (New York: New Directions, 1966), 52.

4. Charles Olson, *Maximus Poems IV, V, VI* (London: Cape Goliard/Grossman, 1968), 79. Qtd. in Paul Christensen, *Charles Olson: Call Him Ishmael* (Austin: Univ. of Texas Press, 1979), 138.

5. Joseph N. Riddell, *The Inverted Bell* (Baton Rouge: Louisiana State Univ. Press, 1974), 14.

6. Olson, *Selected Writings*, 16.

7. Charles Olson, *Letters for Origin*, ed. Albert Glover (New York: Cape Goliard, 1970), 51.

8. Edward Harrison, *Masks of the Universe* (New York: MacMillan, 1985), 123.

9. Donna Jean Haraway, *Crystals, Fabrics, and Fields* (New Haven: Yale Univ. Press, 1976), 178.

10. B.K. Ridley, *Time, Space and Things* (New York: Penguin, 1976), 120.

11. Karl Malkoff, *Escape from the Self* (New York: Columbia Univ. Press, 1977), 66.

12. Gary Zukav, *The Dancing Wu Li Masters* (New York: Bantam, 1979), 200.

13. Ibid., 199.

14. Charles Olson, *The Maximus Poems*, ed. George F. Butterick (Berkeley: Univ. of California Press, 1983), 71. All subsequent references to this edition as *Maximus* in text.

15. Sherman Paul, *Olson's Push* (Baton Rouge: Louisiana State Univ. Press, 1978), 142.

16. Qtd. in Milic Capek, *The Philosophical Impact of Contemporary Physics* (New York: Van Nostrand Reinhold, 1961), 319.

17. Charles Olson, *Human Universe and Other Essays*, ed. Donald Allen (New York: Grove, 1967), 123. Qtd. in Robert von Hallberg, *Charles Olson: the Scholar's Art* (Cambridge: Harvard Univ. Press, 1978), 97.

18. David Bohm, *Wholeness and the Implicate Order* (London: Routledge and Kegan Paul, 1980), 98.

19. Don Byrd, *Charles Olson's Maximus* (Urbana: Univ. of Illinois Press, 1980), 91.

20. See George F. Butterick, *A Guide to the Maximus Poems of Charles Olson* (Berkeley: Univ. of California Press, 1978), 103.

21. See Ibid., 115-16.

22. Qtd. in Paul, *Olson's Push*, 163.

23. Byrd, *Charles Olson's Maximus*, 89.

24. Ibid., 90.

25. Fritjof Capra, *The Tao of Physics* (New York: Bantam, 1977), 69, qtd. in N. Katherine Hayles, *The Cosmic Web* (Ithaca: Cornell Univ. Press, 1984), 19.

26. See Merrill, *Poetry of Charles Olson*, 193-94.

This essay is an expanded version of Steven Carter's "'The Kinetics of the Thing': Charles Olson's Man-within-the-Field" originally published in *Worcester Review* 11.2 (1989): 38-48.

12

"Unfurrowing the Mind's Plowshare": Fiction in a Cybernetic Age

DAVID PORUSH

One of the most pervasive themes in postmodern culture is an urgent concern with an old philosophical question, the mechanism-vitalism problem: Are humans merely machines whose every experience and expression can be described by a formal mechanics? In contemporary terms we call this question a cybernetic one, and concern with it is so ubiquitous and fundamental that it is fair to characterize our era as a cybernetic age.

In the sciences, the answer to this question is not simple, but the general drift is toward the mechanical: human behaviors, including communication in language and thinking, can be expressed in formal, algorithmic, mechanical terms. In the arts, especially in contemporary fiction, the answer is also not simple or unalloyed, but the general tendency is toward the mechanical: there is some quality in humanity that resists mechanical modeling and simulation. As this chapter shows, contemporary literature confronts the cybernetic question not only by dramatizing the problem of humans as machines but also as a matter of style and form; that is, as a matter that can be confronted in the intimate choices of a writer expressing his or her imagination in words. Of course, such self-reflexive concerns are typically postmodern, but in discussing cybernetics they take on particular poignancy for reasons I will explain.

In the exemplary case of Thomas Pynchon's work, which this essay treats, the problem is encapsulated in the question of metaphor. Is metaphor mechanical, can it be parsed in strict formal terms? Or is there some elusive and mysterious quality of intelligence that is uniquely expressed in rich metaphors that help humanity slip out from under the domineering control of the cybernetic project? While the natural response of the humanist would be an urgent affirmative, Pynchon's answer even to this question is ambiguous, for *control, system, pattern, organization, mechanism* are robust and attractive paradigms for the artist as well as for the cyberneticist, and especially for Pynchon, whose imagination seems particularly drawn to considering the systematic aspects of coded communication.

Cybernetics in the Sciences

Because it is fundamental in contemporary culture, the cybernetic question is addressed both in the postmodern sciences and arts. Though it is certainly not unique to American culture (the Japanese appear to be equally obsessed with robots, androids, computers, and cyborgs), it receives in America its most intense, varied, and sustained discussion. Indeed, there is a whole complex of new sciences that have evolved in the last half of this century to attack aspects of the mechanism-vitalism problem: artificial intelligence, cognitive science, neurobiology and neuroscience, information science, decision science and game theory, systems science, behaviorism, general systems dynamics, computational linguistics, cryptanalysis, and all forms of computer modeling.[1] Cybernetics has given us our modern understanding of such terms as *positive* and *negative feedback, entropy, information, noise, sender-receiver, organization,* and *redundancy.* And of course, cybernetics is the single greatest impulse behind the computer and communications revolution of the postwar era, which has had an enormous and growing influence on how we work, play, communicate, and express ourselves. It has also had impact on other sciences and technologies that are busy giving birth to the "posthuman," fueling the drift in biology to biological engineering and such programs as mapping the gene (The Human Genome Project) and the movement in medicine to organ transplants, prostheses and artificial replacement parts for ever more complex organs, for cybernetics shares with these other sciences not only certain techniques of feedback analysis of control mechanisms but also a fundamental commitment to the idea that humans are essentially machines.[2]

The science of cybernetics itself began as an interdisciplinary venture in the 1940s in response to the failure of positivism.[3] The movement in science to prove that a totally deterministic portrait of the universe was possible was most popularly expressed by Bertrand Russell and Alfred North Whitehead's set theory. However, this project received two death blows within four short years from the advent of quantum mechanics in 1927 and Godel's theorem in 1931.[4] The four major figures who were most influential in the evolution of the computer and cybernetics all emerged from strong commitments to determinism—Norbert Wiener, John von Neumann, Claude Shannon, and Alan Turing—although the term *cybernetics* is credited to Norbert Wiener.[5] However, the collective work of Wiener, Neumann, Shannon, and Turing contributed to the cybernetic paradigm. Stated most simply, cybernetics suggests *that everything in the knowable universe can be modeled in a logico-mathematical (formal) system of quantifiable information,* from the phase shifts of subatomic particles to the poet's selection of a word in a poem, to the rent in the fabric of spacetime created by a black hole, to the evanescent images flickering through the brain of a preverbal infant. Norbert Wiener defined cybernetics as the science of control and communication in living beings and machines.[6] But of course, the most riveting consequences of the paradigm are its implications for the human mind.

The consequences of this simple ambition are profound. At the heart of cybernetics is a vision (reflected in the stories we tell ourselves) that our culture evidently finds both deeply threatening and broadly promising. Stated simply, one basic cybernetic assumption is that the richness and spontaneity of the way humans "process information" is specifiable in mechanical terms, and therefore our thought processes can be imitated by, coded in, linked to, or even surpassed or replaced by cybernetic mechanisms. More recently, cybernetics has become receptive to questions regarding the precise status of *consciousness* or *awareness* under its definitions. Cyberneticists today note that the problem of self-consciousness in the human mind (and how to design machines that have it) is shorthand for a whole slew of problems about the distinction between how machines use information and how humans make meaning, between natural languages and artificial codes, between text and context. Clearly, the latter elements of these pairs are not amenable to simple modeling by the former, and many of the inflated claims by AI experts in the 1960s (that self-conscious learning computers were just around the corner), particularly by Marvin Minsky of MIT, have wrecked upon the tricky shoals of self-awareness. Nonetheless, the paradigm grows increasingly strong, fueled by its success in designing computers and implementing them in numerous human domains as "expert systems" and "AI" programs.

Cybernetics in Recent Literature

Our popular culture powerfully registers the still-growing impact of this cybernetic paradigm. The last decade especially has seen an explosion of computerization and the proliferation of robots both in fact and in imaginative works, encouraging even as it reflects this deeply rooted cybernetic drift in our culture. Cyborgs, androids, robots, and superhuman computers like HAL in *2001: A Space Odyssey* (1968) or Rachel, the "replicant" in *Blade Runner* (1983), are eloquent manifestations of this drift. Gobots, Transformers, George Lucas's *Star Wars* "droids," dozens of varieties of cartoon serials, and science fiction movies and novels have been imaginatively preparing our children for the coming roboticization of mankind for decades. Indeed, cybernetic science fiction forms one of the most consistently dominant currents in that growingly influential genre.[7] From Isaac Asimov's *I, Robot* through such recent works of "cyberpunk" as William Gibson's *Neuromancer* (1984), *Count Zero* (1986), and *Mona Lisa Overdrive* (1989), Philip K. Dick's "Do Androids Dream of Electric Sheep" (made into the movie *Blade Runner,*) and Bruce Sterling's *The Artificial Kid* (1980), we see this elaboration of the cybernetic metaphor taken for granted as the shape of our collective future. In fact, some of the most speculative science fiction has trouble keeping up with actual developments in computer and robotics research. For instance, Gibson's 1984 portrait of "cyberspace" in *Neuromancer*—a vast, collective sensory representation of data that the human mind accesses directly and experiences in place of normal sensory reality—is already being researched in rudimentary form by several private ventures, even though Gibson places his vision late in the twenty-first century.[8]

This is not to say that images of automated or artificial people are new. Such imaginings have haunted us since the Greek myths of Talus and Galatea. The eighteenth century was fascinated with automata such as Vaucanson's duck and Swiss clockworks. In Book Three of *Gulliver's Travels*, Jonathan Swift's bitter attack on the attempts by the Royal Society to mechanize language precedes our own fears of automation (quintessentially expressed by Charlie Chaplin in *Modern Times* [1935]) by a good two centuries. What has changed for us, and what has made the dialogue so urgent, is that cybernetics has upped the ante. Now machines imitate not only our muscular actions but the very actions of our minds. Cybernetics challenges us in that soaring dome where we live, in our heads, using weapons essential to our sense of ourselves, our acts of communication, our words.

For these reasons, in the last three decades a powerful counter statement to the advent of cybernetics and its attendant technologies has emerged in American fiction. The rise of cybernetics paralleled and influenced the emergence of a literature that called into doubt its very ability to express anything for certain, a literature that became extremely self-conscious of its own systems of communication. In the 1960s this distrust and dubiety were mistaken for literary "exhaustion," and the hallmarks of postmodernism—its black humor; its ironic undermining of themes, stories and plots; its satirical bent; its distrust of language; its playful love of systems, which it sets about dismantling even as it constructs them; its self-consciousness and embrace of silence—all were mistaken for a perverse failure of imagination, as if authors had used up the things they had to say and were left only with silence.[9]

"It is paradoxical, really," writes Philip Roth in his now classic essay "Writing American Fiction," "that the very prose style which, I take it, is supposed to jolt and surprise us . . . turns back upon itself and the real world is in fact veiled from us by this elaborate, self-conscious language-making. . . . The news I wish to bear is . . . a loss of subject; or if not a loss, . . . then let me say a voluntary withdrawal of interest by the writer of fiction from some of the grander social and political phenomena of our times.[10] From Roth's early suggestion through the reign of deconstruction in literary criticism through the 1980s, the accusation that postmodernism is indifferent to reality or expressed the fundamental epistemological ineffectuality of the text has been the standard in postmodern theory.

However, though in my view postmodernism is persistently concerned with—one might say anxious about—its own epistemological effectuality, its conclusion about the matter is far from clear. Indeed, postmodern fiction cannot help but affirm its own power to describe reality. Even if it does abdicate its authority to describe nature or provide *systematic* meaningfulness, at least it then describes with superior authority the human experience in the face of lost meaning or unworkable systems of explanation. How else to explain the ongoing attempt in postmodern fiction to record the deeper truth of recent history (even if those truths take the form of elaborate and sometimes fantastic fictions like Robert Coover's *The Public Burning* or Pynchon's recent *Vineland* (1990))? How else can we explain the urge to provide a countervailing view to science's version of how the universe and humanity is organized, to register the effects of technological change, to delve into human psychology and motivation? Clearly, writers of fiction continue to feel that fiction is an effective epistemological force. Though—or perhaps because—it lacks the conclusive systematic authority of science, literary expression represents an equally valid alternative route to describing our experience of reality.

An advocate of science might demur that the word "experience" introduces an entire realm of subjectivity that is precisely unepistemological. However, science itself has been forced to face its own inability to banish the observer from the scene of, and calculations about, observation. That was the original attack on determinism that provoked the cybernetic response by Norbert Wiener. As Herbert Simon, a noted artificial intelligence theorist, has said, "All correct reasoning is a grand system of tautologies, but only God can make use of that fact. The rest of us must painstakingly and fallibly tease out the consequences of our assumptions."[11] Hence, from a postmodern view, all narratives, even scientific ones, contain their own refutation. Stephen Toulmin suggests in *The Return to Cosmology* that contemporary science in general is growing more and more postmodern because it calls for a new epistemology that reinserts the human perspective into the model of nature.[12]

In this context, cybernetics earns fiction's special attention because it entails a model for communication. Cybernetic fiction is an expression of literature's need to contest cybernetics' claims for an ultimate description of human communication and thought. In one sense, then, cybernetics and cybernetic fiction can be seen as vying for epistemological superiority: who does the better job of describing how humans think and communicate? In another sense, the two enterprises can be seen as accomplices or collaborators in a larger postmodern mission: defining from opposite sides that gap where humanity remains inexpressible in mechanical terms.

The body of cybernetic fiction, then, includes Kurt Vonnegut, Jr.'s earlier novels, particularly *Player Piano* (1952); William Burroughs's fiction of the 1950s and 1960s, especially *The Soft Machine* and *The Ticket That Exploded*; some of Donald Barthelme's short stories, but especially "The Explanation" (in *City Life*, 1970); several works by John Barth, especially *Giles Goat Boy* (1966) and *Letters* (1979); some works by Robert Coover, but especially "Morris in Chains," (in *Pricksongs and Descants*, 1973); all the novels by Joseph McElroy, but more prominently *Lookout Cartridge* (1974) and *Plus* (1976); Marianne Hauser's *The Talking Room* (1977); and more recently, Don DeLillo's *White Noise* (1985). The exemplary author of this class of fiction is Thomas Pynchon, whose dialogue with various sciences in his novels *V.* (1963), *The Crying of Lot 49* (1967), and *Gravity's Rainbow* (1973) is almost certainly more responsible than any others for leading American literary critics into an engagement with contemporary scientific ideas.[13]

In short, some of the most commonly studied contemporary authors of

American fiction have written cybernetic fiction, and several have done so repeatedly. These overwise arcane texts become most trenchant when we read them as part of a dialogue with a contemporary science. Together they move that far from having exhausted its possibilities, cybernetic fiction, as representative of postmodernism generally, is a robust genre. At the very least, the earlier works of cybernetic fiction seem prophetic because they focused on computers, cybernetics, communication, and information, predicting the direction our technological culture would take in subsequent decades.

Yet, what sets cybernetic fiction apart from every other genre of literature is that *it actually applies cybernetic principles to the construction of the literary text*[14] so that these fictions become "soft machines." This tactic is of course made possible only by the advent of a science, which first proposed principles for such communication. So cybernetic fiction is thereby tangled in—one might say it revels in—a cybernetic loop that is at the same time a typically postmodern conundrum: in its attempt to provide a portrait of human communication and mentation epistemologically superior to that offered by cybernetics, cybernetic fiction finds itself employing cybernetic models and techniques, even if only ironically, in order to expose the limitations of those very models and techniques.

Pynchon and Cybernetics

Understanding the central role played by cybernetics in our contemporary culture, we can then understand the urgency of several of our best postmodern authors to formulate responses to its theories. We can also appreciate postmodern literature's robustness, since it is virtually the only narrative genre that attempts to engage cybernetics on its own ground.[15] It actually applies cybernetic principles to the construction of the text, but perhaps as a sort of inoculation against cybernetic determinism. Thomas Pynchon's work is exemplary of this postmodern turn.

At the root of all of Pynchon's work is a deep skepticism about and mistrust of official systems, a trait in American fiction that we can trace back to James Fenimore Cooper and Herman Melville. It is perhaps *the* quintessential American characteristic, explaining not only American literary motifs, but political themes such as the tension among governmental branches mandated by the Constitution or the addition of the Bill of Rights, which is appended distrustfully to that Constitution. In *Democracy in America* (1835) De Tocqueville commented on the distrust of systems as a ubiquitous American trait (along with the contrary trait that each American seems to have his own system), and it lies at the heart of our politics and national psychology. For Pynchon, any system carries with it the threat of organization, and organization imperializes and controls at the expense of human individuality. In particular, Pynchon compulsively rehearses the drama of individual freedom threatened by some outside— and by definition hostile—agency. Almost always, the tools of that agency are technological. Even apparently neutral and objective (the two terms should not be confused) systems—physics, say, or literary criticism, or the innocent ad hoc systems of individuals searching for meaning in their lives—can be turned into techniques for control and manipulation.

Pynchon's worldview is forged out of the tension between individuals struggling to preserve their freedom and the overlapping systems, grids, patterns, organizations, and technologies that confine them. Ironically, sometimes the patterns and lines of control come from some inner, personal need, including the need to imagine on the part of other individuals. So Pynchon's characters tend to project order onto the world or penetrate the labyrinths of order that others have erected. Mystery and conflicts in Pynchon's stories arise from clashes in teleologies. Control comes from those who have the means to impose their telos on others. Cybernetics gives these forces special techniques to challenge even people's freedom of will and autonomy of expression.

Oedipa Maas of Pynchon's second novel, *The Crying of Lot 49* (1967), is the avatar of this theme. She's a young woman in the middle of a life crisis who becomes the executrix of a wealthy hoaxer's will. Following clues in Pierce Inverarity's will leads her to The Tristero, a subterranean postal society—a communications conspiracy, if you will. Tristero's power seems to grow as she investigates it, even as she has trouble determining its reality. She likens herself to "the dark machine in the center of the planetarium" striving to bring "the Estate into pulsing, stelliferous Meaning all in a soaring dome around her." In other words, Pynchon caricatures through Oedipa the human enterprise of knowledge-seeking. However, the novel offers no resolution: at the end, we await with Oedipa the call of an auctioneer about to "cry lot 49," in which she hopes to find another clue. Like every other clue in the short novel, we know this one will teasingly promise to offer some final insight but will be bound by the laws of Pynchon's universe to engender only further mystery and frustration but with the hint of revelation lying just beyond our event horizon.

Pynchon's primary characters share Oedipa's innocence, her belief in ultimate resolutions, her doubts about her own sanity, her compulsiveness in searching for the truth, her scholarly resourcefulness, and her paranoia. Herbert Stencil of V. sees twentieth-century history as nothing more than a web of intrigue hinting at the identity of V., who is either a spy inexorably turning into an automaton or the code name of a secret rocket developed by the Nazis or one of several other possibilities. Through his eyes, the world becomes Stencilled, stamped with the hero's peculiar and pathological vision of the interconnectedness of everything in the crux of the letter V. In Pynchon's masterpiece, *Gravity's Rainbow,* British intelligence during World War II discovers that an American named Slothrop stationed in London has kept a map of the city with brightly colored pins marking the sites of his amorous conquests. His erotic cartography would be nothing more than a boast, except for the curious fact that each of his affairs corresponds exactly to a site where a Nazi V2 rocket will later explode.

British Intelligence, and eventually Slothrop himself, explore all sorts of systems, from Pavlovian behaviorism to ESP, from statistical mechanics to tarot, from Freudian psychology to physics, in an attempt to establish the remarkable connection between Slothrop's anatomical divining rod and the guidance system in the nose cone of the rocket. Of course, the latter device is the paradigmatic cybernetic mechanism; the Germans call it the *schwarzgerat*—"the dark thing" or "the black box" (i.e., the inexplicable or unnameable).

It seems clear that Pynchon's fundamental interest lies in the relative potency of different epistemologies, different sciences, different narratives of reality, including highly idiosyncratic and personal ones. And somehow, for Pynchon, the laws governing how information is organized into systems—that is, cybernetics—hold the key to it all.[16]

The signs of a deep involvement with cybernetics proliferate across Pynchon's work. First of all, throughout his work we see mechanical organs and parts grafted onto human characters. In *V.,* several characters have prosthetic limbs and organs, and the mysterious, elusive V(ictoria Meroving) herself acquires a growing number of artificial replacements for lost parts until, still barely living, she is gleefully dismantled by urchins of Malta while she lies helplessly pinned beneath a collapsed building. Another character, Bongo-Shaftesbury, calls himself a "clockwork doll." A third character, Fergus, plugs himself directly into a TV set through electrodes on his arm forming a servo-mechanical loop. Pig Bodine gets a job working on SHROUD and SHOCK—two "synthetic human" projects. Shoenmaker, the plastic surgeon who performs a nose job on Benny Profane's girlfriend, feels "himself no more animate than the spanners and screwdrivers he handled."

Pynchon compulsively resorts to cybernetic images and metaphors for human activities and structures. Oedipa looks down on San Narciso Valley and imagines that she has just opened up the back of a transistor radio (a prophesy, perhaps, of Silicon Valley?). Later, her confusion over which version of reality to believe is compared to the feeling of being "trapped between the zeros and ones of a giant computer." What exists in the excluded middle between the zeros and ones of a computer? Pynchon has warned us about "excluded middles": they are "to be avoided at all costs." The titular metaphor of Gravity's Rainbow itself refers to the parabolic arc described by the flight of the V2 rocket, whose ascent we witness in the first passage of the novel, and whose descent we still await at its end, some seven hundred pages later.

Finally, it is clear that Pynchon applies cybernetic principles to the construction of his images and themes with more rigor and consistency than any other author. For instance, Abraham Moles, in his landmark book Information Theory and Esthetic Perception, shows that from the mathematical point of view of the message itself, there is no distinction between noise and signal. Rather, what constitutes noise and what constitutes part of the intended message or code is determined by what system you are using.[18] In terms of human communication, then, it is as if a spy uses encoded marginalia scribbled over a sonnet by Shakespeare to communicate information to his agent in the field. If that text were to fall into the hands of a literature scholar, the marginalia would seem to be distracting marks, just so much noise. But if the intended receiver, the spy, reads it, the sonnet is simply the ground, the background noise, of the "real" message. So what seems like nonsense for one receiver may, in the proper context, be deciphered as highly meaningful information by another. In short, one man's scrabble is another's code. It depends on your point of view or context.

A striking passage in one of Pynchon's works illustrates this neatly. In V. a young German engineer, Kurt Mondaugen, monitors the random electrical noises that are everywhere in the atmosphere and that translate into static on his radio. Placed in psychologically distressing circumstances, Mondaugen returns to his post. Eventually he begins to see in these random noises an emergent pattern. The more he looks at these whistles, bleeps, clicks, risers, etc., the more he seems to discern a message embedded there. Finally, he translates the code into letters, which at first seem like a mere jumble:

DIGEWOELDTIMSTEALALENSWTASNDEURFUALRISKT

He shows it to his superior officer, who immedately sees that if you extract every third letter you uncover a surprising double code. The extracted letters produce

GODMEANTNUURK

which is an anagram of "KURT MONDAUGEN." The remaining letters form a famous quotation from Wittgenstein (in German, of course)

DIEWELTISTALLESWASDERFALLIST

["The world is all that is the case."] This fundamental axiom of Wittgenstein's philosophy of language in turn seems to comment (favorably or unfavorably, it's hard to tell) on the very project Mondaugen is engaged in. Either the world is to be taken for granted, and such decoding is a means of falsifying the world, or the world is everything we can make a case for it being.

In either case, this is typical Pynchonesque maneuvering. The very uncertainty of the status of the code incarnates in the reader a desire to pursue further decodings and interpretations. Is it real or a projection by a troubled mind? Is Wittgenstein correct, in Pynchon's view? What does Pynchon mean by having Wittgenstein's passage appear to Mondaugen, back there in South Africa during the Boer War, before Wittgenstein even penned it (in the 1930s)? In short, we are provoked into reading our own significance into this passage and into the code, with no real hope of coming to any conclusive answers. One thing, however, is certain: we are all Mondaugens when faced with rich uncertainty. For *uncertainty creates a gap where fools and angels alike rush in.*

Of all the literary techniques for creating this dance between uncertainty and interpretation, none is more powerful or enriching than metaphor.

The Cybernetics of Metaphor

Pynchon calls attention to the special status of metaphor throughout his work. Even in one of his earliest stories, "Entropy" (1957), the too-orderly Callisto finds that the informational and thermodynamic entropy in his life creates "a metaphor" that is slowly demolishing his carefully constructed world. In V. Pynchon tells us quite blankly that "metaphor is a device, an artifice," that cloaks the literal truth of the world from humans who are taken in by it. Some view "the laws of physics as legislation," but by contrast, poets, who traffic in metaphor, are alone "with the task of living in a universe of things which simply are, and cloaking that innate mindlessness with comfortable and pious metaphor." In The Crying of Lot 49, we are told that "the act of metaphor was a thrust at the truth and a lie, depending upon where you were: inside, safe or outside, lost."

It is clear why Pynchon has focused on metaphor as the best weapon in his literary arsenal against cybernetic determinism. A real good robust metaphor—what Max Black calls "a strong metaphor—both resonant and emphatic"—explodes under scrutiny.[18] The more we look, the more we see in it. In contrast to most other verbal techniques, the strong metaphor actually aims at introducing uncertainty, at destabilizing the system of signification, at eluding identification or reduction to an algebra of information. In the right context, a strong metaphor is inexhaustible. It can initiate a process of increasing energy or oscillation—positive feedback—that leads the interpreter to the brink of revelation. One character in The Crying of Lot 49, Jesus Arrabal, describes it as "a miracle . . . another world's intrusion into this one." One of Pynchon's favorite metaphors for metaphors is the epileptic seizure, a neuropathic event that several cyberneticists have attributed to positive feedback in the cortex.

Interestingly enough, there have been cybernetic attempts to codify metaphor. The most fascinating of these, because it begins with a most enriched version of metaphor, is Earl MacCormac's A Cognitive Theory of Metaphor. MacCormac provides a superb scholarly analysis of various theories of metaphor and concludes that "finding an algorithmic description of the creative cognitive process by which metaphors are generated seems unlikely" and that "one cannot fully explain metaphor with formal abstractions alone."[19] Nonetheless, and surprisingly, "the major assumption of [his] study . . . [is] the presumption that metaphor itself can best be explained by viewing the human mind as a computational device."[20] And so he proceeds to offer a computational model for metaphor, a complex formal/logical model involving fuzzy sets and many valued logics, and "hierarchical networks in n-dimensional space."[21]

Strong metaphors can give rise to conflicting interpretations and therefore further uncertainty, the occasion for further interpretation. Look at the number of interpretations provoked by Emily Dickinson's elusive poetry, for instance, or the continuing academic unraveling of metaphors in John Donne's "Aire and Angels." Around these precipitating irritants, these motes in the oyster or these nodes of uncertainty, the human reader is compelled to form pearls of meaning, or what Wiener would call "local enclaves of organization." These temporary organizations, however, these new interpretations, in turn alter the context for reading, which in turn invites new interpretation, a spiraling loop of positive feedback in an apparently inexhaustible cycle. Furthermore, as Pynchon often indicates, this process is initiated by a fundamentally mysterious quality in metaphors, which seems to lie at the heart of the human condition of endless uncertainty, endless questing, endless organization and connection-making. Metaphors are good metaphors for how we make meaning in the world.

We encounter one of the best crafted of Pynchon's cybernetic metaphors in a side alley. Oedipa detours (her entire search can be viewed as a digression) into a cul-de-sac of the city streets, where she recognizes an old acquaintance, a drunken sailor. She holds the impression that he might harbor a crucial clue. However, she finds him in the act of unwittingly immolating himself, having lit a cigarette after spilling booze on his mattress. This horrible vision pushes Oedipa over the edge into one of her interpretive seizures.

To her, the sailor's death represents "the massive destruction of information." Pynchon holds us by the hand and takes us through the mental process of someone confronted by a strong metaphor; simultaneously, he induces us to undergo a parallel process:

It was as if she had just discovered the irreversible process [time]. It astonished her to think that so much could be lost. . . . She knew . . . that he suffered DT's. Behind the initials was a metaphor, a delirium tremens, a trembling unfurrowing of the mind's plowshare. The saint whose water can light lamps, the clairvoyant whose lapse in recall is the breath of God, the true paranoid for whom all is organized in spheres joyful or threatening about the central pulse of himself, the dreamer whose puns probe ancient fetid shafts and tunnels of truth all act in the same special relevance to the word, or whatever it is the word [the] is there, buffering, to protect us from. . . . [She recalled] freshman calculus; 'dt', God help this old tattooed man, meant also a time differential, a vanishingly small instant in which change had to be confronted at last for what it was, where it could no longer disguise itself as something innocuous like an average rate; where velocity dwelled in the projectile though the projectile be frozen in midflight, where death dwelled in the cell though the cell be looked in on at its most quick. She knew that the sailor had seen worlds no other man had seen if only because there was that high magic to low puns, because DT's must give access to dt's of spectra beyond the known sun, music made purely of Antarctic loneliness and fright. But nothing she knew of would preserve them, or him. [95-96]

Oedipa and the reader are together sent into a seizure of dt's, an outward-spiraling unraveling of associations that look something like this: DT stands for *delirium tremens.* Pynchon in the next paragraph interprets the experience as "a trembling unfurrowing of the mind's plowshare," which at first glance seems like a poetic gloss but in fact is more a literal interpretation of dt's, for *delire* in Latin means, literally, "to go off the furrow." (Today we would say to have "one wheel on the shoulder" or "one paddle in the water.") *Tremens* means to tremble. Someone who acts strangely has let his plow go off the furrow and left the straight and narrow. But to unfurrow the mind might also allude to smoothing out those wrinkles that comparative anatomists tell us are literal signs of intellect. Or it could also mean to harvest the mind's plowshare of associations, since in harvesting one also tends to un-furrow a plowed field. Does exposure to metaphors hiding in anagrams like DT create the DTs that unfurrow/ harvest the mind's plowshare?

We're not done worrying this bone. The term *dt* plays a special role in Pynchon's calculus. It resonates forward in his work to *Gravity's Rainbow,* where the vanishingly small instant of time represents the rocket frozen in midair that comes screaming across the sky at the beginning of the novel and that is about to land at its end. This in turn shuttles us back to *V.,* a novel and that similarly takes it name (in part) from the German rocket. But through "the high magic to low puns," Pynchon jumps to the more relevant meaning of "dt" as the dimension used in the calculus of information flow, thus opening the door to information theory, which in turn loops us back to the guidance system of the rocket's *schwarzgerat* (Wiener began his cybernetic investigations in trying to refine the guidance systems in antiaircraft gunnery) and to the other rich mines of cybernetic associations throughout Pynchon's fiction. In the vanishingly small interval of time, life is frozen into a caricature of death, the rocket is frozen in midflight, and the cybernetics system ceases to communicate, reduced to the solitary *bit.* The zeros and ones of a computer that Pynchon alludes to later in this novel represent bits. The term is an invention of Claude Shannon, who suggested that a mechanism represents information proportionately to its potential to generate alternatives like "on" (1) or "off" (0). Bit, therefore, designates an irreducible amount of information. Gregory Bateson whimsically called it "the difference which makes a difference." Here, Oedipa finds that each bit of information is the difference that makes, as Derrida would say, a "differance." Rather than helping to achieve resolution, the information she receives from metaphors like this one serves to defer meaning to some other place, outside the system she is in. That is where, I believe, Pynchon wants us to be as well: outside the system we are in. His metaphors are a vehicle for getting us there.

There are many more threads of this elaborated metaphor that we could pursue. We could pick up on other tantalizing phrases and hidden metaphors that wire and connect and echo back and forth not only internally but also to other passages in this text, other texts by Pynchon, other texts generally, and to ideas held out here in the culture at large. But the quantity of information we could generate would not alter the conclusion we come to: the point of such activity is its inconclusiveness. Yet this point should not be confused for a confession of epistemological impotence. Rather, Pynchon offers an alternative version of knowing in which certitude is suspended in favor of ongoing interpretation and a continuous feeding of an inexhaustible desire for new knowledge.

Pynchon doesn't merely portray the techniques and effects of such manipulations, he actually uses them on us, the readers, and tells us as he does so. In order to interpret the phrase "the trembling unfurrowing of the mind's plowshare," we have to experience the unfurrowing of our own mental resources. And so in the grips of this metaphor, the epistemological and the ontological, knowing and being, merge and convert into each other like mass and energy at the speed of light. In essence, Pynchon has deployed the cybernetics of metaphor to reshape the reader's attention into an element in a servo-mechanical positive feedback loop. Such reading in this servo-mechanical loop is a self-engendering activity; the reader experiences postmodern vertigo, trembling on the edge of a revelation of this truth at once frustrating and visionary: "There are no revelations possible as long as you remain within the system of your reading." We are moved away from the vanishingly small instant of time, reduction to single bits that is the object of a well-designed cybernetic system (the negative feedback loop), for such reduction is a form of death, Pynchon tells us. Instead, we are motivated to engage an ever-enlarging orbit of meaning, a spiral up and out of system, toward openness. Though everywhere else in his work Pynchon describes the application of techniques to humans as a form of necrophilia, somehow he works the technique of metaphor to preserve our humanness and enliven the territory.

In coming to this happy conclusion, I don't mean to wave my hands over Pynchon's apocalyptic pessimism nor to wipe away the dark predictions in his satire. Yet, it is clear to me that Pynchon along with other authors of cybernetic fiction sees the value of taking a stand though his art, of expressing a means of temporarily eluding cybernetic determinism, even if it requires using a cybernetic countertechnique of his own and even if it is only temporary. After all, we see many of his characters take just such a stand, and have a good bit of fun along the way, and his novels elaborate that intense and mysterious space defined by the contest between personal freedom and those systems that attempt to construct our reality for us.

Conclusion

Cybernetics was partially born from the desire to answer the uncertainties imported into science by quantum mechanics, to reclaim certainty by showing that how the human mind itself perceives an event and communicates its observations could be described deterministically as a cybernetic mechanism or form of computer. If everything is treated as information, and if information is figured in an equation, and if those equations can be manipulated systematically, then science, it was hoped, will have resubsumed a demonic instrument that has imported uncertainty into the center of scientific realism—the human mind—under a system of positive mathematics. The success of the project has given us computers, expert systems, fascinating new models of the mind and the brain, and a powerful post-Cartesian metaphor: that the human mind in the behaviors it holds most dear—speaking, thinking, observing—is a machine. Naturally, a perspective so challenging to liberal and spiritual views of humanity has been registered and challenged in turn by contemporary fiction. Yet, the posture of postmodern fictions that have directly addressed the question of cybernetics is complex. They tend to exploit and succumb to the seductions of systems of communication and ordering. Yet, at the same time, they pose subtle counterstatements: If you are going to claim that you can describe the human mind and human communication in deterministic forms, you must discount—or, better yet, account for—curiously human features that so far have resisted such determinisms. In what way is self-consciousness mechanical? What are the algorithms for the tendency to make things up, to lie, to use irony, to make metaphors, and to fashion fictions? What are the formal laws governing our infinite capacity to imagine impossible worlds? Precisely unlike artificial intelligence computers or cybernetic devices, we humans have this slippery way of generating our own countersystems, to resist even as we adopt systems of explanation and ordering.

Pynchon uses the machinery of metaphor to activate machinery in the human mind, a link that paradoxically makes us aware of just how we slip out beyond mere mechanism. From one point of view, Pynchon is engaged in a dialogue with science, part of a larger collaborative epistemological project that transcends distinctions between *science* and *literature* and absorbs enormous amounts of our cultural—and indeed global—resources. The purpose of this project is nothing less than to create a positive model of the human mind. In participating in this project as a skeptic, or perhaps even as a member of the guerrilla resistance, Pynchon has nonetheless defined that gap where mechanism does not *yet* work. As an artificial intelligence researcher might note, he has succeeded in creating an enticing map of future projects. Still, in doing so, Pynchon has also succeeded, along with other authors of cybernetic fiction, in that enduring goal of American literature: to use the word as a weapon against system, "or whatever it is the word is there, buffering, to protect us from." At this stage in our cultural evolution, in this point in our cybernetic age, the success of their project testifies to the continuing potency of literature.

Notes

This chapter was originally presented as a panel paper to the MLA in December, 1986 as "Reading in the Servo-Mechanical Loop." It appears in a much abbreviated version, in *Discourse: Journal for Theoretical Studies in Media and Culture* 9 (Spring-Summer, 1987), pp 53-63.

1. See Howard Gardner, *The Mind's New Science: A History of the Cognitive Revolution* (New York: Basic Books, 1985).
2. Interestingly enough, the genetic revolution in microbiology was probably made possible by a new understanding of Shannon's Law, one of the essential principles of information theory. Claude Shannon, working in the 1940s on ways to improve the signal to noise ratio in communications systems at Bell Labs, noted that "all physical channels possess a certain quantifiable capacity to transmit information." Claude Shannon and Warren Weaver, *The Mathematical Theory of Communication* (Urbana, Ill: University of Illinois Press, 1949). Of course, this includes cells and molecules. Joseph Weizenbaum, originally an artificial intelligence researcher at MIT, suggests that genetics was actually first received in cybernetic terms: "The results announced by Watson and Crick fell on soil

already prepared by the public's vague understanding of computers, computer circuitry and information theory. . . . Hence, it was easy for the public to see the "cracking" of the genetic code as an unraveling of a computer program, and the discovery of the double-helix . . . as an explication of a computer's basic wiring diagram." *Computer Power and Human Reason: From Judgement to Calculation* (San Francisco: W.H. Freeman, 1976) p. 156. Interestingly enough, Weizenbaum's own research in artificial intelligence led him to create the popular program ELIZA, an interactive dialogue in which the computer plays the role of psychiatrist by responding to certain verbal cues with stock questions. Later, Weizenbaum came to view the cybernetic paradigm as a threat, and wrote a long analysis of how the embrace of artificial intelligence as a replacement for human intelligence amounted to a descent "from judgement to calculation" (the sub-title of his work).

3. Conventionally, the birth of cybernetics is traced to certain advances in communications technology and theory (Claude Shannon's work at Bell Labs) and the need for more refined guidance and targeting systems in WWII weaponry (Norbert Wiener's work at MIT). But according to Wiener himself, cybernetics arose in the 1940s partly as a response to the uncertainty which Heisenberg's theorem incarnates in the relationship between observer and observed. In other words, the primary impetus to the cybernetic view came from a more fundamental epistemological concern. Scientists felt the need to phrase a response to the troubling new discoveries in quantum physics that put uncertainty at the heart of nature's composition and interposed human indeterminacy between the scientist's theory and reality. Cybernetics was the direct response to what for many, including Einstein and Wiener, was this intolerable situation. It was this intolerable situation that led Einstein to phrase the century's best snappy reply by a physicist, "I cannot be persuaded that God shoots craps with the universe."

This expresses a fundamentally neo-classical urge to banish probabilism or uncertainty from science, to erase the human role in favor of the purely objective mathematical description of information exchanges in nature's mechanics. Wiener reveals the depth to which a Manicheistic metaphysics motivated his theory when he writes about this struggle in *The Human Use of Human Beings*: "This random element, this organic incompleteness [proposed by Heisenbergian physics], is one which without too violent a figure of speech we may consider evil; the negative evil which St. Augustine characterizes as incompleteness" (New York: Doubleday/Anchor, 1954) p. 11. Acting on a suggestion made by Leo Szilard as early as 1922, Wiener—and then Claude Shannon in the 1940s—took the formula for thermodynamic randomness (*entropy*) and used it to define the randomness which provides the necessary precursor for information, and then also called it *entropy*. From there, it was one small step to define information as *negentropy*. In other words, theorists decided to specify that the amount of energy lost in displacing the electron during the attempt to observe it (shining a light on it actually pushes it out of its position, for instance) was made proportionate to the amount of information needed to specify its position. This little trick of nomenclature had powerful consequences. It appropriated the uncertainty that the human introduced into the system and defined such uncertainty as a precondition for having a quantifiable amount of information. Cybernetics thereby managed to subsume the messiness of the observer's role, including his consciousness of a sub-atomic event, into a system of positive math.

4. There is a good discussion of this connection in Rudy Rucker, *Infinity and the Mind* (New York: Bantam, 1983).

5. See Steve J. Heims' excellent biography, *John von Neumann and Norbert Wiener: From Mathematics to the Technologies of Life and Death* (Cambridge: MIT Press, 1980) pp. 58-77. See also John von Neumann, *Theory of Games and Economic Behavior* (Princeton: Princeton University Press, 1953 [c1944]). The cybernetic metaphor that the brain is a machine did not originate with Wiener, of course. A few years earlier, as early as 1936, Alan Turing was exploring the mathematical imitation of computers, but by computers Turing at this point merely meant the only known meaning for the word: humans doing mathematical calculations. Yet even in this early work Turing entertains the idea of a machine capable of imitating those human processes. Earlier that year, Turing attended a lecture course by von Neumann, who was visiting Cambridge University from Princeton, although the course was not about computation by machine but about the pure mathematical underpinning of quantum theory, in which von Neumann was still engaged as part of his battle to find a deterministic solution for Heisenberg's Uncertainty Principle. Turing's biographer speculates that von Neumann's lectures were so influential that they moved Turing to apply for a fellowship at Princeton, which he took the next year (1936). Andrew Hodges, *Alan Turing: The Enigma* (New York: Simon and Schuster, 1983). Von Neumann's explicit attempt to formalize the model of the brain as a computer is *The Computer and The Brain* (New Haven: Yale University Press, 1958).

6. Norbert Wiener, *Cybernetics: Control and Communication in the Animal and in the Machine.* (Cambridge: MIT Press, 1948).

7. See "Cyborgs: Postmodern Phantasms of Body and Mind" by Gabriele Schwab in *Discourse* 9 (Spring-Summer 1987): pp. 64-84.

8. See David Porush, "AI as Alien: William Gibson's Neuromancer" in *Aliens*, ed. by George Slusser and Eric Rabkin (Westport, Conn. Greenwood, 1987). See also the *Scientific American* issue on computing, October, 1987. Professor Michael Benedikt has issued a collection of abstracts from the First Symposium on Cyberspace sponsored at the University of Texas, Austin, May, 1990.

9. See also John Barth's seminal essay, "The Literature of Exhaustion" in *Atlantic Monthly* (August 1967); Susan Sontag's "The Aesthetics of Silence," *Partisan Review* January, 1966; and George Steiner's *The Language of Silence* (New York: Atheneum Press, 1967) p. 14.

10. *Commentary* 31 (March, 1961): 223-33.

11. *The Sciences of the Artificial* (Cambridge, MIT Press, 1969), 15.

12. Stephen Toulmin, *The Return to Cosmology: Postmodern Science and the Theology of Nature* (Berkeley: Univ. of California Press, 1982), p. 210.

13. Cybernetic fiction is not peculiar to America. Italy is well-represented by the noted postmodernist author, Italo Calvino, whose novels since *T-Zero*, including *If on a winter's night a traveller*, *The Castle of Crossed Destinies*, and *Invisible Cities*, exemplify the genre. Michel Butor similarly represents France, as does Samuel Beckett in *The Lost Ones* (originally *Les Depeupleurs* [1973]). Stanislaw Lem, the Polish expatriate living in Vienna, has several cybernetic fictions, including *The Cyberiad Mortal Engines* and his recent *Fiasco* (1987). Page references to *V.* (Philadelphia: J.B. Lippincott, 1963) and to *The Crying of Lot 49* (New York: Bantam Books, 1967) will be given in the text.

14. The term was coined by William Burroughs in his fiction, *The Soft Machine*. I used it in the title to a more extensive exploration of this body of fiction, *The Soft Machine: Cybernetic Fiction* (New York & London: Methuen, 1985).

15. Hyper-synthesized punk music, kinetic sculpture, and some forms of computer-generated art seem to be engaged in the same project.

16. John Stark writes: "Pynchon's work cannot be fully understood without tracing the influence of cybernetics on his work." in his excellent *Pynchon's Fictions and the Literature of Interpretation* (Athens: Univ. of Ohio Press, 1980). William Plater, in a superior study of Pynchon's work writes that cybernetics "incorporates Pynchon's own authorial act and because it is one of the most recurrent themes of his fiction . . . may provide a framework for discovering how various things come together." *The Grim Phoenix: Reconstructing Thomas Pynchon* (Bloomington: Univ. of Indiana Press, 1980]). See also Bruce Herzberg's "Breakfast, Death, Feedback: Thomas Pynchon and the Technologies of Interpretation" in *Science and Literature* (London & Toronto: Bucknell University Press, 1983).

17. Abraham Moles, *Information Theory and Esthetic Perception*, trans. Joel E. Cohen (Urbana, Ill: University of Illinois Press, 1968).

18. See "More about Metaphor" in Andrew Ortony, ed. *Metaphor and Thought* (Cambridge, Eng.: Cambridge Univ. Press, 1979).

19. Earl R. MacCormac, *A Cognitive Theory of Metaphor* (Cambridge: MIT Press, 1985) p. 5.

20. MacCormac, p. 4.

21. MacCormac, p. 4.

13
Turbulence in Literature and Science: Questions of Influence

N. KATHERINE HAYLES

When influence is discussed in literature and science, it nearly always turns out to be the influence of science on literature. If one inquires about the influence of literature on science, one is greeted with such anecdotes as Murray Gell-Man having taken the word "quarks" from *Finnegan's Wake*. Compared with the acknowledged influence of science on literature, these instances are so trivial as to border on the frivolous. Contrast them, for example, with studies discussing the influence of Newton on Blake; Darwin on George Eliot; thermodynamics on Henry Adams. Why is there no comparable list of studies demonstrating the influence of literature on scientists? The answers to this question have important implications for the study of literature and science.

Consider how influence studies in literature and science have traditionally proceeded. Frequently the critic assumes that the scientific theory has discovered the way reality actually is, and that the writer is adapting or interpreting this truth for her own ends. If, as sometimes happens, the writer's version of that truth differs considerably from the scientific source, the critic may take the writer to task for having gotten it wrong.[1] From this standpoint it seems clear why the lines of influence between literature and science are one-way streets. If science is the source of truth to which literature responds, then of course it will influence literature much more than literature will influence it, for it is in direct contact with reality, whereas for literature reality is meditated by science.

This kind of approach ignores at its peril the growing body of work demonstrating that scientific theories are themselves social constructions. For example, in Donna Jean Haraway's analysis of Clarence Ray Carpenter's classic studies of male dominance in primates, she shows how cultural assumptions are transported into the theory through experimental design, theoretical focus, and modes of argumentation.[2] Once it has been scientifically "proven" that male dominance is the governing social principle of primate groups, the theory feeds back into the culture to reinforce the very assumptions that determined it to be a good theory. When scientific theories can be shown to be culturally determined, their privileged position cannot be adequately explained by assuming they map one-to-one correspondences between theoretical constructs and reality. Rather, the privileging of science becomes a social construction to be understood in its own right.[3]

How would the question(s) of influence look from this standpoint? Since it is no longer self-evident why science should influence literature much more than literature influences science, questions addressing this imbalance would need to be asked. What forces within the culture authorize science as the source of truth? How are their interests served by this authorization? How is the ideology of scientific truth propogated and reinforced? What can replications and dissonances between a scientific theory and literary text tell us about the cultural mechanisms at work between the two? What can they tell us about influence studies that attribute dissonance to artistic error and replication to scientific influence? Why do some literary texts and scientific theories accede to the reinscription of cultural assumptions, and other texts and theories resist them? What accounts for whether these reinscriptions and resistances succeed or fail? Asking these questions shifts the focus from influence as such to the social conditions that determine how influence is constituted and replicated in academic discourse. In this view, influence is a construction to be explored rather than a premise to be embraced.

Consider, for example, how this shift in focus would affect how one thought about the correspondence between Gibbs's phase change rule and Henry Adams's theories of historical change.[4] Gibbs demonstrated that phase changes such as the transition of ice to water and water to steam are functions of pressure and temperature. At the critical point where a phase change occurs, the substance continues to absorb (or give off) energy, but no temperature rise (or fall) is observed because the energy is being used to reorganize the substance's molecular structure. At this point different phases exist in equilibrium (for example, ice cubes in a glass of water) until the reorganization is complete and all of the substance exists in the new phase. Gibbs's phase diagrams mapped these transitions and showed where equilibrium areas between different phases occurred. Adams appropriated Gibbs's results to explain changes in social organization.[5] In his view, humankind's ability to tap increasingly powerful energy sources resulted in periodic reorganizations so dramatic that they could aptly be called phase changes. One such phase, the Mechanical, occurred from 1600 to 1900 A.D. Following that was the Electrical, to be succeeded in the twentieth century by the Ethereal, all at exponentially increasing rates of change. In importing the phase change rule into history, Adams did more than recast its terminology. He also altered its underlying meaning, for he sensed that the energy dissipation that nineteenth-century thermodynamicists interpreted to mean the universe was running down had somehow to be reconciled with the increasing complexity so evident in human social organization. The accelerating rate of change was for Adams one expression of this complexity; so were the awesome new energy sources that scientists were discovering, from steam power to X-rays to atomic energy.

Considering the phase change rule and Adams's text as cultural artifacts, one could inquire into their interactions with their culture as well as with each other. One might wonder why the phase change rule became an important concept within thermodynamics while Adams's metaphoric reconstruction of it as a principle of social change was dismissed as wild-eyed conjecture. From a cultural perspective, it could plausibly be argued that the phase change rule was successful because it extended rather than challenged the reigning ideology within thermodynamics, whereas Adams's rule for social change was dismissed because it was incompatible with the accepted view that the world was constantly running down. If Adams had been taken seriously—and there was little chance he would, given the lack of experimental evidence and mathematical rigor in his presentation—the scenario scientists constructed for the universe from the first and second laws of thermodynamics would have to have been drastically revised.

In assessing the play of power between the phase change rule and Adams's rule of acceleration, one quickly becomes aware of how inadequate it would be to argue that the phase change rule succeeded because it was correct, whereas Adams's acceleration rule failed because it was wrong. In fact a revision similar to Adams's formulation eventually took place within science, although when it came, it had nothing to do with *The Education*. A watershed date for the new paradigm is 1968, when it was recognized that phase changes were bound up with the more general phenomena of irreversible processes and the challenge they posed to thinking the world was running down. In 1977, Ilya Prigogine won the Nobel Prize in chemistry for his work showing how dissipative systems with large entropy production can spontaneously reorganize themselves at higher levels of complexity.[6] What was there about Adams's situation that made it possible for him to envision this kind of change for societies seventy years earlier? And after he had written about it, what was there about the situation of his text in the culture that made it fail to become an important focal point for social and scientific change?

My choice of Adams as an example through which to pose these questions is not coincidental. More than most writers and scientists of his time, he understood that questions of influence are themselves social constructions with ideological implications. When he equated the Virgin with the Dynamo in *The Education of Henry Adams*, he was not merely indulging a writer's quaint belief in the power of metaphor. Rather he was recognizing the powerful way that these constructs reinscribed important beliefs for their cultures; he was identifying them as nodes through which the cultural fields resonated. To reduce this profound vision to science's "influence" on Adams is to misread *The Education*. It is also to misunderstand how influence is constituted through and by the culture and how it can be used to interrogate the cultural matrix that bestows upon it its apparent one-way directionality.

The Scandal of Fluid Mechanics

In *This Sex Which Is Not One*, Luce Irigaray speculates in a chapter called "The 'Mechanics' of Fluids" on why there has been a *"historical lag in elaborating a 'theory' of fluids."*[7] Briefly put, her answer posits a *"complicity of long standing between rationality and a mechanics of solids"* (107, emphasis in original). The privileging of solid over fluid mechanics, and indeed the inability of science to deal with turbulent flow at all, she attributes to the association of fluidity with femininity. Whereas men have sex organs that protrude and become rigid, women have openings that leak menstrual blood and vaginal fluids. Although men too flow on occasion—when semen is emitted, for example—this aspect of their sexuality is suppressed; it is the rigidity of the organ that is emphasized, not its complicity in fluid flow. These idealizations are reinscribed in fluid mechanics, which conceives of fluids as laminated planes or other modified solid forms. In the same way that women are erased within masculine conceptions and language, existing only as not-men, so fluids have been erased from science, existing only as not-solids. From this perspective it is no wonder that science has not been able to solve the problem of turbulent flow.

Turbulent flow cannot be solved because the conceptions of fluids (and of women) have been formulated in such a way as necessarily to leave unarticulated remainders.

What do you suppose a fluid dynamicist would make of this argument? From his point of view it could scarcely be anything but scandalous. Not only does it ignore virtually all of the specific formalisms that comprise the mathematics of fluid mechanics, it also implies that these formalisms arose from gender considerations rather than from experimentally informed decisions about the best way to model reality. He would, I suspect, quickly come to the conclusion that Irigaray did not know the first thing about his discipline, and that she is talking through her hat or worse.

There is evidence to support this view. In a footnote to the first page of her chapter, Irigaray airily advises the reader "to consult some texts on solid and fluid mechanics" without bothering to mention any (106). The lack of mathematical detail in her argument forces one to wonder whether she has followed this advice herself. Also conspicuous is the lack of historical detail. Nowhere does she mention a name or date that would enable one to connect her argument with a specific theory of fluids, much less to trace debates between opposing theories. In short, Irigaray's text would seem to be a stellar example of why literature and literary theory do not influence science—at least by the usual rules that govern such games.

But the rules of the game are precisely what is at issue. In her essay "Is the Subject of Science Sexed?", Irigaray makes her challenge to these rules explicit.[8] She begins by musing on how and where one can stand to span different universes of discourse, asking by *what right can one assume a stance outside?*" (73). Rejecting objectivity, she seeks to locate her scientific audience as subjects, saying that if "I were to meet each and every one of you individually, it seems as though I would find a way to say *you, I, we*" (75). This move foreshadows her argument, for she intends to show how the scientific method depends upon intuition, and how intuition is in turn constituted by the reinscription of the male imaginary into scientific models. Her analysis of scientific investigation is thus akin to Haraway's analysis of primatology, in that it aims to unveil a circular dialectic that connects scientific theory with subjects not usually considered to be joined to it.

How does this dialectic work, according to Irigaray? First by constituting the universe as something other than the self, something "in front of oneself" (78); next by imposing a model taken from the self (blindly? Irigaray asks) onto the world, while disavowing any connection between self and model; then by providing the model's universality by consensus between subjects who agree it is so because they are similarly constituted (this move ignores the complicity of subjects in the construction of objects, choosing instead to posit a separation between subject and object, so that the subject touches the world only through the *"meditation of the instrument"* [78, original emphasis]); and finally of avowing that the model's universality constitutes progress (thus authorizing the "schize" between subject and object, discourse and self, that the dialectic both assumes and recreates [78]).

The parentheses that make this last paragraph difficult to read are meant to convey a sense of the elliptical style in which Irigaray writes. In this respect her discourse is quite different from the rational mode of argumentation that Donna Haraway employs in her critique of primatology. The stylistic dissonance between Irigaray's and Haraway's analyses points to an important difference in the assumptions of these two theorists. In keeping with her socialist feminist perspective, Haraway is less interested in the constitution of subjects than she is in the institutional and disciplinary contexts that reinscribe themselves in scientific theories. Her kind of argument challenges scientific objectivity from *within the rules of the game.* Haraway documents her case using evidence that other scholars can verify; she confines her argument to assertions of influence made plausible by her reconstitution of the appropriate contexts; and she analyzes the theories conceptually to reveal their underlying premises. Thus Haraway's analysis accepts the same criteria for judgment as were applied by the scientists in constructing their theories. It differs from normal scientific assessments in broadening the context for judgment to include social and institutional networks. I do not wish to minimize the importance of a broadened context, for it is sufficient to place Haraway at the periphery rather than at the center of normal scientific discourse. Positioning oneself at the periphery is not the same, however, as leaving the game altogether.

Leaving the game is the move that Irigaray makes when she runs the circular dialectic through the self rather than through the culture. It is difficult to articulate her discourse together with that of a fluid dynamicist because they play by different rules. Irigaray takes as given that the constitution of the subject replicates itself in scientific discourse. If this is so, then to play by the rules of that discourse is to lose the game before she starts, for all that one can do within those rules is to reproduce the invisibility of the (male) subject. To render the (male) subject visible to itself, Irigaray posits herself (and women in general) as other than it—fluid where it is solid, interior where it is exterior, silent where it speaks, unwritten where it inscribes, disruptive where it is continuous. Her discourse is fractured, elliptical, nonlinear because it strives to create a space that cannot easily be appropriated into the volumes of male science. In this sense the outrage of our imagined scientist does not signify that Irigaray has failed in her project. For he could comprehend and agree with her argument only if he accedes to opening the space of (his) objectivity to an awareness of (his) interiority. If he insists on maintaining the solidity of his objective position, the fluidity of her subjective one can be processed only as a scandal.

A New Paradigm in Fluid Mechanics

I should like now to undertake what Irigaray declines to do—make the argument for a connection between gender and fluid mechanics from within the rules of scientific discourse, or at least from its periphery. My conclusions will be somewhat different than those Irigaray espouses. Although I think it can be demonstrated that deep cultural assumptions are replicated in the structures of scientific theories, I do not agree that fluids, particularly turbulent fluids, have simple or unified gender identifications. Rather, I take turbulence to be a construction that can be interpreted in different ways under different paradigms. When it moves from one paradigm to another, it undergoes a significant transformation in cultural encoding. I envision turbulence as a highly fissured site within contemporary literary and scientific discourses in which older cultural encodings are overlaid by new ones to create highly complex patterns. Before exploring the dynamics of this transformation, I will need to explain why until very recently turbulence was one of the great unsolved problems of classical mechanics and how the new paradigm circumvents this difficulty.

Often microscopic fluctuations within a flowing liquid cancel each other out, for example when a river flows smoothly within its banks. In this case each water molecule follows much the same path as the one before it, so that water molecules starting close together continue to be close. Sometimes, however, microscopic fluctuations persist and are magnified up to macroscopic level, causing eddies and backwaters to form. Then molecules that began close together quickly separate, and those that were far apart come close together. As a result, it becomes extremely difficult to calculate how the flow will evolve. Kenneth Wilson, who won the 1982

Nobel Prize in physics for his work on modeling turbulence, explains that theorists "have difficulties with these problems because they involve very many coupled degrees of freedom. It takes many variables to characterize a turbulent flow or the state of a fluid near the critical point."[9] The mathematics of turbulence is so complex that even the new supercomputers are inadequate to deal with it. Computation times become unreasonably long after only three or four variables are considered, whereas dozens are necessary to create a model that can simulate turbulence accurately.

Wilson's breakthrough was finding a way to arrive at an analytical (as opposed to an empirical) solution for turbulence. The essence of his approach is to shift the focus from following individual molecules to looking for symmetries between different length scales. Recursive symmetries are characteristic of turbulent flow; large swirls of water have smaller swirls within which are smaller swirls. To model these symmetries, Wilson used renormalization groups. Renormalization had first emerged as a technique in quantum mechanics, where physicists used it to get rid of infinite quantities when they appeared in the equations. Originally the only justification for the procedure was that it made the answers come out right. If you think this sounds suspiciously arbitrary, you are not alone. For years virtually all mathematicians and some physicists regarded renormalization as no more than hand-waving. But Wilson saw its deeper implications.

He knew that in renormalization certain quantities regarded as fixed—for example, particle mass—are treated as if they are variable. He realized that there is a sense in which this is a profound truth rather than an arbitrary procedure. For example, we tend to think of a golf ball as a smooth sphere. But to a mosquito it would appear as a pocked, irregular surface, and to a bacterium, as the Wilson Alps. Renormalization implied that the choice of rule used to measure physical properties affected the answer. At the same time, it revealed that there was something else—something not normally considered—that remained constant over many measurement scales. This was the scaling factor. By combining the renormalization process with the idea of a mathematical group, Wilson arrived at a method whereby this factor could be defined and calculated.

A group, as it is used in mathematics, denotes a set of objects that under certain mathematical operations produce other elements in the same set. One kind of operations that members of a group can undergo is symmetry operations. For example, a cube rotated ninety degrees in any direction appears unchanged in its spatial orientation; it is therefore said to be invariant under right angle rotation and when so rotated produces another element of the same group, that is, another cube. Tetrahedrons are in the same mathematical group as cubes because they also have this property. The purpose of finding a renormalization group is to look for symmetries that are invariant for different measurement scales.

As an illustration of one of these symmetries, consider the classic "middle third" set, first proposed by Cantor in the nineteenth century. Imagine that we draw a line from 0 to 1, as in figure 1.

Figure 1. Cantor's "Middle Third" Set

(1)   0_____1

(2)   0_____   _____1

(3)   0_____   _____   _____   _____1

Now we erase the middle third of line 1. Each of the smaller lines of 2 has the same form as line 1, and multiplying one of these line segments by three gives the original line back again. If we erase the middle third of the small lines of 2, we create the even smaller lines in 3. Each of the two broken lines of 3 has the same form as the entire interval of 2, and multiplying either segment by three gives line 2 back again. If we keep erasing middle thirds, each time the symmetry of the resulting small part mirrors the larger part of the step before, and each time the larger part can be obtained by multiplying the smaller part by three. Sets that have this kind of symmetry are said to possess fixed points. The purpose of defining a renormalization group is to discover the operations and variables that allow fixed point symmetry to emerge.

Groups that display fixed points have physical significance because the symmetry allows coupling to take place between different length levels. When a system possesses fixed points, perturbations on the smallest scale are quickly transmitted throughout the system, affecting even the largest macroscopic level. Imagine a bullwhip moving at just the right frequency so that a small twitch of the handle is transmitted into larger and larger waves all the way to the end, causing the whip to emit a loud and satisfying "CRACK." This kind of transmission and magnification is possible be-cause a system possesses the appropriate kind of symmetry. When fixed point symmetry is present, systems "crack" because the symmetry permits microscopic changes to translate into coordinated movements all through the system. Turbulent flow occurs because the system is configured so as to magnify microscopic deviations into macroscopic chaos. The implicit order that makes an analytical solution sometimes possible derives from the symmetrical couplings between different length scales and the predictable ways in which the onset of chaos occurs.

The generality of Wilson's approach can be appreciated by looking at the range of behavior to which it applies. As we have seen, one area is turbulent flow; another is phase change behavior, as when water turns to steam. The transition from water to steam illustrates how fluctuations at a microscopic level can be translated into dramatic macroscopic changes. Water and steam appear very different; one is liquid, the other gas. But this change in macroscopic properties originates in microscopic changes. At the point where the phase change takes place, the system is characterized by "bubbles of steam and drops of water intermixed at all size scales from macroscopic, visible sizes down to atomic scales."[10] At this critical point, and only at this point, the system undergoes a phase change because it possesses the fixed point symmetry that allows changes at the smallest level to be transmitted all the way up to the largest level. Thus turbulent flow and phase change behavior, different as they are, can both be understood in terms of the scaling symmetries. Additional applications are in quantum field theory, where coupling mechanisms between particles are important.

Implications of the New Paradigms

Implicit in Wilson's approach are new assumptions about how one models a system. To understand what these assumptions are, compare them with the paradigms of classical physics (under which rubric I include Newtonian mechanics and differential and integral calculus). In classical physics the focus is on the autonomy of the individual unit and its behavior through time. For example, in a classical analysis of a hurtling cannonball, the cannonball's parabolic arc is broken into arbitrarily small line segments, each of which occupies a small unit of time. The change across these units is expressed through a differential equation. Adding together the incremental units (or more accurately, taking the limit as the time increments get infinitely small) gives the path as a whole. In its fundamental assumptions, this method closely follows the commonsense intuitions we rely on in figuring out when a running pedestrian will get to the other side of the street. We perceive the figure as a unit (although his hat may be flying off in one direction, his scarf in another), and we project when he will make it to the curb by assuming that he will continue more or less in the same direction he is going.

These assumptions work well for cannonballs. They do not work well for turbulent flow, because turbulence has an extremely complex internal structure. When one concentrates on the paths of individual molecules and tries to express how these paths change over time, the mathematics quickly becomes intractable because each path is changing in an unpredictable way, and in a different way than neighboring paths. Only when the molecules stay in their lanes, so to speak, can the problem of flow be solved in the classical paradigm. Thus classical paradigms can solve laminar flow but not chaotic turbulence. The new paradigm is more successful in modeling turbulence because it does not try to follow individual paths. Instead it concentrates on recursive symmetries between different length levels.

These assumptions have found practical application in fractal geometry. Fractal geometry uses computer technology to create forms that possess recursive symmetries across many length levels.[11] Fractal forms are created by iterating nonlinear differential equations—that is, by using the output of one calculation as input for the next in a cyclic process that allows the forms to move through time. Because the recursive symmetries between different lengths allow small changes to propagate rapidly through the system, very small changes in the iterative formulae can result in very large changes in macroscopic behavior. Hence one can model complex forms and movements through many fewer bits of information than would be required if each change had to be described individually. Fractal geometry shares with Wilson's renormalization groups a focus on recursive symmetries between levels rather than an emphasis on the individual unit. In both models, anthropomorphic time is replaced by computer iteration of mathematical equations.

The change in perspective implicit in these paradigms signals not just the arrival of new scientific theories but a change in the ground of representation itself. The same kind of shift is apparent in many other disciplines besides physics and mathematics. It is so wide-ranging, in fact, that in my view the only adequate explanation for it is to assume that it has been authorized by reconfigurations in the cultural matrix. Compare the assumptions of the new scientific paradigms, for example, to Foucault's archeological analyses of culture.[12] In contrast to older paradigms such as Adam Smith's economies or Hobbes's theory of politics, Foucault is not interested in the behavior of the individual unit. Instead he looks for coupling mechanisms that allow changes at one level or site to be rapidly transmitted through the system as a whole. In his view, individuals do not constitute culture; culture constitutes individuals. Or compare it to Lacan's rewriting of Freudian psychology, in which it is not the "self" so dear to Western thought that matters but coupling mechanisms that control the ruptures and continuities between different stages.

Irigaray is not entirely wrong, then, in conjecturing that fluid mechanics has not developed nearly as quickly as solid mechanics because scientific constructions of flow are gender encoded. Obvious connections do exist between gender constructions and the assumptions that have been encoded into the classical models of Western science, from Newtonian mechanics and calculus to politics and economics. The individual autonomy that is central to these models has its corollary in the hypostatized male of Western culture. Among his identifying characteristics are autonomy, insulation from his environment, and ability to act as a team player.[13] These qualities are reinscribed in the descriptions of fluid mechanics, for they are exactly the characteristics that make laminar flow amenable to classical analyses.

By contrast, turbulent flow cannot be analyzed in the classical model because these assumptions do not hold true. In turbulent flow, the liquid is exquisitely sensitive to tiny fluctuations or uncertainties, which are quickly magnified to macroscopic expression; individual units are decidedly not team players, diverging from each other in unpredictable ways; individual molecules act chaotically because they are coupled to each other by complex symmetry relations. It is not difficult to translate these characteristics of turbulence into gender constructions. One thinks, for example, of the stereotype of the hysterical woman; her sensitivity to her environment; her tendency to let little things quickly build into major disturbances; her misunderstanding of the ethics of team play; and her unpredictable alliances with others of her sex.

Equally important from the point of view of cultural encoding is the disproportionality between cause and effect that turbulence implies. In classical mechanics and in Euclidean geometry, nature is considered "conformable to itself." What holds true on one level is assumed to hold true on every level; if this assumption proves false, then the system is regarded as aberrant or anomalous. As a corollary, small causes are expected to lead to small results. Classical paradigms are thus scale-invariant. By contrast, paradigms in the science of chaos (which includes research in fractal geometry, nonlinear dynamics, meteorology, epidemiology, and irreversible thermodynamics, to mention only a few of the areas contributing to this interdisciplinary field) are *scale-dependent*. These paradigms recognize that what holds true for one level may not hold true for another. And they emphasize that tiny causes can lead to dramatic and irreversible systemic changes.

This shift in assumptions implies a new vision of how the world is structured. One contribution of chaos theory has been to make visible the amnesia at the center of classical science, the forgetfulness that made it consider ordered systems as the rule from which everything else was a deviation.[14] In fact chaotic systems are everywhere in nature, from cream swirling through coffee to global weather patterns. By foregrounding how prevalent chaotic systems are, the science of chaos has delivered a death blow to Laplacian determinism more fatal than that delivered by quantum mechanics. In practice quantum uncertainties cancel each other out so that macroscopic systems remain stable despite quantum fluctuations. By contrast, chaos theory shows that a very large range of *deterministic* systems exhibit chaotic behavior. Linking determinism with unpredictability undercuts the very foundation of an ordered view of the universe, for it implies that chaos can be anywhere, even in the swinging pendulum that Newtonian mechanics took as emblematic of universal order.[15]

With this kind of change in the air, it is no wonder that a theorist like Irigaray is interested in a *rapprochment* with the new science. So, for example, in "Is the Subject of Science Sexed?" she appropriates the dissipative structures of entropy-producing systems as models for female sexuality. Just as Freud had seen in classical thermodynamics authorization for his view of (male) sexuality as essentially conservative, so Irigaray sees in the new science authorization for her view that female sexuality operates according to radically different principles. As is well known, Freud's writing is shot through with hydraulic imagery, virtually always used in a conservative sense: that which engorges an organ and makes it rigid is unavailable for sublimation elsewhere (sublimation in its scientific sense denotes the transformation of a solid into a gas, without becoming a liquid). By contrast, in the fluid realm of female sexuality, turbulence leads not to decay but to *jouissance*, with its connotation of synergistic release that builds on itself to achieve ever more complex expression. It is not difficult to see why the new paradigms seem to be more closely aligned with female sexuality than classical science, for they directly challenge scale-invariance and conservation principles.

How valid are these associations between the feminine and the science of chaos? Do they imply that the new science has inserted the feminine into the dominant male culture, into the hegemony of (masculinist) science itself? I believe that the relation between the science of chaos and the feminine is more complex than this simple one-to-one correspondence would suggest. The displacement of classical assumptions by the new paradigms is not an either/or proposition. Rather, the emergence of new paradigms produces extremely complex configurations in which traces of old attitudes are embedded within new models, creating turbulent vortices that follow no simple dynamics and that vary widely from site to site.

A recent account of the new science will help us explore how the tensions between old attitudes and new models work to shape narratives. In looking at a popular account of scientific research as well as at the research itself, I hope to open passages between literature, science, and culture in which the flow of influence is construed as a turbulent complexity, not a one-way street.

Why Are There Only Men in a Female World?

The emergence of chaos as an interdisciplinary research front is chronicled in James Gleick's *Chaos: Making a New Science*.[16] Gleick, a science writer for the *New York Times,* is interested primarily in the new concepts that chaos theory entails, but he also leavens his account with personal anecdotes and observations drawn from the hundreds of personal interviews he conducted with scientists in his research. He describes his book as a narrative history. He rightly sees it as telling a story, and, like any storyteller, he has shaped his material in ways both obvious and subtle. It is this shaping that I want to explore, for it reveals a complex interplay between cultural attitudes and scientific concepts.

The interplay is most apparent in the curious absence of women in Gleick's text. Hundreds of men are mentioned by name; some dozen are depicted in enough detail so that we almost feel as if we know them. But no women, or virtually none. What are we to make of this absence, this lack? It is possible to argue that Gleick's text simply reflects the prevailing situation within science. Even more than most sciences, chaos theory is heavily dominated by men, especially in America. But the absence of women goes beyond the acknowledged scarcity of distinguished women scientists. It pervades the entire depicted world.

Because the personal realm is where we would expect women to be in the male-dominated world Gleick writes about, their absence is most striking in the personal vignettes that punctuate Gleick's account of the scientific research. These vignettes show what the living quarters of this or that scientist are like; they reveal where one scientist goes for walks, what another likes to eat. But in all this rich detail, women never appear. On one of the few occasions when the anonymous "wives" of the male scientists are mentioned, Gleick implies that their presence signaled the kind of occasion in which it would be impossible for the men to have a serious scientific conversation (141). The impression is that none of these men has a relationship with a woman that is important in his intellectual life; none works with a female collaborator who is an important contributor; and none spends much time with women. The settings in which the male scientists appear reinforce the impression that serious science is a solitary (as well as a masculine) endeavor. Feigenbaum, one of the superstars of chaos, is shown walking away from a group so that he can observe a waterfall; on another occasion, he has a crucial insight when he walks away from a group outdoors and notices that their talk is reduced to babble by the distance. Another scientist likes to take long walks in the desert, sometimes leaving his family behind for weeks at a time. When living quarters are discussed, they are depicted as eccentric or antidomestic. Feigenbaum has no furniture; a group of Santa Cruz graduate students who became important researchers in the field live in a house littered with bean bag chairs. Food is equally rudimentary or odd.

No doubt these details are accurate. But by mentioning them and not others, the text creates an ambiance for the scientific discoveries it describes. As it is shown here, the world of science is first of all genderless— genderless because there is only one gender. It is also solitary, with chance connections made between individuals who discover, often quite by accident, that someone else somewhere in the world is working on the same problem they are. And it is marked by a flow of narrative time in which certain moments are retrospectively identified as decisive, even though they may have seemed ordinary enough when they occurred. Treating time in this way is effective in creating the kind of suspense that keeps readers turning pages; but it also makes time into a series of *agons* marking the junctures at which fate took a different turn. All of these components work together to substantiate Gleick's claim that "no committee of scientists" brought about the new paradigms, only "a handful of individuals" (182).

This view of the scientific enterprise exists in a curiously paradoxical relationship to the larger view of chaos that Gleick presents. For many of the scientists whose words he records, chaos is more than just another theory. It represents an opening of the self to the messiness of life, to all the chaotic unpredictable phenomena that linear science had taught them to screen out. Once roused, they remember that the messiness had always been there and they are able to see it in a new light, perceiving it as central rather than marginal, beautiful rather than aberrant. But these are just the aspects of life that have traditionally been associated with woman. Indeed, chaos itself has often been depicted as female. In the English Renaissance, for example, the male seed was commonly represented as contributing form. The female was thought to contribute raw unshaped *materia*, matter devoid of form or structure. In validating chaos as a scientific concept, Gleick seems to have found it necessary to expunge the female from his world. Why?

I can of course only speculate about the psychological and cultural dynamics underlying this exclusion. Nevertheless, certain aspects are sufficiently clear as to be almost obvious. In the Western tradition, chaos has played the role of the other—the unrepresented, the unarticulated, the unformed, the unthought. In identifying with chaos, the scientists that Gleick writes about open themselves to this otherness, and they perceive their intercourse with it as immensely fructifying, both for their work and disciplines, and for them personally. But otherness is also always a threat, arousing the desire to control it, or even more extremely, to subsume it within the known boundaries of the self, thus annihilating the very foreignness that makes it dangerously attractive.

Both of these impulses are evident in Gleick's text, and probably are at work within chaos theory as well. The desire to control chaos is evident in the search for ways to rationalize it. By finding within it the structures of order, these scientists have in effect subsumed chaos in the familiar. But if this incorporation were entirely successfuly, chaos could no longer function in its liberating role as a representation of the other. Perhaps this is why Benoit Mandelbrot, the inventor of fractal geometry, goes out of his way to emphasize that the rationalization of chaos in fractal geometry can never be entirely successful.[17] For Mandelbrot, some residue of the un-tamable and nonrational should always remain. Thus he urges that the simulation of complex natural forms such as coastlines and landscapes by fractal forms should be achieved not by complete rationalization of the computer algorithm, but by periodic injections of chance. It is worth noting that Mandelbrot has been roundly criticized on this score by Michael Barnsley, who argues that the commercial value of fractal geometry is greatly increased by algorithms that allow for complete control of how the simulated forms will evolve.[18] Already available are fractal T-shirts, fractal calendars, fractal art prints, and fractal coffee table books, as well as fractal coffee mugs. Given the rapid commodification that fractal geometry is undergoing, it is clear which side will win in the argument over how far chaos should remain uncontrolled. The co-optation of fractal geometry into the commodity economy of late capitalism shows how problematic it is to equate the new scientific paradigms with feminist agendas for social change.

A similar problematic between control and chaos is encoded into Gleick's text, especially in his divided response toward the feminine. Representations of actual women and of activities closely associated with them are rigorously excluded from the depicted world. But the feminine principle of chaos is celebrated as having put male scientists into touch with the mysterious otherness of the world and of their own selves. By admitting the feminine as an abstract principle but excluding actual women, Gleick attains control over the polysemy of chaos. Although he does not put it this way, he re-presents chaos as a repository of the Lacanian real at the same time that he strips it of its more dangerous and engendered aspects. As a result, chaos is admitted within the boundaries of scientific discourse, but science itself remains as monolithically masculine as ever.

In achieving this accommodation, Gleick's text engenders a series of paradoxes. It depicts chaos theory as the achievement of extraordinary individuals who stepped out of the mainstream, but this scenario of the solitary man who opens up a frontier is itself deeply a part of the American mainstream. It shows science as an exclusively male domain, but it is the peculiar project of this domain to have intercourse with a female principle. It intimates that scientific discovery is an activity men engage in when they separate themselves from their families and from the larger culture, but the theories these men formulate imply that the individual unit is not important. It represents time as a continuous stream interrupted by fateful moments, but the new paradigms substitute computer input for anthropomorphic time. The complex play among gender, individuality, and scientific theory in Gleick's text indicates that chaos theory is a deeply fissured site within the culture, in which lingering assumptions from older paradigms are embedded within the emerging paradigms of the new science. When there is this kind of complex interplay between science and culture, science cannot be separated from the cultural matrix. Like literature, science is always already cultural and cannot be otherwise.

Opening the Interior: This Volume Which Is Not One

In a provocative essay on the origins of geometry, Michel Serres imagines
Thales standing in the Egyptian desert before one pyramid.[19] Two others
loom in the distance, different and yet somehow the same. The mathematical concept of similarity, Serres suggests, is already encoded into the
scene. Thales stands in the domain of implicit knowledge; all he need do is
make it explicit. Yet the movement from tacit to explicit knowledge is not
trivial. It requires that the particularity of the pyramid's shadow, with all of
its irregularities and local variations, be negated in favor of the ideal form.
When that transformation occurs, Thales will be able to use the length of
the shadow to measure the height of the pyramid, and geometry will have
begun.

For Serres this is a momentous juncture in the history of Western
culture, for it signifies the privileging of order over chaos, information over
noise, that will reign unchallenged in science until the last quarter of the
twentieth century. Serres argues that once the rule of order is established,
the pyramid is rendered transparent to the sun of reason. No longer is its
interior mysteriously inaccessible to the omniscient view of transcendent
knowledge. Instead, the pyramid, and every other geometrical form, is
conceived as a solid that has no interiority. Similarly, shadows are ban-
ished or are represented only as reflections of solid forms. From this point
on, similitudes enter the realm of rigorous correspondence and operate
according to the binary logic of same/different. In Euclidean geometry all
volumes are accessible; all volumes are one in their negation of interiority.

For Irigaray, a crucial difference between man and woman is the
interiority of a woman's body space, a vagina and uterus that is not up front
but inside.[20] She frequently alludes to cultural practices that are designed
to give men control over this interior space—from the suturing shut of the
vagina still practiced in developing countries to the episiotomies still
favored by American obstetricians. One might add to her observations the
fact that "civilized" countries are rarely thought of as having interiors.
Countries like France and the United States have heartlands or midlands,
but they have no interiors because everything is known and accessible. "To
open the interior" or "to penetrate the interior" are phrases reserved for
countries and spaces thought to be available for colonization.

For this masculinist way of thought, turbulent fluids were not just
unsolvable problems but threatening configurations, for they implied the
existence of an interiority so complex that it could not be processed within

classical paradigms. Turbulence signified a shadowy interior that remained inaccessible and unknown, a site that could not be assimilated into the space of similitude. Now that is changing. A new geometry has emerged that validates highly irregular and fragmented surfaces, and a new science of nonlinear dynamics has come forth that sees complex systems and turbulent flows as more prevalent—and more beautiful—than ordered structures. In a sense, the science of chaos restores the interiority that Serres believes was negated with the invention of geometry. It recognizes that volumes have interiors, and it valorizes the fact that these interiors are multiple and complex rather than one and the same.

How far these new ideas will affect the underlying attitudes that characterize a masculinist science is both a complex and an open question. It is likely that the cultural changes that made the women's movement possible also made chaos a thinkable thought. To this extent, I see feminist theory as aligned with the new science. And yet at each of these sites complex internal dynamics operate, as Gleick's representation of the new science demonstrates and as attacks from within the feminist community on Irigaray's essentialism confirm. Change is not unitary or simple any more than the flow of influence between the cultural matrix, the new science, and feminist theory is simple or unidirectional. Flows in these instances are always complex and multidirectional—that is to say, turbulent.

Especially problematic within the new paradigms is the emphasis on recursive symmetries. Since this emphasis replaces the classical focus on individuality, it is possible to see it as a liberating release from the assumptions of individual autonomy that made it easy to think of disciplines as isolated entities analogous to self-determined individuals who existed apart from and above their culture. Yet the symmetrical recursiveness of the new paradigms bears a disturbing resemblance to what Baudrillard has called the precession of simulacra,[21] and what Irigaray criticizes as the repetition of the same.[22] To note the resemblance is not necessarily to conclude that the new paradigms will be as repressive as or more repressive than the old.

Scientific concepts, in and of themselves, are underdetermined in relation to social meaning and value. Only when they are embedded in a particular site and appropriated for specific purposes is it possible to say what they mean for the culture. This implies, of course, that they will mean different things in different contexts. In my view, the flows from the new scientific theories to the culture are still too nascent to say with certainty what they will mean to whom and for what reasons. For example, they mean something to Irigaray; but even though she seems to be influenced by the new science, it is difficult to be sure of how much she knows about it and of whether her knowledge is an implicit valorization of all science or applies more specifically to the new paradigms.[23] Equally problematic is how much the new science was authorized by cultural changes that Irigaray, along with many others, has helped to initiate. However we choose to answer these questions, it is clear that these complexities cannot be adequately represented as simple one-way flows of influence from science to literature.

It remains to say what space I see my essay as occupying within the volume that contains it. Given the current state of the field, a book entitled *American Literature and Science* could be predicted to speak of how literature has been influenced by science. My essay speaks in a different voice, urging us to consider science and literature as two sites within a complex cultural field. Yet even as I write these lines, I recognize that my essay will be read differently because it is inside this volume. Indeed, even if I were not inclined to do so, my argument would compel me to admit that the lines of influence between my essay and others in this book will be multidirectional. I hope that you will read the others differently because of what I have written; I acknowledge you will read me differently because of what the others have written. To recognize the complexity of influence as a social construction is necessarily to acknowledge the limits of authority and the polysemy of meaning. Neither I nor any other writer within this volume can control this turbulence. "In this volume which is not one," I am content if my essay has set up an inner turbulence that reinscribes the complex dynamics characteristic of the interplay between literature, science, and culture.

Notes

1. An example is Robert Nadeau's reading of Nabokov's *Ada* in *Readings from the New Book on Nature: Physics and Metaphysics in the Modern Novel* (Amherst: Univ. of Massachusetts Press, 1981).

2. Donna Jean Haraway, *Primate Visions: Gender, Race, and Nature in the World of Modern Science* (New York: Routledge, 1989), 84-114.

3. This is not to say that science cannot give us meaningful information about our interactions with reality. The social construction of scientific theories does not necessarily invalidate their truth claims. For a fuller version of this argument, see Hayles, "Constrained Constructivism: Locating Scientific Inquiry in the Theater of Representation," in George

Levine, ed., *Realism and Representation: Epistemology in Science and Culture* (Madison: Univ. of Wisconsin Press, 1992).

4. Henry Adams, "A Letter to American Teachers of History," in Brooks Adams, ed., *Degradation of Democratic Dogma* (New York: Macmillan, 1919).

5. Ibid.

6. For an account of the new philosophical synthesis that Prigogine thinks his work makes possible, see Ilya Prigogine and Isabelle Stengers, *Order Out of Chaos: Man's New Dialogue with Nature* (Toronto: Bantam, 1984). A scientific account of the work is contained in G. Nicolis and I. Prigogine, *Self-Organization in Nonequilibrium Systems: From Dissipative Structures to Order Through Fluctuations* (New York: Wiley and Sons, 1977), and in Ilya Prigogine, *From Being to Becoming: Time and Complexity in the Physical Sciences* (New York: Freeman, 1980). Irigaray clearly knows the work by Prigogine and Stengers, since she alludes to "la nouvelle alliance," the title of the Prigogine and Stengers text in the French original. See also the chapter on Prigogine and Stengers in Hayles, *Chaos Bound: Orderly Disorder in Contemporary Literature and Science* (Ithaca: Cornell Univ. Press, 1990).

7. *This Sex Which Is Not One,* trans. Gillian C. Gill (Ithaca: Cornell Univ. Press, 1985), 106; emphasis in original.

8. *Cultural Critique* 1 (1985):73-88.

9. Kenneth G. Wilson, "The Renormalization Group and Critical Phenomena," *Reviews of Modern Physics* 55 (1983):583-600.

10. Ibid.

11. The seminal text for fractal geometry is Benoit B. Mandelbrot, *The Fractal Geometry of Nature* (New York: Freeman, 1983). See also Michael F. Barnsley and Stephen G. Demko, eds., *Chaotic Dynamics and Fractals* (Orlando, Fla.: Academic Press, 1986).

12. See, for example, Michel Foucault, *The Order of Things: An Archaeology of the Human Sciences* (New York: Pantheon, 1970).

13. Evelyn Fox Keller has explored the relation between individual autonomy and scientific objectivity in *Reflections on Gender and Science* (New Haven: Yale Univ. Press, 1985). The male ethic of team play is articulated by Carol Gilligan in *In a Different Voice: Psychological Theory and Women's Development* (Cambridge, Mass.: Harvard Univ. Press, 1982).

14. For a scientific text making this point, see Robert Shaw, "Strange Attractors, Chaotic Behavior, and Information Flow," *Zeitschrift für Naturforschung* 36A (Jan. 1981):79-112. A more accessible treatment can be found in James P. Crutchfield, J. Doyne Farmer, Norman H. Packard, and Robert S. Shaw, "Chaos," *Scientific American* 255 (Dec. 1986):46-57. Also accessible and charmingly illustrated is John Briggs and F. David Peat, *Turbulent Mirror: An Illustrated Guide to Chaos Theory and the Science of Wholeness* (New York: Harper and Row, 1989).

15. A discussion of motor-driven pendulum as a chaotic system can be found in D'Humieries, M.R. Beasley, B.A. Huberman, and A. Libchaber, "Chaotic States and Routes to Chaos in the Forced Pendulum," *Physical Review* 26A (1982):3483-96.

16. (New York: Viking, 1987).

17. Mandelbrot, *Fractal Geometry,* 210.

18. Barnsley, "Making Chaotic Dynamical Systems to Order," in Barnsley and Demko, *Chaotic Dynamics and Fractals,* 49-62.

19. "Mathematics and Philosophy: What Thales Saw . . . ," in Michel Serres,

Hermes: Literature, Science, Philosophy, ed. Josué V. Harari and David F. Bell (Baltimore: Johns Hopkins Univ. Press, 1982), 84-97.

20. *This Sex* and "Science Sexed?"

21. Jean Baudrillard, *Simulations,* trans. Paul Foss, Paul Patton, and Philip Beitchman (New York: Foreign Agent Series, Semiotext(e), 1983).

22. *This Sex.*

23. Naomi Schor argues in "This Essentialism Which is Not One: Coming to Grips with Irigaray," *differences* 1 (1989):38-58, that in contrast to Irigaray's aggressive posture toward psychoanalysts, her attitude toward an audience of scientists is almost deferential in "Is the Subject of Science Sexed?"

Bibliography: American Literature and Science through 1989

The reader will wish to consult the annual bibliographies in *PMLA*, *Isis*, and the new *Quadrant: A Journal for Literature, Science, and Technology*, published by the Johns Hopkins University Press for the Society for Literature and Science. Also essential is *The Relations of Literature and Science: An Annotated Bibliography of Scholarship, 1880–1980*, edited by Walter Schatzberg, Ronald A. Waite, and Jonathan K. Johnson (New York: Modern Language Association, 1987).

In my introductory essay, I emphasized the "permeable boundaries" between the categories of literature, science, and society. In assembling this bibliography, I was necessarily forced to work within boundaries that are not permeable, even though I recognized that many of the listed works cross these boundaries. Works of practical criticism may also contain important theoretical statements. Works dealing with the history of science in America may also contain important discussions of writers, who may also be scientists. I trust, then, that the reader will understand the limits of these necessary bibliography categories. No doubt there are omissions, but I hope that the bibliography provides some guidance for students and scholars in this new field.

History and Theory of Literature and Science

Amrine, Frederick., ed. *Literature and Science as Modes of Expression.* Dordrecht: Kluwer Academic Publishers, 1989. [Essays by G. Beer, G.S. Rousseau, W. Moser, R. Koch, K. Knoespel, G. Von Molnar, J. Neubauer, P. Bynum, J. Slade, M. Orvell, S. Carter.]

Bernstein, Richard J. *Beyond Objectivism and Relativisim: Science, Hermeneutics, and Praxis.* Philadelphia: Univ. of Pennsylvania Press, 1983.

Bronowski, Jacob. *Science and Human Values.* New York: Harper and Row, 1965.

Carlisle, E. Fred. "Literature, Science and Language: A Study of Similarity and Difference." *Pre/Text* 1 (1980): 39-72.

Eagleton, Terry. *Literary Theory.* Minneapolis: Univ. of Minnesota Press, 1983.

Eichner Hans. "The Rise of Modern Science and the Genesis of Romanticism." *PMLA* 97 (1982): 8-30.

Feyerabend, Paul K. *Problems of Empiricism.* Cambridge: Cambridge Univ. Press, 1981.

———. *Against Method: Outline of an Anarchistic Theory of Knowledge.* Atlantic Highlands: New Jersey Humanities Press, 1975.

Foucault, Michel. *The Order of Things: An Archaeology of the Human Sciences.* New York: Vintage, 1973.

————. *The Archaeology of Knowledge.* Translated by A.M. Sheridan Smith. New York: Harper and Row, 1972.

Garvin, Harry R., and James M. Heath, eds. *Science and Literature.* Lewisburg: Bucknell Univ. Press, 1983. [Essays by J. Heath, J. Neubauer, J. Curtis, B. Herzberg, M. Karlow, C. Krance, R. Lund, K. Newell, L. Steinman.]

Geertz, Clifford. "A Lab of One's Own." *New York Review of Books* 37 (Nov. 8, 1990): 19-23.

Green, Martin. *Science and the Shabby Curate of Poetry: Essays about the Two Cultures.* New York: Norton, 1965.

Gutting, Gary. *Michel Foucault's Archaeology of Scientific Reason.* Cambridge: Cambridge Univ. Press, 1989.

Hassan, Ihab. *The Right Promethean Fire: Imagination, Science, and Cultural Change.* Urbana: Univ. of Illinois Press, 1980.

Hesse, Mary. *Models and Analogies in Science.* Notre Dame: Univ. of Notre Dame Press, 1966.

————. *The Structure of Scientific Inference.* Berkeley: Univ. of California Press, 1974.

Holton, Gerald. *Thematic Origins of Scientific Thought: Kepler to Einstein.* Cambridge: Harvard Univ. Press, 1973.

————, ed. *Science and Culture: A Study of Cohesive and Disjunctive Forces.* Boston: Beacon, 1967.

Huxley, Aldous. *Literature and Science.* New York: Harper, 1963.

Irigaray, Luce. *Speculum of the Other Woman.* Translated by Gillian C. Gill. Ithaca: Cornell Univ. Press, 1985.

————. *This Sex Which Is Not One,* trans. Catherine Porter with Carolyn Burke. Ithaca: Cornell Univ. Press, 1985.

————. "Is the Subject of Science Sexed?" *Cultural Critique* 1: 73-88.

Jordanova, Ludmilla, ed. *Languages of Nature: Critical Essays on Science and Literature.* New Brunswick: Rutgers Univ. Press, 1986.

Keller, Evelyn Fox. *Reflections on Gender and Science.* New Haven: Yale Univ. Press, 1985.

Kipperman, M. "The Rhetorical Case Against a Theory of Literature and Science." *Philosophy and Literature* 10 (1986): 76-83.

Kuhn, Thomas. *The Essential Tension: Selected Studies in Scientific Tradition and Change.* Chicago: Univ. of Chicago Press, 1977.

————. *The Structure of Scientific Revolutions.* Chicago: Univ. of Chicago Press, 1970.

Lakotos, Imre, and Alan Musgrave, eds. *Criticism and the Growth of Knowledge.* Cambridge: Cambridge Univ. Press, 1970.

Laudan, Larry. *Progress and Its Problems: Toward a Theory of Scientific Growth.* Berkeley: Univ. of California Press, 1977.

Leavis, F.R. *Two Cultures: The Significance of C.P. Snow.* New York: Pantheon, 1963.

Levine, George. "Literary Science—Scientific Literature." *Raritan* 6 (1987): 24-41.

————, ed. *One Culture: Essays in Science and Literature.* Madison: Univ. of Wisconsin Press, 1987. [Essays by G. Beer, J. Paradis, P. Dale, N.K. Hayles, D. Benson, R. Pearce, D. Bell, R. Young, J. Moore, R. Porter, A. Mellor, S. Shuttleworth.]

Livingston, Paisley. *Literary Knowledge: Humanistic Inquiry and the Philosophy of Science.* Ithaca: Cornell Univ. Press, 1988.

Merrell, Floyd. *Deconstruction Reframed.* West Lafayette: Purdue Univ. Press, 1985.

Neubauer, John. "Literature and Science: Their Metaphors and Metamorphoses." *Yearbook of Comparative and General Literature* 32 (1983): 67-75.

Nicholson, Marjorie Hope. *Mountain Gloom and Mountain Glory: The Development of the Aesthetics of the Indefinite.* New York: Norton, 1963.

——. *Newton Demands the Muse: Newton's Optics and the Eighteenth-Century Poets.* Princeton: Princeton Univ. Press, 1946.

——. *Science and Imagination.* Ithaca: Cornell Univ. Press, 1956.

Paulson, William R. *The Noise of Culture: Literary Texts in a World of Information.* Ithaca: Cornell Univ. Press, 1988.

Peterfreund, Stuart, ed. *Literature and Science: Theory & Practice.* Boston: Northeastern Univ. Press, 1990. [Essays by E. Davenport, J. Bono, E. White, M. Greenberg, S. Peterfreund, F. Burwick, and N.K. Hayles.]

Popper, Karl. *Conjectures and Refutations: The Growth of Scientific Knowledge.* New York: Harper and Row, 1968.

——. *The Logic of Scientific Discovery.* New York: Basic Books, 1959.

Rorty, Richard. *Philosophy and the Mirror of Nature.* Princeton: Princeton Univ. Press, 1979.

Rousseau, G.S. "Literature and Science: The State of the Field." *Isis* 69 (1978): 583-91.

——, ed. *Science and the Imagination, Special Issue of Annals of Scholarship* 4 (1986). Papers from the symposium on Science and the Imagination held at the University of California, Berkeley, Aug. 4-7, 1985. [Essays by Rousseau, S. Peterfreund, N. Helton, M. Greenberg, L. Schachterle, G. Slusser, D. Benson, and J. Woodcock.]

Scholes, Robert. *Structural Fabulation: An Essay on Fiction of the Future.* Notre Dame: Univ. of Notre Dame Press, 1975.

——, and Eric S. Rabkin. *Science Fiction: History, Science, Vision.* New York: Oxford Univ. Press, 1977.

Serres, Michel. *Hermes: Literature, Science, Philosophy.* Edited by David F. Bell and Josué Harari. Baltimore: Johns Hopkins Univ. Press, 1982.

——. *The Parasite.* Baltimore: Johns Hopkins Univ. Press, 1982.

Slade, Joseph, and Judith Lee, eds. *Beyond the Two Cultures: Essays in Science, Technology and Literature.* Ames: Iowa State Univ. Press, 1989. [Essays by Slade, M. Yaross, J. Campbell, S. Weininger, F. Amrine, L. Bergman, E. Denhart, J. Callahan, J. Black, S. Peterfreund, D. Benson, L. Schachterle, E. Zency, P. Sporn, A. Trachtenberg, F. Davenport, L. Steinman, P. Thurman, P. Wilson.]

Slusser, George, and George Guffey. "Literature and Science," in *Interrelations of Literature.* Edited by Jean-Pierre Barricelli and Joseph Gebaldi. New York: Modern Language Association of America, 1982, 176-204.

Snow, C.P. *The Two Cultures and the Scientific Revolution.* New York: Cambridge Univ. Press, 1959.

Super, R.H. "The Humanist at Bay: The Arnold-Huxley Debate," in U.C. Knoeflmacher and G.B. Tennyson, eds., *Victorian Science and Victorian Imagination.* Berkeley: Univ. of California Press, 1977: 230-39.

Suvin, Darko. *Metamorphoses of Science Fiction.* New Haven: Yale Univ. Press, 1979.

Technology, Models, and Literary Study. Special Issue of *New Literary History* 20 (Winter 1989). [Essays by R. Lanham, W. Paulson, N.K. Hayles, R. Aris, R. Ziegfeld, D. Porush, G. Stonum, G. Colomb, E.D. Hirsch, Jr., W. Harker, M.A. Lavin, and I. Horowitz.]

Turner, Frederick. *Natural Classicism: Essays on Literature and Science*. New York: Paragon House, 1985.
University of Hartford Studies in Literature 19 (1987). [Special number on literature and science.]
Whitehead, Alfred North. *Science and the Modern World*. New York: Macmillan, 1925.

History of Science in America

Bell, Whitfield J., Jr. *Early American Science: Needs and Opportunities for Study*. Williamsburg, Va.: Institute of Early American History and Culture, 1955.
Boorstin, Daniel. *The Lost World of Thomas Jefferson*. New York: Holt, 1940.
Bruce, Robert V. *The Launching of American Science: 1846-1876*. New York: Knopf, 1987.
Burnham, John C. *How Superstition Won and Science Lost: Popularizing Science and Health in the United States*. New Brunswick: Rutgers Univ. Press, 1987.
Cohen, B. Bernard. *Revolution in Science*. Cambridge: Harvard Univ. Press, 1985.
Cravens, Hamilton. *The Triumph of Evolution: American Scientists and the Heredity-Environment Controversy, 1900-1941*. Philadelphia: Univ. of Pennsylvania Press, 1978.
Daniels, George H. "An American Defense of Bacon: A Study of the Relations of Scientific Thought, 1840-1855." *Huntington Library Quarterly* 28 (Aug. 1965): 321-39.
————. *American Science in the Age of Jackson*. New York: Columbia Univ. Press, 1968.
————, ed. *Nineteenth-Century American Science: A Reappraisal*. Evanston, Ill.: Northwestern Univ. Press, 1972.
————. "The Process of Professionalization in American Science: The Emergent Period, 1820-1860." *Isis* 58 (1967): 151-66.
————. *Science in American Society: A Social History*. New York: Knopf, 1971.
Davies, John D. *Phrenology, Fad and Science: A Nineteenth-Century American Crusade*. New Haven: Yale Univ. Press, 1955.
Davis, Richard Beal. *Intellectual Life in the Colonial South, 1585-1763*, 3 vols. Knoxville: Univ. of Tennessee Press, 1978.
Debus, Allen G., ed. *Man and Nature in the Renaissance*. Cambridge: Cambridge Univ. Press, 1978.
————. *Science, Medicine, and Society in the Renaissance*. New York: Science History Publications, 1972.
Dupree, A. Hunter. *Asa Gray, 1810-1888*. Cambridge: Harvard Univ. Press, 1959.
————. *Science in the Federal Government: A History of Policies and Activities to 1940*. Cambridge Belknap Press of Harvard Univ. Press, 1957.
Ekerch, Arthur Alphonse. *The Idea of Progress in America, 1815-1860*. New York: Columbia Univ. Press, 1944.
Elliott, Clark A. *Biographical Dictionary of American Science: The Seventeenth through the Nineteenth Centuries*. Westport, Conn.: Greenwood, 1979.
Fleming, Donald. *John William Draper and the Religion of Science*. Philadelphia: Univ. of Pennsylvania Press, 1950.
————. "The Judgement Upon Copernicus in Puritan New England." *Melanges Ala-handre*, 2. Paris: Herman, 1964: 160-175.
Franklin, H. Bruce. *War Stars: The Superweapon and the American Imagination*. New York: Oxford Univ. Press, 1988.

Friedman, Alan J., and Carol C. Donley. *Einstein as Myth and Muse*. Cambridge: Cambridge Univ. Press, 1985.

Furner, Mary O. *Advocacy and Objectivity: A Crisis in the Professionalism of American Social Science, 1865-1905*. Lexington: Univ. Press of Kentucky, 1975.

Gillispie, Charles, ed. *Dictionary of Scientific Biography*, 16 vols. New York: Scribner, 1970-80.

Goetzmann, William H. *Army Exploration in the American West, 1803-1863*. New Haven: Yale Univ. Press, 1959.

———. *Exploration and Empire. The Explorer and the Scientist in the Winning of the American West*. New York: Knopf, 1966.

Greene, John C. *American Science in the Age of Jefferson*. Ames: Univ. of Iowa Press, 1984.

Guralnick, Stanley M. *Science and the Ante-Bellum American College*. Philadelphia: American Philosophical Society, 1975.

Hanley, Wayne. *Natural History in America, from Mark Catesby to Rachel Carson*. New York: Quadrangle, 1977.

Hindle, Brooke, ed. *Early American Science*. New York: Science History, 1976.

———. *The Pursuit of Science in Revolutionary America, 1735-1789*. Chapel Hill: Univ. of North Carolina Press, 1956.

Hofstadter, Richard. *Social Darwinism in American Thought*. 1944; Boston: Beacon Press, 1955.

Hollinger, David A. "American Intellectual History: Issues for the 1980s." *Reviews in American History* 10 (1982): 306-17.

Hovenkamp, Herbert. *Science and Religion in America, 1800-1860*. Philadelphia: Univ. of Pennsylvania Press, 1978.

Kasson, John. *Civilizing the Machine: Technology and Republican Values in America, 1776-1900*. New York: Grossman, 1976.

Kevles, Daniel J. *The Physicists: The History of a Scientific Community in Modern America*. New York: Knopf, 1978.

Kohlstedt, Sally Gregory. *The Formation of the American Scientific Community: The American Association for the Advancement of Science, 1848-1860*. Urbana: Univ. of Illinois Press, 1976.

———, and Margaret W. Rossiter, eds. *Historical Writing on American Science. Osiris.* NS,I,(1985).

Leventhal, Herbert. *In the Shadow of the Enlightenment: Occultism and Renaissance Science in Eighteenth-Century America*. New York: New York Univ. Press, 1976.

Leverette, William E., Jr. "E.L. Youmans' Crusade for Scientific Autonomy and Respectability." *American Quarterly* 17 (1965): 12-32.

Lowenberg, Bert James. *Darwinism Comes to America, 1859-1900*. Philadelphia: Fortress, 1969.

Lurie, Edward. *Louis Agassiz: A Life in Science*. Chicago: Univ. of Chicago Press, 1960.

Manning, Kenneth. *Black Apollo of Science: The Life of Ernest Everett Just*. New York: Oxford Univ. Press, 1983.

May, Henry F. *The End of American Innocence: A Study of the First Years of Our Own Time*. 1959; Chicago: Quadrangle, 1964.

Moore, R. Laurence. *In Search of White Crows: Spiritualism, Parapsychology, and American Culture*. New York: Oxford Univ. Press, 1977.

Morison, Samuel Eliot. *The Intellectual Life of Colonial New England*. New York: New York Univ. Press, 1956.

Nash, Roderick. *Wilderness and the American Mind*. New Haven: Yale Univ. Press, 1982.

Noble, David F. *American by Design: Science, Technology, and the Rise of Corporate Capitalism*. New York: Knopf, 1977.

Numbers, Ronald L. *Creation by Natural Law: Laplace's Nebular Hypothesis in American Thought*. Seattle: Univ. of Washington Press, 1977.

Oleson, Alexandra, and John Voss, eds. *The Organization of Knowledge in Modern America, 1860-1920*. Baltimore: Johns Hopkins Univ. Press, 1979.

Reingold, Nathan. "Clio as Physicist and Machinist." *Reviews in American History* 10 (1982): 264-80.

———, ed. *Science in America Since 1920*. New York: Science History, 1976.

———, ed. *The Sciences in the American Context: New Perspectives*. Washington, D.C.: Smithsonian Institution Press, 1979.

———, ed. *Science in Nineteenth Century America: A Documentary History*. New York: Hill and Wang, 1964.

Roberts, Jonathan H. *Darwinism and the Divine in America: Protestant Intellectuals and Organic Evolution, 1859-1900*. Madison: Univ. of Wisconsin Press, 1988.

Rosenberg, Charles E. *No Other Gods: On Science and American Social Thought*. Baltimore: Johns Hopkins Univ. Press, 1976.

———. "Science in American Society: A Generation of Historical Debate." *Isis* 74 (1983): 356-67.

Rossiter, Margaret. *Women Scientists in America: Struggles and Strategies to 1940*. Baltimore: Johns Hopkins Univ. Press, 1982.

Russett, Cynthia Eagle. *Darwin in America: The Intellectual Response, 1865-1912*. San Francisco: Freeman, 1976.

Stearns, Raymond Phineas. *Science in the British Colonies of America*. Urbana: Univ. of Illinois Press, 1970.

Struik, Dirk J. *Yankee Science in the Making*. New York: Collier, 1962.

Thackray, Arnold. "On American Science." *Isis* 73 (1982): 7-10.

Tobey, Ronald C. *The American Ideology of National Science, 1919-1930*. Pittsburgh: Univ. of Pittsburgh Press, 1971.

Torbell, Dean Stanley, and Ann Tracey Torbell. *Essays on the History of Organic Chemistry in the United States*. Nashville: Folio Press, 1986.

Wachhorst, Wyn. *Thomas Alva Edison: An American Myth*. Cambridge: MIT Univ. Press, 1981.

White, Morton. *Science and Sentiment in America: Philosophical Thought From Jonathan Edwards to John Dewey*. New York: Oxford Univ. Press, 1972.

Wilson, Leonard G., ed. *Benjamin Silliman and His Circle: Studies on the Influence of Benjamin Silliman on Science in America*. New York: Science History, 1979.

Wooster, Donald. *Nature's Economy: A History of Ecological Ideas*. Cambridge: Cambridge Univ. Press, 1985.

Wrobel, Arthur, ed. *Pseudo-Science and Society in Nineteenth-Century America*. Lexington: Univ. Press of Kentucky, 1987. [Essays by Wrobel, T. Stoehr, J. Greenway, M. Legan, R. Delp, H. Aspiz, G. Hendrick, C. Walters, R. Fuller.]

Wynne, James. *Lives of Eminent Literary and Scientific Men of America*. New York: Appleton, 1850.

Zochert, Donald. "Science and the Common Man in Ante-Bellum America." *Isis* 65 (1974): 448-73.

Zuckerman, Harriet. *Scientific Elite: Nobel Laureates in the United States*. New York: Free Press, 1977.

Some General Studies of the Sciences

Atkins, P. W. *The Second Law*. New York: Scientific American Books, 1984.

Barnsley, Michael F., and Stephen G. Demko, eds. *Chaotic Dynamics and Fractals*. Orlando: Academic, 1986.

Bateson, Gregory. *Steps to an Ecology of Mind*. New York: Ballantine, 1972.

———. *Mind and Nature: A Necessary Unity*. New York: Bantam, 1980.

Berman, Morris. *The Reenchantment of the World*. New York: Bantam, 1984.

Bernstein, Jeremy. *Einstein*. New York: Penguin, 1976.

Bohm, David. *Wholeness and the Implicate Order*. London: Routledge and Kegan Paul, 1980.

Bohr, Nels. *Atomic Theory and the Description of Nature: Four Essays with an Introductory Survey*. New York: Macmillan, 1934.

———. *Quantum Theory*. Englewood Cliffs: Prentice-Hall, 1951.

Born, Max. *Einstein's Theory of Relativity*. With Gunther Leibfried and Walter Brem. New York: Dover, 1962.

Brush, Stephen. "Thermodynamics and History." *Graduate Journal* 7 (1967): 477-565.

Burtt, Edwin Arthur. *The Metaphysical Foundations of Modern Physical Science*. Garden City, N.Y.: Doubleday, 1954.

Butterfield, Herbert. *The Origins of Modern Science*. New York: Doubleday, 1952.

Campbell, Jeremy. *Grammatical Man: Information, Entropy, Language, and Life*. New York: Simon and Schuster, 1982.

Capek, Milic. *The Philosophical Impact of Contemporary Physics*. Princeton: Van Nostrand Reinhold, 1961.

Capra, Fritjof. *The Tao of Physics; An Exploration of the Parallels Between Modern Physics and Eastern Magnetism*. Berkeley: Shambhala, Random, 1975.

Cohen, I. B. *Franklin and Newton*. Philadelphia: 1956.

Collingwood, R. G. *The Idea of Nature*. New York: Oxford Univ. Press, 1945.

Davies, Paul. *Other Worlds: Space, Superspace, and the Quantum Universe*. New York: Simon and Schuster, 1980.

———. *Superforce: The Search for a Grand Unified Theory of Nature*. New York: Simon and Schuster, 1984.

Einstein, Albert. *The Meaning of Relativity*. Translated Edwin Plimpton Adams, et al. 5th ed. Princeton: Princeton Univ. Press, 1974.

———, and Leopold Infield. *The Evolution of Physics*. New York: Simon and Schuster, 1961.

Eiseley, Loren. *Darwin's Century: Evolution and the Men Who Discovered It*. Garden City, N.Y.: Anchor, 1961.

———. *The Unexpected Universe*. New York: Harcourt, Brace, and World, 1964.

Elvee, Richard. *Mind in Nature*. San Francisco: Harper and Row, 1982.

Foucault, Michel. *The Birth of the Clinic: An Archaeology of Medical Perception*. New York: Vintage, 1975.

Gillispie, Charles Coulston. *The Edge of Objectivity: An Essay in the History of Scientific Ideas*. Princeton: Princeton Univ. Press, 1960.

Gleick, James. *Chaos: Making a New Science*. New York: Viking, 1987.

Gould, Stephen J. *Ontogeny and Phylogeny*. Cambridge: Harvard Univ. Press, 1977.

Haraway, Donna Jean. *Crystals, Fabrics, and Fields*. New Haven: Yale Univ. Press, 1976.

Harrison, Edward R. *Masks of the Universe*. New York: MacMillan, 1985.

Hawkins, Stephen. *A Brief History of Time: From the Big Bang to Black Holes*. New York: Bantam, 1988.

Heisenberg, Werner. *Across the Frontiers*. Translated by Peter Heath. New York: Harper and Row, 1974.

———. *Philosophical Problems of Nuclear Science*. Translated by F.C. Hayes. London: Faber and Faber, 1952.

———. *Physics and Beyond: Encounters and Conversations*. New York: Harper and Row, 1971.

———. *Physics and Philosophy: The Revolution in Modern Science*. Introduction by E.S.C. Northrop. New York: Harper and Row, 1962.

———. *The Physicist's Conception of Nature*. Translated by Arnold J. Pomerans. 1958; Westport, Conn.: Greenwood, 1980.

Herbert, Nick. *Quantum Reality: Beyond the New Physics*. New York: Doubleday, 1985.

Hofstadter, Douglas R. *Godel, Escher, Bach: An Eternal Golden Braid*. New York: Basic Books, 1979.

Holton, Gerald. *The Scientific Imagination: Case Studies*. New York: Cambridge Univ. Press, 1973.

Jammer, Max. *Concepts of Space*. Cambridge: Harvard Univ. Press, 1954.

———. *The Philosophy of Quantum Mechanics*. New York: Wiley, 1974.

Jantsch, Erich. *The Self-Organizing Universe: Scientific and Human Implications of the Emerging Paradigm of Evolution*. Oxford: Pergamon, 1980.

Judson, Horace F. *The Eighth Day of Creation: Makers of the Revolution in Biology*. New York: Simon and Schuster, 1979.

Mandelbrot, Benoit B. *The Fractal Geometry of Nature*. San Francisco: Freeman, 1982.

Manuel, Frank. *A Portrait of Isaac Newton*. Cambridge: 1968.

Monod, Jacques. *Chance and Necessity: An Essay on the Natural Philosophy of Modern Biology*. Translated by Austryn Wainhouse. New York: Vintage, 1972.

Oldroyd, D.R. *Darwinian Impacts: An Introduction to the Darwinian Revolution*. Kensington, Australia: New South Wales Univ. Press, 1983.

Pagels, Heinz. *Perfect Symmetry*. New York: Simon and Schuster, 1985.

Prigogine, Ilya, and Isabelle Stengers. *Order Out of Chaos: Man's New Dialogue with Nature*. Toronto: Bantam, 1984.

Richards, Robert J. *Darwin and the Emergence of Evolutionary Theories of Mind and Behavior*. Chicago: Univ. of Chicago Press, 1987.

Ridley, B.K. *Time, Space and Things*. Cambridge: Cambridge Univ. Press, 1984.

Rossi, Paolo. *Francis Bacon: From Magic to Science*. Translated by S. Rabinovitch. London: 1968.

Shannon, Claude, and Warren Weaver. *The Mathematical Theory of Communication*. Urbana: Univ. of Illinois Press, 1949.

Toulmin, Stephen. *The Return to Cosmology: Postmodern Science and the Theology of Nature*. Berkeley: Univ. of California Press, 1982.

von Bertalanffy, Ludwig. *General System Theory: Foundations, Development, Applications.* New York: Braziller, 1968.

Weinberg, Steven. *The First Three Minutes.* New York: Bantam, 1984.

Wiener, Norbert. *The Human Use of Human Beings: Cybernetics and Society.* 2nd ed. Garden City, N.Y.: Doubleday, 1954.

Weyl, Hermann. *Philosophy of Mathematics and Natural Science.* Princeton: Princeton Univ. Press, 1949.

Zukav, Gary. *The Dancing Wu Li Masters: An Overview of the New Physics.* New York: Morrow, 1979.

Literature and Science in America:
The Seventeenth and Eighteenth Centuries

GENERAL STUDIES

Clark, Harry Hayden. "The Influence of Science on American Ideas, from 1775 to 1809." *Transactions of the Wisconsin Academy* 42 (1953): 263-303.

Davis, Richard Beale. *Intellectual Life in the Colonial South, 1585-1763.* Knoxville: Univ. of Tennessee Press, 1978.

Hall, Michael G. "Renaissance Science in Puritan New England," in Lewis, Archibald R., ed., *Aspects of the Renaissance: A Symposium.* Austin: Univ. of Texas Press, 1967, 123-36.

Hornberger, Theodore. "Puritanism and Science: The Relationship Revealed in the Writings of John Cotton." *New England Quarterly* 10 (1937): 503-15.

Lemay, J.A. Leo. *Men of Letters in Colonial Maryland.* Knoxville: Univ. of Tennessee Press, 1972.

Lockwood, Rose. "The Scientific Revolution in Seventeenth-Century New England." *New England Quarterly* 53 (1980): 76-95.

Middlekauff, Robert. *The Mathers: Three Generations of Puritan Intellectuals, 1596-1728.* New York: Oxford Univ. Press, 1976.

Miller, Perry. *The New England Mind: From Colony to Province.* Cambridge: Harvard Univ. Press, 1953.

Morison, Samuel Eliot. *Harvard College in the Seventeenth Century.* 2 vols. Cambridge: Harvard Univ. Press, 1936.

Pribeck, Thomas. "'Between Democritus and Cotton Mather': Narrative Irony in 'The Apple-Tree Table.'" *SAR* (1989): 241-55.

Rainwater, Catherine and William J. Scheick. *Seventeenth-Century Poetry: A Reference Guide. Resources for American Literary Study,* 1980.

Stearns, Raymond Phineas. *Science in the British Colonies of America.* Urbana: Illinois Univ. Press, 1970. [John Winthrop, Jr., John Josselyn, Increase Mather, Cotton Mather, Benjamin Colman, Isaac Greenwood, Dr. William Douglas, Dr. John Mitchell, Cadwallader Culden, John Bertram, Dr. Alexander Gardeny, Prof. John Winthrop, and Benjamin Franklin.]

Van de Wetering, John E. "God, Science, and the Puritan Dilemma." *New England Quarterly* 38 (1965): 494-507.

White, Peter, ed. *Puritan Poets and Poetics: Seventeenth-Century American Poetry in Theory and Practice.* University Park: Pennyslvania State Univ. Press, 1985.

Wilson, David Scofield. *In the Presence of Nature.* Amherst: Univ. of Massachusetts Press, 1978.

JOEL BARLOW

Ball, Kenneth R. "Joel Barlow's 'Canal' and Natural Religion." *Eighteenth-Century Studies* 2 (1968-69): 225-39.

WILLIAM BARTRAM

Fagin, Bryllion. *William Bartram: Interpreter of the American Landscape.* Baltimore: Johns Hopkins Press, 1933.

Moore, Hugh. "The Southern Landscape of William Bartram: A Terrible Beauty." *EAS* 10 (1981): 41-50.

BENJAMIN COLMAN

Hornberger, Theodore. "Colman and the Enlightment." *New England Quarterly* 12 (1939): 227-40.

Toulouse, Teresa. "'Syllabical Idolatry': Benjamin Colman and the Rhetoric of Balance." *Early American Literature* 18 (1984): 257-74.

Van De Wetering, Maxine. "A Reconsideration of the Inoculation Controversy." *New England Quarterly* 58 (1985): 46-67.

JOHN COTTON

Hornberger, Theodore. "Puritanism and Science: The Relationship Revealed in the Writings of John Cotton." *New England Quarterly* 10 (1937): 503-15.

JONATHAN EDWARDS

Faust, Clarence H. "Jonathan Edwards as a Scientist." *American Literature* 1 (Jan. 1930): 393-404.

Hatch, Nathan O., and Harry S. Stout, eds. *Jonathan Edwards and the American Experience.* New York: Oxford Univ. Press, 1988.

Hornberger, Theodore. "The Effect of the New Science upon the Thought of Jonathan Edwards." *American Literature* 9 (May 1937).

Laskowsky, Henry J. "Jonathan Edwards: A Puritan Philosopher of Science." *Connecticut Review* 4 (1970): 33-41.

Loewinsohn, Ron. "Jonathan Edwards' Optiks: Images and Metaphors of Light in Some of His Major Works." *Early American Literature* 8 (1973): 21-32.

Martin, Jean-Pierre. "Edwards' Epistemology and the New Science." *Early American Literature* 7 (1973): 247-55.

Miller, Perry. *Jonathan Edwards.* New York: W. Sloane Associates, 1949.

Opie, John, ed. *Jonathan Edwards and the Enlightenment.* Lexington, Mass. Heath, 1969.

Wilson, David Scofield. "The Flying Spider." *Journal of the History of Ideas* 32 (1971), 447-58.

BENJAMIN FRANKLIN

Aldridge, A. Owen. *Franklin and His French Contemporaries.* New York: 1957.

———. *Franklin and Nature's God.* Durham, N.C.: Durham Univ. Press, 1967.

Breitwieser, Mitchell Robert. *Cotton Mather and Benjamin Franklin: The Price of Representative Personality.* Cambridge: Cambridge Univ. Press, 1985.

Cohen, I. Bernard. *Franklin and Newton: An Inquiry into Speculative Newtonian Experimental*

Science and Franklin's Work in Electricity as an Example Thereof. Cambridge: Harvard Univ. Press, 1966.

———. *Benjamin Franklin: Scientist and Statesman.* New York: Scribner, 1975.

ALEXANDER HAMILTON

Micklus, Robert. "The Delightful Instruction of Dr. Alexander Hamilton's *Itinerarium.*" *American Literature* 60 (1988): 359-84.

THOMAS JEFFERSON

Martin, Edwin T. *Thomas Jefferson, Scientist.* New York: Henry Schuman, 1952.

COTTON MATHER

Breitwieser, Mitchel Robert. "Cotton Mather's Pharmacy." *Early American Literature* 16 (1981): 42-49.

Jeske, Jeffrey. "Cotton Mather: Physico-Theologian." *Journal of the History of Ideas* 47 (1986): 583-94.

Levin, David. "Giants of the Earth: Science and the Occult in Cotton Mather's Letters to the Royal Society." *William and Mary Quarterly* 45 (1988): 751-70.

———. *Cotton Mather: The Young Wife of the Lord's Remembrancer.* Cambridge: Harvard Univ. Press, 1978.

DR. JOHN MITCHELL

Berkeley, Edmund, and Dorothy Smith. *Dr. John Mitchell: The Man Who Made the Map of North America.* Chapel Hill: Univ. of North Carolina Press, 1974.

EDWARD TAYLOR

Kehler, Joel R. "Physiology and Metaphor in Edward Taylor's 'Meditation. Can. 1.3.'" *Early American Literature* 9 (1975): 315-20.

Keller, Karl. *The Example of Edward Taylor.* Amherst: Univ. of Massachusetts Press, 1975.

Rowe, Karen. *Saint and Singer: Edward Taylor's Typology and the Poetics of Meditation.* Cambridge: Cambridge Univ. Press, 1986.

Scheick, William J. "Edward Taylor's Herbalism in *Preparatory Meditations.*" *American Poetry* 1 (Fall 1983): 64-71.

———. "Edward Taylor's Optics." *American Literature* 55 (May 1983): 234-40.

———. *The Will and the Word. The Poetry of Edward Taylor.* Athens: Univ. of Georgia Press, 1974.

Sluder, Lawrence. "God in the Background: Edward Taylor as Naturalist." *Early American Literature* 7 (1972–1973): 265-71.

Weathers, Willie T. "Edward Taylor and the Cambridge Platonists." *American Literature* 26 (Mar. 1954): 1-31.

JOHN WINTHROP, JR.

Black, Robert C. III. *The Younger John Winthrop.* New York: Columbia Univ. Press, 1966.

Literature and Science in America—The Nineteenth Century

GENERAL STUDIES

Bell, Ian F.A. "Divine Patterns: Louis Agassiz and American Men of Letters. Some Preliminary Explorations." *Journal of American Studies* 10 (1976): 349-81.

Bender, Bert A. "Let There Be (Electric) Light! The Image of Electricity in American Writing." *Arizona Quarterly* 34 (1978): 55-70.

Bredeson, Robert C. "Landscape Description in Nineteenth-Century American Travel Literature." *American Quarterly* 20 (1968): 86-94.

Chai, Leon. *The Romantic Foundations of the American Renaissance.* Ithaca: Cornell Univ. Press, 1987.

Clark, Harry Hayden. "The Influence of Science on American Literary Criticism, 1860–1910, Including the Vogue of Taine." *Transactions of the Wisconsin Academy* 44 (1955): 179-204; 49 (1960): 249-82.

Connor, Frederick W. *Cosmic Optimism: A Study of the Interpretation of Evolution by American Poets from Emerson to Robinson.* Gainesville: Univ. of Florida Press, 1949).

Cowley, Malcolm. "Naturalism in American Literature," in Persons, Stow, ed., *Evolutionary Thought in America.* New Haven: Yale Univ. Press, 1950, 300-33.

Dahlstrand, Frederick C. "Science, Religion, and the Transcendentalist Response to a Changing America." in Myerson, Joel, ed., *Studies in the American Renaissance.* Charlottesville: Univ. Press of Virginia, 1988, 1-25.

Dean, Dennis R. "The Influence of Geology on American Literature and Thought," in Schneer, Cecil J., ed., *Two Hundred Years of Geology in America.* Hanover: Univ. Press of New England, 1979, 289-303.

Franklin, H. Bruce. *Future Perfect: American Science Fiction of the Nineteenth Century.* New York: Oxford Univ. Press, 1966.

Ketterer, David. *New Worlds for Old: The Apocalyptic Imagination, Science Fiction, and American Literature.* New York: Doubleday; Bloomington: Indiana Univ. Press, 1974.

Limon, John. *The Place of Fiction in a Time of Science: A Disciplinary History of American Writing.* Cambridge: Cambridge Univ. Press, 1990.

Martin, Ronald E. *American Literature and the Universe of Force.* Durham, N.C.: Duke Univ. Press, 1981. [H. Adams, F. Norris, J. London, T. Dreiser.]

Marx, Leo. *The Machine in the Garden: Technology and the Pastoral Ideal in America.* New York: Oxford Univ. Press, 1964.

Millhauser, Milton. "The Literary Impact of *Vestiges of Creation.*" *Modern Language Quarterly* 17 (1956): 213-26.

Pizer, Donald. *Realism and Naturalism in Nineteenth-Century American Literature.* Carbondale: Southern Illinois Univ. Press, 1984.

Tatar, Maria M. *Spellbound: Studies on Mesmerism and Literature.* Princeton: Princeton Univ. Press, 1978. [Includes Hawthrone and H. James.]

Van Leer, David. "Nature's Book: The Language of Science in the American Renaissance," in Cunningham, Andrew, and Nicholas Gardine, eds., *Romanticism and the Sciences.* Cambridge: Cambridge Univ. Press, 1990, 307-21.

Walcott, Charles C. *American Literary Naturalism: A Divided Stream.* Minneapolis: Univ. of Minnesota Press, 1956.

Wrobel, Arthur, ed. *Pseudo-Science and Society in Nineteenth-Century America.* Lexington: Univ. Press of Kentucky, 1987.

HENRY ADAMS

Hamill, Paul J. "Science as Ideology: The Case of the Amateur, Henry Adams." *Canadian Review of American Studies* 12 (1981): 21-35.

Hayles, N. Katherine. "The Necessary Gap: Chaos as Self in *The Education of Henry Adams,*" in *Chaos Bound: Orderly Disorder in Contemporary Literature and Science*. Ithaca: Cornell Univ. Press, 1990, 62-90.

Jordy, William H. *Henry Adams as Scientific Historian*. New Haven: Yale Univ. Press, 1952.

Levinson, J.C. *The Mind and Art of Henry Adams*. Boston: Houghton Mifflin, 1957.

Mindel, Joseph. "The Uses of Metaphor: Henry Adams and the Symbols of Science." *Journal of the History of Ideas* 26 (Jan.-Mar. 1965): 89-102.

WILLIAM C. BRYANT

Glicksberg, Charles I. "William Cullen Bryant and Nineteenth-Century Science." *New England Quarterly* 23 (1950): 91-96.

Ringe, Donald A. "William Cullen Bryant and the Science of Geology." *American Literature* 26 (1954–55): 507-14.

WILLA CATHER

Bender, Eileen T. "Pioneer or Gadgeteer: Bergsonian Metaphor in the Work of Willa Cather." *Midwest Quarterly* 28 (1986): 130-40.

JAMES FENIMORE COOPER

Clark, Harry H. "Fenimore Cooper and Science." *Transactions of the Wisconsin Academy of Sciences, Arts, and Letters* 48 (1959): 179-204; 49 (1960): 249-82.

STEPHEN CRANE

Fitelson, David. "Stephen Crane's *Maggie* and Darwinism." *American Quarterly* 16 (1964): 182-94.

EMILY DICKENSON

Budick, E. Miller. "The Dangers of the Living Word: Aspects of Dickinson's Epistemology, Cosmology, and Symbolism." *ESQ* 29 (1983): 208-24.

Downey, Charlotte. "How the Mathematical Concepts Portrayed in the Language Patterns of Walt Whitman's and Emily Dickinson's Poems Relate to Meaning." *Dickenson Studies* 72 (1989): 17-32.

Howard, William. "Emily Dickinson's Poetic Vocabulary." *PMLA* 72 (1957): 225-48.

Johnson, Greg. "Broken Mathematics: Emily Dickinson's Concept of Ratio." *Concerning Poetry* 13 (1980): 21-26.

Orsini, Daniel J. "Emily Dickinson and the Romantic Use of Science." *Massachusetts Studies in English* 7-8 (1981): 57-69.

Stonum, Gary Lee. *The Dickinson Sublime*. Madison: Univ. of Wisconsin Press, 1990.

THEODORE DREISER

Katope, Christopher. "*Sister Carrie* and Spenser's *First Principles*." *American Literature* 41 (1969): 64-75.

RALPH WALDO EMERSON

Allen, Gay Wilson. "A New Look at Emerson and Science," in Falk, Robert P., ed., *Literature and Ideas in America*, Athens: Ohio Univ. Press, 1975, 58-78.

Berthoff, Warner. "Introduction" to *Nature: A Facsimile of the First Edition*. San Francisco: Chandler, 1968.

Bishop, Jonathan. *Emerson on the Soul*. Cambridge: Harvard Univ. Press, 1964.

Cameron, Kenneth Walter. *Emerson the Essayist*, 2 vols. Raleigh, N.C.: Thistle, 1945.

Clark, Harry Hayden. "Emerson and Science." *Philological Quarterly* 10 (July 1931): 225-60.

Dant, Elizabeth A. "Composing the World: Emerson and the Cabinet of Natural History." *Nineteenth-Century Literature* 44 (1989): 18-44.

Neufeldt, Leonard. *The House of Emerson*. Lincoln: Univ. of Nebraska Press, 1982.

Packer, Barbara L. *Emerson's Fall: A New Interpretation of the Major Essays*. New York: Continuum, 1982.

Paul, Sherman. *Emerson's Angle of Vision: Man and Nature in American Experience*. Cambridge: Harvard Univ. Press, 1952.

Pelikan, Jaroslav. "*Nature* as Natural History and as Human History," in *Nature: A Facsimile of the First Edition*. Boston: Beacon, 1985.

Porte, Joel, ed. *Emerson: Prospect and Retrospect*. Cambridge: Harvard Univ. Press, 1983.

——. *Emerson and Thoreau: Transcendentalists in Conflict*. Middletown, Conn.: Wesleyan Univ. Press, 1966.

Robinson, David. *Apostle of Culture: Emerson as Preacher and Lecturer*. Philadelphia: Univ. of Pennsylvania Press, 1982.

——. "Emerson's Natural Theology and the Paris Naturalists: Toward a 'Theory of Animated Nature.'" *Journal of the History of Ideas* 41 (Jan.-Mar. 1980): 69-88.

——. "*The Method of Nature* and Emerson's Period of Crisis," in Myerson, Joel, ed., *Emerson Centenary Essays*. Carbondale: Southern Illinois Univ. Press, 1982, 74-92.

Sealts, Merton M., Jr. *Emerson's Nature—Origin, Growth, Meaning*. Carbondale: Southern Illinois Univ. Press, 1979.

Shea, Daniel B. "Emerson and the American Metamorphosis," in Levin, David, ed., *Emerson: Prophecy, Metamorphosis, and Influence*. New York: Columbia Univ. Press, 1975, 29-56.

Strauch, Carl F. "Emerson's Sacred Science." *PMLA* 73 (June 1958): 237-50.

Van Cromphout, Gustaaf. *Emerson's Modernity and the Example of Goethe*. Columbia: Univ. of Missouri Press, 1990.

NATHANIEL HAWTHORNE

Baym, Nina. "The Head, the Heart, and the Unpardonable Sin." *New England Quarterly* 40 (1967): 31-47.

Franklin, H. Bruce. "Hawthorne and Science Fiction." *Centennial Review* 10 (1966): 112-30.

Pribek, Thomas. "Hawthorne's Aminidab: Sources and Significance." *Studies in the American Renaissance* (1987): 177-86.

Rucker, Mary E. "Science and Art in Hawthorne's 'The Birthmark.'" *Nineteenth-Century Fiction* 41 (1987): 445-61.

Stoehr, Taylor. *Hawthorne's Mad Scientists: Pseudoscience and Social Science in Nineteenth Century Life and Letters*. Hamden: Archon, 1978.

Uroff, M.D. "The Doctors in 'Rappacini's Daughter.'" *Nineteenth-Century Fiction* 27 (1972-73): 61-70.
Westbrook, Ellen E. "Probable Improbabilities: Verisimilar Romance in Hawthorne's 'The Birthmark.'" *American Transcendental Quarterly* ns 3 (1989): 203-17.

WILLIAM DEAN HOWELLS
Clark, Harry Hayden. "The Role of Science in the Thought of W.D. Howells." *Transactions of the Wisconsin Academy of Sciences, Arts, and Letters* 42 (1953): 263-303.
Marston, Jane. "Evolution and Howellsian Realism in *The Undiscovered County.*" *American Literary Realism* 14 (1981): 231-41.
Pizer, Donald. "The Evolutionary Foundation of William Dean Howells's *Criticism and Fiction.*" *Philogical Quarterly* (1961): 91-103. Rpt. in *Realism and Naturalism in Nineteenth Century American Literature.* Carbondale: Southern Illinois Univ. Press, 1984, 70-85.
―――. "Evolutionary Literary Criticism and the Defense of Howellsian Realism." *Journal of English and German Philology* 61 (1962): 296-304.

HENRY JAMES
Clark, Harry H. "Henry James and Science: *The Wings of the Dove.*" *Transactions of the Wisconsin Academy of Sciences, Arts, and Letters* 52 (1963): 1-15.
Purdy, Strother B. *The Hole in the Fabric: Science, Contemporary Literature, and Henry James.* Pittsburgh: Univ. of Pittsburgh Press, 1977.

SIDNEY LANIER
Anderson, Charles R. Introduction to Anderson, Charles R., ed., *Poems and Poem Outlines,* vol. I of *The Centennial Edition of the Works of Sidney Lanier,* 10 vols. Baltimore: Johns Hopkins Press, 1945.
Beaver, Joseph. "Lanier's Use of Science for Poetic Imagery." *American Literature* 24 (1953-54): 520-33.

HERMAN MELVILLE
Aspiz, Harold. "The 'Lurch of the Torpedo-Fish': Electrical Concepts is *Billy Budd.*" *ESQ* 26 (1980): 127-36.
―――. "Phrenologising the Whale." *Nineteenth Century Fiction* 23 (1968–69): 18-27.
Emery, Allan Moore. "Melville on Science: The Lightning-Rod Man." *New England Quarterly* 56 (1983): 555-68.
Franklin, H. Bruce. *The Wake of the Gods: Melville's Mythology.* Stanford: Stanford Univ. Press, 1963.
―――. "Herman Melville and Science Fiction," in *Future Perfect: American Science Fiction of the 19th Century.* New York, Oxford Univ. Press, 1966.
Smith, Peter A. "Entropy in Melville's 'Bartleby, the Scrivener.'" *Centennial Review* 32 (1988): 155-62.

FRANK NORRIS
Pizer, Donald. *The Novels of Frank Norris.* Bloomington: Indiana Univ. Press, 1966.
Seltzer, Mark. "The Naturalist Machine," in Ruth Bernard Yeazell, ed., *Sex, Politics, and Science in the Nineteenth-Century Novel.* Baltimore: Johns Hopkins Univ. Press, 1986.

EDGAR ALLAN POE

Benton, Richard P. ed. *Poe as a Literary Cosmologer: Studies on Eureka: A Symposium.* Hartford: Transcendental, 1975. [Contains several essays documenting Poe's extensive use of astronomy and other sciences.]

Falk, Doris V. "Poe and the Power of Animal Magnetism." *PMLA* 84 (1969): 536-46.

Maddison, Carol Hopkins. "Poe's *Eureka.*" *Texas Studies in Language and Literature* 2 (1960-61): 350-67.

Monteiro, George. "Edgar Poe and the New Knowledge." *Southern Literary Journal* 4 (1972): 34-40.

HENRY DAVID THOREAU

Adams, Raymond. "Thoreau's Science." *Scientific Monthly* 60 (May 1945): 379-82.

Baym, Nina. "Thoreau's View of Science." *Journal of the History of Ideas* 26 (1965): 221-34.

Harding, Walter. "*Walden's* Man of Science." *Virginia Quarterly Review* 57 (1981): 45-61.

Hildebidle, John. *Thoreau: A Naturalist's Liberty.* Cambridge: Harvard Univ. Press, 1983.

McIntosh, James. *Thoreau as Romantic Naturalist: His Shifting Stance Toward Nature.* Ithaca: Cornell Univ. Press, 1974.

Richardson, Robert D., Jr. *Henry Thoreau: A Life of the Mind.* Berkeley: Univ. of California Press, 1986.

Rossi, William. "'The Limits of an Afternoon Walk': Coleridgean Polarity in Thoreau's 'Walking.'" *ESQ* 33 (1987): 94-109.

———. "Roots, Leaves and Method: Henry Thoreau and Nineteenth-Century Natural Science." *Journal of the American Studies Association of Texas* 19 (1988).

MARK TWAIN

Cummings, Sherwood. *Mark Twain and Science: Adventures of a Mind.* Baton Rouge: Louisiana State Univ. Press, 1988.

Gardiner, Jane. "'A More Splendid Necromancy': Mark Twain's *Connecticut Yankee* and the Electrical Revolution." *Studies in the Novel* 19 (1987): 448-58.

Gellman, Susan. "'Sure Identifiers': Race, Science, and the Law in Twain's *Pudd'nhead Wilson.*" *South Atlantic Quarterly* 87 (1988): 195-218.

Ketterer, David, ed. *The Science Fiction of Mark Twain.* Hamden, Conn.: Archon, 1984.

Poole, Stan. "In Search of the Missing Link: Mark Twain and Darwinism." *Studies in American Fiction* 13 (1985): 201-15.

Waggoner, Hyatt Howe. "Science in the Thought of Mark Twain." *American Literature* 8 (1936-37): 357-70.

Wilson, James D. "'The Monumental Sarcasm of the Ages': Science and Pseudoscience in the Thought of Mark Twain." *South Atlantic Bulletin* 40 (1975): 72-82.

EDITH WHARTON

Schriber, Marysue. "Darwin, Wharton, and 'The Descent of Man': Blueprints of American Society." *Studies in Short Fiction* 17 (1980): 31-38.

WALT WHITMAN

Aspiz, Harold. *Walt Whitman and the Body Beautiful.* Urbana: Univ. of Illinois Press, 1980.

Beaver, Joseph. *Walt Whitman: Poet of Science.* Morningside Heights, N.Y.: King's Crown, 1951.

Scholnick, Robert J. "'The Password Primeval': Whitman's Use of Science in 'Song of Myself.'" in Myerson, Joel, ed., *Studies in the American Renaissance 1986.* Charlottesville: Univ. Press of Virginia, 1986, 385-425.

Literature and Science in America: The Twentieth Century

GENERAL STUDIES

Craige, Betty Jean. *Literary Relativity: An Essay on Twentieth-Century Narrative.* Lewisburg: Bucknell Univ. Press, 1982.

Donley, Carol C., and Freedman, Alan J. *Einstein as Myth and Muse.* Cambridge: Cambridge Univ. Press, 1985.

Elder, John. *Imagining the Earth, Poetry and the Vision of Nature.* Urbana: Univ. of Illinois Press, 1985.

Gefen, Lasylo K. *Ideogram: History of a Poetic Method.* Austin: Univ. of Texas Press, 1981.

Hassan, Ihab. *The Dismemberment of Orpheus: Toward a Post-Modern Literature.* Madison: Univ. of Wisconsin Press, 1982.

Hayles, N. Katherine. *The Cosmic Web: Scientific Field Models and Literary Strategies in the Twentieth Century.* Ithaca: Cornell Univ. Press, 1984.

LeClair, Tom. *The Art of Excess: Mastery in Contemporary American Fiction.* Urbana: Univ. of Illinois Press, 1989. [Pynchon, Heller, Gaddes, Coover, McElroy, Barth, and LeGuin.]

Malkoff, Karl. *Escape from the Self: A Study in Contemporary American Poetry and Poetics.* New York: Columbia Univ. Press, 1977.

Marx, Leo. "Reflections on the Neo-Romantic Critique of Science." *Daedalus* 107 (1978): 61-74. Rpt., *The Pilot and the Passenger: Essays on Literature, Technology, and Culture in the U.S.* New York: Oxford Univ. Press, 1988.

McCaffery, Larry. *The Metafictional Muse: The Works of Robert Coover, Donald Barthelme, and William Gass.* Pittsburgh: Univ. of Pittsburgh Press, 1982.

Nadeau, Robert. *Readings from the New Book on Nature: Physics and Metaphysics in the Modern Novel.* Amherst: Univ. of Massachusetts Press, 1981. [Fowles, Barth, Updike, Vonnegut, Pynchon, DeLillo.]

O'Donnell, Patrick. *Passionate Doubts: Designs of Interpretation in Contemporary American Fiction.* Iowa City: Univ. of Iowa Press, 1986. [Fowles, Barth, Pynchon, and Elken.]

Pearson, Norman H. "The American Poet in Relation to Science." *American Quarterly* 1 (1949): 116-26. Rpt. in Denny, Margaret, and William H. Gilman, eds., *The American Writer and the European Tradition,* Minneapolis: Univ. of Minnesota Press for Univ. of Rochester, 1950, 154-67. [Includes Cummings, Eliot, Frost, Pound, Williams.]

Porush, David. *The Soft Machine: Cybernetic Fiction.* New York: Meuthen, 1985.

Steinman, Lisa M. *Made in America: Science, Technology and American Modernist Poets.* New Haven: Yale Univ. Press, 1987. [W.C. Williams, M. Moore, W. Stevens.]

Stitt, Peter. *The World's Hieroglyphic Beauty: Five American Poets.* Athens: Univ. of Georgia Press, 1985.

Tichi, Cecelia. *Shifting Gears: Technology, Literature, Culture in Modernist America.* Chapel Hill: Univ. of North Carolina Press, 1987. [H. Adams, Bellamy, Dos Passos, Hemingway, Pound, Veblin, and Williams.]

Waggoner, Hyatt Howe. *The Heel of Elohim: Science and Values in Modern American Poetry.* Norman: Univ. of Oklahoma Press, 1950.

Warrick, Patricia S. *The Cybernetic Imagination in Science Fiction.* Cambridge: MIT Press, 1980.

CONRAD AIKEN

Marten, Harry. *The Art of Knowing: The Poetry and Prose of Conrad Aiken.* Columbia: Univ. of Missouri Press, 1988.

Story, Nancy Crucevich. "Aiken's *Preludes:* Starting Fresh." *Essays in Arts and Sciences* 18 (1989): 53-84.

A.R. AMMONS

Bloom, Harold, *A.R. Ammons: Modern Critical Views.* New York: Chelsea, 1986. [See especially essays by Patricia Parker and Frederick Briell.]

Reiman, Donald H. "A.R. Ammons: Ecological Naturalism and the Romantic Tradition." *Twentieth Century Literature* 31 (1985): 22-51.

Wolfe, Cary. "Symbol Plural: The Later Long Poems of A.R. Ammons." *Contemporary Literature* 30 (1989): 78-94.

JOHN BARTH

Harris, Charles B. *Passionate Virtuosity: The Poetry of John Barth.* Urbana: Univ. of Illinois Press, 1983.

Vitanza, Victor J. "The Novelist as Topologist: John Barth's *Lost in the Funhouse.*" *Texas Studies in Language and Literature* 19 (1977): 83-97.

SAUL BELLOW

Weinstein, Norman. "*Herzog,* Order, and Entropy." *English Studies* 54 (1973): 336-46.

ROBERT COOVER

Cope, Jackson I. *Robert Coover's Fictions.* Baltimore: Johns Hopkins Press, 1986.

Hansen, Arlen J. "The Dice of God: Einstein, Heisenberg, and Robert Coover." *Novel* 10 (1976–77): 49-58.

HART CRANE

Giles, Paul. *Hart Crane: The Contexts of "The Bridge".* Cambridge: Cambridge Univ. Press, 1986.

DON DELILLO

Le Clair, Tom. *In the Loop: Don DeLillo and the Systems Novel.* Urbana: Univ. of Illinois Press, 1987.

PHILLIP K. DICK

Warrick, Patricia S. *Mind in Motion: The Fiction of Philip K. Dick.* Carbondale: Southern Illinois Univ. Press, 1987.

ANNIE DILLARD
Filch, Susan M. "Annie Dillard: Modern Physics in a Contemporary Mystic." *Mosaic* 22 (1989): 1-14.

ROBERT DUNCAN
Johnson, Mark. "Robert Duncan's 'Momentous Inconclusions.'" *Sagetrieb* 2 (1983): 71-84.

LOREN C. EISELEY
Angyal, Andrew J. *Loren Eiseley*, in *Twayne United States Authors Series*: 442. Boston, 1983.
Carlisle, E. Fred. *Loren Eiseley: The Development of a Writer*. Urbana: Univ. of Illinois Press, 1983.
Nemerov, Howard. "Loren Eiseley: 1907-1977." *Proceedings of the American Academy of Arts and Letters* 2, no. 29 (1978): 77-81.
Schwartz, James M. "Loren Eiseley: The Scientist as Literary Artist." *Georgia Review* 31 (1977): 855-71.

T.S. ELIOT
Durrell, Lawrence. "Space, Time and Poetry." *A Key to Modern British Poetry*. Norman: Univ. of Oklahoma Press; London: Nevill, 1952, 224-48. [On T.S. Eliot, Joyce, and Woolf.]
Foster, Steven. "Relatively and *The Waste Land*: A Postulate." *Texas Studies in Language and Literature* 7 (1965): 77-95.
Montgomery, Marion. "Eliot and the Particle Physicist: The Merging of Two Cultures." *Southern Review* 10 (1974): 583-89.

WILLIAM FAULKNER
Johnson, Julie M. "The Theory of Relativity in Modern Literature: An Overview and *The Sound and the Fury*." *Journal of Modern Literature* 10 (1983): 217-30.
Miller, J. Hillis. "The Two Relativisms: Point of View and Indeterminary in the Novel *Absalom, Absalom!*" in Craige, Betty Jean, ed., *Relativism in its Arts*. Athens: Univ. of Georgia Press, 1983.

ROBERT FROST
Abel, Darrel. "The Instinct of a Bard: Robert Frost on Science, Logic, and Poetic Truth." *Essays in Arts and Sciences* 9 (1980): 59-75.
Hiers, John T. "Robert Frost's Quarrel with Science and Technology." *Georgia Review* 25 (1971): 182-205.
Rotella, Guy. "Comparing Conceptions: Frost and Eddington, Heisenberg, and Bohr." *American Literature* 59 (May 1987): 167-89.

WILLIAM GADDIS
Sawyer, Thomas M. "*JR: The Narrative of Entropy*." *International Fiction Review* 10 (1983): 117-322.

ROBERT A. HEINLEIN

Franklin, H. Bruce. *Robert A. Heinlein: America as Science Fiction.* New York: Oxford Univ. Press, 1980.

RANDALL JARRELL

Butterfield, R.W. "'The Dark Magnificence of Things': The Poetry of Robinson Jeffers," in Butterfield, R.W. ed., *Modern American Poetry.* London: Vision, 1984; Totowa, N.J.: Barnes and Noble, 1984, 93-109.

ROBINSON JEFFERS

Carpenter, Frederic I. "The Inhumanism of Robinson Jeffers." *Western American Literature* 16 (1981): 19-25.

URSULA K. LEGUIN

Rupert, Peter. *Reader in a Strange Land.* Athens: Univ. of Georgia Press, 1986.

SINCLAIR LEWIS

Land, Mary G. "Three Max Gottliebs: Lewis's, Dreiser's, and Walker Percy's View of the Mechanist-Vitalist Controversy." *Studies in the Novel* 15 (1983): 314-31.

Rosenberg, Charles E. "Martin Arrowsmith: The Scientist as Hero." *American Quarterly* 15 (1963): 447-58.

JACK LONDON

Tavernier-Courbu, Jacquelin, ed. *Critical Essays on Jack London.* Boston: Hall, 1983.

ARCHIBALD MACLEISH

Hartigan, Karelesa V. "Herakles in a Technological World: An Ancient Myth Transformed." *Classical and Modern Literature* 5 (1984): 33-38.

Lane, Lauriat, Jr. "'Intimate Immensity': On the Poetics of Space in MacLeish's *Einstein.*" *Canadian Review of American Studies* 14 (1983): 19-29.

NORMAN MAILER

Finholt, Richard D. "'Otherwise How Explain?' Norman Mailer's New Cosmology." *Modern Fiction Studies* 17 (1971): 375-86.

JAMES MERRILL

Berger, Charles. "Merrill and Pynchon: Our Apocalyptic Scribes," in Lehman, David, and Charles Berger, eds., *James Merrill: Essays in Criticism.* Ithaca: Cornell Univ. Press, 1983.

VLADIMIR NABOKOV

Dembo, L.S. *Nabokov: The Man and His Work.* Madison: Univ. of Wisconsin Press, 1967.

Flower, Timothy F. "The Scientific Art of Nabokov's *Pale Fire.*" *Criticism* 17 (1975): 223-33.

Johnson, D. Barton. "The Ambidextrous Universe of Nabokov's *Look at the Harlequins,*" in Roth, Phyllis A., ed., *Critical Essays on Vladimir Nabokov.* Boston: Hall, 1984, 202-15.

CHARLES OLSON

Butterick, George F. *A Guide to the Maximus Poems of Charles Olson.* Berkeley: Univ. of California Press, 1973.

Byrd, Don. *Charles Olson's Maximus.* Urbana: Univ. of Illinois Press, 1980.

Clarke, Graham. "The Poet as Archaeologist: Charles Olson's Letters of Origin," in Butterfield, R.W., ed., *Modern American Poetry,* London: Vision, 1984; Totowa, N.J.: Barnes and Noble, 1984, 158-72.

Hutchinson, George. "The Pleistocene in the Projective: Some of Olson's Origins." *American Literature* 54 (1982): 81-96.

Merrill, Thomas F. *The Poetry of Charles Olson: A Primer.* Newark: Univ. of Delaware Press, 1982.

Paul, Sherman. *Olson's Push: Origin, Black Mountain, and Recent American Poetry.* Baton Rouge: Louisiana State Univ. Press, 1978.

EZRA POUND

Bell, Ian F.A. *Critics as Scientist: The Modernist Poetics of Ezra Pound.* London: Methuen, 1981.

Douglass, Paul. "Modernism and Science: The Case of Pound's ABC of Reading." *Paideuma* 18 (1989): 187-96.

Kayman, Martin A. "A Model for Pound's Use of 'Science,'" in Bell, Ian F., *Ezra Pound: Tactics for Reading.* London: Vision, 1982; Totowa, N.J.: Barnes and Noble, 1982.

———. *The Modernism of Ezra Pound. The Science of Poetry.* New York: St. Martin's, 1986.

ROBERT PIRSIG

Benson, Donald. "*Zen and the Art of Motorcycle Maintenance:* Technology Revealed." *Iowa State Journal of Research* 54 (1979): 267-73.

THOMAS PYNCHON

Clerc, Charles, ed. *Approaches to Gravity's Rainbow.* Columbus: Ohio State Univ. Press, 1983.

Friedman, Alan J., and Puetz, Manfred. "Science as Metaphor: Thomas Pynchon and *Gravity's Rainbow.*" *Contemporary Literature* 15 (1974): 345-59.

Hume, Kathryn. *Pynchon's Mythography: An Approach to "Gravity's Rainbow."* Carbondale: Southern Illinois Univ. Press, 1987.

Levine, George, and David Leverenz, eds. *Mindful Pleasures: Essays on Thomas Pynchon.* Boston: Little, Brown, 1976.

Moore, Thomas. *The Style of Connectedness: "Gravity's Rainbow" and Thomas Pynchon.* Columbia: Univ. of Missouri Press, 1987.

Olsen, Lance. "Pynchon's New Nature: The Uncertainty Principle and Indeterminancy in *The Crying of Lot 49.*" *Canadian Review of American Studies* 14 (1983): 153-63.

Pearce, Richard, ed. *Critical Essay on Thomas Pynchon.* Boston: Hall, 1981.

Plater, William. *The Grim Phoenix: Reconstructing Thomas Pynchon.* Bloomington: Indiana Univ. Press, 1978.

Schaub, Thomas H. *Pynchon: The Voice of Ambiguity.* Univ. of Illinois Press, 1981.

Seed, David. *The Fictional Labyrinths of Thomas Pynchon.* Iowa City: Univ. of Iowa Press, 1988.

Slade, Joseph. *Thomas Pynchon.* New York: Warner Paperback Library, 1974.

Woodward, Kathleen. "Cybernetic Modeling in Recent American Writing: A Critique." *North Dakota Quarterly* 51 (1983): 57-73.

TOM ROBBINS

Siegel, Mark. "The Meaning of Meaning in the Novels of Tom Robbins." *Mosaic* 14 (1981): 119-31.

THEODORE ROETHKE

Carlisle, Fred E. "Metaphoric Reference in Science and Literature: The Examples of Watson and Crick and Roethke." *Centennial Review* 29 (1985): 281-301.

JACK SPICER

Carter, Steven. "A Place to Step Further: Jack Spicer's Quantum Poetics," in Amrine, Frederick, ed., *Literature and Science as Modes of Expression.* Dordrecht: Kluwer Academic Publishers, 1989, 177-88.

LEWIS THOMAS

Lounsberry, Barbara. "Lewis Thomas and the Revival of Nineteenth Century Literary Tradition." *Markham Review* 13 (1983-84): 7-10.

KURT VONNEGUT

Hume, Kathryn. "The Heraclitean Cosmos of Kurt Vonnegut." *Papers on Language and Literature* 18 (1982): 208-24.

Sheppeard, Sallye. "Kurt Vonnegut and the Myth of Scientific Progress." *Journal of the American Studies Association of Texas* 16 (1985): 14-19.

Sigman, Joseph. "Scientific and Parody in Kurt Vonnegut's *The Sirens of Titan.*" *Mosaic* 19 (1986): 15-32.

WILLIAM CARLOS WILLIAMS

Riddel, Joseph N. *The Inverted Bell; Modernism and the Counterpoetics of William Carlos Williams.* Baton Rouge: Louisiana State Univ. Press, 1974.

Surman, Diana Collecott. "Towards the Crystal: Art and Science in Williams' Poetic," in Terrell, Carroll F. ed., *William Carlos Williams: Man and Poet.* Orono: Univ. of Maine at Orono, 1983, 187-207.

Weaver, Mike. *William Carlos Williams: The American Background.* London: Cambridge Univ. Press, 1971.

Contributors

A. OWEN ALDRIDGE, professor of comparative literature, emeritus, at the University of Illinois, is the author of numerous books and scholarly essays, including *Franklin and His French Contemporaries*, *Benjamin Franklin and Nature's God*, *Voltaire and the Century of Light*, *Thomas Paine's American Ideology*, and *The Reemergence of World Literature: A Study of Asia and the West*.

STEVEN CARTER, Fulbright Lecturer for 1991-92 at the Marie Curie-Sklodowska University in Lublin, Poland, is a member of the English Department of California State University, Bakersfield. His many scholarly articles focus on the relationship of literature and science. In 1989 he won the Schacterle Prize of the Society for Literature and Science.

H. BRUCE FRANKLIN, John Cotton Dana Professor of English and American Studies at Rutgers University, Newark, is author or editor of sixteen books, including *War Stars: The Superweapon and the American Imagination*, *Robert Heinlein: America as Science Fiction*, *The Victim as Criminal and Artist: Literature from the American Prison*, *Future Perfect: American Science Fiction of the Nineteenth Century*, *The Wake of the Gods: Melville's Mythology*, and *M.I.A.; or, Mythmaking in America*.

N. KATHERINE HAYLES, associate professor of English at the University of Iowa, is author of *The Cosmic Web: Scientific Field Models and Literary Strategies in the Twentieth Century*, *Chaos Bound: Orderly Disorder in Contemporary Literature and Science*, and numerous essays. She has served as president of the Society for Literature and Science.

JUDITH YAROSS LEE, is co-editor (with Joseph W. Slade) of *Beyond the Two Cultures: Essays on Science, Technology and Literature* and author of *Garrison Keilor: A Voice of America*. Executive director of the Society for Literature and Science, she serves on the faculties of the E.W. Scrips School of Journalism and the School on Interpersonal Communication at Ohio University.

DAVID PORUSH, professor of literature of Rensselaer Polytechnic Institute, is the author of *The Soft Machine: Cybernetic Fiction* and a collection of short stories, *Rope Dances*, as well as many essays on the interrelations of science and literature. The founding secretary of the Society for Literature and Science, he is currently co-director of Autopoeisis, the artificial intelligence research laboratory at Rensselaer, where he is a Distinguished Teaching Fellow.

CATHERINE RAINWATER is assistant professor of English at St. Edward's University in Austin, Texas. Her publications include *Three Contemporary Women Novelists: Hazzard, Ozick, and Redmon* and *Contemporary American Women Writers: Narrative Strategies*, both co-edited with William J. Scheick. Her essay on the novels of Louise Erdrich (*American Literature*, 62:3) won the Norman Foerster Prize. She is writing a book on the semiotics of contemporary Native American narrative.

ROBERT A. RICHARDSON, JR., Visiting Professor of Letters at Wesleyan University, has taught at Harvard, Denver, Colorado, Queens College, and the Graduate Center of CUNY. His major publications include *Myth and Literature in the American Renaissance* and *Henry Thoreau: A Life of the Mind*. In 1990 he was awarded a Guggenheim fellowship for his current project, a life of Emerson.

DAVID M. ROBINSON, professor of English at Oregon State University, is author of *Apostle of Culture: Emerson as Preacher and Lecturer* and *The Unitarians and the Universalists* and editor of *William Ellery Channing: Selected Writings*, as well as many central articles on the American Transcendentalists.

WILLIAM J. SCHEICK, editor of *Texas Studies in Literature and Language*, is J.R. Millikan Centenial Professor of English and American Literature at the University of Texas, Austin. His wide-ranging publications include *The Will and the Word: The Poetry of Edward Taylor*, *The Writings of Jonathan Edwards*, *The Slender Human Word: Emerson's Artistry in Prose*, *The Half-Blood: A Cultural Symbol in Nineteenth-Century American Fiction*, *The Splintering Frame: The Later Fiction of H.G. Wells*, and *Design in Puritan American Literature*. He was awarded the Pushcart Prize in 1991.

ROBERT J. SCHOLNICK, is professor of English and dean of graduate studies, arts and sciences at the College of William and Mary. As dean, he initiated planning for doctoral programs in American studies (1988) and applied science (1990). His scholarly publications include "'The Password Primeval': Whitman's Use of Science in 'Song of Myself,'" *Studies in the American Renaissance*, *Edmund Clarence Stedman*, and a number of articles. He is the founding president of the Research Society for American Periodicals.

JOSEPH W. SLADE, director of the School of Telecommunications at Ohio University, is author of *Thomas Pynchon* and co-editor (with Judith Yaross Lee) of *Beyond the Two Cultures: Essays on Science, Technology, and Literature*. An NEH Fellow in Humanities and Technology at the National Humanities Institute at the University of Chicago in 1976-77 and holder of the Bicentennial Chair of American Studies at the University of Helsinki, Slade has published some sixty articles and book reviews on technology, literature, film, and communications.

Index

Adams, Brooks, 180
Adams, Henry, 13, 15, 180, 182, 229, 230-32
Adams, John, 58, 59, 67
Aelian, 115
aeronautics: and ballooning, 4, 43-44, 79; Poe's interest in, 79
Agassiz, Louis, 70, 106, 112, 115-16, 121, 123-24, 140
agriculture, as source of national wealth, 62-63, 69
"Aire and Angels" (Donne), 221
Akenside, Mark, 39, 40
Alcott, Amos Bronson, 123
Aldridge, A. Owen, 4, 7
Alembert, Jean Le Rond d', 40, 60
"All You Zombies—" (Heinlein), 163
"American Scholar, The" (Emerson), 100
Ammons, A.R., 16
An 2400, L' (Mercier), 157
Analogy of Religion, The (Butler), 96
Anarchiad, The, 128
Anas (Jefferson), 58
Angel, Myron, 144
animal magnetism, 79
Anstey, Christopher, 39
archy and mehitabel (Marquis), 130
Aristotle: and medicine, 25; and politics, 68; and optics, 80, 82; and naturalism, 115
art: and naturalism, 8-9; definition of, 40; and cybernetic fiction, 228 n 15
"Articles of Belief and Acts of Religion" (Franklin), 52, 53
Artificial Kid, The (Sterling), 212
Asimov, Isaac, 212

astronomy: Poe's interest in, 78; Emerson's interest in, 102-3; Thoreau's interest in, 116; ridicule of, 139-40
Astronomy (Ferguson), 78
Audubon, John James, 119, 130
Augustine (saint), 26, 28
Autobiography (Jefferson), 58
"Autumnal Tints" (Thoreau), 124
Axel's Castle (Wilson), 179
axial tilt, 50-51

Bacon, Sir Francis, 20, 40, 60, 113
Bacon, Roger, 80
ballooning, 4, 43-44, 79
Bangs, John Kendrick, 129
Barbeu Dubourg, Jacques, 43, 44
Barlow, Joel, 65, 128
Barnsley, Michael, 244
Barnum, P.T., 146
Barth, John, 14, 214
Barthelme, Donald, 214
Bartram, William, 116
Bateson, Gregory, 223
Baudrillard, Jean, 247
Baxter, Andrew, 46
Beach, Joseph Warren, 103-4, 106
Beckett, Samuel, 227 n 13
Beer, Gillian, 11
Bell, David F., 3
Bellamy, Edward, 158
Benjamin, Park, 171 n 8
Benson, Ivan, 149-50
"Berenice" (Poe), 80
Berkeley, George, 45
Bernardin de Saint-Pierre, Jacques-Henri, 79

Bernoulli, Jacques, 45, 46
Berthollet, Claude-Louis, 63
Bester, Alfred, 163
Bible, books of: Numbers, 31, 32
Big Money, The (Dos Passos), 172
biology: Dos Passos's interest in, 13, 14, 181, 182-84; Poe's interest in, 79; Crane's interest in, 181
Bishop, Jonathan, 98
Black, Max, 220
Blackburn, Paul, 200
"Black Cat, The" (Poe), 80
Blade Runner (film), 212
Blair, Walter, 141
Blake, William, 179, 229
Blount, Roy, Jr., 152 n 17
Boerhaave, Hermann, 45
Bohm, David, 199-200, 201
Bohr, Niels, 5, 14, 185, 196
Bombast von Hohenheim, Theophrastus (Paracelsus), 20, 21, 25
"Bon-Bon" (Poe), 81, 89
Boorstin, Daniel, 60
Borden, Simeon, 137
Borelli, Giovanni Alfonso, 22
Boston Society of Natural History, 116
botany: Jefferson's interest in, 63; Thoreau's interest in, 116-17, 118, 124
Bowdoin, James, 51-52
Boyle, Robert, 22, 24
Brace, Charles, 123
"Brace of Brief Lectures on Science" (Twain), 134
Bradbury, Ray, 163
"Bravery" (Thoreau), 111
Breithaupt, J.F.A., 146
Brewster, David, 78, 81-89, 100
Bridge, The (Crane), 14, 172, 174, 175, 176-77, 180, 185-87
Brodie, Fawn, 68
Brown, Charles Brockton, 59
Browne, Charles F. (pseud. Artemus Ward), 137
Bruce, Robert V., 4
Brumm, Ursula, 62
Bryant, William Cullen, 59, 70
Buffon, Count George-Louis Leclerc de, 8, 62, 69-70

Burbank, Luther, 182
Burroughs, William, 8, 14, 70, 214, 227 n 14
Butler, Joseph, 96
Butor, Michel, 227 n 13
Butterfield, Herbert, 19, 21
Byrd, Don, 200, 202, 205
Byrom, John, 39

Cabanis, Pierre-Jean-Georges, 53
Cabot, James Eliot, 123
Cabot, Samuel, 123
Cage, John, 203
Call Me Ishmael (Olson), 194
Calvino, Italo, 227 n 13
Cambridge Platonists, 22
Candolle, Alphonse de, 116-17
Cantor, Georg Ferdinand Ludwig Philipp, 237
Capra, Frank, 184
Capra, Fritjof, 206
Carpenter, Clarence Ray, 229
Carter, Steven, 5, 14
Castle of Crossed Destinies, The (Calvino), 227 n 13
Cat's Cradle (Vonnegut), 151 n 7
Chambers, Ephraim, 48
Chambers, Robert, 104
Channing, William Ellery, 16, 120
Chaos: Making a New Science (Gleick), 242
chaos theory, 2, 15, 240-42, 243-45
Chaplin, Charlie, 212
"Chapter of Suggestions, A" (Poe), 77
Chaucer, Geoffrey, 179
chemistry: and medicine, 20, 21, 22; Jefferson's interest in, 63-64; Poe's interest in, 79; shunned by writers, 181, 192 n 34; Pynchon's interest in, 192 n 34
Chernyshevsky, Nikolay, 162
Christographia (E. Taylor), 26
Christ Revealed (T. Taylor), 24, 30-32
Cicero, Marcus Tullius, 68
"Circles" (Emerson), 103
Clark, Harry Hayden, 96
Clark, William, 74 n 10

Clarke, Samuel, 46
classification systems. *See* taxonomy
Clemens, Samuel. *See* Twain, Mark
Cognitive Theory of Metaphor, A
  (MacCormac), 220
Cogswell, Mason Fitch, 35
Cohen, I. Bernard, 40, 42
Colden, Cadwallader, 45, 46, 47, 54
Coleridge, Samuel Taylor, 96
Collinson, Peter, 43, 46
"Colloquy of Monos and Una, The"
  (Poe), 81
*Coloquious dos simples e drogas e sonsas
  medicinas da India* (D'Orta), 25
Columbiad, The (Barlow), 65
Columbus, Christopher, 202
Combe, Andrew, 84, 88
Combe, George, 84, 87, 88
"Compensation" (Emerson), 102
Conchologist's First Book, The, 79
Condillac, Étienne Bonnot de, 63
Connecticut Wits, 35, 128
*Connecticut Yankee in King Arthur's Court,
  A* (Twain), 4, 13, 150, 158-59, 163-67,
  169-70
Conrad, Joseph, 199
Cooper, James Fenimore, 70, 72, 215
Coover, Robert, 213, 214
Cope, Edward Drinker, 143
copyright, 67
Corman, Cid, 196
Cotes, Roger, 79
Count Zero (Gibson), 212
Cowley, Malcolm, 172, 175, 180
Crane, Hart: and integration of science
  and literature, 5, 13-14, 173, 174-77,
  180-81, 184-87, 189-90; and science as
  religion, 172-73, 174, 177, 190 n 9; and
  Romanticism, 176, 179; involvement in
  science, 179-80; influence of Whitman
  on, 180
Crèvecoeur, Hector St. John de, 59, 70
Cromphout, Gustaaf Van, 96
Crucifixion, 31, 32, 33
Crying of Lot 49, The (Pynchon), 151 n 7,
  214, 216, 218, 220, 221-22
Culpeper, Nicholas, 18, 21, 23, 24, 25
cummings, e. e., 180

Cummings, Sherwood, 134
Cuvier, Georges, 116, 117
Cyberiad Mortal Engines, The (Lem), 227
  n 13
cybernetic fiction, 4, 14-15, 209-28 passim

Daniels, George H., 10-11
Dant, Elizabeth A., 97
Dante Alighieri, 19
Darwin, Charles: impact on science and
  religion, 12, 103-4, 181-82; Thoreau's
  interest in, 12, 113, 114, 116-18, 123-24;
  precursors of, 98, 104; Emerson's
  interest in, 103-4, 106; and survival of
  the fittest, 113; scientific method of,
  114; support for, 123, 124; ridicule of,
  128, 132; influence on George Eliot,
  229
Davis, Jim, 130
De Anima (Aristotle), 80
de Broglie, Maurice, 183
Declaration of Independence, 58-59, 62,
  67-68, 71
deconstructionism, 213
Degradation of the Democratic Dogma, The
  (Adams, ed.), 180
DeLillo, Don, 13, 15, 129, 214
Democracy in America (Tocqueville), 215
De Quille, Dan. *See* Wright, William
Derby, George Horatio (pseud. John
  Phoenix), 13, 129-30, 131, 135-41, 143,
  144, 150
Descartes, René, 44, 45
Descent of Man, The (Darwin), 132
Desor, Edward, 123
Dick, Philip K., 212
Dickinson, Emily, 11, 15, 16, 220
Diderot, Denis, 40, 60
Dillard, Annie, 8, 70
*Discourse on the Changes Which Have
  Occurred on Our Globe,* 50
disease theory, 20, 24, 27, 54
Dispensatory (Culpaper), 25
"Dispersion of Seeds, The" (Thoreau),
  124, 125
*Dissertation on the Importance of Physical
  Signs in the Various Diseases of the
  Abdomen and Thorax, A,* 79

Dissertation on the Nature and Propagation of Fire (Voltaire), 53, 55

"Do Androids Dream of Electric Sheep?" (Dick), 212

"Domain of Arnheim, The" (Poe), 87

Donne, John, 19, 221

d'Orta, Garcia, 25

Dos Passos, John: and integration of science and literature, 5, 13-14, 173, 174-76, 177-78, 180-81, 187-89, 190; and science as religion, 172; as a leftist, 178; as a naturalist, 178; involvement in science, 179-80

Dostoyevsky, Fyodor, 162

"Dream-Land" (Poe), 80

Dreiser, Theodore, 15, 182

Drury, Wells, 143, 149

du Bartas. *See* Salluste, Guillaume de (seigneur du Bartas)

Duchesne, Joseph, 27

Dunster, Henry, 23

Eagleton, Terry, 2

Eastman, Max, 179

Edison, Thomas Alva, 164, 168-69, 189

Education of Henry Adams, The (Adams), 180, 231, 232

Edwards, Jonathan, 48, 62

Einstein, Albert: ridicule of, 130; as a cultural deity, 181, 192 n 36; influence on Crane, 185; influence on Olson, 195, 199, 201, 202, 206; and cybernetics, 226 n 3

Elements of the Philosophy of Newton (Voltaire), 42, 43, 50, 53

Eliot, George (pseud. Mary Ann Evans), 229

Eliot, Jaret, 48

Eliot, T.S., 176

Emerson, Ralph Waldo: and separation of science and literature, 6; and Romanticism, 9, 103; changing views of science, 10, 94-95; and unpoetical language of science, 10, 107; opposition to specialization in science, 10-11, 98; influence on Thoreau, 11, 70, 110, 112, 113, 116; and literary imagination, 11; as a preacher, 94, 95, 97; and religion,

94, 99-100, 102, 104, 111; education of, 96; impact of Goethe on, 96, 100, 106; and politics, 102; opposition to technology, 106-7; and precision of scientific language, 118; biography of, 123

Encyclopedia: (Chambers), 48; (Diderot and Dalembert), 40, 55

Encyclopedia Britannica, 144

"End of New York, The" (Benjamin), 171 n 8

English Letters (Voltaire). *See Philosophical Letters* (Voltaire)

"Entropy" (Pynchon), 219-20

Epistola Medica (Galeanus), 23

"Equal, That Is, To the Real Itself" (Olson), 194-95

Essays: First Series (Emerson), 100, 102

Euclid, 80, 178

Eureka (Poe), 77, 78, 81, 84, 85, 90

Evelyn, John, 118

"Experience" (Emerson), 103, 104, 105

Experiments and Observations on Electricity (Franklin), 41, 44, 45, 49

"Explanation, The" (Barthelme), 214

Explication of the First Causes of Action in Matter, and, of the Cause of Gravitation (Colden), 45

"Extraordinary Account of Human Petrification" (Twain), 142

"Fall of the House of Usher, The" (Poe), 80, 81, 82

Farrell, James Thomas, 182

Faulkner, William, 199

Feigenbaum, Mitchell, 243

feminism, 15, 232-48 passim

Ferguson, DeLancey, 149

Ferguson, James, 78

Ferkiss, Victor, 186

Fiasco (Lem), 227 n 13

Figures or Types of the Old Testament (S. Mather), 24, 32

Finegan's Wake (Joyce), 229

Fiske, John, 182

Flaubert, Gustave, 178

Fludd, Robert, 25

fluid dynamics, 2, 232-38

42nd Parallel, The (Dos Passos), 189
Fothergill, John, 54
Foucault, Michel, 21-22, 239
Fourcroy, Antonie-François de, 63
fractal geometry, 2, 15, 239, 244-45
Frank, Waldo, 173
Franklin, Benjamin: opposition to destructive technology, 4, 43-44; and integration of literature and science, 6, 7-8, 44; and theology in science, 40, 41, 46-47, 52; and Newtonian philosophy, 40-41, 44-46, 52, 55; as scientist, 41-43, 44-45, 47-55; and utilitarianism, 43; and morality, 54; charter for American Philosophical Society by, 59
Franklin, H. Bruce, 4, 13
Franklin, Peter, 49
Frederick II ("the Great"; king of Prussia), 46
Freud, Sigmund, 182, 240, 241
"From the 'London Times' of 1904" (Twain), 159-63
Frost, Robert, 5, 15, 194
"Full and Reliable Account of the Extraordinary Meteoric Shower of Last Saturday Night, A" (Twain), 133
"Funeral Tribute, A" (Tompson), 23

Galeanus, Joseph, 23
Galen, 20, 22, 24, 25, 27, 30
Gay, John, 39
Geertz, Clifford, 2
Gell-Man, Murray, 229
"General Aims and Theories" (Crane), 173, 185
geology: Voltaire's interest in, 48, 50; Franklin's interest in, 48-52; Jefferson's dismissal of, 61; Poe's interest in, 79; impact on theology, 95; Emerson's interest in, 105; ridicule of, 142
Gibbs, Willard, 180, 230
Gibson, William, 212
Giles Goat Boy (Barth), 214
Gilpin, William, 118
Gleick, James, 242-45, 247
Glover, Richard, 39
Gnostic philosophy, 25

Godel, Kurt, 210
Goethe, Johann Wolfgang von, 11, 60, 66, 96, 98, 100, 106, 110, 113
Goldberg, Rube, 139
Goodman, Joe, 143
Goodwin, C.C., 143
Gould, Augustus, 116, 123
Gould, Stephen Jay, 16
Grammar of Botany (Smith), 117
Grana, Caesar, 66
Grant, Ulysses S., 135
Gravity's Rainbow (Pynchon), 146, 151 n 7, 192 n 34, 214, 217, 218, 222
Gray, Asa, 123-24
Great American Novel, The (Roth), 146
Great War Syndicate, The (Stockton), 166-67
Green River (Whalen), 181
Gulliver's Travels (Swift), 152 n 14, 212
Guyton de Morveau, Louis-Bernard, 63

Haeckels, Ernest, 182
Haldanes, J.B.S., 182
Halley, Edmund, 39
Hamilton, Alexander, 60
Haraway, Donna Jean, 196, 229, 233, 234
Harrari, Josué V., 3
Harte, Bret, 143
Harvard College, 19, 23, 96, 115-16, 123, 179
Harvey, William, 21, 22, 24, 25
"Haunted Palace, The" (Poe), 81
Hauser, Marianne, 214
Hawthorne, Nathaniel, 4, 15
Hayles, N. Katherine, 2, 15
Head and Heart of Thomas Jefferson, The (Dos Passos), 189
Heart of Darkness (Conrad), 199
Heinlein, Robert A., 163
Heisenberg, Werner, 2, 5, 14, 184, 194, 226 n 3
Helmholtz, Hermann Ludwig Ferdinand von, 182
Helmont, Jean Baptiste van, 24, 25, 26, 27
Herschel, Sir John, 78, 85, 141
Hervey, John (Baron Hervey of Ickworth), 39

Hill, Hamlin, 141
Hindle, Brooke, 61
Hippocrates, 24
History of Nevada (Angel), 144
History of New York . . . By Diedrich Knickerbocker (Irving), 128
History of the Big Bonanza (De Quille), 129-30, 144, 147
History of the Comstock Silver Lode Mines, A (Wright), 144
Hobbes, Thomas, 239
Hoffman, Charles Fenno, 77
Hoffman, Frederick, 187
Holmes, Oliver Wendell, 6, 35
Holton, Gerald, 175
Homer, 59, 64
Hopkins, Lemuel, 35, 128
"Horse's Tale, A" (Twain), 132-33
Howells, William Dean, 134
Huber, Wolf, 119
Hudson River School, 70
"Humanity of Science" (Emerson), 100-101
humor: as antiscientific, 12-13, 128-56 passim; of Franklin, 55; and hoaxes, 141-42, 144-45, 148
humoral theory, 20, 24, 27
Humphreys, David, 128
"Hymn to Science" (Akenside), 39

I, Robot (Asimov), 212
Idealism, 110, 112, 119
If on a winter's night a traveller (Calvino), 227 n 13
Indians. *See* Native Americans
Information Theory and Esthetic Perception (Moles), 218
Innocents Abroad, The (Twain), 134
Inquiry into the Nature of the Human Soul, wherein Its Immateriality is evinced (Baxter), 46
Invisible Cities (Calvino), 227 n 13
Irigaray, Luce, 232-35, 240, 241, 246-48
Irving, Washington, 59, 128
"Is the Subject of Science Sexed?" (Irigaray), 233, 241, 250 n 23

Jackson, Stonewall, 135
James, William, 112

Jeffers, Robinson, 35
Jefferson, Thomas: and literature's contradictory view of science, 4, 8; and integration of literature and science, 6, 7, 8, 59-62, 64-65, 66; writings by, 58; and mortality, 59, 65, 71, 72; as a scientist, 59, 64, 71; and taxonomy, 62; pragmatism of, 64; writing theory of, 65-66; and Romanticism, 67; and religion, 68; and naturalism, 70; lampooned by humorists, 128; Dos Passos's interest in, 189
Jeffersonianism, 69
Jesus Christ, as healer, 20, 26-28, 30-34
Johanson, Donald C., 131
Johnson, Samuel, 7, 40, 60, 66
Jones, Howard Mumford, 61, 70
jouissance, 241
Joule, James Prescott, 182
Journal of Irreproducible Results, 141
Journal of Polymorphous Perversity, The, 141
Jussieu, Antoine-Laurent de, 97

Kahn, Otto, 185
Kalm, Pehr, 116
Kant, Immanuel, 96, 110-11
Keillor, Garrison, 128
Kelvin, William Thomson, 1st Baron Kelvin, 182
Kemble, E.W., 129
Kepler, Johannes, 10, 77, 78, 80, 89-90
King, Clarence, 143
Kouwenhoven, John, 187
Kuhn, Thomas, 62

Lacan, Jacques, 240, 245
la Cosa, Juan de, 201-3, 204, 205, 207
Lamarck, Jean-Baptiste-Pierre-Antoine de Monet de, 98
"Landor's Cottage" (Poe), 87
landscape, 8, 70-71
"Landscape Garden, The" (Poe), 87
Lardner, Dionysius, 87
Lavoisier, Antoine-Laurent, 63-64, 75 n 29
Leakey, Richard E., 130
Leaves of Grass (Whitman), 180
Leavis, F.R., 138

"Lectures on Astronomy" (Derby), 139-40
Lectures on Phrenology (G. Combe), 84
Lee, Judith Yaross, 12-13
Lee, Richard H., 67
Lee, Samuel, 23
Leibniz, Gottfried Wilhem, 45
Lem, Stanislaw, 227 n 13
Lenin, V.I., 189
Leonidas (Glover), 39
Leopold II (king of Belgium), 158
Letters (Barth), 214
Letters From an American Farmer
    (Crèvecoeur), 70
Letters on Natural Magic (Brewster), 82,
    85, 88
Lewis, Meriwether, 74 n 10
Life on the Mississippi (Twain), 152-53 n 19
"Ligeia" (Poe), 80, 81-82
Lindley, John, 116, 118
Linnaeus, Carolus, 63, 116, 117, 118, 120
Literary Bible of Thomas Jefferson, The
    (Chinard), 65
Literary Mind: Its Place in an Age of
    Science, The (Eastman), 179
literature: science as separate from, 1, 6,
    10-12; as fiction, 2; as cultural, 2-3; as
    conducive to science, 3, 4-5; resistance
    to science in, 3-4; contradictory view of
    science in, 4; science as integrated
    with, 6-10; as autonomous way of
    knowing, 11; patronage of, 66;
    legitimacy of commentary on science
    from, 178-79; and scientific expertise,
    179-80; cybernetics in, 211-15;
    exhaustion of, 213; influence of science
    on, 229-50 passim
Livy (Titus Livius), 65
Lock, David Ross (pseud. Petroleum V.
    Nasby), 137
Locke, John, 46, 60, 67-68
Locke, Richard Adams, 128, 141
Logan (Indian chieftain), 72
London, Jack, 182
London College of Physicians, 25
London Dispensatory (Culpeper), 23
Looking Backward (Ballamy), 158, 162
Lookout Cartridge (McElroy), 214
Loomis, C. Grant, 144

Lost Ones, The (Beckett), 227 n 13
Loudon, John Claudius, 116
"Luck of the Roaring Camp" (Harte), 143
Lucretius (Titus Lucretius Carus), 80
Lucas, George, 212
Lyman, Theodore, 123

MacCormac, Earl, 220
Mach, Ernst, 14, 185
Maclaurin, Colin, 42
"Maelzel's Chess Player" (Poe), 91-92 n 11
magic squares and circles, 45
Magirus, Johannes, 19
Magnalia Christi Americana (C. Mather),
    24
Malebranche, Nicolas de, 45
Malkoff, Karl, 197
Mandelbrot, Benoit, 244
Manhattan Transfer (Dos Passos), 183, 184
manufacturing, Jefferson's mistrust of, 69
Marbois, François, 68
"Marginalia" (Poe), 78, 79, 87
Mark Twain's Western Years (Benson), 149
Marquis, Don, 130
Marsh, Othniel Charles, 131-33
Martin, Ronald, 182
Marxist criticism, 2-3
mathematics: Franklin's aversion to, 41,
    44-45; Poe's interest in, 79, 113;
    Thoreau's interest in, 113; ridicule of,
    138
Mather, Cotton, 23, 35
Mather, Increase, 23
Mather, Samuel, 24, 32, 34
Maupertuis, Pierre Louis, 42
Maximus Poems, The (Olson), 5, 14, 195,
    197-207
Maximus Poems IV, V, VI (Olson), 207
McClellan, George B., 135
McElroy, Joseph, 214
McLuhan, Marshall, 184, 187
McPhee, John, 8, 70
McPherson, James, 67
medicine: and literature, 6, 18-38;
    metaphysical, 18, 20, 21; and religion,
    18, 19-20, 23-27; chemistry in, 20, 21,
    22; competing theories of, 20, 24-27,
    30; modernization of, 21; education in,

23; Franklin's view of, 54; Poe's interest in, 79, 83-84

"Meditations" (E. Taylor). *See Preparatory Meditations* (E. Taylor)

"*Meleagris Gallopavo*—The American Turkey" (Anon.), 130

"Mellonta Tauta" (Poe), 77

Melville, Herman, 215

Memoirs (Franklin), 42, 45

Mendel, Gregor Johann, 182

Mendeléyev, Dmitry Ivanovich, 63

Meno (Plato), 80

"Men Who Murdered Mohammed, The" (Bester), 163

Mercier, Loùis-Sebastian, 157

Merrill, Thomas F., 194-95

"Mesmeric Revelation" (Poe), 78, 83

mesmerism, 79

Metallographia: An History of Metals (Webster), 25

metamorphosis, 10, 103, 104, 107

metaphors, 219-24, 225

Meteorologica, 80

meteorology, Franklin's interest in, 48

Méthod de nomenckature chimique (Lavoisier et al.), 63

Method of Nature, The (Emerson), 102, 103

Method of Science, The (Sargent), 41

"Metzengerstein" (Poe), 80

Michaux, André, 74 n 10

Micromegas (Voltaire), 52

Miller, Perry, 7

Minsky, Marvin, 211

Mitchell, John (of Cambridge, England), 49

Mitchell, John (of Virginia), 49

Mitchell, Jonathan (of Harvard College), 23

"Modern Poetry" (Crane), 191 n 14

Modern Times (film), 212

Moles, Abraham, 218

Mona Lisa Overdrive (Gibson), 212

Monroe, Harriet, 189

Mont St. Michel and Chartres (Adams), 180

Moore, Henry, 203

Moore, Marianne, 15, 16

Morison, Samuel Eliot, 19

"Morris in Chains" (Coover), 214

Morton, Charles, 24

Moses, 31, 32, 33

Muir, John, 8, 70, 143

Munson, Gorham, 174

"Murders in the Rue Morgue, The" (Poe), 77, 86

Mussolini, Benito, 150

Nasby, Petroleum V. *See* Locke, David Ross

Native Americans, 68, 72

Natural History Extract Notebook (Thoreau), 124

Natural History of Intellect, The (Emerson), 106

"Natural History of Massachusetts, The" (Thoreau), 111, 120

naturalism: of Jefferson, 8; and religion, 8-9, 95-97, 111-12; of Thoreau, 111-12; impact of modern science on, 182

"Naturalist, The" (Emerson), 98

Natural Religion (Paley), 96

"Nature" (Emerson), 104-6

Nature (Emerson), 97, 98-100, 103, 112

Neufeldt, Leonard, 106-7

Neuromancer (Gibson), 212

"New System of English Grammar, A" (Derby), 138

Newton, Sir Isaac: and integration of literature and science, 7, 39; and naturalism, 8; and vision theory, 9, 78, 82-84, 110; philosophy attributed to, 40, 41; and theology, 40, 46; influence of Franklin and Voltaire, 41-46, 52-55; and metaphysics, 45-46; influence on Jefferson, 60-62; influence on Emerson, 100; compared to Einstein, 181; influence on Blake, 229

Nichol, John Pringle, 10, 78, 102-3

Nicholson, Marjorie Hope, 24

Norris, Frank, 182

Notes from the Underground (Dostoyevsky), 162

Notes on the State of Virginia (Jefferson), 8, 58, 59, 62, 63, 67, 68-73

Novak, Barbara, 8, 12

Observations on Mental Derangement (A. Combe), 84
Oegger, Guillaume, 100
"Official Report" (Derby), 135-37, 150
Oken, Lorenz, 106
Olson, Charles: and integration of science and literature, 5, 14, 195; interest in science, 194-207 passim
Ong, Walter J., 35
On the Origin of Species (Darwin), 12, 118, 123, 124, 128, 144, 181
Oppenheimer, J. Robert, 179
Opticks (Newton), 45, 78, 82, 83
optics. *See* Poe, Edgar Allan: and vision theory
Ouspensky, P.D., 186
"Oval Portrait, The" (Poe), 80
Overland Monthly, 142, 143
Owen, Sir Richard, 106
"Oya Life These Days" (Keillor), 128

Packer, Barbara, 100
Paige, James W., 171 n 9
paleontology: Poe's interest in, 79; ridicule of, 132-33, 135
Paley, William, 96
Paracelsians, 20, 22, 24-28, 30-33
Paracelsus. *See* Bombast von Hohenheim, Theophrastus
Parva naturalia (Aristotle), 80
"Passage to India" (Whitman), 180
patents: Jefferson's interest in, 67; ridicule of, 135, 139
Paul, Sherman, 99, 198
Pearson, Karl, 14, 185
Peden, William, 68
Pemberton, Henry, 39, 42, 46
perception, 9-10, 79-80, 84-90
Percival, James Gates, 35
Percy, Walker, 6, 35
Perelman, S.J., 138
"Petrified Man" (Clemens), 128, 134, 142
"Petrified or the Stewed Chicken Monster" (Wright), 142
Pharmacopaeia Londinensis (Salmon), 24-25
Philosophical Letters (Voltaire), 44
"Philosophy of History" lecture series (Emerson), 100

Philosophy of Mathematics and Natural Science, The (Weyl), 194
Phoenix, John. *See* Derby, George Horatio
Phoenixiana (Derby), 129, 135
phrenology, 79, 81-82
Phunny Phellows, 13, 129, 137-38
physics: Crane's interest in, 13, 181, 184-86; Olson's interest in, 14, 194, 195, 196-97, 199; in works of cybernetic fiction, 14-15, 224; Poe's interest in, 78-79; Dos Passos's interest in, 181, 183; and positivism, 210; and new scientific paradigm, 238-39
Physiocrats, French, 62
Physiologiae Peripateticae (Magirys), 19
Pickering, Timothy, 58, 67
Pickett, George E., 135
Pindar, 174, 186
Pinkering, Timothy, 67
Planck, Max Karl Ernst Ludwig, 183
Plato: and vision theory, 9, 80-82, 85, 89; and medicine, 25; influence on Emerson, 96, 99
Player Piano (Vonnegut), 214
Pliny, 115, 125
plow, moldboard, 67
Plus (McElroy), 214
Poe, Edgar Allan: and separation of science and literature, 6, 10, 77-78; and Romanticism, 9; and vision theory, 9, 80-90; and perception, 9-10, 79-80, 84-90; and Newtonian optics, 78, 82-84, 86-87; interest in the sciences, 78-80, 89; and Platonic optics, 80-82, 85, 89; and wave theory of light, 83; Thoreau compared to, 113
"Poet, The" (Emerson), 118
Poetic Renaissance, 175
"Poetry and Imagination" (Emerson), 94, 106, 107
Poincare, Jules-Henri, 14, 185
polygraph, 76 n 46
Poor Richard's Almanack (Franklin), 52
Pope, Alexander, 39, 52, 61
Porush, David, 4, 14-15
positivism, 210

postmodernism, 189, 196, 207, 209, 210, 213, 215
Pound, Ezra, 176
Practice of Physick, The (Riviere), 25
pragmatism, 64
Preparatory Meditations (E. Taylor), 19, 24, 25, 26, 27, 28-30, 31, 32, 33, 34
Pricksongs and Descants (Coover), 214
Priestley, Joseph, 55, 64
Prigogine, Ilya, 2, 5, 15, 231
Principia (Newton), 39, 40, 41, 42, 45, 78, 83
Principles of Physiology, The (A. Combe), 84, 88
Principles of Zoology (Agassiz and Gould), 123
"Projective Verse" (Olson), 196
Projectivist verse, 196-97
prosody, 65
psychology, 79
Public Burning, The (Coover), 213
Pultenay, William, 116
Puritanism, 19-20, 22-26, 30, 65
Pynchon, Thomas: as humorist, 13, 129, 146; cybernetic fiction of, 14, 209-10, 214, 215-25; interest in chemistry, 192 n 34; as postmodern chronicler, 213
Pytheas, 50

quantum physics. *See* physics

Raffinesque, Constantine, 181
Rainwater, Catherine, 6
rationalism, 19, 21, 22
Ratner's Star (DeLillo), 151 n 7
"Reflexion, The" (E. Taylor), 27, 31
"Relation of Man to the Globe, The" (Emerson), 98
religion: and naturalism, 8-9, 95-97; impact of Darwin on, 12; and medicine, 18, 19-20, 23-27; and Newtonians, 40; and natural theology, 49
"Remarkable Discoveries in Oregon and Washington Territories" (Derby), 141
Representative Men (Emerson), 106
Return to Cosmology, The (Toulmin), 214
Richardson, Robert D., Jr., 11-12
Richardson, Samuel, 65

Riddell, Joseph N., 196
Ridley, B.K., 196
Riemann, Bernard, 194
Rittenhouse, David, 59
Riviere, Lazare, 25
Robinson, David, 10
Rock, The (Eliot), 176
Rockefeller, John D., 182
Romanticism, 9, 66-67, 103, 176, 179
Rotella, Guy, 5
Roth, Philip, 146, 213
Roughing It (Twain), 134
Rousseau, Jean-Jacques, 43, 62
Rush, Benjamin, 35, 64, 67
Russell, Bertrand, 210

Saadi (Sa'di), 125
Sacks, Oliver, 6, 35
Saint-Hilaire, Geoffroy, 106
Salluste, Guillaume de (seigneur du Bartas), 49
Salmon, William, 24
Sanborn, Franklin Benjamin, 123
Sanctorius, Sanctus (Santorio Santorio), 22
"San Francisco Antiquarian Society, and California Academy of Arts and Sciences" (Derby), 140-41
San Francisco *Golden Era*, 142, 143
Sargent, John, 41
Sartre, Jean-Paul, 177
Savage, Derek, 176
Scheick, William J., 9
Schelling, Friedrich Wilhelm Joseph von, 96, 111, 119
Schleiermacher, Friedrich Ernst Daniel, 111
Schrödinger, Erwin, 183
science: as separate from literature, 1, 6, 10-12, 61-62; critical analysis of, 1-2; as cultural, 2, 15, 175, 178, 245; as fiction, 2, 15; objectivity of, 2, 233-34; as destructive, 4, 12, 13, 106-7, 149-50, 167-70, 175-76; definitions of, 7, 39-40, 60; specialized vocabularies in, 8, 11, 62, 117, 120, 137, 138; and naturalism, 8-9; amateur versus professional, 10-11, 62, 64, 73;

specialization in, 10-11, 59, 60-61, 62, 64, 69, 98, 115; public attitude toward, 12-13; and gender, 15, 232-48 passim; as natural philosophy, 39; experimentation in, 41, 60; ridicule of, 128-56 passim; and cybernetics, 210-11; influence on literature, 229-50 passim
Science and the Modern World (Whitehead), 119, 179
Selzer, Richard, 6, 35
Sénarmont, Henri Hureau de, 146
Sennert, Daniel, 24
Serres, Michel, 3, 246, 247
"Sewing Machine—Feline Attachment" (Derby), 139
Shakespeare, William, 65, 218
Shannon, Claude, 211, 222, 225 n 2, 226 n 3
Sherman, Gen. William Tecumseh, 135
Sidney, Sir Philip, 68
Silliman, Benjamin, Jr., 133
"Silver Man, A" (Wright), 142, 144-46, 147, 149
Simon, Herbert, 214
Skipwith, Robert, 65
Slade, Joseph W., 5, 7, 8, 13-14
slavery, 8, 68, 72
Sloane, Hans, 42
Smith, Adam, 62, 239
Smith, Sir J.E., 117
Smith, John, 200-201
Smith, Robert, 83
Smollet, Tobias George, 65
Snow, C.P., 2, 60, 138
Social Darwinism, 182
Soft Machine, The (Burroughs), 214, 227 n 14
"Solar Armor, The" (De Quille), 147-50
"Some Learned Fables for Good Old Boys and Girls" (Twain), 131, 133, 135
"Sonnet—to Science" (Poe), 77
Sontag, Susan, 66
Soulavie, Abbé Jean Louis Giraud, 51, 52
Sound and the Fury, The (Faulkner), 199
"Sound of Thunder, A" (Bradbury), 163
space flight, 52. *See also* aeronautics
"Spectacles, The" (Poe), 84, 85, 89
Spencer, Herbert, 182

Spengler, Oswald, 173
"Sphinx, The" (Poe), 84, 85
Spinoza, Baruch, 181
Squibob, John P. *See* Derby, George Horatio
Squibob Papers, The (Derby), 135
Standish, Miles, 201
Star Wars (film), 212
Statute of Virginia for Religious Freedom, 58, 68
Stearns, Raymond, 45
Stegners, Isabelle, 2, 5, 15
Steinman, Lisa, 185
Steinmetz, Charles Proteus, 188-89
Sterling, Bruce, 212
Sterne, Laurence, 65
Stevens, Wallace, 14, 184
Stevenson, James, 130
Stevenson, Polly, 44, 45, 49, 54
Stiles, Ezra, 39
Stockton, Frank, 166
Stoehr, Taylor, 4
Stoever, Dietrich H., 116
Strauch, Carl F., 96, 103-4
Stress Analysis of a Strapless Evening Gown, 141
Struik, Dirk Jan, 70
Studies of Nature (Bernardin de Saint-Pierre), 79
"Succession of Forest Trees, The" (Thoreau), 12, 124, 125
Surgeons Mate, The (Woodall), 23, 25, 27
Swedenborg, Emanuel, 106
Swift, Jonathan, 152 n 14, 212
Synopsis of Natural History with Human and General Physiology and Biology, A, 79
System of Phrenology, A (G. Combe), 84, 87, 88
Szeyepovik, Jan, 159, 162

Tacitus, Cornelius, 65, 75 n 39
"Tale of the Ragged Mountains, A" (Poe), 81, 82
Talking Room, The (Hauser), 214
tall tales, 145
taxonomy: Jefferson's interest in, 62, 63, 69; Emerson's interest in, 95, 97-98,

101, 106; Thoreau's interest in, 118; and
chaos theory, 241
Taylor, Edward: and integration of
literature and science, 6; as physician-
writer-minister, 6, 20, 23, 24, 34-35;
scientific milieu of, 18-22; education of,
19, 23; and reconciliation of science
and theology, 22-24, 26-35
Taylor, Thomas, 24, 30, 32
technology. *See* science
"Tell-Tale Heart, The" (Poe), 80
Tesla, Nikola, 168
Thales of Miletus, 246
Thentetus (Plato), 80
theology. *See* religion
This Sex Which Is Not One (Irigaray), 232
Thomas, Lewis, 16, 35
Thoreau, Henry David: and separation of
science and literature, 6, 11-12, 114,
118, 120-21; and naturalism, 8, 102, 111,
112-15, 119; and Romanticism, 9;
spoiled by Emerson and Agassiz, 70;
and facts, 110, 112-15, 120, 121, 122-23;
compared to Emerson, 110-11; and
religion, 111; and morality, 112-13, 119;
scientific method of, 114, 119, 120,
124-25; and precision of scientific
language, 118, 120, 122
Thoreau, Sophia, 119
"Three Thousand Years among the
Microbes" (Twain), 128, 134
Tichi, Cecilia, 188
Ticket That Exploded, The (Burroughs),
214
Timaeus (Plato), 80
time, changing conception of, 157-58,
162-63, 198, 202, 205
Tocqueville, Alexis de, 215
"Tom Edison's Shaggy Dog" (Vonnegut),
151 n 7
Tompson, Benjamin, 23
Torrey, John, 123-24
Toulmin, Stephen, 214
Traité élémentaire de Chimie (Lavoisier), 63
Transcendentalism, 11, 12, 110-12, 120,
124, 125
"Traveling Stones of Pahranagat Valley,
The" (De Quille), 146-47

Treatise on Astronomy (Herschel), 78
Treatise on Optics (Brewster), 83
Trumbull, John, 128
Turing, Alan, 211, 227 n 5
Twain, Mark (pseud. Samuel L.
Clemens): resistance to science from,
4, 13, 132, 134, 144, 150; as humorist,
128, 129, 131-37, 139, 142, 143, 144,
146-47; and time travel, 157-71
2001: A Space Odyssey (film), 212
two cultures, 2, 60, 138
T-Zero (Calvino), 227 n 13

uncertainty principle, Heisenberg's, 2, 5
Unitarianism, 96
U.S.A. trilogy (Dos Passos), 14, 175, 176,
182-84, 187-89, 190
"Uses of Natural History, The"
(Emerson), 98

V. (Pynchon), 151 n 7, 214, 217-19, 220,
222
Vendler, Helen, 16
Vesalius, Andreas, 21
Vestiges of the Natural History of Creation
(Chambers), 104
View of Sir Isaac Newton's Philosophy
(Pemberton), 39, 46
Views of the Architecture of the Heavens
(Nichol), 78, 102
Vineland (Pynchon), 213
Virgil, 64
Virginia City (Nevada) *Territorial
Enterprise*, 128-29, 142, 143-44, 146,
147, 150
Vis Inertiae, 46
vitalism, 18-19
Voltaire (François-Marie Arouet):
compared to Franklin, 7, 41-44, 46-48,
50-55; as contemporary of Jefferson,
60, 62
Vonnegut, Kurt, Jr., 14, 151 n 7, 214
von Neumann, John, 211, 227 n 5
Voyage of the Beagle (Darwin), 116

Waggoner, Hyatt, 176
Walden (Thoreau), 70, 118, 121, 122, 124,
125

Walker, Franklin, 143
Ward, Artemus. *See* Browne, Charles F.
"Water" (Emerson), 98
Wealth of Nations, The (Smith), 62
Weber, Max, 62
Webster, John, 25
Week on the Concord and Merrimack Rivers, A (Thoreau), 111, 112, 115
Weismann, Gerald, 35
Wells, H.G., 173
Westinghouse, George, 168
Weyl, Hermann, 194
Whalen, James, 181
Wharton, Edith, 178-79
What Is To Be Done? (Chernyshevsky), 162
Whitefield, George, 54
Whitehead, Alfred North, 119, 179, 181, 186, 195, 210
White Noise (DeLillo), 151 n 7, 214
Whitman, Walt, 11, 15, 62, 180
Wiener, Norbert, 194, 211, 214, 221, 226 n 3
"Wild Fruits" (Thoreau), 124

Williams, William Carlos, 6, 14, 15, 35, 184, 185, 188
Wills, Garry, 59
Wilson, Edmund, 70, 179
Wilson, Kenneth, 235-36, 238, 239
Winthrop, John (1714–79), 39
Winthrop, John, Jr. (1606–76), 23, 35
Wittgenstein, Ludwig Josef Johan, 219
women, perspective on science, 15, 16, 232-48 passim
Woodall, John, 23, 25, 27
Wright, William (pseud. Dan De Quille), 13, 129, 130, 137, 142-50
"Writing American Fiction" (Roth), 213

Yale Scientific Expeditions of 1870–1874, 131
Youmans, Edward, 182
Young, Edward, 39
Young, Thomas, 83

Zinsser, Hans, 181
Zola, Émile, 178
Zukav, Gary, 197